Critical Acclaim for *Best Dives of the Caribbean*, first edition

Acknowledgments

The authors thank all of *Best Dives'* contributors, correspondents, photographers and researchers (identified throughout the book) for their enormous effort in preparing material for this edition.

A special thanks to Lissa Dailey and Michael Hunter of Hunter Publishing and to Dr. Stephen Brenner; Gary Flink; Anita, Amanda, Neal and Ken Liggett, Underwater Sports of NJ; Rick and Lisa Ocklemann, Puerto Rico and Guadeloupe; JoAnn and Jonathan Pannaman, BVI snorkeling; Alvin Jackson, Honduras; Bret Gilliam, Joe Giacinto, Dive BVI; Barbara Swab, Frank Holler, Holler Swab & Partners; Auston MacLeod, Julian Rigby, Kenneth Samuel, H.V. Pat Reilly, Marilyn and Tim Benford, Ellis Chaderton, St. Kitts and Nevis; Mark Padover, St. Eustatius; Bob Di Chiara; Susan and Rick Sammon, CEDAM; Dr. Susan Cropper; Wendy Canning Church; Dee Scarr, Touch the Sea, Bonaire; Brenda Fine; Karen and Dennis Sabo, Landfall Productions; Cathy Rothschild, Dive Safaris, NY; Castro Perez, Aruba Tourism; Christopher Lofting, Maria Shaw, Cayman Brac; Mike Emmanuel, Little Cayman; Lucy Portlock, Pelagic Pleasure, USVI; Dave Farmer, Michael Young, Barbados; Erwin F. Eustacia, Ivan Englentina, and Eva Van Dalen, Michel Angelo Harms, Curacao Tourism; Dominique & Leroy French, St. Martin; Tom Mc Kelvey; Finn Rinds, Tobago; Gareth Edmonson-Jones, Jose E. Rafols, Efra Figueroa, James Abbott, Puerto Rico; Iain I. Grummitt, Thomas L.C. Peabody, Anguilla; Jim Spencer; Joan Borque, Saba; Karolin Kolcuoglu, St. Lucia; Luana Wheatley, Michelle Pugh, Mike Meyers, Monica Leedy, Myron Clement, Guadeloupe; Tom Burnett, Walter Frischbutter, Dominican Republic; Christopher Wright, Jamaica.

BEST DIVES
of the
CARIBBEAN

Second Edition

Joyce & Jon Huber

HUNTER
PUBLISHING

Hunter Publishing, Inc.
130 Campus Drive, Edison NJ 08818
(732) 225 1900, (800) 255 0343
Fax (732) 417 0482
e-mail: hunterpub@emi.net

In Canada
1220 Nicholson Rd., Newmarket, Ontario
Canada L3Y 7V1, (800) 399 6858

ISBN 1-55650-798-4

©1998 Joyce & Jon Huber

Maps by Joyce Huber
Cover photo: Jon Huber
Barrier Reef off Placencia, Belize

For complete information about the hundreds of other travel guides and language courses offered by Hunter Publishing, visit our Web site at:

www.hunterpublishing.com

1   2   3   4   5

Contents

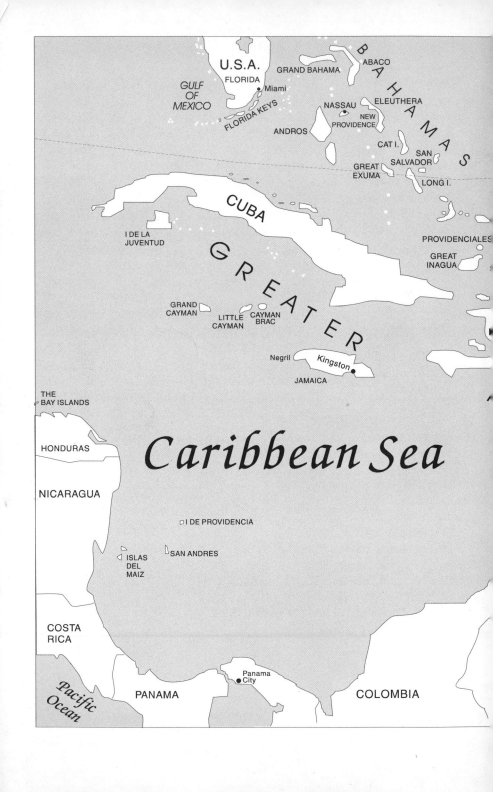

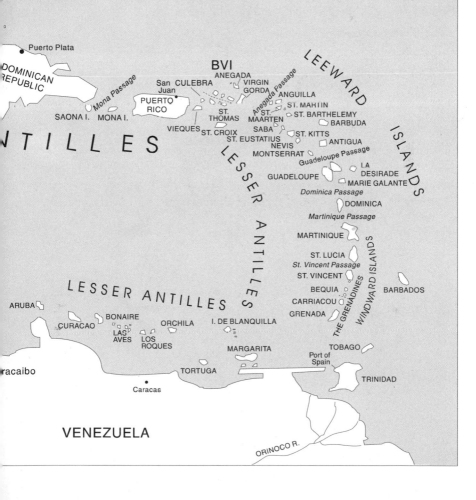

0 ——— MILES ——— 450

0 ——— KM ——— 450

TROPIC OF CANCER

Atlantic Ocean

KS & CAICOS ISLANDS
ORTH CAICOS
GRAND CAICOS
EAST CAICOS
  GRAND TURK

Puerto Plata

DOMINICAN
REPUBLIC

Mona Passage

San CULEBRA
Juan

PUERTO
RICO

SAONA I.   MONA I.

VIEQUES ST. CROIX

NTILLES

BVI
ANEGADA
VIRGIN
GORDA

ST.
THOMAS

ST.
MAARTEN
SABA
ST. EUSTATIUS
NEVIS
MONTSERRAT

LEEWARD

Anegada Passage

ANGUILLA
ST. MARTIN
ST. BARTHELEMY
BARBUDA
ST. KITTS
ANTIGUA

Guadeloupe Passage

ISLANDS

LA
DESIRADE
MARIE GALANTE

GUADELOUPE

Dominica Passage

LESSER

DOMINICA

Martinique Passage

ANTILLES

MARTINIQUE

ST. LUCIA
St. Vincent Passage
ST. VINCENT

BEQUIA
CARRIACOU
GRENADA

THE GRENADINES

WINDWARD ISLANDS

BARBADOS

LESSER ANTILLES

ARUBA

CURACAO

BONAIRE

LAS
AVES

LOS
ROQUES

ORCHILA   I. DE BLANQUILLA

racaibo

TORTUGA

Caracas

MARGARITA

Port of
Spain

TOBAGO

TRINIDAD

VENEZUELA

ORINOCO R.

Starfish Ratings

Each best dive and snorkeling site has been given a rating of from one to five starfish by prominent divemasters of the area.

☆☆☆☆☆ Five Starfish

Best of the best for diving – best visibility and water clarity, best marine life, best wreck or reef dive.

☆☆☆☆ Four Starfish

Fantastic dive. Outstanding for marine life or visual interest.

☆☆☆ Three Starfish

Superb dive. Excellent visibility and marine life or wreck.

☆☆ Two Starfish

Good Dive. Interesting fish and plant life; good visibility.

☆ One Starfish

Pleasant dive. Better than average.

Map Symbols

Dive Site

Shipwreck

Snorkeling area

Airport

Introduction

Before the creation of underwater viewing equipment, early Caribbean travelers caught merely a glimpse of the world beneath the sea. But, once they did, the idea of subsea exploration really caught on. By the 1930's, rubber goggles with glass lenses and face masks became a standard part of many a tropical traveler's wardrobe and a new wave of adventure travel took root. And, though much has changed since those early days, the fascination of the sea and its splendid inhabitants are still romancing and captivating visitors the way they always have.

Dive vacations have since evolved into a major part of Caribbean travel. There are now resorts, travel agents, tour operators and yacht charters that cater exclusively to divers and snorkelers. Many all-inclusive resorts have added scuba lessons and tours. There is even a cruise ship with an all-dive itinerary. Sailing afficionados find hull-to-hull pick-up service offered by the dive shops. Novice sailor-divers can rent a yacht with a captain who doubles as a dive instructor and a reef-and-wreck tour guide. The biggest consideration left for the traveler is deciding where to go.

Best Dives of the Caribbean is designed to help you wade through this endless wonder of vacation choices. Whether you are a snorkeler, a novice diver or an experienced ocean explorer you'll find a unique choice of destinations, diver-friendly accommodations and dive services to pick from. We've added several adventure destinations to this edition and expanded others to include more dive and snorkeling sites, a wider choice of accommodations, eateries and après-dive activities.

You'll find suggestions for the best time of year to visit each island and where to write, call or fax for additional information.

Dive and snorkeling sites have been carefully described and rated for various skill levels by the top dive operators of each area and double-checked by a member of our own US-based panel of dive-travel experts. Rules and etiquette for diving individual marine parks and reserves are listed throughout the guide.

If we've overlooked one of your favorite spots, write and tell us about it and we'll take another look for the next edition. In the meantime we hope you find **Best Dives of the Caribbean** a useful addition to your diver's bookshelf.

E-mail for Best Dives should be addressed to: bestdives@juno.com or jonhuber@worldnet.att.net.

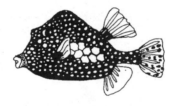

Planning Your Trip

To plan your best dive vacation, consider first the type of trip that interests you most. It may be a stay at a luxury resort, a week's tour on a live-aboard yacht or an excursion into the wilderness. Then check the best time of year to go. A week of bad weather or rough seas can turn any vacation sour. Most areas experience a predictable rainy season. And, though no one can guarantee the weather, each chapter discusses local weather patterns and suggests a best time of year to go.

Finally, consider your budget. You'll note a wide range of live-aboards and land accommodations throughout this guide, plus the appropriate contact for additional information at the end of each chapter.

SCUBA CERTIFYING ORGANIZATIONS

Locations for scuba instruction near your home may be obtained from one of the following organizations.

IDEA, International Diving Educators Association, P.O. Box 8427, Jacksonville, FL 32239-8427. ☎ (904) 744-5554.

NASDS, National Association of Scuba Diving Schools, 1012 S. Yates, Memphis, TN 38119. ☎ (800) 735-3483; (901) 767-7265. Web site: divesafe.com.

NAUI, National Association of Underwater Instructors, P.O. Box 14650, Montclair, CA 91763. ☎ (800) 553-6284; (909) 621-5801. Lost cards (909) 621-6210; fax (901) 621-6405. Web site: www.naui.org.

PADI INTERNATIONAL, Professional Association of Diving Instructors, 1251 E. Dyer Rd., Suite 100, Santa Ana, CA 92705-5605. ☎ (800) 729-7234; (714) 540-7234. Web site: www.padi.com.

PDIC INTERNATIONAL, Professional Diving Instructors Corporation 1554 Gardener Ave, Scranton, PA 18509. ☎ (717) 342-9434; fax (717) 342-1480. E-mail: info@PDIC-INTL.com. Web site: www. pdic-intl. com.

SSI, Scuba Schools International , 2619 Canton Court, Fort Collins, CO 80525. ☎ (800) 892-2702; (303) 482-0883. E-mail: admin@ssiusa. com or ssilen@aol.com

YMCA, National YMCA Scuba Program, Oakbrook Square, 6083-A Oakbrook Parkway, Norcross/Atlanta, GA 30093. ☎ (770) 662-5172; fax, (770) 242-9059. E-mail: scubaymca@aol.com. Web site: www.webcom. com/cscripts/-ymca/ymca.html.

CRUISES AND PACKAGE TOURS

Hundreds of dollars may be saved by choosing a package tour, offered by dive-tour operators, airlines, resorts and dive shops. For example, one package to Guadeloupe includes airfare and hotel for $100 less than the airfare alone. Package tours with diving are listed throughout this guide.

Be sure to read the fine print carefully when you are comparing tours. Transfers, sightseeing tours, meals, auto rentals, acceptable accommodations, and taxes. Tanks and weights may or may not be included. Also ask whether extra airline weight allowances are included for dive gear.

Off-the-beaten-track expeditions are offered by specialty organizations like **CEDAM** (Conservation, Ecology, Diving, Archaeology, Museums) which offers programs as varied as an underwater archaeological dig on an ancient shipwreck or a mapping tour of the Galapagos. For information write to Membership Chairman at CEDAM International, 1 Fox Road, Croton, NY 10520. ☎ (914) 271-5365 or fax (914) 271-4723. E-mail: cedamint@ aol.com. Web site: http://www.cedam.org.

Oceanic Society Expeditions, a non-profit environmental group, offers research-oriented snorkel trips and dolphin swims. ☎ (415) 441-1106 or (800) 326-7491 or write to the Oceanic Society, Fort Mason Center, Bldg. E, San Francisco, CA 94123. Web site: www.oceanic-society.org.

Landfall Productions offers hassle-free, money-saving tours for groups and individual divers to the Bahamas, Bonaire, Belize, BVI, Cozumel, Dominica, St. Vincent & the Grenadines, Bay Islands, Honduras, St. Kitts, St. Lucia, Turks and Caicos and the Pacific. Owners, Karen and Dennis Sabo, both divers and underwater photographers, personally check out each resort and live-aboard to insure quality service. ☎ (800) 525-3833. E-mail: lndfall@aol.com. Web site: http://ecotravel.com/land-fall.

Dive Safaris offers deluxe dive tours to Puerto Rico and most Caribbean destinations, as well as the Pacific, Africa and Indonesia. Owner Cathy Rothschild initiated shark diving/photo expeditions in cages. ☎ (800) 359-0747, (212) 662-4858; fax (212) 749-6172. E-mail: rothschild@divesafaris.com. Web site: http://www.divesafaris.com.

ICS Scuba books cruise-ship scuba vacations – money-saving group and individual tours to all points in the Caribbean, Austrailia, New Zealand, Indian Ocean and most other exotic destinations. They specialize in consolidating air travel and offer remarkably low fares to far-away spots for groups and individuals. ☎ (800) 722-0205 or (516) 797-2132. E-mail: TheICSGang@aol.com. Web site: www.icstravel.com.

Scuba Voyages features package trips to Saba, Roatan, Cozumel and Tobago. ☎ (800) 544-7631. E-mail: scubavoy@ix.netcom.com. Web site: www.scubavoyages.com.

HANDICAPPED DIVERS

Handicapped divers will find help and information by contacting the **Handicapped Scuba Association** (HSA). The association has provided scuba instruction to people with physical disabilities since 1975. Over 600 instructors in 24 countries are HSA-trained. HSA has developed the "Resort Evaluation Program" to help handicapped divers select a vacation destination. They check out facilities and work with the staff and management to ensure accessibility. Once a resort is totally accessible it is certified by HSA.

For a list of HSA-certified resorts, group-travel opportunities and more information on HSA's programs, instruction and activities send $2 with a stamped, self-addressed legal size envelope to: HSA International, 1104 El Prado, San Clemente, CA 92672. ☎ (714) 498-6128. E-mail: 103424.3535 @compuserve.Web site:www.ourworld.compuserve.com/hompeges/hsahdq/members.htm.

MONEY

Most large resorts, restaurants and dive operators will accept major credit cards, although you risk being charged at a higher rate if the local currency fluctuates. Traveler's checks are accepted almost everywhere and often you'll get a better exchange rate for them than cash. It's always a good idea to have some local currency on hand for cabs, tips and small purchases.

INSURANCE

Many types of travel insurance are available covering everything from lost luggage, trip cancellations and medical expenses. Since emergency medical assistance and air ambulance fees can run to several thousand dollars it is wise to be prepared. Trips purchased with some major credit cards include life insurance.

Divers Alert Network (DAN) offers divers' health insurance for $35 a year plus an annual membership fee of $25, $35 for a family. Any treatment required for an accident or emergency which is a direct result of diving, such as decompression sickness (the bends), arterial gas embolism or pulmonary baro-trauma is covered up to $125,000. Air ambulance to the closest medical care facility, recompression chamber care and in-patient hospital care are covered. Non-diving travel-related accidents are NOT covered.

Lacking the ability to pay, a diver may be refused transport and may be refused treatment. For more information write to DAN, P.O. Box 3823, Duke University Medical Center, Durham, NC 27710. ☎ (919) 684-2948. For emergencies worldwide call collect ☎ (800) 446-2671 or (919) 684-4DAN (4326). E-mail: dan@dan.ycg.org. Web site: http://www.dan.ycg.org.

International SOS Assistance is a medical assistance service to travelers who are more than 100 miles from home. For just $55 per person for seven to 14 days, or $96 per couple, SOS covers air evacuation and travel-related assistance. Evacuation is to the closest medical care facility, which is determined by SOS staff doctors. Representative Michael Klein states that SOS has and will send out a private LearJet if necessary to accommodate a patient. Hospitalization is NOT covered. Standard Blue Cross and Blue Shield policies do cover medical costs while traveling. For individual and group information write to International SOS Assistance, Box 11568, Philadelphia, PA 19116. ☎ (800)-523-8930 or (215) 244-1500. E-mail: jfahy @intsos.com. Web site: www.intsos.com.

Lost luggage insurance is available at the ticket counter of many airlines. If you have a homeowner's policy, you may already be covered. Be sure to check first with your insurance agent.

Keep a list of all your dive equipment and other valuables including the name of the manufacturer, model, date of purchase, new price and serial number, if any, on your person when traveling. Immediately report any theft or loss of baggage to the local police, hotel security people or airline and get a copy of that report. Both the list and the report of loss or theft will be needed to collect from your insurance company. Do not expect airlines to cheerfully compensate you for any loss without a lot of red tape and hassle. Regardless of the value of your gear the airline pays by the weight ($9 per pound) of what is lost. Be sure to tag your luggage with your name and address. Use a business address if possible.

DOCUMENTS

Carry your personal documents on you at all times. Be sure to keep a separate record of passport numbers, visas, or tourist cards in your luggage.

SECURITY

Tourists flashing wads of cash and expensive jewelry are prime targets for robbers. Avoid off-the-beaten-track areas of cities, especially at night. Do not carry a lot of cash or wear expensive cameras or jewelry. Keep alert to what's going on around you. Stay with your luggage until it is checked in with the airlines. Jewelry should be kept in the hotel safe.

Rental cars have become a target for robbers, more so in the U.S. than the Caribbean, but a few incidents of "bump-'n-rob" crimes have been reported in the islands. To avoid problems, try to rent a car without rental agent markings. If someone bumps into your car, do not stop. Drive to a police station and report the incident. Do not stop for hitchhikers or to assist strangers.

DRUGS

Penalties for possession of illegal drugs are very harsh and the risk you take for holding even a half-ounce of marijuana cannot be stressed enough. Punishment often entails long jail terms. In certain areas, such as Mexico, your embassy and the best lawyer won't be much help. You are guilty until proven innocent. Selling drugs is still cause for public hanging in some areas.

CAMERAS

Divers traveling with expensive camera gear or electronic equipment should register each item with customs *before* leaving the country.

SUNDRIES

Suntan lotion, aspirin, antihistamines, decongestants, anti-fog, or mosquito repellent should be purchased before your trip. These products are not always available and may cost quite a bit more than you pay for them at home.

FIRST AID

Every diver should carry a small first aid kit for minor cuts, bruises or ailments. Be sure to include a topical antihistamine ointment, antihistamine tablets, seasickness preventive, decongestant, throat lozenges, band aids, aspirin and diarrhea treatment.

SUNBURN PROTECTION

Avoid prolonged exposure to the sun, expecially during peak hours, 10 am to 3 pm. Since most dive trips occur during peak hours, whenever possible, opt for trips on dive boats with sun canopies, use sunblock lotions or a sunscreen with a protection factor of at least 15, select hats with a wide brim and wear protective clothing of fabrics made to block the sun's ultraviolet rays. The following manufacturers offer catalogs featuring comfortable, protective clothing: **Sun Precautions Inc.**, Everett, WA, ☎ (800) 882-7860; **Solar Protective Factory**, Sacramento, CA, ☎ (800) 786-2562; **Koala Konnection**, Mountain View, CA, ☎ (888) 465-6252.

DIVER IDENTIFICATION

Most dive operations require that you hold a certification card and a logbook. A check-out dive may be required if you cannot produce a log of recent dives.

GEAR

Uncomfortable or ill-fitting masks, snorkels, and other personal diving gear can make your dive a miserable experience. You can greatly reduce the possibility of these problems by buying or renting what you need from a reliable dive shop or specialty store before departure. Snorkeling gear, especially, is often expensive to rent.

Packing Checklist

___ MASK
___ SNORKEL
___ FINS
___ REGULATOR
___ DEPTH GUAGE
___ BOUYANCY
COMPENSATOR
(stab jacket)
___ WET SUIT, SHORTIE
OR LYCRA WET SKIN
___ WET SUIT BOOTS
___ MESH CATCH BAG
___ U/W DIVE LIGHTS
___ DRAMAMINE or other
seasickness preventative
___ GEAR MARKER
___ DIVER CERTIFICATION
CARD (C-card)
___ DIVER LOG BOOK
___ SUNGLASSES
___ SPARE MASK STRAP
___ DIVE KNIFE OR SHEARS

___ SPARE SNORKEL
RETAINER RING
___ SPARE STRAPS
___ SUBMERSIBLE
PRESSURE GAUGE
___ WATCH/BOTTOM TIMER
___ WEIGHT BELT
(no lead)
___ DE-FOG SOLUTION
___ REEF GLOVES
(not for use in marine parks)
___ CYALUME STICKS
(chemical light sticks)
___ U\W CAMERA AND FILM
___ FISH ID BOOK
___ DIVE TABLES
___ PASSPORT or proof of
citizenship as required
___ DIVE TABLES
(or computer)
___ SUNTAN LOTION
___ HAT (with visor or brim)

Note: Global warming has changed Caribbean weather. Islands normally free from winter storms have experienced colder air and water temperatures during January and February. Desert islands, normally dry year round, have been hit with storms and shifting winds for the first time in February.

If you plan a vacation during January or February, check weather in your planned destination before packing. You may want to consider a full wetsuit.

Anguilla

Anguilla (pronounced Ann-GWIL-A) is one of the Caribbean's best-kept secrets. Though sailing buffs have enjoyed its secluded bays and coves for decades, divers are just discovering its rich coral walls, great wrecks and miles of shallow snorkeling gardens.

Sitting just five miles from St. Martin and 190 miles east of Puerto Rico, Anguilla is the northernmost of the Leeward Islands in the Eastern Caribbean. It is small, just 16 miles long and three miles wide, with one main road that threads through picturesque villages, rows of Indian cottages, and colorful fruit and vegetable stands. Scattered along its craggy coast are 30 white sand beaches.

Delightfully tranquil, this crown colony is devoid of mammoth shopping centers, casinos, and crowds. Just 7,000 residents and a few thousand free-roaming goats comprise the local population.

Physically, Anguilla is predominantly low-lying, formed of limestone and coral with patches of mangrove and fresh-water ponds. Small cliffs on its north side are habitat to a variety of tropical birds, as are nearby out islands where you can spot the red-billed tropic bird, royal terns, kingfishers, laughing gulls, frigates and blue-faced boobies.

Anguilla's capital, The Valley is a tiny strand of pastel shops, government buildings and colorful houses.

Sandy Ground—just west of The Valley—on the northwest end, is the main yacht and cruise-ship harbor. It is the jumping-off point for sail-snorkeling cruises and west-end dive trips. Adjacent to Sandy Ground is Road Bay, a small strip of land with an ocean beach on one side and a maze of salt ponds that attract a multitude of tropical birds on the other.

When to Go

The best time to visit Anguilla is from mid-December to May. Tropical storms bringing an annual rainfall of 35 inches are a threat from late July to October, though most storms occur during September.

Contributors: Thomas L.C. Peabody, Iain I. Grummitt, The Dive Shop.

Air and water temperatures are agreeable for diving year-round. Average air temperature is 80° F. Water temperatures range from 79° to 85° F.

Best Dives and Snorkeling Sites

Wreck diving and out-island snorkeling prevail over Anguilla's subsea activities, though new sites are being opened on the east end of the island where coral caves and chutes shelter a robust fish population.

Eight of the 25 sites regularly visited by The Dive Shop, the island's west-end operator, are wrecks that were intentionally sunk to create artificial reefs. Anguillan divemasters boast the largest number of diveable wrecks in the eastern Caribbean—all in warm, clear water.

☆☆☆ The wreck of the **M.V. Oosterdiep** is one of the newest sites. It is a 130-ft freighter resting at 80 ft about 2½ miles out from Road Bay. Intact and upright, it attracts schooling yellowtail, schoolmaster snapper, Atlantic spadefish, flying gurnard, stingrays and small fish. Penetration is not allowed without specialty certification and under the supervision of local divemasters.

☆☆☆ **Sandy Deep**, a mini wall and the favorite reef dive, is lush with hard and soft corals, gorgonians, and abundant fish life and lobster (no collecting). Not recommended for snorkeling, but good for the novice, with depths from 15 to 60 ft. Sea conditions vary depending on the time of year.

☆☆☆ **Frenchman's Reef**, a collapsed limestone cliff off the southern point of West End Bay, is Anguilla's best snorkeling and novice-diver spot. Depths are from the surface to 40 ft. The submerged terrain is mixed coral, boulders and sand. There are spectacular swim-throughs, ledges and caverns—a "Whitman's Sampler" of West Indies marine life. Seas are calm and visibility is good.

☆☆☆☆ The wall at **Dog Island**, 10 miles north west of Road Bay, is an outstanding dive with depths from 15 to 80 ft. The wall's rock and coral face is riddled with nooks and crannies where you'll find octopi, turtles, arrow crabs, basket sponges, slender tube sponges, shrimp and lobster. Seafans and gorgonians abound. Fish include horse-eye jacks, chub, parrotfish, huge grey and French angels, blacktip and nurse sharks.Stingrays bury themselves in the sandy bottom. The surface over the wall is usually too choppy for snorkeling, but other areas around Dog Island—Bay Rock, for example—are popular snorkeling spots when seas are calm. The boat ride is about 30 minutes.

☆☆ **Little Bay Reef** is a sheltered 15- to 25-ft reef, ideal for novice divers, students and snorkelers. The bottom is a mix of coral, sand and turtle grass. There is excellent micro-life, including nudibranchs and lettuce slugs, sea horses, turtles, octopi, barber shrimp and lobster. The reef is a stone's

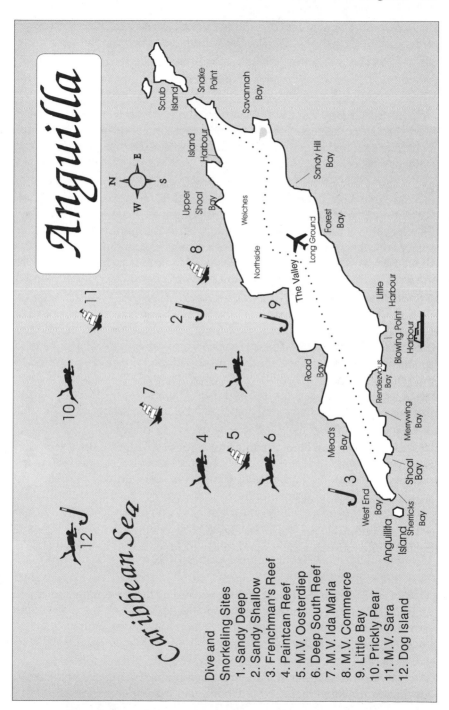

Anguilla

Caribbean Sea

Dive and
Snorkeling Sites
1. Sandy Deep
2. Sandy Shallow
3. Frenchman's Reef
4. Paintcan Reef
5. M.V. Oosterdiep
6. Deep South Reef
7. M.V. Ida Maria
8. M.V. Commerce
9. Little Bay
10. Prickly Pear
11. M.V. Sara
12. Dog Island

throw from shore but access other than by boat entails a rugged climb down a rocky footpath to the beach. The Dive Shop, Ltd. offers snorkelers drop-off and pick-up service to the beach at Little Bay.

Noted underwater photographer, Paul Humann, shot extensively here for his famous book *Reef Creatures*.

☆☆☆ **Shoal Bay East** is the best water-entry snorkeling and scuba site. There are two reefs, one directly off the beach that parallels the beach for some distance and another one a little further out. Depths range from the surface to 80 ft.

☆☆ The wreck of the *M.V. Commerce* is another freighter scuttled by divemasters Peabody and Grummitt. This 130-ft ship was sunk in 1986 off Limestone Bay on the Northwest coast. Depth is 45 to 80 ft. Great for photography, dramatic remains of the ship are astir with schools of shimmering barracuda, golden sergeant majors, queen angels, green and spotted morays, sting rays and spiny lobster. Macro subjects proliferate. Seas are variable; usually a light chop with an occasional current. Bottom terrain is boulder coral and sand.

☆☆☆☆ Marine life is superb at **Deep South Reef**, a patch reef displaying beautiful brain-coral formations. A profusion of soft, pastel corals and gorgonians blend with the vibrant reds and oranges of the reef. Purple tube sponges, barrel sponges and sea fans are abundant. Triggerfish, trumpetfish, parrotfish, angels, jacks, southern stingrays, spotted drums, wrasses, blue tangs, crabs and lobster are in residence. Depths are 55 to 80 ft. Good visibility. Seas vary with winds. Deep South is a short boat trip, about a mile, from the south end of Road Bay.

☆☆☆☆ **Paintcan Reef** is named for colorful splashes of strawberry and vase sponges which adorn the magnificent hard-coral structures of this patch reef. Fish life, too, is excellent with glimpses of black durgon, blacktip and nurse shark, walls of grunts, morays, jacks, copper sweepers, barracuda, and schools of silversides and sergeant majors. Pink-tipped anemones, and iridescent tube sponges cluster along the walls of the reef. Hawksbill turtles are recurrent visitors. Paintcan is about three miles north of Road Bay, a 15-minute boat trip. Depths are from 55 ft to 80 ft. Sea conditions vary. Recommended for experienced divers.

☆☆☆☆ The *M.V. Sara,* a freighter scuttled by the government to create an artificial reef, is impressive by size alone—over 230 ft long. The *Sara* provides a fantastic backdrop for underwater photographs. Grunts, goatfish, barjacks, stingrays and small schooling fish frequent the area. Depth is 80 ft. It is about 2½ miles north of Road Bay. Seas are usually choppy.

☆☆☆ Another favorite of macro photographers is the wreck of the *M.V. Ida Maria*. Scuttled in 1986 by divemasters Peabody and Gummitt, this

Grunts.

110-ft freighter sits on the sand at 60 ft. The deteriorating hull is overgrown with plate, pencil and clinging corals, anemones and sponges—home to sea horses, octopi, urchins, arrow crabs, banded cleaner shrimp, lavender shrimp and sea cucumbers. Huge green moray eels and lobsters peek out from the cracks along the bottom. Fish life and visibility are outstanding. Seas vary with weather. The *Ida Maria* is about six miles north of Limestone Bay.

☆☆☆ **Prickly Pear Reef** is an underwater canyon characterized by ledges and caverns. One formation resembling a chimney is a beautiful backdrop for underwater portraits. There are schooling goatfish, crabs, lobster, barracuda, friendly angels and grouper, squirrel fish, longnose butterfly fish, tarpon, mangrove snapper and grunts. Nurse sharks rest on the sandy bottom under the ledges. Depths range from 40 to 70 ft. Prickly Pear is west of the *M.V. Sara*—about six miles out from Long Bay.

☆ **Sandy Shallow** is recommended for novice divers. A garden of soft corals and gorgonians slopes from 30 to 70 ft. Seas are usually calm. Small schooling tropicals and invertebrates populate this spot.

Snorkeling

Catamaran and mono-hull sailboats leave Road Bay daily for snorkeling/picnic jaunts to **Little Bay,** on Anguilla's northwest coast; **Prickly Pear Cays,** six miles out of Road Bay; **Shoal Bay**, on the south end of Anguilla; **Scilly Cay; Dog Island,** 10 miles north of Road Bay and **Sandy Island,** the most popular out-island snorkeling destination. Tiny Sandy Island is surrounded by living reef from waist deep to 10 ft.

Beach snorkeling is good at **Barnes Bay**, West End, if you don't mind climbing down the crag from the Coccoloba Hotel. When winds and seas are calm, good snorkeling exists off the beach behind **Shoal Bay Villas**.

Note: Spearfishing and collecting is prohibited in Anguilla.

Dive Operators

The Dive Shop, Anguilla Ltd. is a PADI, five-star dive center offering reef and wreck tours for divers and snorkelers; certification and advanced training. Divemaster Thomas Peabody recommends use of a pony bottle and a safe second when diving the deep wrecks. Rates are $45 for a one-tank dive, $80 for a two-tank. Dive/accommodation package tours with any of the hotels can be arranged with The Dive Shop. ☎ (809) 497-2020; fax (809) 497-5125. Write to The Dive Shop Ltd., P.O. Box 247, The Valley, Anguilla, British West Indies. E-mail: peabodyt@zemu.candw.com.ai.

Anguillan Divers, Ltd. in Island Harbour dives the reefs and drop-offs on the east end of Anguilla. PADI certifications. Rates are $50 for a one-tank dive, three one-tank dives for $135, $70 for two one-tank dives. Snorkelers may join the trips for $15. Special snorkeling excursions that include a beach barbecue are offered. Prices vary with meal choice. ☎ (809) 497-4750. E-mail: axadiver@candw.com.ai.

Additional snorkeling cruises can be arranged through **Enchanted Island Cruises, Ltd.,** Road Bay. Enchanted Island operates a 50-ft catamaran, *Wildcat,* and a 31-ft monohull, *Counterpoint.* Local ☎ 497-3111; **Sandy Island Enterprises**, Road Bay with three *Shauna* power boats and a 26-ft sailboat, *Ragtime.* ☎ 497-6395; and **Suntastic Yacht Services**, Road Bay aboard a 37-ft yacht, *Skybird* and 30-ft powerboat, *Sunrise.* ☎ 497-6847.

Accommodations

Accommodations range from low- to mid-priced inns and cottages to luxurious resorts. A 10% service charge is added to resort bills in lieu of gratuities, and 8% government tax is added onto rooms only. Diving and snorkeling packages are offered through the dive operator. Web site for more hotels: http://galaxy.cau.edu/anguilla/hotels.html.

Syndans Apartments are clean, attractive studios overlooking Sandy Ground Beach and Road Salt Pond. Winter rates are $60 per day. ☎ (809) 497-3180, fax (809) 497-5381.

Shoal Bay Villas is a small, intimate, beach-front condominium hotel. Units feature full kitchen, split-level bedroom/living room and a private patio with hammock. Restaurant, tennis, jacuzzi. Snorkeling and scuba off the beach. Fresh-water pool. Winter rates are $265; summer $180 per night for two people. Boat and unlimited shore-dive packages offered. ☎ (800) 722-7045; (809) 497-2051; fax (809) 497-3631.

The Mariners is a West Indian-style, beachfront cottage complex at Sandy Ground. Choose from rooms or cottages, each with a verandah, refrigerator, ceiling fan, telephone and private bath. Winter rates for a double are $190-$320, summer, $125-$165. Dive packages, tennis, pool, restaurant. Romantic. ☎ (800) 848-7938 or (809) 497-2671; fax (809) 497-2901. Write P.O. Box 139, Sandy Ground, Anguilla, BWI. E-mail: sternj@candw.com.ai.

Anguilla Great House Beach Resort, built in the style of a West-Indian plantation house, sits on Rendezvous Bay where you can see St. Martin on the nearby horizon. Features include an open-air restaurant, pool, beach bar and snorkeling off the mile-long beach. Suites have well-equipped kitchenettes. Winter rates per day for double occupancy, are from $200 per day for a room; $440 with meals for two; summer, $130 for a room (double), $360 with meals. Money-saving packages available. ☎ (800) 583-9247 or (809) 497-6061; fax (809) 497-6019. E-mail flemingw@zemu.candw.com.ai.

La Sirena is an intimate hideaway overlooking Mead's Bay on the southwest portion of the island. Choose between individually-designed rooms and villas, all with ocean views, balcony, ceiling fans, phone and minibars. Restaurant, bar and two freshwater pools on site. Rates for a double are from $95 to $110 in summer; $180 to $215 in winter. Villas for one to four persons are from $160 in summer and from $290 in winter. Packages. ☎ (800) 331-9358 US and Canada; ☎ (800) 331-9358; fax (809) 497-6829. Write to P.O. Box 200, Mead's Bay, Anguilla BWI. E-mail: masshardt@ candw.com.ai.

The Ferryboat Inn is a small family-operated inn on the south side of the island. Snorkeling and swimming off the beach. Well-equipped apartments are adjacent to the beach. Restaurant. Rates are from $140 per day in winter, $78 in summer, for a one-bedroom apartment, double occupancy. Rooms are clean, modern and attractive. ☎ (809) 497-6613; fax (809) 497-6713.

The most romantic and luxurious hotel on Anguilla is the **Malliouhana,** which sits high on a rocky cliff over Meads Bay on the Southwest shore surrounded by two miles of sand beaches. This tastefully appointed resort features an exercise hall and massage room, three pools, boutique, shops, hair salon, French gourmet restaurant, tennis courts with night lights, and impeccable service. Complimentary snorkeling and fishing gear, water skiing, cruises, windsurfing, Sunfish and catamarans are included in the rates for rooms and suites. Doubles, winter, $480 to $1,080 per day. Summer, $240 to $565 per day. $25 to $50 extra for child. ☎ (800) 835-0796 or (809) 497-6111; fax (809) 497-6011. Write to P.O. Box 173, Anguilla, Leeward Islands, BWI.

Cinnamon Reef Beach Club in Little Harbour offers villa suites with spacious, split-level bedroom/living rooms, private patios and hammocks. Award-winning restaurant. Beautiful beach, tennis, jacuzzi. Winter rates, breakfast included, are from $250 to $325; summer, $150 to $225. ☎ (800) 346-7084; (809) 497-2727; fax 497-3727. E-mail: cinnamon-reef @candw.com.ai.

The Inns of Anguilla are a group of 23 hotels, guests houses, apartments and villas offering attractively-priced accommodations from $65 per night. Week-long packages from $380. For a list, description, brochures and rates of the inns, ☎ (800) 553-4939; fax (809) 497-2710 or write to The Anguilla Tourist Office, P.O. Box 1388, Factory Plaza, The Valley, Anguilla. BWI. In the UK: Anguilla Tourist Office, WINDOTEL, 3 Epirus Rd, London SW 67UJ, ☎ 01-937-7725; fax 071-938-4793. E-mail: atbtour@candw.com.ai.

Other Activities and Sightseeing

Sailing, deep-sea fishing, sunset cruises, birdwatching at Little Bay and Crocus Bay, shelling and relaxing are the mainstay of activity on Anguilla. Plans for a movie theater and museum are in the works.

Anguilla's sightseeing spots are the **Wallblake Historic House** near the Roman Catholic Church; the **prison at Crocus Hill**, the old **Warden's Place** in the Valley; the **Fountain Cave area**, the **Devonish Cotton Gin Gallery**, **Road Bay** and **Sandy Ground** where you'll find the dive shop and fishing boats.

Anguilla does not have a tourist-oriented nightlife, but a 15-minute ferry ride to St. Martin brings you to a wealth of duty-free shops, casinos and evening entertainment. Ferries leave Blowing Point for Marigot, St. Martin every 40 minutes from 7:30 am till 11:00 pm. ☎ 6853.

For guided archaeological tours write to P.O. Box 252, Anguilla in advance of your trip. Deep-sea fishing can be arranged at Road Bay and Island Harbor, glass bottom boat cruises are from Shoal Bay and Island Harbour (☎ 4155); sunset cruises to out islands are offered by Enchanted Island Cruises, ☎ 3111.

Dining

Anguilla's leading French eatery, **Hibernia** at Island Harbour offers dining on a huge veranda overlooking the sea. Choice menu picks include smoked Caribbean fish, grilled crayfish in lemongrass sauce, grilled snapper in honey and garlic, and chestnut ice cream. Open for lunch and dinner. ☎ 4290. Major credit cards.

Uncle Ernie's in Shoal Bay is a laid-back beach bar and restaurant where you can get a beer for one dollar. Selections include barbecued chicken, fish or ribs with chips. ☎ 3907.

Reefside, a friendly beachfront complex adjacent to Shoalbay Villas, opens every day for breakfast, lunch and dinner. Offers grilled lobster, steaks, steamed shrimp and tropical drinks. Catch the beach barbecue on Wed, Fri and Sun from 12 to 3 pm. ☎ 2051. Major credit cards.

Fat Cat in George Hill packages hors d'oeuvres, entrées, salads, and desserts ready to heat in the oven or microwave. Call ahead for picnics, special entrées or special-occasion cakes. ☎ 2307. American Express.

Ships Galley on the beach at Sandy Ground, features sumptuous West-Indian dishes—stewed whelks (shellfish) with sweet potatoes, scampi, grilled snapper and lobster. Open for breakfast, lunch and dinner. ☎ 2040. Major credit cards.

Vegetarian dishes with a Mexican flair are offered at **Que Pasa** in Sandy Ground, where the chef whips up stuffed mushrooms, chili-potato soup, enchiladas in red chili sauce, quesadillas and burritos for lunch and dinner. Lobster, chicken, pork and beef are available for all dishes. Take-out and delivery service. ☎ 3171. Major credit cards.

Snorkel off the beach, then lunch under the seagrape trees at **La Fontana** in Shoal Bay. This garden of delights is open all day from 8 am till 10 pm and offers Caribbean and Italian specialties. Dinner favorites are *Rassa alla Zio Mario*—duck breast with blueberries and barolo wine—and *Lobster Conte Panuss*, lobster in fresh herbs and wine. ☎ 3491. Major credit cards.

For American food stop at the **Paradise Cafe** in Katouche, ☎ 3200 or enjoy luxurious Anguillian surroundings at **The Old House** at George Hill ☎ 2228. **KoalKeel**, in The Valley, specializes in Caribbean seafood. ☎ 2930.

Facts

Helpful Phone Numbers: Police, ☎ 2333. Hospital, ☎ 2551/1552.

Nearest Recompression Chamber: SABA (38 miles).

Airlines: Wallblake Airport. International airports serving Anguilla are St. Maarten, San Juan and Antigua. St. Kitts and St. Thomas also have scheduled feederline services. WINAIR has flights from St. Maarten, St. Thomas. American Eagle links with flights from San Juan. LIAT connects to St. Kitts and Antigua. Flying time from St. Maarten is 7 minutes, San Juan and Antigua, one hour; St. Thomas, 45 minutes; St. Kitts, 35 minutes.

Ferry Service: From Marigot Bay, St. Martin to Blowing Point, 15-20 minutes. Ferries depart at approximately 40-minute intervals during the day. There is one evening ferry that departs Blowing Point at 6 pm and Marigot, St. Martin at 7:30. Fare: US $10 day; US $12 night.

Driving: On the left. Driver's license required. US $6 for 3-month permit. May be obtained at the police station or any car-rental agency.

Documents: Passports are required of all visitors except US and Canadian citizens who may present proof of citizenship in the form of card or official photo I.D. such as driver's license along with an original birth certificate with a raised seal. Onward ticket required.

Customs: Visitors may bring in duty-free one carton of cigarettes or cigars, one half-pound of tobacco, one bottle of liquor, four ounces of perfume.

If you are sailing your own boat you must clear customs and immigration at Blowing Point, across from Marigot, St. Martin or at Sandy Ground.

Currency: The EC (Eastern Caribbean) dollar. $2.68 EC to US $1.

Language: English.

Climate: Average temperature is 80° F. Rainfall averages 35 inches per year.

Clothing: Lightweight casual dress. Nudity, topless swimming and sunbathing are forbidden. Wearing swimwear off the beach is frowned upon.

Electricity: 110 volts, 60 cycles.

Time: Atlantic Standard (Eastern Standard + 1 hr).

Departure Tax: US $10 Airport; US $2, Ferry Port.

Religious Services: Methodist, Anglican, Baptist, Seventh Day Adventist, Roman Catholic, Church of God and the Apostolic Faith Churches.

Additional Information: Anguilla Tourist & Information Office, P.O. Box 1388, Factory Plaza, The Valley, Anguilla BWI. ☎ (800) 553-4939; fax (809) 497-2710. *In the UK,* Anguilla Tourist Office, WINDOTEL, 3 Epirus Rd, London SW 67UJ, ☎ 01-937-7725; fax 071-938-4793. E-mail: atbtour@candw.com.ai. Web site: http://galaxy.cau.edu./anguilla/.

Antigua & Barbuda

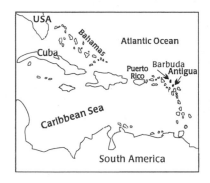

Set smack in the center of the Caribbean, Antigua and Barbuda, a two-island nation, offer visitors the best of England's charm, great diving and a wealth of enticing resorts.

Antigua, a 108-square-mile island, populated by 76,000 people, is the largest of the two and of the Leeward Islands. Its capital, St. John's, is the hub of tourist activity with a bustling cruise-ship terminal, duty-free shops, full-service dive shops, fast food and gourmet restaurants. Formerly a thriving sugar cane producer, the island has given way to a booming tourist industry since its independence from the British Crown in 1981. Physically, the island is circular and ringed by 365 secluded beaches, coves, bays and small harbors. Gentle hills to the south slope down to a beautiful turquoise sea pierced by miles of coral shoals. Beneath the surface lies a rocky terrain of coral cliffs, caves and buttresses, an oasis to thousands of fish, rays and shellfish. Shallow reefs and countless wrecks surround the island.

Barbuda, 26 miles north of Antigua, is considered one of the last frontiers of the Caribbean. It is a beautifully undeveloped and pristine low-coral island where there are no paved roads, few hotel rooms and only a handful of restaurants. Miles of secluded, untouched pink sand beaches meld into a sea of well-developed reefs teeming with lobster, hawksbill turtles, conch, and fish. Conservation efforts protect large tracts of coral banks with marine-park status. Barbuda is also habitat to the Frigate Bird Sanctuary, one of the largest in the world.

History

The islands' history dates back to 1775 BC when the Siboney tribe inhabited the land. In 1493, on his second voyage to the New World, Christopher Columbus sighted and named Antigua, in homage to the miracle-working saint, Santa Maria de la Antigua of Seville. More than a century later, in 1632, an English party from St. Kitts landed on the island and claimed it for the Crown—a relationship that would remain until 1981 when Antigua gained full independence.

Contributor: Gilbert Gjersvik

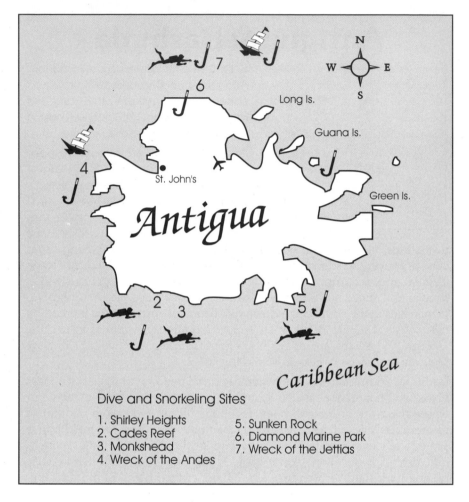

Dive and Snorkeling Sites

1. Shirley Heights
2. Cades Reef
3. Monkshead
4. Wreck of the Andes
5. Sunken Rock
6. Diamond Marine Park
7. Wreck of the Jettias

Best Dive and Snorkeling Sites

ANTIGUA

Antigua's dive and snorkeling sites are one to two miles offshore, no more than a five-minute boat ride, in most cases, along a barrier reef that surrounds most of the island. Dive shops frequent the south- and west-coast reefs where visibility is good, seas are dependably calm and currents mild, but new areas are continually opening up. Depths range from shallow to drop-offs of more than 2,000 ft. Dive shops offer both scuba and snorkeling tours. Scuba divers must show a certification card.

☆☆☆ **Shirley Heights**, off the south coast, is one of the island's most spectacular areas. Jagged cliffs, coral buttresses, huge boulders and sheer drop-offs form the subsea terrain. Residents include eagle rays, schools of spade fish and turtles with frequent sightings of mantas and dolphins. Huge mackerel and kingfish pass through. Depths are from 10 to 100 ft. Visibility is usually excellent.

☆☆☆ **Cades Reef**, a five-mile shelf off Antigua's southwest corner, is Antigua's largest reef structure. It has 25 or more different dive and snorkeling sites that vary in depth from 20 ft to 90 ft. Examples are **Lemon Ridge**, with depths from 20 to 45 ft; **The Chimney**, home to huge pillar coral formations inhabited by margate, squirrelfish, nurse sharks, morays; and the **The Pillars**, at 50 to 80 ft, where you'll see queen angel fish, trigger fish, black durgons, spotted and green moray eels.

Cades' ridges and valleys are shot through with small caves hiding lobster, crabs and small fish. Forests of elkhorn and staghorn coral provide shelter to an abundant fish population, including huge grouper, eagle rays, throngs of grunts and sergeant majors, parrotfish, sting rays, snapper and barracuda. Visibility often exceeds 100 ft when seas are calm.

☆☆☆☆ **Monkshead** is a sandy coral passage in the center of Cades which is populated by garden eels, large stingrays and jacks. Spearfishing, or collecting shells, shellfish and coral are prohibited.

The Wreck of the *Andes*, an old freighter, lies in 20 ft of water at the bottom of Deep Bay, 100 yds off the west coast. She went down in 1905 when a cargo of cotton and pitch caught fire. Abundant with fish, the hull and scattered remains are overgrown with plate corals and red sponges. Good for snorkeling and diving during summer. Visibility during a swell can go down to zero.

☆☆☆ **Sunken Rock**, just five minutes off the south coast, is perhaps the island's most popular dive when sea conditions permit. The dive starts at 30 ft and drops off to 150 ft. Hundreds of coral crevices and ledges attract huge rays, amberjack, and barracuda. Recommended for experienced ocean divers.

☆☆☆ **Diamond Bank,** located 2½ miles off the north coast of Antigua, is a large shallow barrier reef complex riddled with small caves, boulders, overhangs and canyons. Marine life is prolific with huge rays, nurse sharks, morays, lobster, queen helmuts, conch, and tropicals. Depths range from shallow to about 100 ft. Trips are weather-dependent. Usually choppy.

Wreck of the *Jettias*, a 310-ft steamship that hit the reefs in 1917, rests in 25 ft of water and offers dramatic photo opportunities when weather and visibility permits. This area is subject to swells and silting during high winds. Summer is the best time to dive the *Jettias*.

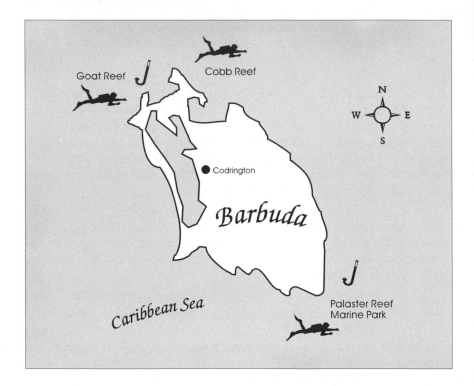

Snorkeling Antigua

When seas are calm, good shore snorkeling may be found in Half Moon Bay in Saint Philip Parish, off the beaches of the Galley Bay Hotel at Deep Bay, Pineapple Beach Hotel at Long Bay on the Southeast coast, the Hawksbill Beach Resort at Five Islands Village just south of Deep Bay and the Sandpiper Reef Hotel. (The Galley Bay and Sandpiper hotels were not open at press time, but you can still use the beaches). Check with local dive shops for wind and current conditions before entering the water.

Boone's Reef, located one mile offshore from Dickenson Bay, is a protected reef area, good for beginning and experienced snorkelers. The reef starts at two ft and drops off to 25 ft. Lots of juvenile and schooling fish. Visibility varies with sea conditions. Glassbottom and snorkeling boats depart from Dickenson Bay.

Snorkeling trips to **Prickly Pear Island,** a tiny coral-fringed island off Beggars Point on the North coast, can be arranged through Miguel Holiday Trip Adventures at ☎ 461-0361.

BARBUDA

The dense reefs fringing Barbuda are largely unexplored. There are no dive shops on the island, but experienced snorkelers can swim to Palaster Reef, off Palmetto Point on the southwest tip of the island. More than 100 shipwrecks have been documented off Barbuda's coast. Charter day trips from Antigua can be easily arranged.

Antigua Dive Operators

Note: Area code changed from 809 to 268 as of 3/97.

Aquanaut Diving Centres are at the St. James' Club, ☎ (268) 460-5000 and the Galleon Beach Club, ☎ (268) 460-1450. Or try **Dive Antigua** at the Rex Halcyon Cove Hotel in Dickenson Bay. ☎ (268) 462-3483, VHF channel 68. **Dockyard Divers** at English Harbour visits the south coast dive and snorkeling sites, ☎ (268)-460-1178, fax (268)-460-1179, VHF channel 68; **Jolly Dive** at Club Antigua, ☎ (268) 462-0061; **Pirate Divers** at the Lord Nelson Beach Hotel, ☎ (268) 462-3094.

Catamarans such as the **Wadadli Cats** (☎ 462-2980) offer excellent sail-snorkeling trips. Lunch, drinks and equipment are included in the price. For a snorkeling trip to Prickly Pear Island contact **Miguel Holiday Trip Adventures** at ☎ 461-0361. The day trip departs from Hodges Bay next to the Pelican Club on the north-east side of the island. This trip departs three times a week, but special trips can also be arranged.

Accommodations

Antigua is not a "diver's island" and has no dedicated dive resorts, but those listed either have dive operators on the premises, are associated with diving, or are located near popular dive or snorkeling areas.

Note: A 7% room tax and 10% service charge are added to accommodation rates. Some resorts include them in their package rates. Some do not. Check with individual operations. Web site: www. interknowledge.com/antigua-barbuda/index.html.

Antigua

Curtain Bluff Resort sits on a dramatic, 13-acre seaside bluff on Antigua's southern shore. This all-inclusive resort is the closest jump-off point to Cades Reef diving. The property slopes down to two coves, one calm and good for snorkeling, the other with rolling surf. Amenities include 61 beachfront rooms and suites. Dive shop on premises offers boat tours only. Certification courses, if desired, can be arranged with nearby shops. Rates cover the room, all meals for two, bar service, afternoon tea and hors d'oeuvres, mail service, water-skiing, scuba diving (two dives per day—gear included), snorkeling trip to Cades Reef each morning, deep-sea fishing, sailing, tennis, golf, squash and croquet. Summer and fall rates (Oct 18 to Dec 18, April 15 to Oct 17th), $525 for two per day; winter rates (Dec 18 to April 14), $655 per day for two. 10% gratuities and 8% tax not included. ☎ (888) 289-9898 or (212) 289-8888, direct (268) 462-8400, fax (268) 462-8409.

Set on Antigua's southernmost tip, the **Galleon Beach Club and Hotel** offers one- and two-bedroom cottages and suites with fully equipped kitchens. Rooms overlook Freemans' Bay and English Harbour. Dive shop, restaurant and bar on premises. Winter rates for a one-bedroom suite start at $210 per night. Two-bedroom cottage for up to four people, $230 per night. Diving and meals are extra. ☎ (268) 460-1024, fax (268)-460-1450 or book through your travel agent.

The **Copper and Lumber Store Hotel** is a charming 17th-century brick building restored as an intimate 14-suite hostelry, located in Nelson's Dockyard. Each individually decorated room features beamed ceilings and dormer windows overlooking the harbour with luxurious Persian rugs, period antiques, four-poster beds and mahogany baths with brass fixtures. Ferry service to Galleon Beach for swimming and scuba. Dive shop on premises. Learn-to-dive packages offered at $985 (winter), $700 (summer), include seven nights accommodations, airport transfers, a four-day certification course, equipment. For experienced divers: $885 (winter), $ 620 (summer); includes seven nights accommodations, airport transfers, five two-tank dives, dive-boat pickup, weights, belts, tanks. ☎ (268) 460-1058 or book through your travel agent.

The lagoon off **The Galley Bay Hotel** is a favorite snorkeling spot. The resort does not offer scuba, but can arrange for reef trips through nearby shops. Galley Bay is a 30-room, all-inclusive resort set on 40 acres of landscaped ground between a half-mile sandy beach and a lagoon. A variety of accommodations feature ceiling fans, refrigerator, cottages with grass roofs, and a gourmet restaurant. Rates per couple start at $275 per day and include all meals, drinks, and taxes. ☎ (800) 345-0356, direct (268) 462-0302.

Another snorkelers' favorite, though expensive, is **Jumby Bay,** an exclusive, yet accessible, luxury resort on its own island, two miles north of Antigua. Off the beach are beautiful coral patches and throngs of tropicals. Jumby Bay offers 38 suites, all with ocean views and secluded beaches. Rates include three meals, afternoon tea, unlimited cocktails, laundry and picnic service. Three snorkeling trips are made to Bird Island each week. Facilities include tennis, water-skiing and instruction, snorkeling, Sunfish sailboats, bicycles, croquet and instruction, putting green, bar and laundry service. Rates include three meals, afternoon tea, unlimited cocktails, laundry and picnic service. For seven nights: winter, $1,050 per night, per couple; summer

Triggerfish.

$650 per night per couple. 18% tax not included. Scuba diving extra, arranged at the desk. ☎ (800) 421-9016; (268) 462-6000.

Long Bay Hotel, on Long Bay, offers 18 rooms and six cottages. Dive trips with the Long Bay Dive Shop visit nearby reefs and wrecks. Snorkeling trips, tennis, two restaurants, pretty beach. Their boat takes a maximum of three people on a dive offering personal attention and total flexibility. Winter hotel rates average $255 per day. ☎ (800) 291-2005, fax (268) 463-2439. Dive shop: ☎ (268) 463-2005, fax (268) 463-2439.

Pineapple Beach Club is an all-inclusive 125-room hotel located on Long Bay Beach. There is good snorkeling on a shallow coral reef off the hotel beach. Scuba can be arranged with local shops but is not included in the resort's all-inclusive package rates. Winter rates, per night, per couple start at about $390 for a double; summer at $320 for a double, including all meals for two, drinks, wind surfing, sailboats, snorkeling equipment, fishing, fitness center, tennis, beach, pool, nature trails and evening entertainment. Room tax is included. Reserve through travel agents or ☎ (800) 345-0356 or (268) 463-2006.

Rex Halcyon Cove Resort on Dickenson Bay offers a choice of first-class rooms. Standard rooms at $185 per day for a double in summer, $260 per day in winter, have double beds, shower, ceiling fan, phone and terrace. Superior rooms include a mini-fridge, cable TV, air-conditioning. Dive Antigua on premises offers dive tours, PADI training and gear rentals. Snorkeling pro, Tom Paterson, operates the resort's *Splish Splash* glass bottom boat and offers trips to Paradise Reef. Recreational facilities include tennis, beach volleyball, shuffleboard and table tennis. Water-skiing, scuba and fishing are charged separately. Restaurants offer casual or fine dining. ☎ (800) 255-5859, direct (268) 462-0256, fax (268) 462-0271.

The **Royal Antiguan Beach & Tennis Resort,** located on Deep Bay at the entrance of St. John's Harbor, features three restaurants, four bars, eight tennis courts, a watersports center, freeform pool with swim-up bar, white sand beach, children's activities and nightly entertainment. It has 282 spacious rooms (12 poolside cottages), each with air-conditioning, telephones, color TV, key card locks. Marker buoys for the wreck of the *Andes*, 100 yds offshore, can be seen from the *al fresco* restaurant on Andes Bay. Diving is arranged by the desk with nearby dive shop. Room-only rates for a double are $150 in summer, $190 in winter. Hotel ☎ (800) 345-0356, fax (407) 994-6344. Write to Box 1322, Deep Bay, Antigua, WI. E-mail: VeryCaribb@aol.com.

Sandals Antigua, a luxurious resort village on Dickenson Bay, features lavish round suites known as *rondovals*, dive shop, fitness center, five restaurants, five pools, five whirlpools, gorgeous white sand beach, swim-up bar, outdoor dancing and dining. Diving and snorkeling are part of its all-inclusive package, which also includes meals, land and watersports. Three-night rates start at $870 per person in winter, $830 in summer; $1,020 for beachfront in winter, $965 in summer; six-night all-inclusive packages start at $1,520 in winter. Book through your travel agent or ☎ (800) SANDALS; Canada (800) 545-8283; UK 44-171-581-9895. Web site: http://www. sandals.com.

Sonesta Beach Resort, formerly the Casablanca Resort, retains a Byzantine motif with Arabian-style arches and patterns, Moroccan pools, and open-air restaurants. Situated on Rendezvous Bay, the resort has two tennis courts, pool, powder-white beach on Rendezvous Bay. Rooms feature satellite TV, mini-bar, porch or patio. Diving may be arranged at the desk, but not offered by the resort. Rates are from $290 per room, double occupancy, to $750 in winter. From $180 for April through mid-December. ☎ (800) SONESTA.

St. James Club, on 100 acres of private peninsula, features 73 two-bedroom villas, 20 suites, 85 rooms, all with ocean or bay view. Amenities include three pools, two beaches, seven tennis courts, water-skiing, sailing, windsurfing, horseback riding, gym and children's facilities, three restaurants, night club, casino, salon and shops. Scuba school, fishing and private marina. All-inclusive rates including meals and accommodations (not diving) for two are from $500 per night. Aquanaut Divers on property. ☎ (800) 274-0008.

Budget-minded divers will find lower rates and comfortable, air-conditioned accommodations at the **Falmouth Harbour Beach** apartments in the English harbour area ☎ (800) 621-1270, and **Sunset Cove Resort** on Runaway Bay. ☎ (800) 766-6016.

Barbuda

Palmetto Hotel, Barbuda. Located on Palmetto's Peninsula, to the southwestern side of Barbuda, this resort consists of a 63-room luxury hotel and 67 villas facing the ocean. The surroundings insure complete privacy and comfort. Two restaurants. Book through your travel agent or ☎ (268) 460-0440.

For additional Antigua accommodations contact the Antigua & Barbuda Department of Tourism (see chapter end for listings).

Other Activities

A number of leisure cruises, most of which last the better part of a day and include lunch, sightseeing, snorkeling and other entertainment, sail Antigua's jagged coast. The *Servabo Fun Cruise*, a 70-ft Brixham gaff-rigged ketch based off the shore of Dickenson Bay, departs from Antigua Village. The *Jolly Roger Pirate Cruise* (☎ 462-2064), Antigua's largest two-masted schooner, offers daily and Saturday evening cruises. The *Falcon*, an elegant catamaran, offers sunset and day snorkeling cruises to Barbuda and Bird Island, a tiny, uninhabited island that is a nesting ground for red-billed tropic birds, sooty terns, brown noddies, and brown pelicans. Outstanding shallow snorkeling reefs skirt Bird Island's beach. Most hotels can arrange for any of these cruises.

Antigua's northeast trade winds are ideal for windsurfers of all abilities. The island's sheltered west coast is perfect for beginners, while on the east coast, the giant "Atlantic rollers" are challenging even for advanced surfers.

Windsurfing lessons for novices, intermediate, and advanced board surfers are offered at several hotels, including **Jolly Beach Hotel's Windsurfing Sailing School** and **Patrick Scales Water Sports** at Lord Nelson Beach Hotel.

Water-skiing, jet skiing, and parasailing are offered at the **Wadadli Watersports Centre** at Buccaneer Cove and **Unlimited Hydro Sports** at Dickenson Bay and Jolly Beach.

Deep-sea fishing charters can be arranged through most hotels. Tennis courts are everywhere. Viking Tennis Club, ☎ 462-2260, is a private club that offers temporary membership for visitors. **Temo Sports,** ☎ 460-1781, a tennis and squash complex, has synthetic grass courts and two glass-backed squash courts. Squash is also offered at the **Bucket Club,** ☎ 462-3060.

Golf enthusiasts will enjoy Antigua's fine 18-hole, par-72 course at **Cedar Valley Golf Club,** ☎ 462-0161. This course has panoramic views of Antigua's northern coast and surrounding areas. Daily greens fees are $20 for 18 holes, $15 for nine holes; carts are $25 for 18 holes and $13 for nine.

Escorted horseback beach and cross-country tours are arranged at the **Wadadli Stables,** ☎ 462-2721 in St. John's.

Antigua's exquisite scenery, varied terrain and well-preserved monuments make excellent walking and hiking territory. The capital of St. John's is filled with interesting attractions and shops, and the national park at Nelson's Dockyard provides historic sightseeing opportunities. Mond's Hill, Boggy Peak, Fig Tree Drive, and Megaliths at Greencastel Hill are just a few of the hiking areas for adventurous souls.

Bicycles are another way to view Antigua's scenery. Mountain bikes can be rented for $10 per day from **Sun Cycles**. ☎ 461-0324.

Sightseeing

ANTIGUA

Two major sightseeing areas are the capital city of St. John's on the northwestern side of the island and English Harbour on the south side. St. John's, with a population of 35,000, is the center of business and visitor activity. More than half of the country's hotels surround the capital city.

Situated on a hilltop overlooking the center of town, **St. John's Cathedral** was originally constructed in 1683 and replaced in 1745. It was rebuilt and reconsecrated in the 19th century, after a shattering earthquake. Its unusual architecture features two Baroque-style towers. The **Museum of Antigua & Barbuda**, located in the Old Courthouse, exhibits artifacts tracing the rich history of the sister islands, from pre-historic times through independence. **Government House** is the official residence of the Governor General for Antigua in St. John's. As such, it is not regularly open to the public, but is a fine example of 17th-century colonial architecture. **Fort James**, which once defended the entrance of St. John's Harbor, features weapons and other military details dating back to the American Revolution.

Other interesting things to see in and around St. John's include the **Public Market**, a semi-open-air mart that provides much local color and the opportunity to sample native produce. The **Antigua Rum Distillery,** which may be toured with prior arrangement, is located at Deep Water Harbour. Cavalier and Old Mill Rums are made here. **Heritage Quay,** a shopping complex and cruise ship pier, offers a wide variety of duty-free shops, a casino, and a hotel. **Redcliffe Quay**, a restored arsenal, now houses shops and restaurants.

Many more historical buildings can be found on the other side of the island within the confines of **Nelson's Dockyard**. Built in 1784 at **English Harbour**, it served as the headquarters for Admiral Horatio Nelson, the commander of the Leeward Islands Squadron, during the days when a man's worth was measured in how quickly he could reload his musket.

Landmarks of the seamen's commitment to Antigua have been painstakingly restored and the area is now a national park. One landmark in particular is the **Copper and Lumber Store Hotel,** the former center of activity for purchasing construction materials. While the bottom served as a supply store, the upper floors were used as quarters for sailors whose ships were being hauled for repairs. Today, those early quarters are elegant rooms of a Georgian hotel, filled with period furnishings. Two other buildings, the old **Capstan House** and the **Cordage and Canvas Store,** have been restored for additional hotel space by the Copper and Lumber owners. The **Admiral's Inn and Restaurant** also provides accommodations and the opportunity for leisurely investigation.

The complex has two museums. **Admiral's House,** with its bust of Nelson framing the doorway, is an original structure full of Nelsonian mementos reminiscent of his era. **Clarence House**, the former home of Prince William Henry, Duke of Clarence, who later became King William IV, is a graceful Georgian stone residence overlooking the Dockyard. Now home to Antigua's Governor General, when he is not in residence, it is open to the public, and the caretaker provides visitors with a lively lecture on the house's origins and history. In modern times, it has served as the vacation residence of Princess Margaret.

To the north are the stately ruins of Shirley Heights, named for General Thomas Shirley, the former governor of the Leeward Islands. The fortress includes extensive fortifications, barracks, and powder magazines which serve as great "lookout" points. On Sunday afternoons, Shirley Heights is a gathering spot where visitors can enjoy local reggae and steel bands and a tasty barbecue meal, as they watch the sunset over the dockyard area. On the southern side of the Harbour, about a 10-minute walk from the dockyard, are the remains of **Fort Berkeley**, a small outpost with eight cannons.

In the center of the island lies Antigua's pioneer sugar plantation **Betty's Hope Estate**, which introduced large-scale sugar cultivation and innovative methods of processing sugar. It was founded in the 1650's by Governor Keynell and granted to Christopher Codrington in 1688. The Codrington family had interest in Betty's Hope for more than 250 years until 1920. Both Christopher Codrington and his son served as Governor General of the Leeward Islands, developing the plantation as the seat of government during the late 17th and early 18th centuries. Two old windmill towers still stand, together with the walls and arches of the plantation's boiling house. A conservation project was recently completed that has handsomely refurbished this historic site.

BARBUDA

After the magnificent reefs that surround the island, Barbuda's **Frigate Bird Sanctuary** tops the list of sightseeing favorites. It is located at the north end of Codrington Lagoon, and is only accessible by small boat. Here, the *Fregata Magnificens* brood their eggs in mangrove bushes that stretch for miles. In olden days, sailors called the frigate bird the "man-o-war bird" and the "hurricane bird," because their eight-foot wingspan gives them enough power to easily soar as high as 2,000 ft. Although visitors can see the birds throughout the year, the mating season, from September to February, is a brilliant spectacle when the male frigate inflates a crimson pouch at his throat and breast in an attempt to attract the female frigate. Chicks hatch from December to March and remain in the nest for up to eight months until they are strong enough to fly.

A visit to the Sanctuary is a 45-minute trip in a wooden rowboat powered by a small outboard motor. The boats are piloted by Barbudians who cautiously navigate through the mangroves.

Barbuda's dry climate attracts many other species of birds, including pelicans, warblers, snipes, ibis, herons, kingfishers, tropical mockingbirds, oyster catchers, and cormorants. Other wildlife found roaming the island are white-tailed deer, boar, donkeys, and red-footed tortoises. Unique to its marine life is the Barbudian lobster.

Besides snorkeling and bird watching, Barbuda offers some interesting attractions and activities. **Highland House** is the former estate of Sir William Codrington, the first lessee of Barbuda, when the annual rent to the crown was "one fatted sheep, on demand." **Dark Cave** has deep pools of clear water that extend approximately one mile underground, and at the **Caves at Two Foot Bay** visitors can climb down into a circular chamber through a hole in the roof to view faded Arawak drawings on the walls.

Several Antigua-based companies offer day tours of Barbuda. Tour prices are approximately $120 per person. They include round-trip airfare, a tour with a visit to the Frigate Bird Sanctuary and lunch.

Dining

The cuisine of Antigua and Barbuda has evolved from the tastes and foods of the many groups that make up the islands' West Indian heritage: Carib Indians, French, English, Africans, Spanish, Portuguese, Indian, Lebanese, and Syrian. The influence of these cultures, and the diversity of locally grown fruits and vegetables, combine to create a cuisine that will satisfy the most discerning palate.

A trip to the public market in St. John's is a delectable opportunity to sample the real riches of Antigua and Barbuda. Visitors will find a variety of fruits and vegetables, some that are familiar to many in North America, but known by a different name. For instance, a *green fig* is a small green banana that must be cooked before eating. *Christophine*, a large squash with pale green flesh, is boiled and served hot. The *breadfruit* is rounded with a hard green skin and soft inside, and is cooked and served as a vegetable or made into bread, pie, or pudding. The islands' most famous fruit is the *Antigua Black Pineapple,* a smaller, sweeter version of the Hawaiian variety.

Lobster, conch, cockles (mollusks), grouper, and red snapper are other local seafood delights.

Coconut Grove Beach Restaurant (☎ 462-0806) sits beneath swaying palm trees at the water's edge on Dickenson Bay, and offers fresh lobster, seafood and Caribbean dishes. Open for breakfast, lunch and dinner.

In St. John's, **Brother B's** is an inexpensive spot for local dishes— dumpling and mackerel, curried conch, or fresh fish, hamburgers, or salads.

Tasty island dishes such as spicy land crab backs, saltfish balls and fish at reasonable prices are served at **18 Carat**, Lower Church Street, St. John's (☎ 462-0016), a porch and garden restaurant in the heart of town. Top it off with a piece of freshly made rum cake.

Situated high on a hilltop with a spectacular panorama view is Antigua's newest restaurant, **Jaws**. This lively spot features an indoor/outdoor dance floor with live entertainment. The kitchen, open till midnight, offers light fare.

Alberto's at Willoughby Bay offers dining in a giant gazebo cooled by the Caribbean breeze. Local seafood, prepared with an Italian accent, includes conch salad, lobster, and pasta dishes, and the wine list features many Italian favorites.

Facts

Nearest Recompression Chamber: None on island.

Getting There: American Airlines from the United States; Air Canada direct from Canada; British Airways direct from London; BWIA direct from the US and Canada. Lufthansa direct from Frankfurt. LIAT flies inter-island. Bird International airport accommodates large aircraft, and passengers are served by a new and modern terminal.

Driving: British-style, on the left. A valid driver's license will secure a temporary license in Antigua at a nominal cost (US $12).

Documents: Visitors from the US, Canada, UK and Germany require proof of citizenship such as a passport or birth certificate. Also required is an onward or return ticket.

Customs: Arriving passengers are allowed 200 cigarettes, one quart of liquor, and six ounces of perfume.

Currency: Antigua & Barbuda use the Eastern Caribbean dollar, also known as the "Bee Wee." The currency is tied to the US dollar at an average exchange rate of EC $2.65 for US $1, subject to fluctuation. Most major credit cards accepted.

Taxes: Airport Departure tax for stay-over visitors is US $10. A 7% government tax is added to all hotel bills. There is a 10% service charge added to bills in lieu of tipping. Elsewhere tipping is discretionary.

Climate: Antigua's temperatures range between an average of 76° F in January/February to 83° F in August and September. Rainfall averages 45 inches per year with relatively low humidity. The rainy season is September, October and November, but there are usually only short showers.

Clothing: Casual light, loose-fitting cotton clothes are suggested. Generally informal, but some hotels and casinos require jackets at night. Ladies are requested to wear skirts or slacks rather than abbreviated shorts or swimwear while in the city. Use a light wetsuit or wetskin for diving during winter.

Electricity: Dual voltage available in major hotels, 220 and 110 AC, 60 cycles.

Language: English with an island lilt—"No big ting."

Religious Services: Protestant, Roman Catholic, Seventh-Day Adventist.

Additional Information; *In the US,* Antigua & Barbuda Department of Tourism, 610 Fifth Ave., Suite 311, NY, NY 10020. ☎ (212) 541-4117 or 121 S.W. First St., Suite 1001, Miami, FL 33131, ☎ (305) 381-6762

In Canada, Antigua & Barbuda Department of Tourism and Trade, 60 St. Clair Ave. East, Suite 205, Toronto, Ontario, MT4 IN5, ☎ (416) 961-3085.

In Europe, Antigua House, 15 Thayer St., London W1, England, ☎ 01-486-7073; Postfach 1147 Minnholzweg 2, 6242 Kronberg 1, Germany, ☎ 06173-5011.

Aruba

Vacationers discovered Aruba in 1957, when the first cruise ship, *Tradewinds,* arrived. The island has since developed into a top tourist destination. Easy to reach, it is just 18 miles from Venezuela's coast—yet far enough away to escape the hustle and bustle of civilization.

And, it's easy to explore, both above and below the sea. Just 20 miles long and six miles wide, its luxury hotels and dive boats line up neatly along the western (leeward) shore—minutes from popular reef and wreck dives. The shops and sights of the capital, Oranjestad, are nearby too.

Aruba's sub-seascapes encompass dramatic wrecks, rocky shoals, and reefs. Coastal scenery is impressive with miles of white, soft sand beaches along the western and southern shores. Huge rocks dot the eastern windward coast where a natural coral bridge rises from the sea to 25 ft and stretches more than 100 ft long. On shore, windswept divi divi trees (*watapana*) beautymark the rocky cliffs and wind-sculpted sand dunes.

Inland, Aruba presents a unique Caribbean landscape of cactus and aloe with gigantic boulders strewn about. Very low humidity and an average annual rainfall of only 20 inches explain the desert-like countryside. On the southeastern tip is Aruba's other city, San Nicolas.

Arubans themselves may be their country's best advertisements. Long secure in a solid economy with good education, housing and health care, the island's population of about 88,000 regard tourists as welcome guests. Even the national anthem celebrates a high regard for hospitality. The line "Grandeza di bo pueblo ta su gran cordialidad" translates as "The greatness of our people is their great cordiality." Thousands of past visitors would agree.

History

Aruba's history is a tale of varied influences. The Spaniards had relatively low regard for the land they discovered and claimed in 1499. Like its neighbors, Bonaire and Curacao, Aruba was officially declared an *isla inutil* (useless island). The Spanish found Arawak Indians of the Caiquetio tribe living there, just as they had in the Stone Age, and promptly shipped them off to Santo Domingo to work in the gold mines. About 11 years later, its

Contributors: Castro Perez, Dive Specialist, Aruba Tourism Authority; Hiske Versteeg, Red Sail Sports; Captain Christian Lyder, Red Sail Sports.

discoverers turned Aruba into something of a large cattle ranch and some of the original inhabitants were brought back to work it.

For awhile the Indians regained control of their land, but in 1636 it was taken over by the Dutch, who have remained in power ever since. Through 300 years of changing economic fortunes and various immigrations, the ABC islands (Aruba, Bonaire and Curacao) were part of the Netherlands Antilles, whose governor reported directly to the queen.

Europeans began to immigrate to Aruba in the late 1700s. At this time, Oranjestad was founded and named after the reigning Royal House of Orange. During the 19th century, many Venezuelans arrived, adding a decidedly Spanish influence to the small country.

In 1824, gold was discovered in Aruba. Visitors can still see remains of the smelting works at Bushiribana and Balashi. When gold mining no longer proved profitable, Aruban aloe plantations flourished. Then, in the 1920s, the oil industry arrived. The Lago refinery, a subsidiary of Standard Oil, was established just outside San Nicolas and remained the island's most important employer until its closing in the spring of 1985. Its influence is likely to be permanent, however. The resulting influx of Americans and others has made English a prominent second language, and Aruba's main thoroughfare, L.G. Smith Boulevard, is named for Lago's one-time general manager.

Politically, Aruba has made quiet and peaceful change. On January 1, 1986, the nation left the Netherlands Antilles to become a separate entity within the Kingdom of the Netherlands. Now Aruba has its own governor, appointed by the queen. Local government is democratic, with an elected 21-member parliament and Council of Ministers.

Tourism in Aruba began in 1959 when the first hotel/casino, the Aruba Caribbean (restored to its former prominence by the Radisson company), opened its doors. However, the world truly began to discover the island in the mid-1960s. Hotels, casinos, restaurants, dive boats, shops and amusements have been popping up ever since.

Diving and Snorkeling Sites

Except for Sonesta Island, access to most of Aruba's dive and snorkeling sights is easiest by boat. All are a few minutes ride from shore on the leeward west and south coasts. Dive shops divide the area into north end (wrecks and rocks), and south end (reefs and artificial reefs). Three spots on the south shore are close enough to swim to, but attempting to find the channels and cuts through the shallow reefs is futile without a local guide.

☆☆ **Arashi**, a rocky reef offshore from the lighthouse at the northwest corner of the island, delights novice divers and snorkelers with throngs of juvenile fish, elkhorn and brain corals. Visibility is always 60 ft or better. Depths range from the shallows to 40 ft. Nice! Seas are calm with an occasional light surge. Boat access. Good for novice divers and snorkelers.

☆ **Arashi Airplanes** denotes a twin-engine Beechcraft at 35 ft and a Lockheed Lodestar at 60 ft—both purposely scuttled to create an artificial reef. Visibility is good enough to see the Beechcraft from the surface. Both wrecks are broken up. Small fish inhabit the engines and fuselages. Boat access. Good for new divers.

☆ A short distance from Arashi lies **Blue Reef** and *Debbie II*, a small tugboat at 70 ft. The reef starts at 50 ft and drops to a sandy shelf at 90 ft where huge lobsters and a couple of stingrays hide out. In 1992, a 120-ft fuel barge was sunk as an additional attraction. The wreck attracts schooling fish. Purple, orange and green sponges decorate the reef. Depths are from 40 ft to 90 ft.

☆☆☆☆ Just south of Blue Reef sits one of Aruba's most unusual sights and most popular dives, the wreck of the 400-ft German freighter, *Antilla*. The ship was scuttled new in 1940, when Germany invaded Holland.

Locally referred to as the "ghost ship", it is covered by giant tube sponges and brilliant orange cup corals. Her twisted, rusting steelwork extends upward from the main section to above the surface, making for intriguing photo opportunities. The remains of the hull are surrounded by big lobsters and angelfish, moray eels and throngs of silversides. Octopus and puffers are common. Outside, schools of yellowtail and sergeant majors sway with the gentle current.

The wreck lies about a mile offshore, just north of Palm Beach in 60 ft of water. Visibility is between 50 and 70 ft. Snorkelers can circle the *Antilla's* superstructure.

☆☆ Just west of Palm Beach lies the wreck of the *Pedernales*, an oil tanker torpedoed by a German sub during WWII, then later cut into three pieces by the US military. The bow and stern were salvaged, towed to the US and welded together to create a new vessel, which joined the Normandy invasion fleet. The center section was left behind and now rests at 25-40 ft. A favorite of novice divers, the wreck is populated by parrotfish, yellowtail, grunts, squirrel fish, trumpet fish and a profusion of silversides. Boat access.

☆☆ **Barcadera Reef,** four miles south of Oranjestad, ranges from 20 to 90 ft. Excellent for snorkelers and divers, the reef supports dense stands of elkhorn and staghorn corals, finger corals, home to wrasses, scorpion fish, blue and stoplight parrot fish, French angels, damsel fish and pink-tipped anemones. The reef lies 600 yards from the shore at Barcadera Harbor (boat dive).

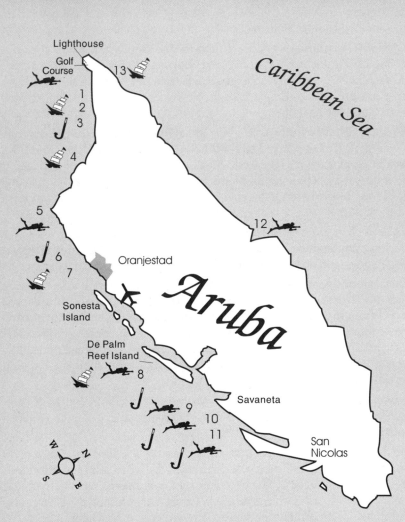

Dive and Snorkeling Sites

1. Arashi Marine Park
2. Wreck of the Antilla
3. Malmok
4. Wreck of the Pedernales
5. South Airplanes
6. Harbour Reef
7. Tugboat Wreck
8. Barcadera Reef
9. Mike Reef
10. Mangel Halto Reef
11. Isla de Oro Reef
12. Natural Bridge
13. California Wreck

Dive guide, Hiske Versteeg, Red Sail Watersports.

☆☆☆☆ **Mangel Halto** ("tall mangrove"), three-fourths of a mile south of Barcadera Harbor, can be reached by swimming out from the Mangel Halto Beach for 120 yards, but it's easier from a boat. The reef slopes from 15 ft to ledges and ridges at 110 ft that support an array of hard corals and encrusting sponges. Fish life includes copper sweepers, grunts, sergeant majors, lobsters, blue tangs, butterfly fish, stingrays and jacks. At depth, green morays, nurse sharks, tarpon and large barracuda inhabit small caves and overhangs. Nice for snorkeling and diving.

Just south of Mangel Halto lies the *Jane Sea*, an impressive 250-ft cement freighter intentionally sunk by local dive masters to attract fish. *Jane Sea's* bottom rests upright in 45 to 90 ft of water. Good for photography.

☆☆ **Isla de Oro Reef** lies off Savaneta, an old Aruban fishing village, near the south end of the island. This site is close to the mangrove-lined shore and is challenging for novice and experienced divers. There is always some current running; visibility is usually excellent. Resident yellow sting rays, lobster, Spanish hogfish and French angelfish race the walls of star, brain and plate corals. At depth, sheet and leaf corals form ledges and caves—home to large morays and parrotfish. The reef begins at 20 ft and drops down to 125 ft. Boat access.

DePalm Island

First-time snorkelers (of all heights) will find waist-high snorkeling outside of DePalm Island, located one-quarter mile offshore from the Water & Electricity Plant—four miles south of Oranjestad along L.G. Smith Boulevard. A ferry ($5) to DePalm leaves the mainland every half-hour.

Snorkelers are immediately greeted by a dozen or more two-ft blue parrot fish looking for a handout. These fish meet you at the dock stairs and will leap up out of the water to eat offerings of bread or whatever munchies you tote. One surprised small snorkeler was chased back up the dock staircase by a voracious few. Feed with caution, they have sharp teeth!

More adventurous snorkelers swim out about 30 yards to find a dense coral reef, which gets more interesting the further out you swim. The reef supports an abundance of fish—blue tangs, blue and stoplight parrot fish, triggerfish, sergeant majors, yellowtail and grunts. Depths range from 4 ft to a drop-off of 120 ft about 400 yards out.

Facilities on DePalm include a good bar and grill, showers, changing facilities and a snorkeling equipment rental shack. The restaurant sells fish food for $1. DePalm reef is great for scuba too, but more easily reached from a dive boat.

Sonesta Island

Sonesta Island, a watersports outpost owned by Sonesta Resorts at Seaport Village, is reached by a short shuttle boat ride. Guests of the Sonesta may use the island for free. Others pay $25 for the day, which includes the shuttle to and from the resort, lunch and one cocktail. Coupons for the island are sold in the Sonesta lobby. Snorkeling gear, rented on the island by Redsail Sports (☎ 861603) costs $10 for a day's use. Moorings for dive kayaks were in the plans at press time. Island facilities include a dive shop, beach restaurant, air-conditioned fitness center. Three separate beaches cater to families or adults (topless), with a special cove for honeymooners, divers and snorkelers.

☆☆☆ **South Airplanes**, 50 yards from the Sonesta Island main beach, is the site of two vintage twin-engine, aircraft wrecks—both unclaimed drug runners—sunk to form an artificial reef and a fun dive. The wrecks, a Beechcraft 18 and a Convair 400, are intact and may be penetrated by divers. Inside are octopuses, moray eels, lobsters and crabs. The Beech sits in 15 ft of water on a sloping reef, the Convair lies in 40- 60 ft. The oxidizing fuselages, good for video and still photography, are covered with a thin layer of clinging corals and hydroids. Red Sail Sports on the island rents equipment and offers guided tours and lessons. Normally calm with one- to two-foot swells and a mild current. Snorkelers can see the Beechcraft from the surface.

☆ **The Barge**, in 12 ft of water lying about 100 yards off Sonesta Island's main beach, makes a fun snorkeling spot. Crowds of fish swarm the wreckage. Usually calm with a one- to two-ft swell and light current. Check with the dive shop for current conditions. Swimming and snorkeling outside the protected lagoon is not recommended for small children, though swimming inside the lagoon is fine.

Bucuti Beach Resort.

Windward Side Dives

☆☆☆ The *California* wreck off the northwest tip of the island is for experienced divers and then recommended only during periods of extreme calm. Resting at 40 ft, the scattered remains of the wooden ship are draped in orange and yellow sponges, plate corals and anemones. Huge grouper, jewfish, lobster, shark and barracuda frequent the area. A dense reef of staghorn and pillar corals forms a breakwater beyond the wreck.

☆☆☆ The **Natural Bridge,** another north-shore adventure dive, rises from monster-size boulders adorned with black and soft corals. Gigantic basket sponges rise from the bottom. Depths from 20 ft to 110 ft. Rough water and currents make this a choice for advanced divers only.

Beach Snorkeling and Scuba

The best beach snorkeling from the mainland is off Malmok. Get there by driving north from Palm Beach along L.G. Smith Boulevard, the main coast road. There is usually a snorkeling boat moored offshore, which makes it easy to spot, or if you look straight out to sea you'll see the top of the *Antilla.* Park anywhere and walk down to the beach. Swim out from the shore about 10 ft to the rocks, where you'll find hordes of small reef fish. Beware the spiny urchins hiding in the rocks. Always calm. Good for children.

All of Aruba's beaches are open to the public, but a narrow strip directly behind the houses is private. Most homeowners have a sign marking where their back yard ends and the public beach begins.

Beach dives are best off Sonesta Island, but possible off the local beaches on the south end of the island at **Mangel Halto**—swim straight out to the breakwater, then about 45 yards to the reef; **Pos Chiquito**—swim to the left once out of the lagoon; **Santo Largo**—walk out about 200 yards till the water is deeper. All require a fairly long swim or walk through shallow water and you must be accompanied by an Aruban dive operator. **Baby Beach**, outside the breakwater, is listed everywhere, including Aruba's Web site, as a great beach dive, but it's usually too rough and the current too strong. Inside the breakwater there is nothing but sand on the bottom, no fish, no coral. If you ignore our suggestion to pass it up and want to try it as a shore dive, wait for a day when seas are calm and expect the current to carry you up the coast all the way to the Marina Pirata Country Club. Start from the southernmost corner of the parking lot.

Dive Operators

Most Aruban dive shops offer scuba and/or snorkeling trips, certification and resort courses. One-tank dive trips start at $45; snorkeling tours from $25. Mask, fins and snorkel rent for about $12 per day, but may be included at no extra charge on a sail tour.

Sail-snorkel cruises are offered by **DePalm Tours** (☎ 824400 or 837643); **Red Sail Sports** (☎ 861603; E-mail, info@redsail.com); **Pelican Watersports**, (☎ 831228/fax 832655); **Mi Dushi** (snorkel/sail yacht, ☎ 826034); and **Wave Dancers** (☎ 825520).

Scuba courses and trips may be arranged through any hotel or direct through **Red Sail Sports**, ☎ 824500, or (800) 255-6425; **Pelican Watersports**, ☎ 831228, fax 832655; **Aruba Pro Dive**, ☎ 825520, fax 837723; **Dax Divers**, ☎ 821270, fax 834389; **S.E.A. Scuba**, ☎ 834877, fax 834875; **DePalm Watersports**, ☎ 824545, fax 823012; **Mermaid Sports Divers**, ☎ 835546, E-mail mermaid@mail.SETARnet.aw; **Native Divers**, ☎ 834763; **Scuba Aruba**, ☎ 834142; or **Unique Watersports**, ☎ 823900, fax 860096.

Red Sail and Pelican are full-service shops. Pelican is located on Palm Beach behind the Holiday Inn and offers gear rental, sail-snorkeling tours, courses amd dive tours.

Red Sail Sports offers an unlimited seven-day dive package for $175. No refunds for unused portions.

Red Sail Sports also tempts guests with water-skiing, jet skis and wave runners, tubing, banana boat rides, Hobie Cat rentals, instruction and sailing with a captain, Sunfish and paddleboat rental and Sea Searcher floats. Their 35-ft catamaran, *Balia*, sets sail for morning snorkeling tours as well as sunset and dinner cruises. Red Sail is on the beach between the Americana Aruba Beach Resort and the Hyatt. They are also on Sonesta Island and have a shop in Seaport Village. Dive tours are top notch with a full pre-dive briefing, underwater guides and a rescue diver who remains on the boat. E-mail: info@redsail.com.

The smaller operators offer custom dive tours from the beach, if desired, and visit the reefs off the south end of the island.

Accommodations

Note: a 12-15% service charge and 5% government tax are added to the hotels' bills.

Aruba's resorts come in two varieties—low rise and high rise. The low rise, dive-friendly resorts, Talk of the Town, Bucuti Beach and Manchebo Beach are near town and the Seaport Village, home to hundreds of beautiful shops and trendy waterfront bars and restaurants—all set in charming, pastel, gingerbread architecture. The high rise resorts—Hyatt, Holiday Inn, Las Cabanas Beach Resort, further north—are nearer to Malmok and the Lighthouse.

Best Western Bucuti Beach Resort touts beautiful Spanish architecture, a gorgeous, powder white beach and The Pirates' Nest, a unique restaurant built to resemble an 18th-century ship. Other amenities include an outdoor fitness center, pool, activities desk that will book dive and snorkeling excursions and on-site car rental. The resort's 71 guest rooms range from $120 to $170 per night in summer; $200 to $270 in winter. All are clean, very comfortable and modern, with cable TV, phone, air conditioning, safe, king or queen size beds, complimentary coffee and tea service, ceiling fan, small refrigerators and a min-bar. Adjacent Mermaid Dive Shop visits the south end sites. Friendly staff members attend to guests' every want. Meal plans for $40 per day include a full American breakfast daily and three-course meal at the Pirate's Nest or a choice of nine popular outside restaurants. Dive packages with Dive Aruba for four nights, three one-tank dives in summer (3/31-12/20) are $252 per person for a double; in winter the same package is $972. No refunds for unused portions. ☎ (800) 344-1212, or (011) 297-8-31100, fax (011) 297-8-25272. E-mail: int1233@ mail.setarnet.aw. Web site: www.olmco.com/aruba/bucuti.html.

Best Western's Manchebo Beach Hotel, next to the Bucuti Beach Resort, offers dive packages (south end only) with on-site Mermaid Diving. The recently remodeled resort has attractive, clean, modern rooms with cable TV, air-conditioned, direct-dial phones, safes and in-room refrigerators. On-site are Bistro Aruba, a patio restaurant, French Steak House and Pega Pega, a beachside bar and grill open all day. Great beach! Summer room rates are $120 for a standard to $135 for a superior; winter, $175 and $190 per room, per day. For three meals daily add $50 per person. ☎ (800) 223-1108, fax 310-440-4220 or direct (011) 2978-023444, fax (011) 2978-33667. Children under 16 stay free in room with parents. Gift shop, car rental, laundry, pool and snack bar.

The 360-room **Hyatt Regency Aruba Resort & Casino** has teamed up with **Red Sail Sports** and developed the "Dive Into It" package. Summer price for seven nights is $2,398 for two people. Package includes

Arashi Airplane Wreck.

accommodations, daily two-tank boat dives, tanks, weights and belt, sunset sail aboard the 53-ft *Balia* catamaran, T-shirt, one-year subscription to *Scuba Times* magazine and 10% discount on clothing at Red Sail sports shops. ☎ (800) 233-1234, (800) 255-6425, (011) 2978-61234, fax (011) 2978-65478.

Red Sail Sports offers dive accommodation packages with the **Bucuti Beach Resort** and **Stauffer Hotel**. Both include accommodations, daily two-tank boat dives, dive transfers, lockers. A two-tank dive trip can be traded for two one-tank dives or a night dive, if available. Rates for two people for seven nights at the Bucuti Beach Resort are $1,495 in summer, $2,166 in winter. At the Stauffer Hotel for two people, seven nights, $1,139 in summer, $1,453 in winter. ☎ (800) 255-6425. E-mail: info@redsail.com.

Talk of the Town and **Manchebo Beach Hotel** properties offer dive packages, though rates were unavailable at press time. Talk of the Town room rates per night are $118 in summer, $155 in winter; Manchebo Beach rooms are $135 per night in summer, $190 in winter. ☎ (800) 223-1108.

Divi Aruba Beach Resort offers diving and snorkeling trips with RedSail Watersports. The oceanfront resort features 203 shell-colored rooms with a spacious balcony, two pools, baby-sitting, laundry and dry cleaning services, salon, car rental, shopping arcade. Suites have air-conditioning, ceiling fan, satellite TV. Room rates, $180-$240. Meal/accommodation packages available. ☎ (800) 554-2008 or (011) 297-8-23300, fax (011) 297-8-34002.

Holiday Inn Aruba Beach Resort & Casino meets the needs of dive fanatics with **Pelican Watersports.** The 600-room hotel offers frequent specials with rates as low as $79.95 per night. Normal room rates are $109.95 per night, double occupancy. Room rates with meals are $145 per person. For reservations, ☎ (800) HOLIDAY, fax (011)-2978-65165.

Las Cabanas all suites, a modern, (800) suite luxury resort complex offers packages with Pelican Watersports, on premises. Air-hotel specials are offered through Liberty Travel with offices across the US.

Check weekly newspaper travel ads. Or book through your travel agent.

Sonesta Beach Resort, a beautiful hotel at Seaport Village, sits amidst 120 shops, restaurants, casinos, cafés, and entertainment facilities. The 300-room resort features two pools, a swim-up bar and water shuttle to their own 40-acre Sonesta island. ☎ (800) SONESTA. Call for rates. Dive packages offered by Red Sail, ☎ (800) 255-6425.

Additional hotels with dive operations on the premises are the **Port of Aruba Palm Beach Resort & Casino**; the **Aruba Caribbean Resort** and **Harbour Town Beach Resort & Casino** (S.E.A. SCUBA).

For a complete list of resorts, contact your travel agent or The Aruba Tourism Authority, L.G. Smith Blvd. 172, Eagle, Aruba or ☎ (800) TO-ARUBA. In the US , 1000 Harbor Boulevard, Weehawken, NJ. ☎ (201) 330-0800, fax (201) 330-8757. E mail for brochures: brochures@toaruba.com. Web site: www.interknowledge.com/aruba/anahome.htm.

Other Activities

Outdoor lovers will enjoy visiting Aruba's National Park—where flamboyant scenery, tropical foliage and even wild goats and donkeys await. The **Arikok National Park** has two hiking trails. Free admission. Guided tours are through **DePalm Tours** (☎ 824545) and **Eco Destination Management** (☎ 26034).

One of the island's newest sport attractions is **Happy Surf Aruba**, a windsurfing operator at Fishermen Huts, just north of Palm Beach. Aruba's constant trade winds create ideal conditions for windsurfing off eastern shores. ☎ 863940. Rentals from $20 per hour. Private lessons $125 for two hours.

E-mail: arubaboardsailing@mail setarnet.aw. Web site: discoveraruba. com/ArubaBoardSailing.html.

Additional windsurfing rentals and instruction are offered by **Sailboard Vacations**, (☎821072), *Roger's* (☎ 821918), **Divi Winds** (☎ 835000).

Board a glass bottom boat with **DePalm Watersports** (☎ 824545), **Pelican Watersports** (☎ 832128), **Red Sail Sports** (☎ 861603) and **Scuba Aruba** (☎ 834142).

Cave tours to view prehistoric Indian art may be arranged through **Aruba Transfer Tours and Taxi** (☎ 821149); **Tiny Tours** (☎ 847449; **Sea & Sea Tours**

The road to the Chapel of Alto Vista.

(☎ 31228) and **Private Safaris** (☎ 834869). Archaeologist **E. Boerstra** (☎ 841513) of **Marlin Booster Tracking Inc.** also offers tours that highlight Aruba's prehistoric Indian cultures.

Sunset cruises, deep-sea fishing, island tours, para-sailing, and sightseeing can all be easily arranged at your hotel.

Tennis is widely available. There are two golf courses, one 18-hole professional calibre Tierra del Sol course and a nine-hole with oiled sand greens, the trade winds and an occasional goat as a live hazard. Equestrians can ride along the beach at **Rancho El Paso, ☎** 873310.

While nightlife to many divers equates with suiting up after sunset for yet another dive, others will find endless entertainment on shore in the form of casino gambling, limbo shows and discos.

Those traveling with young children will enjoy a picnic at **Baby Beach** on the southwest tip of the island. This is a beautiful, natural lagoon with shallow, calm water. Baby Beach is listed in many tour guides as a "great snorkeling beach" but, in fact, don't waste your energy carrying a mask or snorkel. There is absolutely nothing on the bottom but white sand, three juvenile yellowtails and an old sneaker, which may be gone by press time. Outside the breakwater there is a nice coral reef, but seas are often very rough and currents too strong to swim back to shore.

California Lighthouse

Sightseeing

A walking tour of Oranjestad would include the **harborside fruit market**; **Fort Zoutman** and **King Willem III Tower**, home to a Aruban heritage museum; the **Numismatic Museum** and the **Archaeology Museum**. Shopping abounds.

If you are opposed to organized tours, grab a road map and rent a car to tour the island. Directly east of the high-rise hotel strip, on the north shore, you'll find the **Chapel of Alto Vista**, high above the sea on a most peaceful spot. It was built by Spanish missionary, Domingo Antonio Silvester, and serves as a ceremonial center. Stations of the cross line the steep, cactus-bordered road to the chapel. Driving east to Andicuri from Oranjestad will lead to the **Natural Bridge** (the largest of eight on the island), complete with gift and snack shops. The road is unpaved and bumpy in spots, but very scenic. Very photogenic at sunrise. Also worth a visit are the Casibari and Ayo rock formations—monstrous boulders which mystify geologists. Casibari is about halfway (three miles) between the Natural Bridge and Oranjestad. Ayo is approximately two miles from the Natural Bridge toward Casibari. At Casibari stone steps give access to a viewing platform on top. At the entrance a formation resembling and named "Dragon Mouth" can be seen. You can climb on top and, on a clear day, see all of Aruba and the coast of Venezuela.

The California Dunes and **California Lighthouse** are at the northernmost tip of the island. The dunes are sand, but most of this area is barren and rocky. High winds have carved some interesting shapes in the rocks. Views from the lighthouse ridge are magnificent.

Dining

Expect to spend between $60 and $100 (US) on dinner for two at the hotel and seaside restaurants. Most eateries add a 15% service charge, which does not cover the tip. Tips are usually just a couple of dollars for good service. For divers on a budget, fast food chains are widely available. Hotel meal plans average $40 to $50 per person, per day, and may include vouchers which are accepted by many outside restaurants. Check with your hotel.

All hotels have coffee shops and snack bars. Most also feature specialty restaurants that serve American, Continental and regional food. For outstanding native seafood dishes, don't miss **Brisas Del Mar Restaurant**, six miles south of Orangestad at Savaneta 222, ☎ 847718 (turn right after the Esso station) or **The Waterfront Crabhouse** at Seaport Marketplace, ☎ 835858. Additional country flavor is at **The New Old Cunucu House Restaurant,** Palm Beach 150, which is set in a 70-year-old Aruban home, ☎ 61666, or **Boonoonoos** on Wilhelmastraat #18, ☎ 831888. Or enjoy seafood or steaks inside a Dutch windmill, first built in 1804 in Holland then reconstructed on Aruba in 1960. This is the **Mill Restaurant** at J.E. Irausquin Blvd # 330 (open from 6 pm till 11), ☎ 862060—walking distance from the high-rise hotels.

The Pirates' Nest at the Bucuti Beach Resort features a nice beach bar and breakfast buffet for $13. An endless choice of fried foods and island drinks are offered by **Papa's & Beer,** 184 Palm Beach Rd—Aruba's favorite "California" hang-out restaurant. Menu favorites are empanaditas (fried pastries filled with cheeses and meat), Filipino chicken wings, cheese nachos and chips with salsa and guacamole, deep-fried ice cream (very carefully).

Entertainment nightly. It is a short walk from the hotel strip. Look for the big neon sign!

The best steaks are found at **El Gaucho,** Wilhelmastraat 80, ☎ 823677, the **Holiday Inn Restaurant** and the French restaurant at the **Manchebo Beach Hotel**. Other notable dining spots are spread throughout the **Seaport Village.**

Bon Bini Bagels down the street from the Manchebo Beach Resort offers excellent New York bagels and bagel-egg sandwiches for a reasonable price. Open from 8 am till 2 pm.

Fast foods are served at **Burger King** on Nassaustraat 81 in Oranjestad; **Charlies Bar** on Zeppenfeldstraat 56, San Nicolas; and **Wendy's** on L.G. Smith Blvd. 90-92. Additional chains around the island are **Hooters**, **Kentucky Fried Chicken, Pizza Hut** and **Houlihans**.

Facts

Helpful Phone Numbers: Police/ambulance, ☎ 824000. Airport, ☎ 824800. Hospital, ☎ 826034.

Nearest Recompression Chamber: Curacao. None on Aruba.

Getting There: American Airlines (☎ (800) 433-7300) offers direct daily flights from New York, twice daily from Miami and San Juan, Puerto Rico with connections from Boston, Philadelphia, New Jersey, Baltimore, Miami, Raleigh, Washington, Hartford, Providence, Chicago, Dallas, Detroit, Pittsburgh and other major US cities. Air Aruba has direct flights from Newark and Miami. From Venezuela, Avensa; from Europe KLM; from Toronto via Air Canada; from Miami, and Curacao via ALM.

Car Rentals: Hertz, ☎ 824545, 824400, airport 824886; Dollar, ☎ 822783, 831237, airport 825651; Budget, ☎ 828600, airport 825423; AC&E Jeep, ☎ 876373.

Driving: Traffic moves on the right.

Language: The official language is Dutch, but residents speak Papiamento—a blend of Dutch, Spanish, Portuguese and English. English and Spanish are widely spoken.

Documents: Passport, official birth certificate, certificate of naturalization for US and Canadian citizens. Return or continuing ticket.

Customs: If you have been out of the US for 48 hours or more and have not claimed any exemption within 30 days, you may bring in $400 tax-exempt products including 100 cigars (**no cuban cigars**) and 200 cigarettes, and for those 21 or older, one liter (33.8 oz.) of alcoholic beverages.

Canadians after 48 hours absence may bring in goods to the value of $100. After seven days absence you may bring in goods to the value of $300. A person aged 16 or over may include up to 200 cigarettes and 50 cigars. If you meet the age requirements of the province through which you re-enter, you may include up to 1.14 (40 oz) of wine or liquor.

Currency: The Aruba florin=US $1.77.

Credit Cards: Widely accepted.

Service Charges: There is a 12-15% service charge on room rates. The service charge on food and beverage is 12-15%, which should not be considered a tip. Tips are extra.

Climate: Dry and sunny with a year-round average temperature of 82° F. Showers of short duration are frequent during November and December. Aruba is outside the hurricane belt.

Clothing: Lightweight casual cottons. Informal for the most part, but dress-up clothes are advisable for a night out in one of the elegant restaurants, night clubs or casinos. Jackets are required for men at night in some casinos, night clubs and restaurants. Note: Persons under 18 are NOT permitted in the casinos.

Airport Departure Tax: $15 US.

Electricity: 110-120 volts AC, 60 cycles (same as in US).

Time: Atlantic Standard Time. Same as Eastern Daylight Saving time, all year round.

Religious Services: Roman Catholic. Protestant (Dutch Reformed, Anglican, Evangelican, Methodist, Seventh Day Adventist, Church of Christ, Baptist), Jewish, Baha'i Faith.

Additional Information: Aruba Tourism Authority, L.G. Smith Blvd. 172, Eagle, Aruba, ☎ 2978, 23777, fax 2978 34702.

Aruba Tourism Authority, 1000 Harbor Boulevard, Weehawken, NJ 07047. ☎(201) 330-0800, fax (201) 330-8757.

Web site: http://www.interknowledge.com/aruba/.

Barbados

Barbados, a tiny island just 21 miles long and 14 miles wide, offers remarkable contrasts, from its boulder-strewn northern coast to its serene Caribbean coastline. Inland, hilly forests slope down to golden fields of sugarcane, corn, sweet potatoes, and yams. Stunning white sand beaches rim the island.

The eastern-most island of the Lesser Antilles, Barbados boasts a unique range of natural and historic attractions, from its exquisite plantation "great houses" to vast caves filled with prehistoric formations. Its quaint colonial capital, Bridgetown, surprises visitors with upscale shopping and gourmet dining.

Despite 30 years of independence from Great Britain, Barbados still exudes a British atmosphere. A statue of Admiral Nelson graces Bridgetown's Trafalgar Square, and afternoon tea remains a custom for many hotels. Good diving and snorkeling exists off the southwestern shores. Gorgeous reefs flank the rocky east coast, but pounding seas and strong currents usually limit access to this area.

When to Go

Divers, both novice and experienced, are advised to visit Barbados between April and November, when they can expect fabulous visibility on the barrier reef and calm seas. This changes from December through March, when a "North Swell" decreases visibility near shore and on the outer reefs.

During spring, summer and fall the island's shallow shipwrecks offer a variety of dive experiences. The best wrecks are found on the offshore barrier reef that extends along Barbado's western coast. The wrecks are camouflaged by soft corals, sea fans, and sponges, home to thriving communities of fish and other marine animals. Barbados presents snorkelers with miles of

Area Contributors: Dave Farmer, Jolly Roger Watersports; and Michael Young, Underwater Barbados.

white-powder sand beaches and shore-access coves with a wide range of corals and friendly fish.

Best Dive and Snorkeling Sites

☆☆☆☆☆ **Dottins Reef,** a half-mile off the coast of St. James Parish on the west coast, drifts along the shore from St James to Bridgetown. It is the prettiest reef in Barbados with visibility at 100 ft or better. Basket sponges, sea fans, gorgonians, and thickets of staghorn and brain coral adorn the reef's canyons and walls. Depths start at 65 ft with some drop-offs to 130 ft. Reef residents include rays, turtles, barracuda, parrotfish, snapper and large grouper. Seas are generally calm.

☆☆☆ **Sandy Lane,** a deeper area off Dottin's Reef, is usually a drift dive. The walls, dotted with sponges and vibrant, clump corals, drop to 90 ft. Superb marine life abounds. A good spot for video photography. For experienced divers only.

☆☆☆ **Wreck of the *Pamir*,** located just 200 yds offshore, it is easily accessible from the beach and is very open and uncluttered. This 150-ft ship was sunk in 30 ft of water by the Barbados dive shop operators to form an artificial reef. The ship's superstructure breaks the usually calm surface, making it perfect for snorkelers and snorkel-swimmers. Swarms of sergeant majors and butterfly fish inhabit the wreck. Nearby, about 60 yds out, is a small reef. Although visibility varies, seas are always calm. Dive operators request no spear fishing or collecting. An excellent dive for novices.

☆☆☆ **Bright Ledge Reef** is a narrow reef that wraps around the island's northern tip. Depths average 60 ft with deep drop-offs on either side. Unsuitable for novices but generally a safe dive and particularly good for photography. Encounters with gigantic pelagics, turtles and rays are frequent, with dependable sightings of parrotfish, snapper, grouper, porgy, grunts, and glass eye snapper. The sea is generally calm unless there is a stiff wind or storm.

☆☆☆ The ***Stavronikita*,** a 360-ft freighter, was gutted by a fire at sea 14 years ago. After towing the sinking ship closer to shore, the government of Barbados sunk the smoldering mass where it would benefit divers and fishermen as an artificial reef. The wreck sits in 130 ft of water, the deck at 80 ft. Although the depth discourages most novice explorers, the ship is one of the island's most interesting dives. Its hull, covered with a colorful patchwork of small sponges and clinging corals, attracts schools of silversides and large pelagics. Very appealing to photographers.

☆☆ Nearby in shallow water lie the ***Conimara*,** an old P.T. boat, and the ***Lord Combermere*,** an old tug boat—both in 30-40 ft of water. Visibility

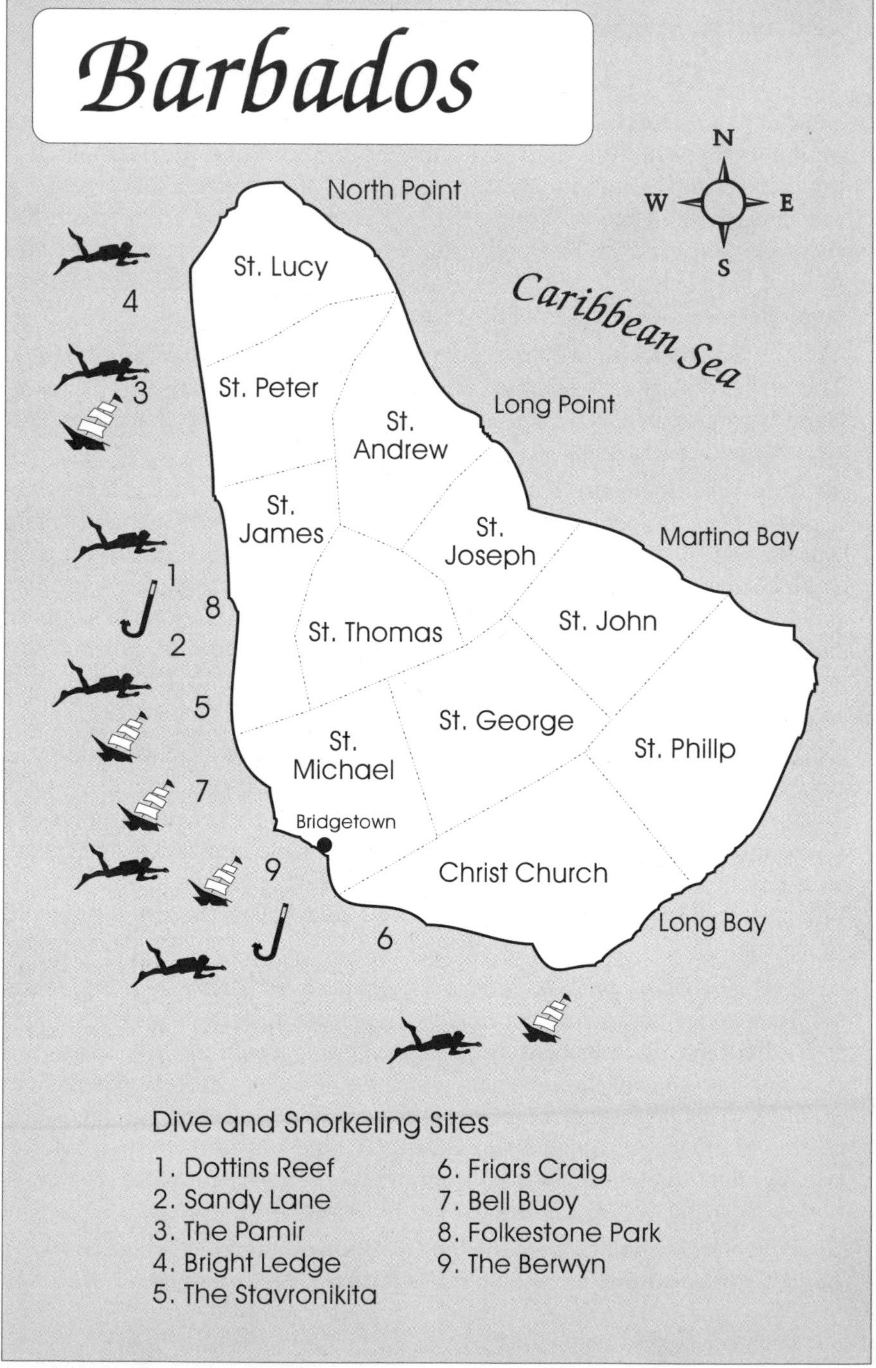

Barbados

North Point

St. Lucy

N
W — **E**
S

St. Peter

Caribbean Sea

Long Point

St.
Andrew

4

3

St.
James

St.
Joseph

Martina Bay

1

8

St. Thomas

St. John

2

5

St. George

St.
Michael

St. Phillp

7

Bridgetown

9

Christ Church

6

Long Bay

Dive and Snorkeling Sites

1. Dottins Reef
2. Sandy Lane
3. The Pamir
4. Bright Ledge
5. The Stavronikita

6. Friars Craig
7. Bell Buoy
8. Folkestone Park
9. The Berwyn

varies. Good photo opportunities abound here as well. The wrecks can be reached from the shore after a 600-yd swim.

☆☆ *Friar's Craig* is a good dive for the novice although strong current may be occasionally encountered. This is another purposely sunken wreck. It lies in just 60 ft of water with the bridge at 30 ft, making it more accessible than the *Stavronikita*. Nearby, **Asta Reef**, a shelter for throngs of fish, is often combined with a Friar's Craig dive. A short 600-yd swim from the southwest corner of Christ Church Parish will put you over the wreck and an adjacent reef, **Castle Bank.** Exercise extreme caution and check the current before diving. Numerous fish and usually great visibility.

☆☆☆ **Bell Buoy Reef**, located off St. Michael's Parish on the island's southwest, is a wall dive with a shelf at 40 ft, dropping off to a sandy bottom at 70 ft. The reef is alive with small critters amidst the shadows of large brain coral heads, sea fans, and vase sponges. Schools of small reef fish, turtles, and an occasional ray are in residence. During windy periods this spot can be wiped out by strong currents.

☆☆☆ **Caribbee Reef**, off the Caribbee Hotel is a section of the fringing reefs that parallel the southwest shore. Lots of fish, giant barrel sponges, tube sponges and sea fans. Usually good visibility. Light surge. Good for experienced divers. Depths are 60 to 120 ft. This is a boat dive.

☆☆☆ **Folkestone Park** is the favorite beach/snorkeling site in Barbados. An underwater trail has been marked around the inshore reef. It is also the favorite area for boaters and jet skiers, so the swimming and snorkeling area has been roped off to insure safety. Snorkel with or near a group. A 200-yd swim from the sandy beach will take you to a raft anchored over the wreckage of a small barge sitting in 20 ft of water. During winter when the North Swell rises, visibility can drop drastically for as long as two days. During the rest of the year, Folkestone is the number one snorkeling choice.

☆☆ The **Wreck of the *Berwyn*** is a 45-ft-long French tugboat that sunk in the early 1900s. It sits at the bottom of Carlisle Bay, 200 yds off the island's southwest shore at a depth of 25 ft. Encrusted with plate corals, the wreck is host to sea horses, frogfish, wrasses, arrow crabs and other small creatures. It is a favored snorkeling photo site with good visibility and calm sea conditions.

☆☆ The **Wreck of the *Eillion***, a former drug boat, was sunk June 8, 1996 to form part of the Carlisle Bay Marine park. The wreck, located near the *Berwyn*, sits at 110 ft, with the top at 55 ft. Lots of fish.

The **Ce-Trek,** an old cement-constructed boat at a depth of 40 ft, sits near the *Berwyn*. A favorite of re-entry divers, the *Ce-Trek* has attracted hordes of fish and invertebrates since its sinking in 1986. She sits 300 yds offshore.

The *Berwyn, Eillion, Ce-Trek* and *the Fox* (a small wreck) are possible to see on one dive.

Two nice spots for beginning snorkelers are Mullins Beach and Paynes Bay. Both offer calm waters and ample parking.

Dive Operators

Dive shops are located along the southwest shores.

Bubbles Galore Barbados Dive Shop at the Sandy Beach Island Resort, Worthing, Christ Church, offers all levels of PADI training, two-tank dives every morning and afternoon. Complimentary drinks served on board their custom 31-ft Bertam dive boat. Night dives upon request. Specialty courses in Dan O2 Provider, Basic Nitrox, underwater photography, and navigation. All are offered in English, German, Italian, Spanish, French, Swedish, Norwegian and Russian. ☎ (246) 430-0354, fax (246) 430-8806. E-mail: bubbles @caribsurf.com.

The Dive Shop Ltd., celebrating its 30th year on the island, offers daily trips at 10 am and noon with night dives twice a week. All staff members are certified by PADI, NAUI and/or ACUC. They are also DAN O2 certified. All levels of certification courses are taught. Shipwrecks *Berwyn* and *Ce-Trek* sit 300 yds from the shop. Rates are $55 for a one-tank dive, $90 for a two-tank dive. A 10-dive package costs $300 with equipment, $260 with your own equipment. Hotel/dive packages are available at the Island Inn Hotel and Cacrabank Beach Apartments. For additional information write or call Haroon Degia, The Dive Shop Ltd. Aquatic Gap, Bay Street, St. Michael, Barbados WI. ☎ (246) 426-9947 or (800) 348-3756, fax (246) 426-2031. Web site: www.caribnet.net/diveshop. E-mail: hardive@carib net. net.

Underwater Barbados, a PADI five-star dive shop in Carlisle Bay Centre, visits all the best sites aboard a 31-ft pirogue boat. Staff are medic first-aid trained and are experienced dive instructors and guides. All levels of instruction. Demonstrations and instruction are offered at the Carlisle Bay Centre on Bay Street in St. Michaels's Parish, Coconut Court Beach Hotel, Asta Beach Hotel, Long Beach Club, Sam Lords, Welcome Inn Beach Hotel. ☎ (246) 426-0655, fax (246) 426-0655. Write to: Michael Young, Underwater Barbados, Carlisle Bay Centre, St. Michael, Barbados, WI. Web site: www.ndl.net/~uwb/. E-mail: myoung@ndl.net.

Coral Isle Divers, on the Careenage in Bridgetown, operates a custom 40-ft power catamaran dive boat with a changing room, on-board washroom and shower, dry storage areas and plenty of deck space. They offer PADI and NAUI instruction. Complimentary soft drinks. ☎ (246) 431-9068. E-mail: coralis@caribnet.net.

Atlantis Submarine.

Blue Reef Water Sports, St. James, offers reef and wreck trips, resort and certification courses. Their 28-ft boat carries 12 divers. ☎ (246) 422-3133, fax 246-422-3133.

Hightide Watersports touts a new custom-built, 30-ft dive boat, *Flyin' High*. This PADI shop offers one- and two-tank dives, night dives, snorkeling trips, and PADI instruction. Equipment sales and rentals, video camera. Gear storage. ☎ (246) 432-0931.

WestSide Scuba Centre, next to The Sunset Crest Beach Club, Holetown, St. James, offers PADI courses, dive and snorkeling tours. Free transportation to and from your hotel. ☎ and fax (246) 432-2558.

Beginning and advanced dive tours and certification courses are also offered at **Willies Watersports**, St Michael, ☎ (246) 425-1060 or (246) 422-4900; at **Dive Boat Safari** at the Barbados Hilton, St. Michael, ☎ (246) 427-4350; and at **Scotch & Soda**, ☎ (246) 435-7375.

Hazell's Water World Inc., in the Sandy Bank complex, Hastings, Christ Church, sells a wide range of scuba and snorkeling equipment. Repair service on dive equipment. ☎ (246) 426-4043.

Atlantis Submarine dives to 150 ft, exploring the reefs and wrecks for 90 minutes. Divers on scooters outside the sub interact with the surroundings and can communicate with submarine guests. Located in Bridgetown. ☎(246) 436-8929.

Atlantis' 65-ft glass-hulled **Seatrec** (Sea Tracking and Reef Exploration Craft) features advanced glass-bottom viewing with in-cabin video monitors.

Reserve sail-snorkeling, sunset, lunch and dinner tours through **Jolly Roger Cruises**, Bridgetown, ☎ 436-6424, fax 429-8500; **Tiami Catamaran Sailing Cruises**, Bridgetown, ☎ 427-7245, fax 431-0538; **Secret Love**, ☎ 432-1972; or **Irish Mist**, ☎ 436-9201. Mask and snorkel included.

Accommodations

Most hotels and nightlife exist on the south and central western coast of the island. There are no dedicated dive resorts, but all will arrange for diving. Several guest houses, cottages and apartments may be rented for $30 per night and up. A list with current rates is available from the Barbados Board of Tourism. In the US, ☎ (800) 221-9831; in Canada, ☎ (800) 268-9122 or (416) 512-6569, fax (416) 512-6581. In Barbados, ☎ (246) 427-2623/4, fax (246) 426-4080. Web site: www.barbados.org.

To book on the Internet, go to the Web site, then hotels. Click on E-mail to book reservations with the hotel of your choice.

Before booking on your own, check the travel section of your Sunday newspaper. Money-saving packages including airfare and choice hotels in Barbados are frequently featured by the large travel companies.

Divi Southwinds Beach Hotel sits on a half-mile of white sand beach near the St. Lawrence Gap. It is surrounded by 20 acres of tropical gardens and features 166 guestrooms and air-conditioned suites, all having a patio and pool or ocean views. Beachside restaurants offer local and international dishes. Pool-side bar and snackery. You are within walking distance of restaurants and nightlife. ☎ (800) 367-3484, (607) 277-3484 or write Divi Resorts, 6340 Quadrangle Drive, Suite 300, Chapel Hill, NC 27514-8900.

Almond Beach Club, an all-inclusive resort, features 131 air conditioned guestrooms and suites with ocean or pool views. Gourmet meals are served at the elegant beachside restaurant; refreshments at a swim-up bar adjacent to the twin pools. Dive trips are arranged with the Blue Reef Dive shop. All-inclusive rates per couple, per day, include meals, drinks, snorkeling, fishing, windsurfing, kayaking. Winter (Dec 18 to Mar 31) rates per day, per couple, start at $470 for a standard room; summer rates start at $380. ☎ (800) 4ALMOND.

Grand Barbados Beach Resort is a luxury, beachfront resort with scuba facilities on the premises. Located in Carlisle Bay, one mile from Bridgetown, the resort is just minutes from reef and wreck dives. Features are a fitness center, shopping arcade, coffee shop, two restaurants and bars, satellite TV, hairdryers, mini-safes, radio, phone, balconies, and meeting facilities. Mistral Windsurfing School. ☎ (246) 426-4000, fax (246) 429-2400.

Coral Reef Club, a small, luxury, beachfront resort with its own dive shop (Les Wooten's Watersports) sits in 12 acres of gardens adjacent to a superb, white sand beach. All 70 lovely, air-conditioned cottages and rooms feature secluded patios or balconies. Activities available to guests include cruises on the club's own 30-ft catamaran. Amenities include tennis court, pool, and shops. Alfresco restaurant overlooks the sea. Special nights including Bajan buffets and barbecue dinner with steel band, flaming limbo and exotic calypso dancers. ☎ (246) 422-2372, fax (246) 422-1776.

Asta Beach Hotel in Christ Church, 1½ miles from Bridgetown, offers 67 beachfront rooms and suites. Diving with Underwater Barbados. All rooms are air-conditioned with private bath, kitchen, TV and telephone. Restaurant and bar, two pools. Free bus to city weekdays. Rates are from $65 per person daily, double occupancy in summer; from $120 in winter. ☎ (246) 427-2541, fax (246) 426-9566. Book through your travel agent or the Internet.

Coconut Court, a family-owned hotel two miles from Bridgetown, features ocean views, gift shop, restaurant. TV in rooms. Rates start at $55 per day in summer, $95 in winter. ☎ (246) 427-1655.

Crane Beach Hotel sits on four acres overlooking a half-mile of beautiful coral sand beach. A gourmet restaurant, refreshment bar and four tennis courts are on the estate. Rates start at $100 per day per person. ☎ (246) 423-6220, fax (246) 423-5343.

Crane Beach Mansion, a four-bedroom luxury mansion on the property, features a large swimming pool and a fully equipped two-bedroom guest house. Cottage & mansion (six bedrooms) rent for $1,000 per day from April 1 to Dec 21. Book through your travel agent.

Long Beach Club on Chancery Lane in Christ Church features 24 rooms. Rates are from $51 to $100 per person daily. ☎ (246) 428-6890, fax (246) 428-4957.

Sandy Beach Island Resort, Worthing, Christ Church, offers 128 air-conditioned, beachfront rooms. Diving with Bubbles Galore Dive Shop. Rates per person are $85 to $125 in summer, $120 to $200 in winter. ☎ (246) 435-8000, fax (246) 435-8053.

Sam Lord's Castle, a luxurious, waterfront Marriott resort in Long Bay, on the Atlantic east coast, St. Phillip, features 234 air-conditioned rooms with all amenities. Tennis courts. ☎ (800) 228-9290 or (246) 423-7350, fax (246) 423-5918. Diving with Underwater Barbados.

Welcome Inn Beach Hotel, Maxwell Coast Road, Christ Church, offers 110 rooms, diving with Underwater Barbados. Rates are $75 per person per day in summer, $110 in winter. ☎ (246) 428-9900, fax (246) 428-8905.

For villas and home rentals contact **Island Hideaways**. ☎ (800) 784-2690 or (202) 232-6137, fax (202) 667-3392.

Crewed luxury yacht charters are offered by **Alleyne, Aguilar and Altman Ltd.**, St. James (none have compressors on board). ☎ (246) 432-0840, fax (246) 432-2147.

Other Activities

Horseback riding is offered by **Brighton Riding Stables**, ☎ 425-9381; **Caribbean International Riding Centre**, ☎ 433-1453; **Riding Beau Geste Farm**, ☎ 429-0139; or **Ye Olde Congo Road Stables**, ☎ 423-6180. Stables are near Bridgetown.

The **Sandy Lane Golf Course** at the Sandy Lane Hotel is a well-maintained 18-hole course. **Royal Westmoreland Golf & Country Club** offers contrasting challenges, stunning scenery and a succession of "feature holes." **Almond Beach Resort** features a par-3, nine-hole layout. It's straightforward, requiring only a nine iron, wedge, sand wedge and putter. ☎ 422-4900. **Club Rockley** resorts offers an 18-hole layout, with a second nine holes playable from varying tee positions. ☎ 435-7873.

Deep-sea fishing for dorado, wahoo, sail fish, tuna and marlin is easily arranged by the hotel desks. Call **Blue Jay Charters**, ☎ 422-2098 or 230-3832, fax 425-2819, or **Deep Sea Adventure**, ☎ 428-5344.

Skyrider Parasail features a 32-ft boat with an integrated, self-contained launching and landing platform. ☎ 435-0570.

Windsurfing off the south coast can be arranged at the **Barbados Windsurfing Club** at Maxwell and **Silver Rock Windsurfing Club** at Silver Sands. ☎ 428-2866.

Submarine tours of the reefs are offered aboard the 28-passenger *Atlantis*. ☎ 436-8929.

Sightseeing

Ride on an electric tram into **Harrison's Cave** (☎ 438-6640) to explore beautiful underground water falls, Mirror Lake and The Rotunda Room, where the walls of the 250-ft chamber glitter like diamonds. Or view exotic tropical birds and native monkeys at the **Oughterson House Barbados Zoo Park**. History buffs will delight in finding 17th-century military relics like antique cannons and signal towers around the island.

The Barbados National Trust offers an open house program where **Historical Great Houses** are open for public viewing between 2:30 and 5:30 pm. Entrance is $6. A bus tour that includes entrance and transportation from hotels is $18. ☎ (809) 426-2421.

A Heritage Passport Program offers visitors special admission to many of the island's historic attractions for only $35. Short-stay visitors can opt for the $12 mini-passport. Children under 12 accompany adults for free.

Shopping

Barbados abounds with boutiques, galleries and shops, with department stores such as **Harrison's** and **Cave Shepherd & Co**. offering goods from around the world, particularly diamonds and Italian gold. Island specialties include handmade puppets and clay and wood figures along with colorful silk-screened prints and fabrics. Pepper sauce and Barbados rum are also high on the list of popular take-homes. Most shops are in or near Broad Street, Bridgetown.

Dining

West Indian specialties and native seafood dishes like grilled flying fish and lobster are featured throughout the island. Bajan delicacies include *cou-cou* (a cornmeal and okra dish), pepperpot, a spicy stew, and *jug-jug*, a mixture of Guinea corn and green peas. Whether you're looking for a romantic five-star restaurant, beach-front café or Bajan buffet, Barbados has an endless number of dining options for every palate and budget. Restaurants range from small, front-porch cafés to large, luxury hotel dining rooms. Many hotels—Sandy Lane for example—offer a barbecue served to the music of steel bands or open-air discos. Fast food afficionados will enjoy **Chefette Drive-Thru**, Barbados' answer to the golden arches, open weekends from 10 am on Friday to midday Sunday. Chefette restaurants are located in Rockley, on Harbour Road, in Oistins, Holetown, Six Cross Rds, Broad St. and on Marhill St.

Josef's, located in St. Lawrence Gap, Christ Church, serves fabulous gourmet fish and continental cuisine in a grand native home with a garden overlooking the sea. Meals are under $25. ☎ 435-6541.

Pisces Restaurant, located in the St. Lawrence Gap on the waterfront, is noted for West Indian specialties and fabulous rum pie. ☎ 435-6564.

Waterfront Café, The Careenage, Bridgetown, serves Bajan specialties and Creole cuisine, including pepperpot and melts, plus tapas. Meals run between $25 and $40. Nice view of the docks. ☎ 427-0093.

"Nu-Bajan" cuisine is served at **Koko's** on Prospect, St James. Meals are under $25. ☎ 424-4557. Seating overlooks the ocean.

Creole cuisine lovers should be sure to try the **Brown Sugar Restaurant** at the Aquatic Gap in St. Michael. Popular buffet lunch served in an old Barbadian home. Under $25. ☎ 427-2329

Atlantis, Bathsheba, St. Joseph features a Bajan buffet on Sundays. Breathtaking views of the Atlantic surf. Under $25.

Additional favorites are **39 Steps** wine bar in Hastings, **Raffles** gourmet restaurant in Holetown, ☎ 432-6557, and the **Round House Inn** in Bathsheba for great margaritas, and gorgeous views of the Atlantic coast, ☎ 433-9678.

Facts

Helpful Phone Numbers: Police, ☎ 112; ambulance, ☎ 115.

Recompression Chamber: Located in St. Annes, Fort Garrison, St. Michael. Contact Dr. Brown or Major Gittens at ☎ 436-6185.

Getting There: British West Indies Airlines (BWIA), ☎ 800-327-7401, offers regular service from London, Frankfurt, Stockholm, Zurich, New York, Miami, and Toronto. American Airlines, ☎ 800-433-7300, from New York. Air Jamaica from US. Air Canada and American Airlines from Canada. Inter-island service: BWIA, LIAT, Carib Express and Air Martinique. Barbados' Grantley Adams International Airport is modern and well kept.

Island Transportation: Taxi service is available throughout the island. (Note: cab fares should be negotiated before accepting service.) Local auto-rental companies are at the airport. **National,** ☎ (246) 426-0603, **P&S,** ☎ 424-2907; **Corbins,** ☎ 427-9531; **Drive-A-Matic,** ☎ 422-3000; **Courtesy Rent A Car,** ☎ 431-4160.

Driving: Traffic keeps to the left in Barbados.

Documents: Canadian and US citizens require a birth certificate with a current photo ID or passport and return ticket in order to enter Barbados. Entry documentation is good for three months.

Customs: Personal effects of visitors, including cameras and sports equipment, enter duty free. Returning US citizens may take back free of duty articles costing a total of US $600 providing the stay has exceeded 48 hours and that the exemption has not been used within the preceding 30 days. One quart of liquor per person (over 21 years) may be carried out duty free. Not more than 100 cigars and 200 cigarettes may be included.

Note: Cameras and dive equipment should be registered with Customs **before** you leave the US.

Currency: Barbados dollar (BD)=US $2.

Climate: Temperatures vary between 75 and 85° F. Average rainfall is 59 inches.

Clothing Lightweight casual clothing is recommended. A jacket for men may be desirable for visiting nightclubs or dressy resort restaurants. Swim suits, bikinis and short shorts are not welcome in Bridgetown shops or banks.

Electricity: 110 volts AC, 50 cycles.

Time: Atlantic Standard (EST + 1 hr).

Language: English with a local dialect.

Taxes: A 10% service charge is added to the bill at most hotels. A sales tax of 5% is also added to hotel and restaurant bills.

Religious Services: Anglican, Baptist, Catholic, Methodist, Moravian, Seventh Day Adventist, Jehovah's Witnesses.

For Additional Information: Barbados Board Of Tourism, 800 Second Ave., NY, NY 10017, ☎ (800)-221-9831; in NY (212) 986-6510. *In Florida:* 150 Alhambra Circle, Suite 1270, Coral Gables, FL 33134. ☎ 305-442-7471, fax 305-567-2844. *In Barbados:* Harbour Road, Bridgetown, WI. ☎ 246-427-2623/2624 or 800-744-6244, fax 246-426-4080. Web site: http://barbados.org.

Belize

Fascinating and exotic, Belize offers a world of tropical adventure to divers and snorkelers. It is a preserve for the largest barrier reef in the western hemisphere, second only to the Great Barrier Reef in Australia, the magnificent Blue Hole, a 1,000-ft ocean sinkhole, and home to three beautiful atolls—Lighthouse Reef, the Turneffe Islands and Glovers Reef. Within the reef system are hundreds of uncharted islands.

Just 750 miles from Miami, Belize lies on the Caribbean coast of Central America between Guatemala and Mexico. Populated by a mere 200,000 people, it is a country of approximately 9,000 square miles. It has inland mountain ranges with peaks over 3,500 ft, dense tropical jungles, a coastline of mangrove swamps, and 266 square miles of offshore coral islands. The 185-mile-long barrier reef parallels the shore from 10 to 30 miles out, with prime diving locations around the out islands.

Tours to Belize are labeled "expedition" or "safari" rather than "vacation." Its offshore accommodations and facilities are considered primitive by Caribbean standards—few TVs, phones or automobiles on most of the islands—yet Belize's jungles and unspoiled reefs lure intrepid divers back again and again.

Visitors arriving in Belize City will find a safer environment than in the past, thanks to a special Tourist Police Force formed in 1995 that has reduced crimes against tourists by 72%. Despite the improvement, it's still wise to avoid flashing expensive cameras, jewelry, or money around.

On the mainland outside Belize City one finds fairly rugged and varied terrain, alive with yellowhead parrots, giant iguanas, monkeys and a curious creature called the gibnut—described by Belizean author, Robert Nicolait, as a cross between a fat rabbit and a small pig.

The heart of dive tourism is Ambergris Caye, a bustling resort and fishing community, the largest of the out islands or "cayes." Its main town, San Pedro, is a few hundred yards from the Hol Chan Marine Preserve, the northernmost point of the Barrier Reef, and is the jump-off point to Belize's smaller cayes and atolls. Ambergris is just 20 minutes by air from Belize City or an hour and 15 minutes by ferry (see end of chapter for transportation details). The northern portion of Ambergris is accessible by boat only, but plans for a road are under consideration. Transportation on Ambergris and the other islands is by golf cart or on foot.

A new area for divers is Placencia, a quaint fishing village located on a 16-mile coastal peninsula, 100 miles south of Belize City. There are some coral heads off the beaches, but a half-hour boat ride will bring you to Laughing Bird Caye, a small island surrounded by pristine reefs, and the remains of old wrecks. Several Spanish galleons went down in this area over the years and occasionally a gold piece washes up on the beach. Placencia is an intriguing new place to explore.

Visit Belize during the dry season, from February to May. Annual rainfall ranges from 170 inches in the south to 50 inches in the north. Heaviest rainfall is from September to January. August is frequently dry.

The climate is sub-tropical, with constant brisk winds from the Caribbean Sea. Summer highs are rarely above 95° F, winter lows seldom below 60°. Bug repellent is always needed as mosquitoes and sand flies are a constant annoyance.

Belize has a long history of stable government. It is a member of the British Commonwealth, with a democratically elected government. The people are Creoles (African-European), Garifuna (African-Indian), Mestizo (Spanish-Indian), Maya and European. English is the official language and is widely spoken, as is Spanish.

History

Early inhabitants of Belize were the Maya, whose territory also included Mexico, Guatemala, Honduras and El Salvador. They left behind great ceremonial centers, pyramids and evidence of a dynamic people with advancements in the arts, math and science. The Maya inhabited Belize as early as 9000 BC and flourished as a master civilization until most of them mysteriously disappeared about 1000 AD. Theories about their fate range from massive death by natural disaster to speculation about spaceship travel to other planets. Remnants of this ancient culture show that Belize was a major trading center for the entire Mayan area. Today, a small population of Mayan descendants inhabit the countryside.

At Altun Ha (30 miles north of Belize City), an excavated Maya center, spectacular jade and stone carvings have been unearthed, including an ornately carved head of Kinisch Ahau, the Mayan Sun God. This head, weighing 9¾ pounds and measuring nearly six inches from base to crown, is believed to be the largest Maya jade carving in existence. Also uncovered was the Temple of the Green Tomb, a burial chamber that contained human

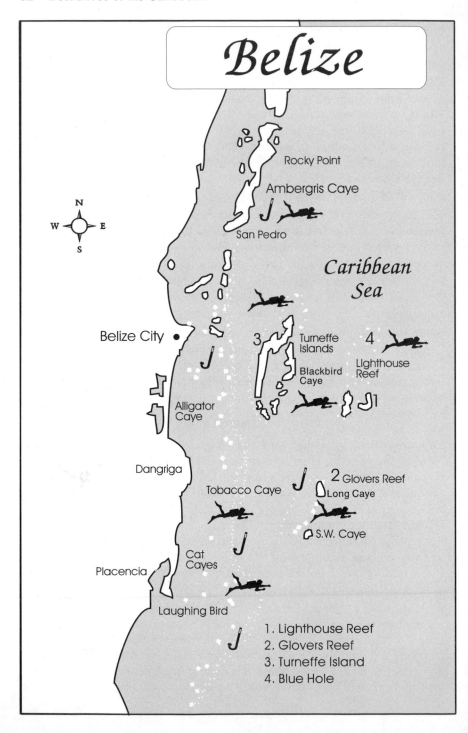

Belize

Rocky Point

Ambergris Caye

San Pedro

Caribbean Sea

Belize City

3 Turneffe Islands

4 Lighthouse Reef

Blackbird Caye

1

Alligator Caye

Dangriga

Tobacco Caye

2 Glovers Reef

Long Caye

S.W. Caye

Cat Cayes

Placencia

Laughing Bird

1. Lighthouse Reef
2. Glovers Reef
3. Turneffe Island
4. Blue Hole

remains and a wealth of jade pieces, including pendants, beads, figures and jewelry. Side trips to this and other jungle archaeological sites are offered by most dive-tour operators.

During the 17th century, Belize was colonized by the British and the Spanish. In 1862, the settlement became an English colony known as British Honduras. It gained independence in 1981. Today, it is the only Central American nation where English is widely spoken.

Best Dive and Snorkeling Sites

THE BARRIER REEF

☆☆☆ **Hol Chan Marine Preserve**, a five-square-mile reef area off the southern tip of Ambergris Caye, is characterized by a natural channel or cut that attracts and shelters huge communities of marine animals. Maximum depth inside the reef is 30 ft, allowing unlimited bottom time. The outside wall starts at 50 ft, then drops to beyond 150 ft. Schools of tropicals line the walls, with occasional glimpses of big turtles, green and spotted morays, six-ft stingrays, eagle rays, spotted dolphins and nurse sharks.

A constant flow of sea water through the cut promotes the growth of large barrel and basket sponges, sea fans, and beautiful outcroppings of staghorn and brain corals. Check tide charts before diving on your own; currents can be very strong in the channel at outgoing tides.

Diving all along the barrier reef is extraordinary. There are caves, dramatic overhangs, and pinnacles, all with superb marine life, though commercial fishing has taken its toll on the really big grouper, shark and huge turtles that were commonplace 10 years ago. The subsea terrain is similar throughout the area, with long channels of sand running perpendicular to the overall reef system. These cuts run to seaward allowing a constant change of nutrient-rich sea water to cleanse and feed the coral.

The inner reef, that area facing land, is shallow, with coral slopes that bottom out between 20 and 40 ft. Amidst its forests of stag horn and elkhorn are throngs of juvenile fish, barracuda, invertebrates, spawning grouper, stingrays, conch, nurse shark and small critters.

Diving the outer reef brings a better chance to see mantas, permits, jacks, black durgons, tuna, dolphin, turtles and sharks. Visibility is exceptional too. The reef profile outside is typically a sloping shelf to between 25 or 40 ft, which then plunges to 2,000 ft or more.

Live-aboard yachts that explore the entire coast are extremely popular in Belize, though local guides and tourist officials are working to attract more divers to their shore facilities and après-dive attractions.

The Atolls

Atolls are ring-shaped coral islands or island groups surrounding a lagoon. Most are in the South Pacific and are often the visible portions of ancient, submerged volcanoes. But those in Belize are composed of coral and may have been formed by faults during the shifting of land masses.

All three, Lighthouse Reef, Glovers Reef and the Turneffe Islands, are surrounded by miles of shallow reefs and magnificent, deep dropoffs. The sheltered lagoons are dotted with pretty coral heads and are great for snorkeling and novice divers. Outside, visibility exceeds 150 ft and marine life is unrivaled. Generally, the islands are primitive, remote and largely uninhabited, with the bulk of the population made up of free-roaming chickens, though each location has at least one dive resort and a resident divemaster.

☆☆☆☆ **The Turneffe Islands**, 35 miles from Belize City and beyond the barrier reef, are a group of 32 low islands bordered with thick growths of mangroves. The lower portion of the chain forms a deep V shape with Cay Bokel at the southernmost point. Reef areas just above both sides of the point are the favorite southern dive spots. Cay Bokel is where you'll find the Turneffe Island Lodge, a quaint resort offering dive services. West of the southern point are sheltered, shallow reefs at 20 to 60 ft depths. Along the reef are some old anchors overgrown with coral, a small, wooden wreck, the *Sayonara,* and a healthy fish population. Seas are rougher, currents stronger and the dives deeper to the east, but more impressive coral formations and large pelagics are found. The ridges and canyons of the reefs are carpeted by a dense cover of sea feathers, lacy soft corals, branching gold and purple sponges, anemones, seafans and luxurious growths of gorgonians. Passing dolphins and rays are the big attraction as they upstage the reef's "blue collar workers"—cleaner shrimp, sea cucumbers, patrolling barracuda, defensive damsel fish, schooling yellowtail, grunts and coral crabs. Snorkeling and diving are excellent, with outstanding water clarity, protected areas, and diverse marine life.

Rendezvous Point at the northernmost point is equal in sub terrain and diver interest, but is more often visited by fishermen. Much of the northern area is shallow mangrove swamp where tarpon, bonefish, shrimp and lobster proliferate.

☆☆☆☆☆ The most popular atoll, and that most visited by dive boats, is **Lighthouse Reef.** It lies 40 miles from Belize City and is the outermost of the offshore islands within the Belize cruising area. Lighthouse is a circular reef system featuring several islands and small cayes. On its southeast boundaries is a beautiful old lighthouse and Half Moon Caye Natural Monument, the first marine conservation area in Belize and a bird sanctuary for colonies of the red-footed boobie, frigate birds, ospreys, mangrove warblers and white-crowned pigeons.

Half Moon Caye Natural Monument has white sand beaches with a drop-off on the north side and a shallow lagoon on the south end. A dock with a pierhead depth of about six ft and an area for amphibious aircraft are on the north side of the island. Dive boats are required to anchor in designated areas to prevent reef damage. All boaters must register with the lighthouse keeper upon arrival. Coordinates of an approved anchorage for craft with a beam length of less than 120 ft are 17° 12' 25" N 87° 33'11"W.

The lighthouse, situated on the tapering eastern side of Half Moon Caye, was first built in 1820. It was later replaced by another in 1848 and since reinforced by a steel-framed tower in 1931. Today the lighthouse is solar-powered. A climb to the top offers a spectacular view.

Endangered loggerhead turtles and hawksbill turtles come ashore to lay their eggs on the sandy southern beaches.

To the north is the Lighthouse Reef Resort, an air-conditioned colony of English villas catering to divers and fishermen.

☆☆☆☆☆ Near the center of Lighthouse Reef is the **Blue Hole**, Belize's most famous dive spot. From the air it looks like an apparition. The cobalt blue of the Caribbean abruptly changes to an azure blue circle. The heart of the circle is an indigo blue.

Approaching by water is not as breathtaking, but beautiful nonetheless. You know you are somewhere special. It is an almost perfect circle, 1,000 ft in diameter in the midst of a reef six to 18 ft below the surface. Inside the shallow reef, the walls drop suddenly to a depth of 412 ft, almost completely vertical for the first 125 ft. Here they turn inward and slightly upward. At 140 ft you reach an awesome underwater "cathedral" with alcoves, archways and columns. It is a huge submerged cave with 12- to 15-ft-wide stalactites suspended 20 to 60 ft from the cavern ceiling. Formed thousands of years ago, perhaps during the Ice Age, the cave was once above sea level. This is always a guided dive and should be attempted only by experienced divers, but novice divers are as entertained by the shallows surrounding the crater's rim as are those venturing down to the cave. Note: The nearest decompression chamber is in Belize City.

Travel time to and from the Blue Hole and the cost of your trip will vary according to the location of your accommodations. If you are staying on Ambergris Caye the trip will take an entire day and cost about $150. From the Turneffe Islands, travel time to and from is about half a day and the cost is included. If you are on a live-aboard, one of your stops will surely be the Blue Hole.

☆☆☆☆ South of the Turneffe Islands and Lighthouse Reef is the third and most remote atoll, **Glover's Reef**. It is a reef system formed by coral growing around the edges of a steep limestone plateau. An almost continuous barrier reef encloses an 80-square-mile lagoon that reaches depths of 50 ft. The lagoon is an outstanding snorkeling spot, with over 700 coral heads. Outside, the reef starts at 30 ft and drops to more than 2,000 ft. Visibility exceeds 150 ft. Grouper, queen trigger fish and parrot fish are in abundance. Mantas, pods of dolphins, spotted eagle rays and sea turtles are occasionally seen on the reefs. It is a spectacular diving and snorkeling spot, with more than 25 coral species to be explored and thousands of sheltered spots. The reefs remain largely unexplored and are seldom visited by live-aboards. Two dive/fishing resorts, Glovers Reef Resort and Manta Reef Resort, offer experienced guides and services.

Accommodations

Rates listed are for winter, in US dollars, and are subject to change. Most resorts and restaurants accept US dollars, travelers checks, and major credit cards.

Note: Direct dial service is available between Belize and the US and Canada. To call Belize, dial (011) 501, drop the first zero from the local number, then dial the remaining numbers. E-mail, where available, may be used to book direct.

Ambergris Caye

There are flights between Belize City and San Pedro, the main town on Ambergris Cay, every 30 minutes from sunrise to sunset.

Ramon's Village in San Pedro offers 20 lovely, air-conditioned, thatched-roof bungalows with double beds and full baths. The resort has a nice poolside bar, saltwater pool, restaurant, and fully equipped dive shop offering reef trips and basic rentals. Relaxed atmosphere. Daily room rates start at $125 daily for a double, to $245 for a suite. ☎ (800) MAGIC 15 or (601) 649-1990, fax (601) 425-2411; or write P.O. Drawer 4407, Laurel MS 39441. Web site: www.ramons.com.

Money-saving dive-accommodation packages at Ramon's Village with breakfast, five nights and eight boat dives are $640 per person; seven nights with 12 boat dives for $899 through Landfall Productions, ☎ (800) 525-3833, fax (510) 794-1599. Discounts for groups. Dive packages with air from the US also offered. Web site: http://ecotravel.com/landfall; E-mail: lndfall@aol.com.

Victoria House, on its own nine-acre beach, features 31 casually elegant rooms, suites, apartments and villas. An on-site PADI dive shop, restaurant and tour desk make this deluxe resort a popular spot with divers—coupled with the fact that the barrier reef lies three-quarters of a mile directly in front of the hotel. Day rates for standard air-conditioned rooms are from $110 for a double. Seven-night packages with airfare from the mainland included range from $1,142 (varies with season). Kayaks, windsurfers, Sunfish and a small catamaran may be rented. ☎ (800) 247-5159 or (504) 865-0717, fax (504) 865-0718. Local 026-2067, fax 026-2429, or write to Victoria House, Ambergris Caye, Belize, Central America. Web site: www.belize.com/victoriahouse.html. E-mail: victoria@bze.com or victoria@ communique.net.

Belize Yacht Club, within easy walking distance of San Pedro Town and restaurants, features modern, Spanish-style, air-conditioned, one- and two-bedroom suites with fully-equipped kitchens. Amenities include a freshwater pool, marina, bar, dive shop, fishing, snorkeling excursions. No restaurant. Book through Belize International Expeditions, ☎ (800) 633-4734 or write to International Expeditions, Inc., One Environs Park, Helena, AL 35080.

Coral Beach Hotel and Dive Club, situated on the main street of town, is a dive shop with 19 adjacent rooms. Accommodations are plain and simple, some with air-conditioning, some with fans. The hotel bar, The Tackle Box, sits over the sea. Dive packages, snorkel-sail trips, airport pickup. Room rates per day, per person start at $45, with meals $80. ☎ (011) 501-26-2013, fax (011)501-26-2864. E-mail: forman@btl.net.

Caribbean Villas Hotel, three-quarters of a mile from San Pedro, features 10 air-conditioned beachfront luxury rooms and suites. Nice pier and beach. Hot tubs, elevated perch for bird watching. ☎ (800) 633-4734 or direct (011) 501- 26-2715, fax (011) 501-26-2885. Winter rates range from $85 for a room to $245 for a suite. E-mail: c-v-hotel@btl.net.

Paradise Resort Hotel, at the north end of San Pedro, features 24 charming tropical rooms, some with air-conditioning. Rates are $60 for an air-conditioned room in summer, $120 in winter. ☎ (800) 451-8017

Paradise Villas Beachfront Resort Condos offer one- and two-bedroom deluxe apartments with ceiling fans, air conditioning, TV and kitchenettes. Restaurant. Rates are $90 to $150 per night plus 7% tax. No service charge. ☎ (501) 792-2639, fax (510) 791-5602. E-mail: susan@belize.com.

Captain Morgan's Retreat is a thatched-hut village on the beach. Cabanas are private, with ceiling fans and solid mahogany floors. Modern baths. Roomy. The resort, 3½ miles north of San Pedro, is reached by water taxi. Diving and fishing packages. Accommodations are from $95 for a single to $135 for a triple from May-Dec; $143 for a single to $209 for a triple from

Dec-April. Dive packages available. ☎ (800) 447-2931 or (218) 847-3012, fax (218) 847-0334. E-mail: information@captainmorgans.com.

Journey's End, is an outstanding, beachfront hotel just 500 yds from the Barrier Reef. The 50-acre resort is accessible by water taxi—10 minutes from the airstrip. Guests stay in luxurious beach cabanas, poolside villas, or waterfront rooms. All have been recently renovated. Amenities include a gourmet restaurant, tennis courts, beach bar, and freshwater Olympic pool with swim-up bar and grill. All watersports are offered. The 125-member staff caters to guests' every whim. Rates in summer (May-Dec 13th), seven nights, for a pool/garden room are $882, three nights $471; in winter (Jan 5-Apr 15) seven nights, from $872; three nights, from $432. Package includes round-trip air from Belize International Airport to San Pedro, land transfers to hotels, welcome cocktail, accommodations, continental breakfast and dinner daily, taxes, service charges. ☎ (800) 447-0474, (800) 365-6232 or (281) 996-7800, fax (281) 996-1556.

Rocks Inn is on the beach within walking distance of San Pedro, restaurants, bars, and shops. The hotel offers attractive air-conditioned suites with modern appliances. No restaurant. Day rates are from $100 for a double. Dive-travel packages available. ☎(501) 26-2326, (501) 26-2358. E-mail: rocks@btl.net.

Sunbreeze Beach Hotel, a 39-room, air-conditioned beachfront hotel, teams up with Belize Undersea Adventures to offer a seven-night package for $683 including accommodations, five two-tank boat dives and transfers from Belize City. Rooms have private bath, ocean views, balconies, phone, cable TV. ☎ (800) 327-8150 or (954) 462-3400, fax (954) 462-4100. E-mail: nealwatson@aol.com or sunbreeze@btl.net. Web site: www.twofin.com/twofin/belize.htm.

Caye Caulker

Tropical Paradise Resort features standard rooms with fans, traditionally constructed from local woods. suites with telephones, refrigerator, AC and TV. Amenities and services include restaurant and ice cream parlor, diving, snorkeling and fishing available. A good spot for getting away from the world. Day trips to San Pedro easily arranged. Book through International Expeditions, ☎ (800) 633-4734.

St. George's Caye

St. George's Lodge is the only commercial establishment on Saint George's Caye. The lodge, which is beautifully hand-crafted of exquisite local hardwoods, houses a dining room, rosewood bar, secluded sundeck and 12 private rooms cooled by tradewinds. In addition, there are four new thatched cottages, each with a private veranda overlooking the sea. All rooms and cottages feature private bath with shower, and windmill-powered electricity. (A 110-V AC converter is located in the lodge for recharging strobes, etc.) Gourmet meals featuring fresh lobster, broiled native fish, and outstanding conch chowder, followed by fabulous desserts created with local fruits, are the fare of the day at this lodge. Diving takes place on a shallow wall ranging from 40 to 100 ft, where there is a wide variety of corals and endless schools of fish. Visibility exceeds 100 ft. Rates per person, per day, include round-trip ground and boat transportation from Belize International Airport, private bath, three meals daily, tanks, weights, full diving privileges, two trips daily and maid service; $293 (cottages); $271(lodge). Non-divers $201.25 (lodge), $213 (cottage). Non-divers may swim from dive boats on a space-available basis. Nitrox diving available. Instruction extra. ☎ (800) 678-6871, local 02-44190, fax 02-30461. St. George's Lodge, P.O. Box 625, Belize City, Belize, C. A. E-mail: belize@teleport.com. Web site: www. teleport.com/~belize.

Villas at Banyan Bay in San Pedro are deluxe, with two bedrooms and two baths, ocean views, air conditioning, phone, cable TV, microwave, washer/dryer, security storage. Rates for two sharing a villa are $175 per villa per night; for four, $225 per night. Add 7% tax. ☎ (800) 382-7776 or (011) 501-26-3739, fax (011) 501-26-2766. E-mail: bztravel@compassnet. com or divebze@compassnet.com.

South Water Caye

Escape the masses on this private 18-acre island off Dangriga, 35 miles south of Belize City. Transfers from the mainland are by the Blue Marlin Lodge launch or by charter flight. By boat, the trip takes about 90 minutes. Driving from Belize City to Dangriga takes about 2½ hours, or by air, 20 minutes.

The big plus for this pristine spot is easy beach diving and snorkeling on the barrier reef that sits 120 ft offshore. Sounds like a short swim, but actually the water is so shallow between the shore and the drop-off, that it's a short walk. Despite Belize's current trend towards marine conservation, spearfishing is allowed here.

The Blue Marlin Lodge, South Water Caye's sole resort, spreads over six acres. Catering primarily to divers and fishermen, the all-inclusive rustic lodge features nine clean, modern rooms (each with two double beds) cooled by ceiling fans and three air-conditioned cottages on the water's edge. All rooms have a private bath with hot and cold running water. The lodge produces its own 110 volt, 60 cycle power and has a desalinization plant to produce pure water. The restaurant and bar serve three sumptuous meals daily. Fresh fish, shrimp and lobster are nicely prepared. Snacks and beverages are served all day. The bar is always stocked with fine Caribbean rums and an assortment of other liquors and beers. No phones and no TV in the rooms or cottages, but there is a phone in the office that guests may

Maya Ruins.

use, and the bar has one satellite TV and a VCR. The lodge's dive office has an air compressor, tanks, weights and a small supply of gear. Bring your own personal equipment and snorkeling gear.

Dive/snorkel trips are aboard a fast Pro 42 dive boat or one of two 26-ft power boats. Fishing trips are aboard a 28-ft Mako.

All-inclusive dive packages for $1,443 per person, based on a double, from Saturday to Saturday, include pick-up in Dangriga, standard accommodations, three meals daily plus snacks, two boat dives daily (six days), unlimited shore dives. Add $180 for an air-conditioned cottage. ☎ (800) 798-1558, (011) 501-52-2243 or (011) 501-52-2296. E-mail for reservations: blue marlin @netrunner.net. E-mail to resort: marlin@btl.net. Web site: www. belize net.com/marlin.html.

The Turneffe Islands

Turneffe Island Lodge accommodates guests either in 12 air-conditioned beachfront cottage rooms with private bath or at the main lodge. Cellular and fax service (no phones). American-owned and -operated, this delightful outpost lies approximately 30 miles from Belize City—a two-hour boat trip supplied by the lodge. Lodge rooms feature tropical decor and screened porches facing the Caribbean. Specialties from the gourmet dining room include local fish dishes, conch, and island-grown fruits and vegetables.

A sheer coral wall that starts at 40 ft and drops to more than 2,000 ft surrounds the entire island. Outstanding snorkeling reefs lie about 350 yards off the resort beach. Get there by either paddling one of the resort's four sea kayaks, sailing a Sunfish or taking the skiff. Rates per person of $1,350 for seven nights, seven days, include round-trip transfers from the Belize City airport, three meals daily, 17 single-tank dives, day trip to the Blue Hole, Half Moon Wall and Long Caye Wall, use of sea kayaks, windsurfer, sailboat, volleyball, horsehoes and lodging. Non-divers pay $1,095. Tanks and weights supplied. Bring your own personal gear. ☎ (800) 874-0118, fax (770) 534-8290. Write to P.O. Box 2974, Gainesville, GA 30503. E-mail: info@turneffelodge.com. Web site: www.turneffelodge.com.

Dive/hotel/airfare packages from the US are offered through Landfall Productions, ☎ (800) 525-3833. E-mail: lndfall@aol.com.

Blackbird Caye Resort, located 35 miles from Belize City within the Turneffe Reef Atoll on Blackbird Cay, defines "ecotourist paradise." Unique and exciting, with miles of deserted beaches and jungle trails, the island sits close to 70 impressive dive sites with depths from 20 to 80 ft. Reefs are spectacular with huge tube and barrel sponges, dramatic overhangs, large loggerhead turtles, dolphins, perfect coral formations. Lots of groupers and reef fish. Manatee sightings. Great snorkeling lies just 400 yds offshore, a five-minute swim. Calm waters inside the reef make it a safe spot for novices. Rate for an all-inclusive package is $1,350 for seven nights. Packages include airport reception, boat transfers, lodging, all meals (excellent buffet-style), trails, three dives per day, air, tanks and weights. Dive shop on property. Morning and afternoon snorkeling excursions. Boat to the island departs from Ramada docks in Belize City promptly at 3:30, Sept to Mar; 4:30 pm, Apr-Aug. Travel time is four-five hours.

Accommodations are in thatch-roofed cabanas with ceiling fans and private baths. ☎ (888) 271-DIVE (3483) or (310) 937-6470, fax (310) 937-6473. E-mail: dive@blackbirdresort.com. Web site: http://dive.blackbirdresort. com.

Lighthouse Reef

Lighthouse Reef Resort on Northern Cay, a private island at the northern end of the Lighthouse Reef Reserve, boasts a protected lagoon perfect for snorkelers of all ages. For experienced divers, the resort's custom-built cruiser takes off for the best of Belizean adventure dives, including the fabulous Blue Hole and Lighthouse Reef where 15 x 10 ft basket sponges, kelp-like gorgonians and sea fans up to nine ft across thrive.

The resort offers luxury air-conditioned rooms and villas. Tropic Air meets incoming flights at Belize International Airport and transports guests to the resort's private airstrip. Flight time is 20 minutes. Diving packages, $1,200 (non-divers $1,050), run from Sat to Sat and include air-conditioned room with bath, three meals per day and snacks, three boat dives per day, night dives, tanks and weights. A fishing and diving package may be combined for $1,400. ☎ (800) 423-3114. Write: P.O. Box 26, Belize City, C.A.

Glovers Reef

Manta Reef Resort, a 2½-hour boat trip from Belize City, sits on 12 palm-studded acres at the southern tip of Glovers Reef Atoll, conveniently perched over a deep coral wall with easy beach entry. Guests unwind in modern, though simple, mahogany cabanas with private baths and showers. A spacious waterside restaurant and bar decorated with hand-rubbed native woods, fast dive boats, an E6 photo lab and gift shop fill most divers' vacation wishes. Rates are $1,295 per week (Sat to Sat), per person, double occupancy, including round-trip transfers from the mainland aboard their 48-ft boat, three meals daily, three boat dives per day, two night dives, unlimited beach dives. Fishing packages also available. ☎ (800) 326-1724, local (011) 501-232767, fax (011) 501-234449. E-mail: dive@blackbird resort.com. Web site: http://dive.blackbirdresort.com.

Placencia

Placencia is a great spot for divers seeking off-the-beaten-track adventures and especially for those on a low budget. Forty cayes between the mainland and the barrier reef offer pristine diving and snorkeling. Placencia Village has guest rooms for as low as $10 per night. Affordable open air bars serve pizza, chili and Creole fish dishes. Camping is available at the Bonaventure Resort in Seine Bight Village. For complete listings contact the Belize Tourist Board, ☎ (800) 844-3688.

Rum Point Inn, a NAUI and PADI Dream Resort, three miles from Placencia Village, comprises 10 seaside cabanas, a main house and a small sandy swimming beach. E-6 processing. Pro-42 "Auriga" dive boat. Rates per person, per day, for a double are $90 for accommodations, $112 including meals. Children under 12, $35; $50 with meals. Add 7% hotel tax and 15% service charge on meals. Dive courses available. ☎ (800) 747-1381 or (011) 501-6-23239, fax (011) 501-6-23240. Or book through International Expeditions, ☎ (800) 633-4734 or (205) 428-1700. E-mail: 76735@compu-serve.com.

Turtle Inn, a mile north of Placencia Village, offers six thatch-roofed cabanas along 500 ft of Caribbean beachfront. Cabanas have private baths, solar-generated lighting and kerosene lanterns. Guests are offered a number of dive, snorkeling and jungle trips. Book through International Expeditions, ☎ (800) 633-4734 or (205) 428-1700. E-mail: 76735@ compuserve.com.

Nautical Inn, the newest resort on the Placencia peninsula in Seine Bight Village, features beachfront rooms with private baths, the Oar House

Restaurant, transfers from Placencia airstrip, a gift shop, salon, scooter rentals, canoeing, scuba, snorkeling and jungle tours. Rooms that sleep two are $109 per day. Dives are $67 for two one-tank dives. ☎ (800) 225-6732 or (011) 501-6-22310. E-mail: seaexplore-belize@worldnet.att.net.

Singing Sands Inn features private individual thatch-roofed cabanas, modern on the inside, with private bathrooms. Excursions for diving, snorkeling and day-trip visits to Maya ruins and the Cockscomb Jaguar Preserve are offered. Book through International Expeditions, ☎ (800) 633-4734 or (205) 428-1700. E-mail: 76735@compuserve.com.

Soulshine Resort dive tours take off to Laughing Bird Caye, Ranguana Caye and Little Caye. This small dive resort offers clean accommodations, breakfast and dinner, five two-tank dives, transfers for rates starting at $1,060 per person, double occupancy. ☎ (800) 890-6082. Web site: www. soulshine.com.

The Placencia Dive Shop specializes in friendly service, dive and snorkeling trips such as their Creole seafood feast and snorkel trip to nearby French Louis Cay. ☎ (501) 62-3313 or (501) 62-3227, fax 501-62-3226.

Sightseeing

Day trips to Belize's archaeological sites, the rain forest and Belize Zoo are offered by local tour companies in Belize City and Ambergris Caye or can be arranged as part of your trip in advance. Day rates are from $65 to about $200 from Ambergris Caye to inland sites, depending on where you are headed.

Altun Ha is the most popular Maya Ruin and least expensive from Ambergris Caye. Tour operators include a picnic lunch, ground and sea transportation.

Xunantunich (Maiden of the Rock) is on the west coast about 80 miles from Belize City. This is the largest ruin unearthed in Belize. Impressive views are had from the top of El Castillo, the main pyramid. Xunantunich is accessible only by ferry, which runs from San Jose Succotz daily from 8 am to 5 pm. Trips often include a tour of the Belize Zoo and a drive around Belmopan, Belize's capital.

Animals at the **Belize Zoo** are housed in naturalistic mesh and wood enclosures. The animals—jaguars, pumas, toucans, spider and howler monkeys, and the "mountain cow"—are all indigenous to Belize. They were originally gathered for a wildlife film. The zoo is 30 miles west of Belize City.

From Belize City, driving up the Western Highway to Mile Marker 21 will bring you to **Gracie Rock,** one of the sites used in the movie *Mosquito Coast*, where you'll find the remains of the huge icemaker blown up by Harrison Ford.

Guanacaste Park, about 50 miles southwest of Belize City, is a 50-acre parcel of tropical forest located in the Cayo District at the junction of Western Highway and Hummingbird Highway. It is named for the huge Guanacaste tree, which can reach a height of 130 ft with a diameter in excess of six ft. More than a hundred species of birds have been spotted here.

The Blue Hole National Park & St. Hermans Cave are 12 miles southeast of Belmopan. This inland "Blue Hole" is a popular recreational spot where water, on its way to the Sibun River, emerges into the base of a collapsed sinkhole about 100 ft deep and 300 ft in diameter. St Hermans Cave is 500 yards from the Hummingbird Highway and is accessible via a hiking trail from the Blue Hole. The nearest of the three known entrances is impressive—a large sinkhole funneling to a 65-ft entrance. Mayan pottery, spears and torches have been found here.

Dining

Divers staying on Ambergris Caye will find restaurants in the village of San Pedro offering fresh seafood and local dishes such as conch chowder, conch fritters, broiled snapper, shrimp, lobsters, and rice dishes, often accompanied by home-baked breads or soups. Chinese food is also extremely popular. **Ramon's Village Restaurant**, ☎ 26-2071, offers a variety of fresh seafood in Chinese, Cajun and island dishes (breakfast, lunch and dinner). Or try the **Celi's**, ☎ 26-2014, next to the Holiday Hotel for fabulous fish in beer batter and key lime pie (beach barbecue on Wednesdays), **Little Italy**, ☎ 26-2866, for great pizza, pasta and seafood (open for lunch and dinner), or **Elvi's Kitchen**, ☎ 26-2174, for lobster, conch and shrimp (open for lunch and dinner).

If you are staying at an out-island resort, meals are included in the price of the stay. Local fish, conch and chicken dishes are the usual.

Shopping

Small shops at the airport and resorts offer T-shirts, straw crafts and native carvings from mahogany, rosewood and ziricote, a two-toned wood indigenous to Belize.

Tours

The following tour companies offer diving and/or combination diving/jungle expeditions of Belize. There are pre-planned packages for groups and individuals, or design your own and they will make all the arrangements. Most Belize tours from the US depart from Houston or Miami. Package rates for week-long trips are usually much lower than buying air, accommodations, diving, meals and transfers separately.

Landfall Productions features well-planned, money-saving, all-inclusive dive vacations from the US, including transfers, diving and accommodations for seven nights to the Turneffe Island Lodge ($1,350), St. George's Lodge ($1,349), Ramon's Village on Ambergris Caye ($829), Lighthouse Reef Resort ($1,350) and live-aboard vacations on the *Wave Dancer* ($1,495) and *Belize Aggressor* ($1,595). Call for group rates. ☎ (800) 525-3833. E-mail: lndfall@aol.com.

International Expeditions Inc. offers custom-guided trips for the naturalist. Tours are well organized to consider both the skilled diver and novice snorkeler. ☎ (800) 633-4734 or (205) 428-1700; write to Number One Environs Park, Helena, AL 35080.

CEDAM (Conservation, Ecology, Diving, Archaeology, Museums) is a non-profit organization that organizes scientific expeditions. ☎ (914) 271-5365 or fax (914) 271-4723. Write to 1 Fox Road, Croton, NY 10520.

Ocean Connection offers snorkeling, fishing and diving trips, with a choice of islands and hotels. Beach and jungle treks, Mayan ruins and Belize national park tours are their specialty. Budget rates. Combination tours with Mexico are possible. ☎ (800) 934-6232, (713) 996-7800, fax (713) 996-1556; or write 211 E. Parkwood #108, Friendswood, TX 77546.

Magnum's Belize features dive and fishing packages to Ambergris Caye, Placencia, Corozal, Caye Caulker and Lighthouse Reef. ☎ (800) 447-2931. Write to 718 Washington Ave., Detroit Lakes, MN 56502. Web site: www. magnumbelize.com/Dive.html.

American Canadian Caribbean Line Inc. features luxurious, small ship cruises from San Pedro to the Rio Dulce, Guatemala and cays between. No scuba, but they make several snorkeling stops at the best spots. $2,100 per person for 12 days. Airfare extra. ☎ (800) 556-7450.

Live-Aboards

Belize live-aboards offer access to these pristine diving areas and are popular among those who thrive on 24-hour diving.

Peter Hughes Diving operates the 120-ft *Wave Dancer*. ☎ (800) 932-6237 or (305) 669-9391. Or write 1390 S. Dixie Highway, Waterway II, Suite 2213, Coral Gables, FL 33146. Packages, ☎ (800) 525-3833.

Belize Aggressor II is a 110-ft luxury yacht that carries 18 passengers. It offers all the amenities of a dive resort: air-conditioned private rooms, photo shop, film processing, mini movie theater, plus fast cruising speeds. ☎ (800) 348-2628 or write Aggressor Fleet Ltd., P.O. Drawer K, Morgan City, LA 70381. Packages through Landfall, ☎ (800) 525-3833.

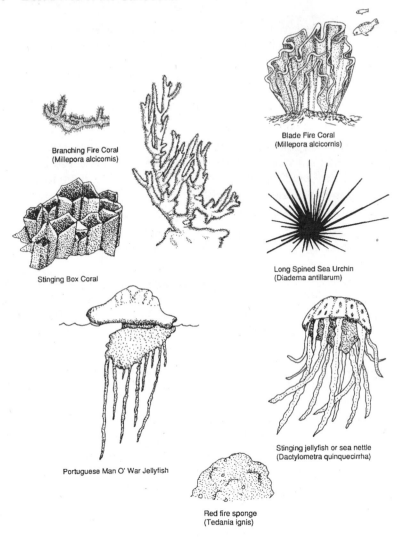

Branching Fire Coral
(Millepora alcicornis)

Blade Fire Coral
(Millepora alcicornis)

Stinging Box Coral

Long Spined Sea Urchin
(Diadema antillarum)

Portuguese Man O' War Jellyfish

Stinging jellyfish or sea nettle
(Dactylometra quinquecirrha)

Red fire sponge
(Tedania ignis)

Stinging Corals and Marine Animals

Facts

Helpful Phone Numbers: Police and ambulance: *Belize City,* ☎ 90; *San Pedro,* ☎ 02-82095; *Placencia,* ☎ 06-23129. 911 works in some areas. Hospital: *Belize City,* ☎ 02-77251 or 90. Tourist board: ☎ (800) 422-3435 or (501) 26-2012, fax (011) 501-26-2338. Coast Guard: ☎ 02-35312. Philip S.W. Goldson International Airport: ☎ 02-52014. Maya Airways: ☎ 2-44032/45968/44234 (service throughout Belize).

Nearest Recompression Chamber: Belize City. Emergency helicopter service from atolls. Dial 90 for assistance.

Health: Anti-malaria tablets are recommended for stays in the jungle.

Airlines: Scheduled commercial service from the US and Canada is by American Airlines, ☎ (800) 433-7300, Continental, and TACA. Tropic Air flies from Cancun, Mexico. ☎ (800) 422-3435 or (501) 26-2012, fax (011) 501-26-2338. In Belize, Tropic Air, ☎ 2302; in San Pedro, 2012 or 2439, services major cities, Ambergris Caye and the out islands. Additional Belize cities are served by Island Air, ☎ 2219 or 2435, or Maya Airways, ☎ 2336; in San Pedro, 2515.

Private Aircraft may enter Belize only through the Phillip Goldson International Airport in Belize City. Belizean airspace is open during daylight hours. Pilots are required to file a flight plan and will be briefed on local conditions. Landing fee for all aircraft.

By Car: Belize can reached from the US and Canada via Mexico, though reports of hold-ups on the roads deter most motorists. You must possess a valid driver's license and registration papers for the vehicle. A temporary permit will enable use of your vehicle without payment of customs. A temporary insurance policy must be purchased at the frontier to cover the length of stay in Belize. After three days, visitors must obtain a Belize driving permit, for which they need to complete a medical form, provide two recent photos and pay $20.

Private Boats must report to the police or immigration immediately. No permits are required. Boaters need documents of the vessel, clearance from last port of call, four copies of the crew and passenger manifest and list of stores and cargo.

Documents: Visitors are permitted to stay up to one month, provided they have a valid passport and have a ticket to their onward destination. For stays longer than 30 days, an extension must be obtained from the Immigration Office, 115 Barrack Road, Belize City.

Transportation: Bus service around Belize City is readily available via Batty Brothers, ☎ 02-72025; or Z-Line, ☎ 02-73937/06-22211. Since few cars are available on the islands, transportation is usually arranged by the resorts. On the mainland, reservations can be made through National (☎ 800-CAR-RENT; in Belize, 2-31650) or Budget (☎ 800-927-0700; in Belize, ☎ 2-32435 or 33986). Reserve prior to trip. Jeeps and 4WD vehicles are mandatory on back roads. Avoid local car rental companies or carefully check vehicles for scratches or dents and have them documented by the rental copany beforehand.

Ferries: Ambergris Caye can be reached by ferry boat from Belize City. The *Andrea I and Andrea II* operate from Belize City to San Pedro, leaving the docks of the Bellevue Hotel at 4 pm from Mon to Fri and 1 pm on Sat, returning to Belize at 7 am. Also available to San Pedro is the *Miss Belize*, which runs daily. Tickets may be purchased from the Universal Travel Agency in Belize City. *Miss Belize* departs from the docks behind the Supreme Court building. Travel time to San Pedro is one hour and 15 minutes. US $10 one way.

Departure Tax: US $10.

Customs: Personal effects can be brought in without difficulty, but it is best to register cameras, videos and electronic gear with customs before leaving home. American citizens can bring home $400 worth of duty-free goods after a 48-hour visit. Over that, purchases are dutied at 10%. Import allowances include 200 cigarettes or ½ lb tobacco; 20 fluid oz of alcoholic beverages and one bottle of perfume for personal use. Note: removing and exporting coral or archaeological artifacts is prohibited. Picking orchids in forest reserves is illegal.

Currency: Belize dollar=US 50¢.

Climate: Belize has a sub-tropical, humid climate. Average temperature 79° F. The rainy season is from Apr to Dec. Hurricanes form during late summer. Best time to visit is Feb through May, though summer diving when weather permits (mid-Aug) is often done in calm seas with excellent visibility.

Clothing: Lightweight clothing with long sleeves to protect against sunburn and a light sweater for evening wear. The dive resorts are extremely casual. Leave dress wear at home. Those who want to combine an expedition into the jungle with their diving vacation should check with the tour company. Bring mosquito repellent.

Gear: Divers' rental equipment is limited in Belize so be sure to bring all of your own personal equipment. The resorts do supply weights and tanks, but little else.

Electricity: 110/220V 60 cycles. Most island resorts run on generators, which are out of service for at least part of the day. Air-conditioning is limited on the out islands.

Time: Central Standard Time.

Language: English

Additional Information: Belize Tourist Board, 421 Seventh Ave, New York, NY 10001; ☎ (800) 624-0686, (800) 563-6011, fax (800) 563-6033. In Belize, 83 North Front St, P.O. Box 325, Belize City, Belize, C.A. Web site: www.belize.com.

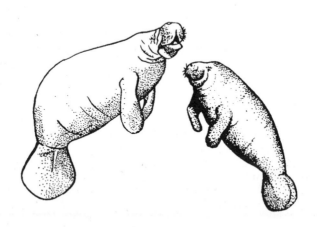

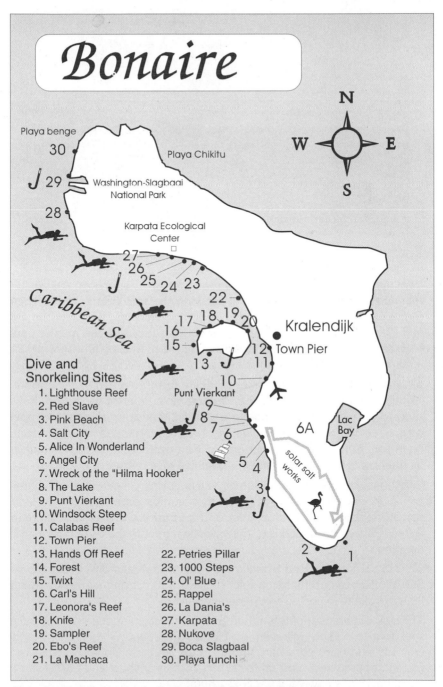

Bonaire

N
W   E
S

Playa benge
30
Playa Chikitu
J 29
Washington-Slagbaai
National Park
28

Karpata Ecological
Center
27
26
J   25 24 23
22
17 18 19 20
16
15   Kralendijk
13   12 Town Pier
11
10
Punt Vierkant
9
8
7   6
5   4
3
2   1

Caribbean Sea

Lac
Bay
6A
solar salt works

Dive and Snorkeling Sites
1. Lighthouse Reef
2. Red Slave
3. Pink Beach
4. Salt City
5. Alice In Wonderland
6. Angel City
7. Wreck of the "Hilma Hooker"
8. The Lake
9. Punt Vierkant
10. Windsock Steep
11. Calabas Reef
12. Town Pier
13. Hands Off Reef
14. Forest
15. Twixt
16. Carl's Hill
17. Leonora's Reef
18. Knife
19. Sampler
20. Ebo's Reef
21. La Machaca
22. Petries Pillar
23. 1000 Steps
24. Ol' Blue
25. Rappel
26. La Dania's
27. Karpata
28. Nukove
29. Boca Slagbaal
30. Playa funchi

Note: Bonaire sites are periodically closed down for rejuvenation.
Check with local dive shops for availability before diving on your own.

Photo by Jon Huber

Salt Pier.

see Bonaire's reefs. They grow to the surface in many areas and are visible from the shore. Excellent beach dives exist along the shores on the leeward side where channels have been cut allowing access to deeper water. These reefs slope down to a narrow ledge at 30 ft, then drop off to between 100 and 200 ft. Expect to pay a $10 "annual" fee for using the marine park. Most of the resorts and dive shops offer guided snorkeling trips that include a map and instructional text materials.

☆☆☆ **Lighthouse Reef** takes its name from the nearby Willemstoren Lighthouse and is located at the southernmost point of the island. It is a shore dive, which can be entered at the lighthouse or at most any point west. Due to the surf, this dive is only recommended to experienced open-water divers. During calm seas, however, this site can also be dived by the novice if accompanied by a qualified dive master or instructor.

Lighthouse sparkles with sea plumes, sea fans, star, yellow-pencil, and brain corals. Marine life tends to be larger than at most other sites and includes parrotfish, schoolmasters, snappers, and sea turtles. Old anchors and chains rest in this area, the remains of ships wrecked prior to the lighthouse's 1838 opening.

☆☆☆☆ To reach **Red Slave** drive south from Kralendijk, past the Solar Salt Works beyond the second set of slave huts. Strong currents and surf limit this site to experienced open-water divers.

The size and number of fish at Red Slave is spectacular. It is not unusual to spot four-foot tiger, yellowfin, or Nassau groupers. Gorgonians, orange crinoids, and black corals are found on the southern slope. Artifacts from pre-lighthouse wrecks rest on the slope, such as anchors and ballast stones from the 1829 shipwreck *H.M.S. Barham*.

☆☆☆☆ **Pink Beach,** named for the unusual pinkish tint of the sand, is either a boat or shore dive. Drive south from Kralendijk, past the Solar Salt Works, to the rock marked "Pink Beach." Park along the road and walk north to the beach. The mooring offshore marks the start of the dive.

Seaward of the mooring are clumps of staghorn coral and gorgonians. Schools of goatfish, porgies and horse-eye jacks feed in this area, with many large barracuda.

☆☆☆☆☆ One of the favorite boat dive areas is **Alice in Wonderland,** a double-reef complex, separated by a sand channel and extending from Pt. Vierkant south toward Salt Pier. A number of good dive sites exist within this reef system, all marked by dive buoys. Angel City, the most popular, starts at about 30 ft, then drops off to a deep channel. Swim down the first reef slope to a narrow sand channel, keeping right. One of the largest purple tube sponges you will ever see is at the channel's northern end.

Scattered throughout the shallow terrace are stands of staghorn, star, giant brain, and flower corals—home to goatfish, jacks, groupers and trunkfish. Farther down is a garden-eel colony, queen conchs, and swarms of fish. Initially, the garden eels look like a bed of grass, but will retract into the sand if you wave your arm over them.

☆☆☆ Boat dives in Bonaire are inexpensive ($16 and up) and very convenient, but if you miss the boat, **Angel City** may be reached by swimming from shore. Drive to the Trans World Radio transmitting station, south of Kralendijk—its huge tower is easy to spot. Follow a track before the station entrance which leads to the shore. From there, enter opposite the Angel City buoy.

☆☆☆☆ **Salt City** is a boat or shore dive located at the southern end of "Alice in Wonderland." To reach Salt City, drive south from Kralendijk past the salt loading pier (very visible). You'll spot a large buoy south of the pier. Enter along the left "bank" formed by the large "sand river," a wide, sand stretch that eventually drops off the shallow terrace into a short, reef slope "island."

The terrace is landscaped with star, fire, elkhorn and staghorn corals. Sea life is superb, featuring scad, palometa, big groupers, snappers, garden eels, tilefish and French angelfish.

☆☆☆ **The *Hilma Hooker*,** a 250-ft freighter, lies right offshore just north of Angel City Reef. Reached from the beach or by boat, this is Bonaire's most spectacular and notorious shipwreck. The ship was seized during a drug raid when a member of the Antillean Coast Guard discovered a false bulkhead. The crew abandoned the freighter and fled the island. Because of an unmanageable leak, Bonaire law enforcement agents were afraid that the ship would sink and damage the reefs, so they towed the ship out to

Diving the Cruise Ship Pier.

where she now lies, creating an intriguing dive site. The wreck rests on a sandy bottom at 91 ft. Divers should stay outside the wreck and monitor bottom time.

☆☆☆☆ **The Lake** is yet another part of the "Alice in Wonderland" complex. Sea plumes, purple tube sponges and a profusion of groupers, coneys, rock hinds and moray eels are in residence.

☆☆☆ **Punt Vierkant** is marked by the first buoy past the small lighthouse north of the "Alice in Wonderland" complex. To reach the site, drive south from Kralendijk past the Belnam residential area and toward the lighthouse. On the swim out you'll be joined by trunkfish, groupers and snappers. As you descend, the fish are larger and the rays more numerous. Pastel gorgonians and sponges decorate the wall.

☆☆☆ **Windsock Steep** is known for great snorkeling. This dive is off the small sand beach opposite the airport runway. Watch out for fire coral as you explore the shallow terrace. The bottom is sandy, but stacked up with sergeant majors, angelfish, snappers, trumpetfish and barracuda.

☆☆☆☆ **Calabas Reef**, just off the beach in front of the Divi Flamingo Resort, is reached by swimming over a sand shelf. Giant brain and star corals grow from the slope. Old anchors are scattered about. To the north is a small sailboat wreck. The hotel pier is well lit after dusk, making it an easily accessible and attractive night-dive spot.

Bonaire's beach dive sites are marked by yellow "sign" rocks.

Reef inhabitants are parrotfish, French angels, damsels, Spanish hogfish and yellow snappers. Spotted, goldentail and chain morays peek out from the crevices.

☆☆☆☆ **Town Pier** refers to the "old pier" in the center of town, between the customs office and the fish market. Both the Town Pier and the neighboring, new cruise-ship pier are popular for night dives. Bright sponge crabs and several species of decorator crabs materialize with darkness, disappear with daylight. Because water entry and finding one's way around the maze of pilings gets tricky, we find this site more interesting, and much more fun as a guided tour, with Bonaire's "Touch-the-Sea" guru, Dee Scarr. She knows where to find all the good stuff. For details, contact Dee from the US, ☎ (011) 599-7-8529.

For safety reasons, diving under the piers is subject to permission from the Harbormaster. All divers must check into the Harbormaster's office, located at the old fort with the cannon, next to the main government building ☎ 8151. Double-check with the tugboat captain on duty before entering the water.

☆☆☆ Off the main road, in front of the Habitat dive shop is **La Machaca**. Ideal for night and warm-up dives, this site is named after a small, wrecked fishing boat. Every variety of fish found in Bonaire's waters can be seen here by divers and snorkelers. Mr. Roger, a huge green moray, an old tiger grouper, friendly rock beauties, and two black margates inhabit the wreck.

☆☆☆ **Petries Pillar** derives its name from the colony of pillar coral that grows on the reef face. To reach this site travel north toward Gotomeer, turn left about 4/10 of a mile after the last house onto an unpaved road. Follow that road down to the sea. Fine for boat or shore entry.

☆☆☆☆☆ **1000 Steps (Piedra Haltu)** may be either a boat or a shore dive, though a boat dive may be easier and will definitely save you carrying your gear down the (actual count, 67) steps. To reach 1000 Steps, drive north from town along the scenic road towards Gotomeer until you reach the entrance of the Radio Nederland transmitting station. On your left are steep concrete steps leading down the mountainside to a sandy beach and the dive site.

Swim through the marked channel to a sandy shallow terrace. Gorgonians and flower corals are abundant. Lavender shrimp, barracuda, black durgons, yellowtail snappers, horse-eye jacks and schoolmasters populate the reef.

☆☆☆☆ **Ol' Blue**, a favorite with snorkelers for its walls of reef fish, cleaning stations and calm waters, may get choppy when the wind kicks up. Get there by driving north along the scenic road to Gotomeer past the transmitting station to the white coral-rubble beach. The dive site is at the point where the road descends to the ocean and the cliff bends away from the road.

☆☆☆☆☆ **Rappel**, one of the best dives on the island, was named for its sheer cliff face. Divers have been known to "rappel" down the wall. Usually a boat dive, it may also be reached by swimming out from Karpata.

Rappel's exceptional marine life includes orange seahorses, green moray eels, spiny lobster, squid, marbled grouper, orange tube coral, shrimp, encrusting sponges, black coral and dense pink-tipped anemones.

☆☆☆☆☆ **Nukove** lies off a little road between Boca Dreifi and Playa Frans. It is a particularly nice shore dive with a channel cut through the jungle of elkhorn coral which grows to the surface.

Numerous juveniles, shrimp and anemones may be seen in the cut. To the south are huge sponges, black coral, crinoids and sheet and scroll corals. Scrawled filefish, black durgons, grouper, wrasses and barracuda are in residence.

☆☆☆☆ **Boca Slagbaai** provides opportunity to see the best examples of buttress formations in Bonaire water. In addition, green morays, white spotted filefish, tarpon and barracuda are in abundance. Slagbaai boasts six concrete cannon replicas, halved and buried for the 1974 film, *Shark Treasure.*

To reach this dive, drive through the village of Rincon into Washington/Slagbaai National Park, where you will follow the green arrows to Slagbaai. The center of the bay is sand, but a swim to the north brings you across ridges and valleys of coral. Excellent snorkeling is to the south, where two real cannons may be viewed at the southernmost point of the bay.

☆☆☆☆ **Playa Funchi**, located in Washington/Slagbaai National Park, is another popular snorkeling area. From Rincon, follow the green or yellow signs. Enter next to the man-made pier and swim north for the best snorkeling. Rays, parrotfish, rock hinds, jacks, groupers and angels swim through fields of staghorn coral. On shore, picnickers are greeted by hoards of fearless lizards in search of scraps.

KLEIN BONAIRE

The dive sites surrounding Klein Bonaire are great for both diving and snorkeling. Some may be closed down for rejuvenation.

☆☆☆☆☆ **Leonora's Reef**, on the north side, is a snorkeler's paradise heavily covered with yellow pencil coral, fire coral, star coral and elkhorn stands on a narrow shallow terrace. West of the mooring are pillar coral formations. Expect to be greeted by masses of fish. "Attack" yellowtail snappers and tiny royal blue fish are joined at cleaning stations by tiger, yellowmount and rare yellowfin groupers.

☆☆☆☆ **Hands Off Reef** was named in 1981 when an experiment was conducted to determine whether inexperienced and camera-carrying divers do more damage to the corals than others. "Hands Off," as the name implies, was not to be dived by photographers or resort course classes, designated solely as a control for later comparison to unlimited-access dives.

The reef slope is alive with black margate, grouper, rockhinds, parrots. Some of the narrow valleys of the drop-off zone contain the remains of coral-head "avalanches" worth exploring.

☆☆☆☆ Nearby is **Forest**, another fabulous snorkeling and diving spot. The reef starts at 15 ft, dropping off to undiveable depths. This site is named for the abundant black coral "trees" growing from the wall at 60 ft. Two-ft queen triggerfish, morays, filefish, black durgons, puffers and an abundance of small critters roam the "forest."

☆☆☆☆☆ **Twixt** is just north of Forest, around the southwest bend of Klein Bonaire. It provides excellent opportunities for wide-angle photography, with huge basket sponges, sea whips, black coral, enormous pastel fans, tube sponges and star corals. Depths range from 15 to 100 ft. The coral wall slopes down to a sandy bottom. Seas are almost always calm and flat here.

☆☆☆☆☆ Large groupers frequent the pillar coral cleaning station at the upper edge of **Carl's Hill**. Named after photographer Carl Roessler, this spot is great for snorkeling and diving. The drop-off begins at 15 ft and drops sharply to 80 ft, creating a narrow precipice called Venus Mound. An occasional strong current cleanses the huge purple finger sponges on the slope. West of the mooring divers will find a buttress and sand valley, lined with coral rocks and cleaning stations—areas where fish line up to have barber or "cleaner" shrimp pick parasites from their mouths.

☆☆☆☆ **Ebo's Reef** (aka Jerry's Jam) is superb for video and still photography. Shallow enough for snorkeling, the drop-off starts at 20 ft and slopes off to a sandy bottom at 150 ft. Dramatic overhangs of black coral grow in less than 30 ft of water. Masses of grunts, Spanish hogfish, groupers, sergeant majors, parrotfish and yellowtail swarm the shelf. Small tunnels along the shelf are good hiding places for juvenile fish and small critters.

☆☆☆☆ **Knife Reef** is excellent for snorkeling and diving. A shallow, half-circle of elkhorn coral creates a mini "lagoon" protecting star coral heads, gorgonians, and a multitude of fish. Bermuda chubs, peacock flounders, lizardfish and yellowhead jawfish rove the shallow terrace. The drop-off zone is fairly barren (the result of reef slides), but gorgonians, stinging coral, and yellow pencils thrive.

☆☆☆☆ Another snorkeler's delight is **Sampler**. Resident spotted eels and hordes of tamed, friendly fish will charm you as you investigate the lovely pillar- and staghorn-coral formations.

Touch the Sea

Learn to pet moray eels, tickle sea anemones, get a manicure from a cleaner shrimp, massage the tummy of a "deadly" scorpionfish and befriend marine animals from which one normally keeps a safe distance. Diving with Touch-the-Sea creator, Dee Scarr, is an experience divers won't soon forget.

Ms. Scarr recommends that divers not try these antics without first participating in her program, which includes classroom and underwater time. Bring or rent a camera; you'll enjoy shooting these normally hard-to-get-close-to creatures.

Arrangements to dive with Dee Scarr must be made prior to your trip to Bonaire by writing to her c/o Touch the Sea, P.O. Box 369, Bonaire, Netherlands Antilles, or calling 8529 on the island. From the US, ☎ (011) 599-7-8529. A maximum of four divers may participate in one dive. Touch the Sea programs close from Mar to Oct.

In the US, specialized land programs are offered for universities and groups.

"Touch the Sea" is a PADI Specialty Certification available to all certified divers. Environmentalist Dee Scarr is author of *Touch the Sea, Coral's Reef,* a children's book, and *The Gentle Sea.*

Dive Operators

Bonaire Scuba Center, at the Black Durgeon Inn, offers reef and wreck diving trips by reservation. Resort and certification courses. ☎ (011) 599-7-5736, fax (011) 5-997-8846. Write to: P.O. Box 200 Bonaire, NA.

Carib Inn Dive Shop is a full service dive shop at the Carib Inn. Reef trips; resort, certification and advanced courses. Equipment sales, rental and repair. ☎ (011) 599-7-5295, fax (011) 599-7-5295, or write P.O. Box 68, Bonaire, NA. E-mail: caribinn@bonairenet.com.

Dee Scarr's "Touch the Sea" meets at the town pier and features personalized dives with an opportunity to interact with reef fish, moray eels. Super photo opportunities. Closed from Mar to Oct. ☎ (011) 599-7-8529.

Dive Inn, next door to the Sunset Inn, offers scuba packages, PADI courses, reef trips, picnic trips. Six days of unlimited shore diving costs $99; add six boat dives for a total of $175. ☎ (011) 599-7-8761, fax (011) 599-7-8513.

write Kaya C.E.B. Hellmund 27, Bonaire, NA. E-mail: diveinn @caribbeans. com.

Peter Hughes Dive Bonaire, at the Divi Beach Resort & Casino specializes in reef trips; resort, certification and advanced courses; underwater photo and video courses. Daily E-6 and color print processing. Equipment sales, rental, and repair. Dive packages. ☎(800) 367-3484; in Bonaire 8285.

Sand Dollar Dive and Photo, within the Sand Dollar Condominium Resort complex, offers PADI certification, advanced, rescue, and divemaster courses. Reef trips, park trips, underwater photo and video courses. Same-day E-6 and print processing. Equipment sales, rental and repair. Fishing, sailing, snorkeling, water skiing. ☎ (800) 345-0805 or (011) 599-7-5252, fax (011) 599-7-8760, or write: P.O. Box 175, Bonaire, NA.

Sunset Beach Dive Center, at the Sunset Beach Hotel, offers full PADI certification, six days of shore diving for $99; add six boat dives for a total of $175. E-mail: sundive@caribbeans.com.

Great Adventures Bonaire, at the Harbour Village Resort, offers certification and underwater photography programs, boat and shore dives, night dives and equipment rental. ☎(800) 424-0004, (011) 599-7-7500, fax 7505. E-mail: harbourvil@aol.com.

Jerry Schnabel & Suzi Swygert's Underwater Photo Tours can be arranged through Captain Don's Habitat. ☎ (011) 599-7-5390, fax (011) 599-7-8060.

Peter Hughes Dive Bonaire, on the beach at the Divi Flamingo Beach Resort, features comfortable dive boats, snorkeling tours, equipment rentals, courses. ☎(011) 599-7-8285, fax (011) 599-7-8238.

Habitat Dive Center at Captain Don's Habitat is a PADI facility offering resort, certification and advanced courses, reef trips and 24-hour shore diving. ☎ (800) 327-6709, (011) 599-7-8290, fax (011) 599-7-8240, or write P.O. Box 88, Bonaire, NA. E-mail: maduro@netpoint.net.

Accommodations

Bonaire's entire tourist trade revolves around its beautiful reefs. All but three of the island's hotels were built in the last 20 years and especially to accommodate divers. All have dive shops attached or nearby. Money saving dive/accommodation packages can be arranged through any hotel listed below. Rates listed are winter prices.

Buddy Beach & Dive Resort sits just north of Kralendijk, offering 40 luxury oceanfront apartments with TV, air-conditioning, fully-equipped kitchens, nicely furnished living rooms. Restaurant and PADI five-star training facility on premises. Drive and dive packages from $782 for seven nights include six boat dives, unlimited airfills for six days, vehicle rental (often a pick-up truck). ☎ (800) 359-0747 for Rothschild Dive/Travel packages, (800) 786-3483 for Caribbean Dive Tours, direct (011) 599- 7- 5080, fax (011) 599-7-8647.

Bruce Bowker's Carib Inn is one of Bonaire's most intimate dive resorts. Oceanfront accommodations are air-conditioned and have cable TV. Maid service, pool. Full-service scuba facilities. Studio/one-bedroom, $79-$139. ☎(011) 599-7-8819 or write P.O. Box 68, Bonaire, NA. E-mail: carib inn@bonairenet.com.

Divi Flamingo Resort & Casino is a luxury resort on the beach overlooking Calabas Reef. A few have balconies directly over the water where you can view the reef and see fish swimming by. All rooms are air-conditioned with private bath. Two pools, tennis, jacuzzi. Two excellent open-air restaurants, casino, dive shop. Room rates for one or two in summer: standard, $84; superior, $100; deluxe, $115. In winter: standard, $150, deluxe, $185. Credit cards accepted. ☎ (800) 367-3484 or write Divi Hotels, 6340 Quadrangle Drive, Suite 300 Chapel, NC 27514.

Lions Dive Hotel Bonaire (formerly the Coral Regency) features 31 ocean-view, one- and two-bedroom apartments with patio or balcony, each with a fully equipped kitchen. Amenities are fresh-water pool with sundeck, waterfront restaurant and dive shop, diving and fitness school. Rates for a one-bedroom suite are from $150-$180 per day, a two-bedroom suite from $315. ☎ (888) 546-6734 or (011) 599-7-5580, fax (011) 599-7-5680.

Plaza Resort Bonaire, a 224-unit luxury hotel, offers divers full service through the on-premises Toucan Diving shop and school, offering IDD, PADI, and NAUI instruction, custom dive boats, rental equipment and classroom facilities. The Sports and Entertainment Department offers snorkeling, water-skiing, banana boating, knee boarding, tube rides, windsurfing, kayaking, tennis, beach volleyball, aqua jogging, water-polo, body-fit training and has Boston Whalers and catamarans for rent. The casino features 80 slot machines, roulette, and card games. Recent additions to this plush resort include a Mexican restaurant, racquetball and squash court, basketball court, mini-market, first-aid center, jogging track, playground, still and video camera rental. Jr. suite rates per day in winter (Dec 18-Apr 15) are $180-$200 for a double or single, $210 for a triple, $305-$365 for a two-bedroom villa. Off-season per day rates (Apr 16-Dec 17) are $125-$145 for a double or a single, $245 to $305 for a two-bedroom villa. Add three meals per day per person for $60. A 10% service charge and $6.50 per night tax are added to the rates. Dive packages are $104 covering six days unlimited air for beach dives and use of weights, $182 for six days of one boat dive per day, unlimited air and weights. Group rates available. ☎ (800) 766-6016 or (800) 786-DIVE.

Off Klein Bonaire.

Sunset Beach Hotel, located on Playa Lechi Beach (one of Bonaire's loveliest), features recently renovated rooms, all air-conditioned with cable TV, and telephone. Restaurant, beach bar, gift shop, tennis, dive shop. Laundry, dry-cleaning and baby-sitting services available. Private bath. Reef dives and snorkeling off the hotel beach. Very comfortable. Rooms are $125 to $185 plus 10% service charge and $5.50 per day. ☎ (800) 344-4439 or (011) 599-7-8291, fax (305) 225-0572, or (011) 599-7-4870. Money-saving package tours are offered by Caradonna Caribbean Tours starting at $999 with airfare from Miami for seven nights. ☎(800) 328-2288.

Harbour Village Beach Resort sits opposite Klein Bonaire on a powdery sand beach close to town. Seventy-two spacious air-conditioned rooms, one- and two-bedroom suites with French doors leading to patios or terraces, cable TV, telephones, hair dryers. Pool, three restaurants, bar, marina, dive shop. Meeting and banquet facilities. Rooms are $275-$405; suites, $445-$705. Third person, $40 per day. Seven-night packages from $825 in summer, per person, double occupancy. Winter rates for a dive package are $1,683, including seven nights accommodations, five days of one-tank boat diving and unlimited shore dives, buffet breakfast daily, rental car for one day, transfers, tanks, weights and belts. Non-diving companions pay $1,408. Add $4.50 per person per night taxes and 15% service charges. Credit cards accepted. ☎ (800) 424-0004, (800) 786-DIVE or (305) 567-9509, fax (305) 567-9659; in Bonaire, 7500, fax 7507. E-mail: harbourvil @aol.com.

Captain Don's Habitat offers deluxe, oceanfront cottages, cabanas, villas, studios. Package rates, per diver, start at $840 for seven nights in a Jr. suite, including 12 boat dives. Non-divers pay $570. Per day accommodation rates are from $195 to $280 daily. Entire villas from $420-$485 daily. Dive shop, open-air restaurant, bar, pool, gift shop. Credit cards accepted. ☎(800) 327-6709 or (011) 599-7-8290; fax (305) 438-4220 or (011) 599-7-8240, or write P.O. Box 115, Bonaire NA. Guests who are certified divers can take out tanks and dive the reef off the beach 24 hours a day. Web site: www.bonaire.org/habitat.

The Sunset Inn, overlooking Kralendijk Bay, comprises five double rooms and two suites within walking distance of town. Accommodations are air-conditioned, have refrigerators, electronic safes and remote cable TV. ☎ (800) 328-2288, (407) 774-9000 or (011) 599-7-8291, fax (011) 599-7-8118; or write Caradonna Caribbean Tours, P.O. Box 3299, Longwood, FL 32779. Dive packages available.

Sand Dollar Condominium Resort features luxurious oceanfront condominiums—all air conditioned, with kitchens, private baths, cable TV, balcony or terrace. Dive shop on premises with excellent diving and snorkeling off the beach. Tennis, pool bar, grocery store, sailing, babysitting. Studios, $155 summer, $165 winter; one-bedrooms, $180 summer, $215 winter; two-bedrooms, $200 summer, $215 winter. Packages in a studio for seven nights, six days diving start at $890 per person in winter. ☎ (800) 288-4773, (407) 774-9322 or (011) 599-7-8738, fax (011) 599- 7-8760 or write P.O. Box 3253 Longwood, FL 32779. Credit cards.

Happy Holiday Homes rent one- , two- or three-bedroom homes with air conditioning, living room, with US cable TV and radio, dining room, fully equipped kitchen, patio and barbecue area. All are close to southern beaches. Bungalow rates start at $65 per day. Call for brochure: ☎(610) 459-8100, ext. 204, or (011) 599-7-8405, fax (011) 5997-8605. E-mail: 103665,1405@compuserve.com. Web site: www.interknowledge.com/bonaire/happy-holiday.

Other Activities

Exploring Washington-Slagbaai Park is a nice day's alternative to diving. One of the first national parks in the Caribbean, it is home to over 190 species of birds, thousands of towering candle cacti, herds of goats, stray donkeys, lizards and more lizards. The park covers the entire northern portion of the island. Its terrain is varied and those who are ambitious enough to climb some of the steep hills are rewarded with sweeping views.

Cars can be taken through the park, and the two driving trails offer visitors the choice of a thorough tour of the park or a shorter excursion. A map, available at the entrance gate, indicates points of interest. The park is open from 8 am to 5 pm, though no one is permitted to enter after 3:30 pm. Small entrance fee. Visitors are advised to bring a picnic lunch, binoculars, a

Boca Slagbaai, Washington/Slagbaai National Park.

camera, sunscreen and plenty of drinking water. Opportunities for exotic bird photography are outstanding.

Driving south you'll pass roadside cliffs with 500-year-old Arawak Indian inscriptions. Just beyond is Rincon, the island's oldest village. A drive to the southern tip of the island will bring you past primitive stone huts that were once homes to slaves working the salt flats. It is hard to imagine how six slaves shared one hut when you see the small size of them. Nearby, 30-foot obelisks were built in 1838 to help mariners locate their anchorages. Further down is the island's oldest lighthouse, Willemstoren, built in 1837.

The salt ponds at Gotomeer are always occupied with resident flamingos, but flamingo watching is best at the solar salt flats on the southern end of the island. You can only watch from the road as the area is a sanctuary, but the huge bird population (10,000 to 15,000) en masse makes a spectacular display. Every day at sunset, the entire flock flies the short trip to Venezuela. During spring, a highlight is seeing the fluffy gray young. It is only after months of consuming brine shrimp that they attain their characteristic pink color. Since the birds are extremely shy, bring binoculars.

Guided bus tours of the national park or entire island are available through **Bonaire Sightseeing Tours**. ☎ 8778.

Ernest van Vliet's **Windsurfing Bonaire** features top-of-the-line equipment and classes for beginners to advanced board sailors. Production or custom

Flamingos at the Salt Flats.

boards can be rented by the hour, day or week. He even provides transportation to and from island resorts twice a day.

Tours through the tiny capital city of Kralendijk ("coral dike" in Dutch) are highlighted by the colorful, well-preserved buildings such as Fort Oranje, Queen Wilhelmina Park, Government House and the miniature Greek temple-style fish market. The town pier makes for an interesting stop as do any one of Kralendijk's open-air bars and restaurants. Sunset watching is best from Pink Beach at the south-eastern part of the island.

Dining

Restaurants in Bonaire offer a unique selection of local, creole and seafood dishes. Enjoy a delicious Cantonese dinner at the **China Garden Restaurant** (☎ 8480)—an old restored mansion at 47 Kaya Grandi; or Caribbean seafood and steak dishes at the **Chibi Chibi** (☎ 8285) an open-air restaurant (located at the Divi Flamingo Resort); or **Banana Tree Restaurant** (☎ 2500) at the Plaza Resort. A few miles north of Kralendijk on the coast road brings you to the **Bonaire Caribbean Club** (☎ 7901) for a cozy seaside and caveside lunch or dinner (bring bug repellent). Chefs at the **Beefeater Restaurant** (☎ 7776), Playa Grande no. 3, will prepare a banquet of fish or steak dishes at your table. Vegetarian favorites are found at **Je Mar Terrace** (☎ 5012), Kaya Grandi 5.

Stop by the Sunset Beach Hotel office for a schedule of beach barbecues, frequently put on by the resort's **Playa Lechi Restaurant** (☎ 5300). Carry-out and sit-down casual meals are offered by the **Green Parrot Restaurant** at the Sand Dollar Caribbean Resort (☎ 5454).

Local foods include *juwana*, a stew or soup made from local iguana; *piska hasa*, a fried fish dish served with funchi and fried plantains; *tutu*, funchi with frills—cornmeal mush with black-eyed peas; and goat stew made with onions, peppers, tomato, soy sauce and spices.

*Board sailing
off Kralendijk.*

In Kralendijk, local dishes are served at the **Supercorner** on Kaya Simon Bolivar (☎ 8115); **Seumar's** on Kaya Simon Bolivar; and **Kunuku Warahama** on Kaminda Lac. Fast food lovers will delight in finding **Kentucky Fried Chicken** and **Cozzoli's Pizza** in the Harborside Mall.

Facts

Helpful Phone Numbers: Police, ☎ 8000; taxi, ☎ 8100; airport, ☎ 8500; San Francisco Hospital, ☎ 8000 or 8900.

Nearest Recompression Chamber: San Francisco Hospital on the island.

Getting There: ALM Antillean Airlines offers regularly scheduled service to Bonaire's Flamingo International Airport from Miami and Atlanta. Air Aruba offers direct service out of Newark, Baltimore and Tampa. American Airlines offers regularly scheduled service to Curacao with connections via ALM to Bonaire. Guyana Airways from La Guardia connects with ALM in Curacao.

Driving: Foreign and international licenses accepted. Traffic to the right.

Language: The official language for Bonaire is Dutch, but residents speak Papiamento—a blend of Dutch, African and English. English and Spanish are widely spoken.

Documents: US and Canadian citizens may stay up to three months providing they prove citizenship with a passport, birth certificate or a voter's registration card accompanied by a photo identification.

All visitors must have a confirmed room reservation before arriving and a return ticket. A visa is required for visits over 90 days.

Customs: US citizens may bring home $400 worth of articles including one quart of liquor and 200 cigarettes. Canadian citizens may bring in C $300 of goods once each calendar year.

Currency: Netherlands Antilles florin or guilder, but US dollars are widely accepted. US $1=NA fl 1.77.

Credit Cards: Widely accepted.

Climate: Mean temperature 82° F year-round; 22 inches rainfall annually.

Photo by Joyce Huber

Clothing: Casual lightweight. A wetsuit is not necessary most of the year, but water temperatures occasionally drop down in mid-winter, especially late January and February.

Electricity: 127 volts, 50 cycles. Adapters are necessary.

Time: Atlantic (EST + 1 hr).

Tax: Airport departure tax.

Religious Services: Roman Catholic, Seventh Day Adventist, Jehovah's Witnesses.

Additional Information: Tourism Corporation Bonaire, 10 Rockefeller Plaza, Suite 900, NY, NY 10020. ☎ (800) U-BONAIR (826-6247). E-mail: 102372. 3337@compuserve.com. Web site: www.interknowledge.com/bonaire.

British Virgin Islands

Windswept and wildly beautiful, the British Virgins encompass more than 60 sparsely inhabited islands and rocks that lie 60 miles east of Puerto Rico. Most tourist activity centers around the four larger islands—Tortola, Anegada, Virgin Gorda and Jost Van Dyke. Except for Anegada, which is a flat coral slab surrounded by shallow reefs, the islands are mountainous and of volcanic origin. The highest point is 1,781-ft Mt. Sage on Tortola.

The capital and chief port is Road Town on Tortola, the largest island and home to 80% of the BVI residents, with a population of 17,000. A toll bridge connects Tortola to Beef Island and the international airport. An efficient ferry service, In some cases a short hop by light aircraft, takes visitors to the other main islands of Virgin Gorda, Jost Van Dyke and Anegada. Other BVI islands include Cooper Island, Ginger Island, The Dogs, Great Camanoe, Necker Island, Guana Island, Mosquito Island and Eustatia Island.

Save for a few clubs and discos that come to life on weekends, nightlife consists of stargazing and moonlit dives. The islands, devoid of casinos or high-rise hotels, offer a relatively untouched panorama of land, sea and sky. Overall, BVI life is relaxed, yet retains some British formality in terms of dignity and manners. Crime is rare and nudity is not encouraged. Visitors are asked to respect the residents' wishes by covering up in town and dressing "appropriately" in restaurants and bars.

The BVI's prime attractions are its hundreds of sheltered coves, isolated beaches and protected marine parks. Superb snorkeling and diving exists around the out islands with towering coral pinnacles, underwater caves, canyons, massive boulders, lava tunnels and almost 200 different wrecks. Most areas have little or no surge and only gentle currents. Visibility may reach anywhere from 50 to over 100 ft.

Clustered around the Sir Francis Drake Channel and protected from high wind and waves, the islands are enormously popular with sailors. In fact, half the BVI tourist "beds" are aboard the hundreds of yachts in Tortola's marinas.

Area Contributors: Gayla Kilbride, Jeff Williams, Joe Giacinto, Kara Dugan,FCB.

The best time to visit the BVI is between Oct and June, with warmest water temperatures between mid-March and early Dec. Reduced rates at hotels and on charter boats are available from July through mid-Dec. Hurricane season is from July through Oct. Air temperature ranges between 80° and 90° F year-round with an occasional drop in February.

History

In 1493 Christoper Columbus discovered the islands and named them *St. Ursula y las Once Mil Virgenes* (St. Ursula and the Eleven Thousand Virgins.) At that time peaceful tribes of Indians roamed the BVI and remained its principal residents until the turn of the 17th century.

During the 1500's, pirates set up base on Tortola, an ideal spot to attack ships trying to navigate the treacherous reefs of Sir Francis Drake Channel. Buccaneers such as Blackbeard Teach, Bluebeard, and Sir Francis Drake became legendary.

By 1672, the pirates were forced out by English planters who, with slave labor, developed the land for farming. They thrived on the export of bananas, sugarcane, citrus fruits, coconuts, mangoes and root crops until slavery was abolished in the early 1800's. Today, tourism has replaced agriculture as the islands' largest employer. Politically, the islands are a British colony administered by an executive council with a governor.

Best Dive and Snorkeling Sites

☆☆☆☆☆ Wreck of the **R.M.S. *Rhone***, featured in the movie *The Deep*, is by far the most popular dive in the BVI. Struck by a ferocious hurricane in October, 1867, the Royal Mail Steamer, *Rhone* was hurled onto the rocks at Salt Island as its captain, Robert F. Wooley, struggled desperately to reach open sea.

The force with which the 310-ft vessel crashed upon the rocks broke the hull in two, leaving two superb dive spots, a great snorkeling area at the stern, which lies in 30 ft of water amid rocks and boulders, and a good area for diving at the bow, 80 ft down on a sandy bottom. The top of the rudder sits just 15 ft below the surface. Its superstructure, encrusted with corals, sponges, and sea fans, provides a dramatic setting for underwater photography.

Fish greet divers and snorkelers as they enter the water. Living among the wreckage is a 300-pound jew fish, a very curious 4½-ft barracuda, named Fang, schools of snappers, grunts, jacks, arrow crabs, squirrel fish, and yellow tail. The *Rhone* is a boat-access dive. Sea conditions are usually calm; recommended for novices. Visibility is usually excellent, from 50 to over 100 ft. Also, the *Rhone* is a national park and off-limits to coral collecting

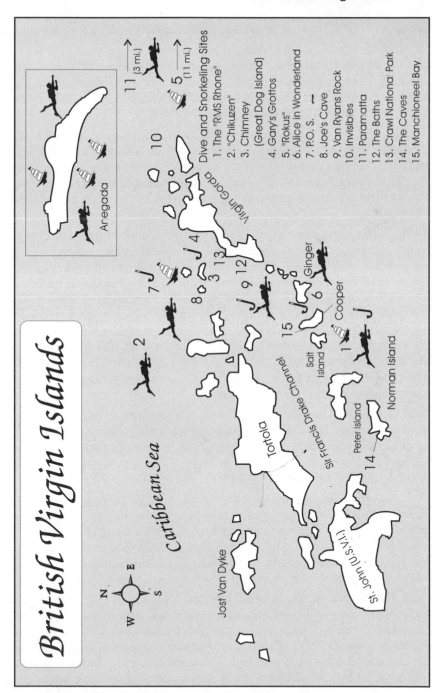

British Virgin Islands

Caribbean Sea

Dive and Snorkeling Sites
1. The "RMS Rhone"
2. "Chikuzen"
3. Chimney
   (Great Dog Island)
4. Gary's Grottos
5. "Rokus"
6. Alice in Wonderland
7. P.O. S.
8. Joe's Cave
9. Van Ryans Rock
10. Invisibles
11. Paramatta
12. The Baths
13. Crawl Nationa' Park
14. The Caves
15. Manchioneel Bay

Aregada

Virgin Gorda

Ginger

Cooper

Salt
Island

Norman Island

Peter Island

Tortola

Sir Francis Drake Channel

Jost Van Dyke

St. John (U.S.V.I.)

11 (3 mi.)
5 (11 mi.)

and spear fishing. The wreck is located off Black Rock Point on the southwest tip of Salt Island.

☆☆☆☆ *The Chikuzen*, a 268-ft steel-hulled refrigerator ship that went down off Tortola's east end in 1981, lies in 75 ft of water. Currently in use as a fish condominium, the wreck is blessed with visibility so good that you can stand on the bow and see the stern.

Tenants of the *Chikuzen* include several large sting rays, occasional black tip sharks, schools of yellowtail, filefish, barracuda, octopus, drum fish, and jew fish. The ship rests on her port side allowing easy entry. Coral covers the hull. A fine choice for novice divers. By boat access only. The outstanding visibility and large number of marine animals make for excellent photography.

☆☆☆ **The Chimney**, located at Great Dog Island off the west end of Virgin Gorda, is a spectacular coral archway and canyon covered with a wide variety of soft corals, sponges and rare white coral. Hundreds of fish follow divers and snorkelers along the archway to a coral-wrapped, tube-like formation resembling a huge chimney. Inside the Chimney are circling groupers, crabs, brittle starfish, spiny lobster, banded coral shrimp, queen angels, tube sponges and schooling fish. This is a favorite spot for close-up photography. Maximum depth of the Chimney is 45 ft. The many shallow areas and protected-cove location make this a "best snorkel dive" as well as a good selection for the scuba diver. Boat access only. Some surge and currents when wind is out of the north.

☆☆☆ **The M/V *Inganess Bay***, a new wreck sunk by BVI dive operators as an artificial reef after a storm snapped its anchor chain, lies off the southern tip of Cooper Island. The 136-ft freighter lies in 95 ft of water, its masts at 45 ft. Two national park moorings mark the sight. A good show of invertebrates and fish inhabit the wreck. Boat access.

☆☆☆ **Gary's Grottos** lies near the shoreline, four miles north of Spanish Town on Virgin Gorda. It is a shallow reef characterized by three huge arches which give the feel of swimming through a tunnel. At the end of the "tunnel" divers find a cave guarded by a friendly moray. This rocky area is teeming with shrimp, squid and sponges. Protected from wind and waves, the cove is also a choice spot for a night dive. The average depth is 30 ft.

☆☆ **The Wreck of the *Rokus***. On New Year's Eve, 1929, the Greek ship *Rokus* hit the reef on the southeast tip of Anegada. She sank in 40 ft of water with much of her hull remaining above the surface until hurricane Frederick struck in 1979. Remains of her cargo of animal bones can be found scattered around the wreckage. The reef surrounding the hull is pretty, with large formations of elkhorn and staghorn as well as brain coral. An enormous eel has been spotted under the wreck by a number of divers.

During the winter months, February through March, the song of migrating humpback whales can be heard from this site. This area is occasionally rough with small surges.

☆☆ **Great Dog Island's** south side drops off to a shallow reef with 10-to-60-ft depths. Nice elkhorn stands hide spotted and golden moray eels, spiny lobster and barber shrimp. Good for novice divers when seas are calm.

☆☆☆☆☆ **Alice in Wonderland**, a coral wall at South Bay off Ginger Island, slopes from 15 ft to a sandy bottom at 90 ft, with most interest at 50 ft. Named for its huge mushroom corals, villainous overhangs, and gallant brain corals, this ornate reef shelters longnose butterfly fish, rays, conch and garden eels. Visibility is good and seas are usually calm. Alice in Wonderland is a boat dive, good for photography, free diving, and novice through expert scuba diving.

Private yachts should choose the eastern mooring which is closer to the larger coral ridges.

☆☆☆☆ **P.O.S.** was named after "Project Ocean Search," a Cousteau project. The reef which follows the shoreline of Cockroach Island (one of the Dog Islands) is a "must" for every underwater photographer. Beautiful, towering pillar, staghorn, and elkhorn corals at 35 ft are swept by huge silvery tarpon, French angels, crabs, lobsters, and schooling fish. The "Keyhole," a hole in one of the coral walls, is just big enough to frame a diver for an underwater portrait.

☆☆☆ **Blonde Rock**, a pinnacle between Dead Chest and Salt Island, starts at 15 ft below the surface. Coral-encrusted tunnels, caves and overhangs support a wealth of crabs, lobsters and reef fish. Good for novice divers when seas are calm. Boat access.

☆☆ **Santa Monica Rock**, a sea mount, sits about a mile south of Norman Island. Depths range from 10 to 90 ft. Currents attract spotted eagle rays, sharks and other pelagics.

☆☆☆ **Joe's Cave,** an underwater cavern on the west side of West Dog Island, can be explored by swimming from the entrance at 20 ft down to 75 ft, where you'll find a magnificent opening to the sky. Corals and boulders form the cave's outer walls. Eels abound. Rough bottom terrain accents the masses of gleaming copper sweepers inside. This is a protected area with no current or surges. A good choice for divers of all levels.

☆☆ **Van Ryan's Rock**, in Drake's Channel, sits between Beef Island and Virgin Gorda. The top is at 16 ft and the bottom at 55 ft, with boulders and coral leading down to a sandy plain. Nurse sharks, eels, huge turtles, lobster, jacks, spade fish, and barracuda circle it. Divers and snorkelers should take care to avoid the huge clumps of fire coral. A light current is occasionally encountered.

Anemones.

☆☆☆ **Invisibles**, a sea mount off Tortola's northeast tip, is a haven for nurse sharks, eels, turtles and all types of reef fish from the smallest to the largest. Diver Gayla Kilbride describes this area as a "Symphony of Fish." Depths go from three ft to 65 ft, a nice range for both snorkeling and diving.

Snorkeling

Snorkeling gear may be rented or borrowed from most hotels and charter boats, although it is best to have your own to insure a comfortable fit. Be sure to bring your camera. Snorkeling trips are offered by the dive shops.

☆☆☆☆☆ **Wreck of the *Paramatta*** which ran aground on her maiden voyage in 1853, rests at 30 ft off the southeast end of Anegada. The ship is on a dense coral reef—perfect for snorkelers. If you stand on the ship's engine, you'll be shoulder-deep. Enormous reef fish swim around the wreck, including a 200-pound jew fish, 30-pound groupers, butterfly fish, turtles, and rays. Still remaining are the stern and bow sections, long chain, port holes, and cleats of the wreck, all sitting amid beautiful elkhorn and staghorn coral formations, large sea fans, brain corals and red and orange sponges. This is a great spot for underwater portraits.

☆☆☆☆ **The Baths**, at the southern tip of Virgin Gorda, encompasses the islands' most famous beaches. The area, a natural landscape of partially submerged grottoes and caves formed by a jumble of enormous granite boulders, is a favorite beach-access snorkeling area and one of the biggest tourist attractions in the BVI. The caves shelter a variety of tropical fish. Find this area by taking the trail which starts at the end of the Baths Road. A small bar just off the beach rents snorkel equipment. Beware of dinghies! The Baths is a favorite of cruise ship visitors.

☆☆ **Spring Bay**, neighboring the Baths, has a gorgeous sandy beach and good snorkeling.

☆☆ **Crawl National Park**, a great spot for beginning snorkelers, also on Virgin Gorda, is reached via a palm-lined trail from Tower Road, just north of the Baths. A natural pond created by a boulder formation is ideal for children.

☆☆☆ **Smugglers Cove,** off the beaten path on the northwest end of Tortola, may be tough to find but is well worth the effort. The last mile leading to this spot is rough driving. There are two lovely reefs, about 100 ft

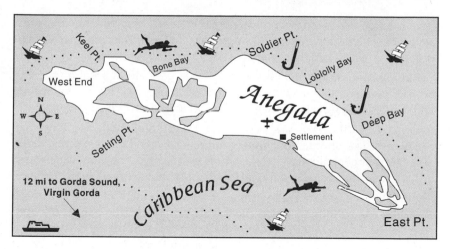

out, with crowds of grunts, squirrel fish, parrot fish and some good-sized trunk fish to keep you company. Depths are shallow and seas usually calm. Good for children. The beach is shaded by palms and sea grape trees. No rest rooms or changing facilities, but there is an honor bar with sodas, beer and some snacks and a phone with a couple of taxi numbers.

Guests of the neighboring **Long Bay Beach** Resort are shuttled to Smugglers Cove twice a day.

☆☆ **Brewers Bay**, on Tortola's north coast road, has two good snorkeling sites, one to the left along the cliffs with depths from eight to 10 ft, the other in the center of the beach opposite the rock wall edging the road. The reef starts close to shore and stretches out in shallow depths for a long way. Schools of trumpet fish, barracuda, octopus, stingrays and sergeant majors inhabit the area.

☆☆☆☆ **The Caves** at Norman Island are accessible by boat. It is a favorite snorkeling-photo site, bright with sponges, corals and schools of small fish. The reef slopes down to 40 ft. Norman Island is rumored to have inspired Robert Louis Stevenson's *Treasure Island* and the Caves are reputed to be old hiding places for pirate treasure. Moorings are maintained by the National Park Trust.

☆☆ **Manchioneel Bay,** Cooper Island, has a beautiful shallow reef with packs of fish around the moorings.

☆☆☆☆☆ **Loblolly Beach,** on Anegada's northern shore, is one of the best shore-entry snorkeling spots in the Caribbean when winds are calm. Coral heads teeming with fish and invertebrates are close to shore. Visibility can exceed 100 ft. There is usually some surf, but it breaks on the front of the reef, which is quite a distance from shore. The Big Bamboo bar and restaurant on the beach is worth the trip. Owner Aubrey Levons welcomes everyone with island stories and hospitality. Loblolly Beach is reached by taxi, bike or jeep from the Anegada Reef Resort docks.

Avoid this area during strong winds. The sea gets stirred up and visibility drops from super to silty, while the beach becomes a sand blast area. Spring and summer are usually the best times to dive and snorkel Anegada.

Anchoring on Anegada Reef is prohibited. Dive and snorkeling day trips can be arranged through the dive operators. Dive BVI offers a particularly nice snorkeling trip aboard their fast 45-ft *Sea Lion* to Anegada, which also includes beachcombing and a local lobster lunch at the Anegada Reef Hotel.

Additional excellent snorkeling sites are found on the northeast corner of **Benures Bay**, Norman Island, or the **Bight** and **Little Bight**, also off Norman Island. At Peter Island, try the south shore at **Little Harbor** and the western shore at **Great Harbor**. **Diamond Reef** on the southeast side of Great Camanoe can be reached by dinghy fom Marina Cay. The shallow reef sits straight out from the utility pole on the shore.

Long Bay, near Smugglers Cove, Tortola, has pretty corals and the biggest fish, but water entry is difficult as the coral grows to the surface.

Note: A wetsuit top, shortie, or wetskin is recommended for night dives and winter diving. Snorkelers should have some protection from sunburn. The BVI reefs are protected by law, and no living thing may be taken. "Take only pictures, leave only bubbles."

Dive Operators

Dive BVI Ltd., a PADI five-star shop, operates out of Leverick Bay, Virgin Gorda Yacht Harbour, Peter Island and Marina Cay. Owner Joe Giacinto has been diving and snorkeling the BVI for 29 years and knows all the best spots. Rates are $85 for a two-tank dive, $225 for three two-tank dives. Will rendezvous with boats. Snorkeling trips are offered to Anegada and other spots aboard the *Sealion*, a fast 45-ft wave-piercing catamaran. Resort courses up through certification are available. Write: P.O. Box 1040, Virgin Gorda, BVI. ☎ (284) 495-5513/(800) 848-7078, fax (284) 495-5347. E-mail: dbvi@caribsurf.com.

Underwater Safaris, at the Moorings Mariner Inn on Tortola and Cooper Island, offers fast 42- and 30-ft dive boats, full service, rendezvous with yachts, PADI certification. The Tortola shop is the largest retail dive shop in the BVI. Rates: $55 for a one-tank dive, $80 for a two-tank tour. Hotel/dive and sail packages. Write: P.O. Box 139, Road Town, Tortola. ☎ (800) 537-7032 or (284) 494-3235, fax (284) 494-5322.

Baskin in the Sun at the Prospect Reef Resort Marina has two dive boats which can accommodate 10 and 20 divers comfortably. Rates: $60 for a one-tank tour; $80 for a two-tank; $25, snorkel trip. Super service—you never carry a tank or gear. PADI five-star dive center. Package tours can be booked through Baskin in the Sun, P.O. Box 8309, Cruz Bay, St. John, USVI 00831. ☎ (800) 233-7938 or (284) 494-2858/9, fax (284) 494-4303. E-mail: baskin@usmall.com.

Blue Water Divers, located at Nanny Cay on the south side of Tortola, serves divers staying at Sugar Mill or the Windjammer. Blue Water Divers operates a 47-ft catamaran and a 27-ft dive boat. Dive tours are to the eastern sites in the BVI, such as Jost Van Dyke, as well as all the sites in the channel. ☎ (284) 494-2847. Write: P.O. Box 846, Road Town, Tortola, BVI. E-mail: bwdbvi@caribsurf.com.

Island Diver Ltd at Village Cay Marina, Road Town, offers reef and wreck tours, resort courses and snorkeling. ☎ (284) 494-3878/5236-7.

Kilbride's Underwater Tours, now owned by Sunchaser Scuba Ltd., located at the famous Bitter End Yacht Club on Virgin Gorda, features a variety of dive packages, courses and services. Their boats take you to 50 different dive locations. Despite a change in ownership, you will still be escorted by any one of 16 diving Kilbrides. As personal friends of the "better mannered fish," the Kilbrides provide a diving tour that is educational as well as entertaining. Tours can be booked by writing to Sunchaser Scuba, Box 46, Virgin Gorda, BVI. ☎ (800) 932-4286 or (284) 495-9638; fax (284) 495-7549. Mail may take as long as six weeks so write early. Kilbrides serve the North Sound resorts and their tours cover all the islands. Resort courses through PADI certification and open water checkouts are available. Rates:

Photo by Jonathon Pannaman

The Baths, Virgin Gorda.

$60 for a one-tank dive; $80-$90 for a two-tank tour. Rates include all equipment except wetsuits. Non-divers can join for a small fee.

Rainbow Visions Photography at Prospect Reef offers underwater, still and video camera rentals. Processing. Custom videos and portraits. ☎ (284) 494-2749. Write: P.O. Box 139, Road Town, Tortola, BVI.

Sailing and Scuba Live-Aboards

Sail-dive vacations are an easy way for divers to enjoy a variety of sites and destinations. Live-aboard yachts are chartered with captain, captain and crew or "bare" to qualified sailors. Navigation is uncomplicated; you can tour most of the area without ever leaving sight of land. Most boats carry snorkeling gear as standard equipment; some of the large craft have compressors. And every dive shop offers some type of arrangement to accommodate seafarers.

With sailing almost a religion in the BVI, it is easy to customize a live-aboard dive or snorkeling vacation. If you are an experienced sailor and diver you can charter a bareboat and see the sights on your own. If you've never sailed before or have limited experience, you can "captain" a crewed yacht to find the best dive spots. If you've never sailed or dived, but want to learn both, you can charter a yacht with a crew that includes a divemaster (often the captains are qualified dive instructors) or arrange to rendezvous with a dive boat. Or you can book a week-long cruise on a commercial live-aboard where you'll meet other divers. Prices on private charters vary with the number of people in your party. With four to six people, a crewed yacht will average about the same cost as a stay at a resort.

Cuan Law

One of the world's largest trimarans (105 ft), *Cuan Law* was specifically designed with the scuba diver in mind. As with most live-aboards, you are offered "all the diving you can stand." *Cuan Law* accommodates 18 passengers in 10 large, airy double cabins, each with private head and shower. Rates from April through December start at $1,495 per person for seven days and six nights. Transfers, tips, alcohol and scuba instruction are NOT included.

Cruises are booked up from three months to a year in advance. ☎ (800) 648-3393 or write Trimarine Boat Company, P.O. 4065, St. Thomas, USVI 00803.

The Moorings Ltd. offers "Cabin 'N Cruise" tours for those wishing to enjoy a fully crewed sailing vacation without having to charter an entire yacht. ☎ (800) 535-7289. Dive arrangements must be made separately. See listing below.

Bareboating

Private sailing yachts with diving guides and instructors are available from most of the charter operators listed below. You can arrange for your own personal live-aboard diving or snorkeling vacation. Be sure to specify your needs before going.

Bareboating can be surprisingly affordable for groups of four or more. Boats must be reserved six to nine months in advance for winter vacations and at least three months in advance for summer vacations.

Experience cruising on a similar yacht is required and you will be asked to fill out a questionnaire or produce a sailing resume. Instructor-skippers are available for refresher sailing. A cruising permit, available from the Customs Department, is required. For a complete list of charter companies contact the BVI Tourist Board at ☎ (800) 835-8530 or write 370 Lexington Ave., Suite 1605, New York, NY 10017.

The Moorings Ltd., Tortola, has been operating for 18 years. Their charter boats include Moorings 35, 38, 51, 50, 432 (43 ft), and 433 plus 39- and 42-ft catamarans. A Moorings 51, Morgan 60 or Gulfstar 60 may be chartered, but with crew only. The Moorings' book *Virgin Anchorages* shows through aerial photographs the best anchorages in the British Virgin Islands.

A three-day sailing vacation can be combined with a four day resort/diving vacation at the Moorings Mariner Inn. Write to The Moorings, Ltd., 19345 US Hwy 19 N, Clearwater, FL 34624. ☎ (800) 535-7289 or (813) 535-1446.

Offshore Sailing School uses the Moorings boats and offers a Sail 'N Dive vacation with the Prospect Reef Resort. The package includes the complete Learn to Sail course and PADI Dive certification, eight nights accommodations and all course materials. Classroom and on-water instruction is held Monday through Thursday alternating between midday and afternoon. On-water instruction is held Monday through Thursday in half-day sessions. They also offer a Learn to Sail vacation (from $1,195 per week), which can be mixed with dive expeditions through the Prospect Reef Resort. Rates for the Sail 'N Dive course and accommodations are $1,643 based on a double in summer, April 20th to Dec 20th; $1,743 from Dec 12 to April 19; $1,594 from Oct 13 to Nov 16. ☎ (800) 221-4326.

A Fast Track to Cruising course, offered by Offshore Sailing School, includes the complete Learn to Sail course and Moorings/Offshore Live Aboard Cruising course on consecutive weeks. Available starting Sundays year-round (two-person minimum for Live Aboard cruising), the package includes 10 days/nine nights accommodations ashore, six days/five nights aboard a Moorings yacht, Learn to Sail and Live Aboard Cruising courses, textbooks, certificates, wallet cards, logbook, full day practice sail, split yacht provisioning during onboard portion of Live Aboard Cruising course (five breakfasts, five lunches, three dinners), graduation dinners ashore, airport or ferry transfers in Tortola. Per-person rates for a double between Dec 22 and April 4 are $2,895; from April 20 to Dec 20, $2,595. ☎ (800) 221-4326 or (941) 454-1700, fax (941) 454-1191. Write to: Offshore Sailing School, 16731 McGregor Blvd., Ft. Myers, FL 33908.

Yacht Promenade, a sleek, 65-ft tri-hull sailing yacht for couples or groups of six to 12, features on-board scuba facilities, spacious air-conditioned cabins, full breakfasts, lunches, cocktails, hors d'oeuvres and three-course gourmet dinners. There are five guest staterooms, one in each outer hull and three at the rear of the center hull, three queen-sized berths and two that are larger than king and can be converted into four single berths. A 20-ft Wellcraft launch wisks divers off to all the best spots. Cost of $1,450 per week per diver includes use of 11-ft kayaks, a sailing dinghy, and a windsurfer. Non-divers' discount $100. For 12 divers the price drops to $1,195 per person. Gear rental, $90 per week. Pick up at Village Cay Marina, Road Town, Tortola. ☎ (US) (800) 526-5503 or (284) 494-3853, fax (284) 494-5577. E-mail: promcruz@caribsurf.com.

Mooring Buoys

In order to protect the BVI's fragile coral reefs, boats are required to use National Parks Trust (NPT) mooring buoys when visiting the following areas: The Baths, The Caves, The Indians, Pelican Island, Carrot Shoal; also dive or snorkeling sites at Peter, Norman, Ginger and Cooper Islands, the Wreck of the *Fearless*, Dead Chest, Blonde Rock, the Dogs, Guana Island, the wreck of the *Rhone* and the *Rhone's* anchor. All users of the moorings must have a valid NPT moorings permit, which can be obtained at their office in Road Town, or at BVI Customs Offices, local charter boat companies and brokerages.

Mooring buoy colors indicate the use for that mooring. White is for scuba diving only; orange or red are for snorkeling or any day use; yellow moorings are for commercial dive operations only; blue are for dinghies.

Note: Mooring on the reefs surrounding Anegada is prohibited.

Accommodations and Anchorages

Web site: www.britishvirginislands.com/divebvi.

Tortola

Every type of accommodation is available in the BVI from tents to cottages, guesthouses, condos, luxury resorts to live-aboard sailboats and motor yachts. Reservations can be made through your travel agent or the BVI Tourist Board at ☎ (800) 835-8530, or in New York, (212) 696-0400. Locally owned properties start at $40 per night for a room. For a copy of the Intimate Inns brochure, ☎ (US) (800) 835-8530. Web site: www.carib.com/carib/bvi.

Island Hideaways rents upscale private homes and villas. ☎ (800) 784-2690 or (202) 232-6137, fax (202) 667-3392.

Long Bay Beach Resort on Tortola's north shore has 82 deluxe hillside and beachfront accommodations. Transfers, three two-tank dives, beach, restaurant, tennis, pitch & put golf. Rates start at $899 per person per week for a seven-night dive vacation with hillside accommodations, breakfasts, four dinners, one-day car rental, airport transfers and shuttle to diving. Dive packages with Baskin' in the Sun. ☎ (800) 729-9599. Write: P.O. Box 433, Road Town Tortola, BVI.

The Moorings-Mariner Inn, Tortola, is home port to The Moorings charter boat operation. It has no beach. The poolside bar and restaurant are just a few steps from Underwater Safaris, the largest retail shop in the BVI.

The resort offers a new Shore 'N Sail vacation with three nights aboard a luxurious sailing yacht (snorkeling only) with your own skipper and provisions and four nights at the resort diving with Underwater Safaris. ☎ (800) 535-7289, (284) 494-2332, fax (813) 530-9747, or write The Moorings-Mariner Inn, 1305 US 19 S., Suite 402, Clearwater, FL 34624. E-mail: yacht@moorings. Web site: www.moorings.com

Maria's By the Sea, Road Town, is a new 20-room hotel on the water. Most rooms have balconies with ocean views and a kitchenette. Diving is with Underwater Safaris on nearby Cooper Island. One package includes seven nights at Maria's, two morning dives for five days, airport transfers and ferry to and from the dive center on Cooper Island. The dive portion is $365. Winter room rates are $75 to $95 per day. To book the package call Underwater Safaris at ☎ (800) 537-7032. For hotel reservations only, call (284) 494-2595. Write P.O. Box 206, Road Town, Tortola, BVI.

Nanny Cay Resort & Marina, two miles southwest of Road Town, has 41 air-conditioned rooms from $180 per day in winter; $110 in summer. TV, mini bars, phones, pool, restaurant, bar, tennis, windsurf school and on-site dive operation, Blue Water Divers. Winter dive packages start at $635 per person for four nights accommodations and three two-tank boat dives, $1,101 for seven nights with six two-tank dives. ☎ (800) 74CHARMS or (800) 742-4276 or (284) 494-4895, fax (914) 424-3283. Write: P.O. Box 281, Road Town, Tortola, BVI.

Prospect Reef Resort is a sprawling 10-acre resort located on the west end of Road Town, Tortola, facing Sir Francis Drake Channel. The resort has over 130 rooms ranging from studios to standard rooms, full apartments, and luxury villas. This resort is the largest on Tortola and offers six tennis courts, miniature golf, two restaurants for casual food and drinks, and three pools. Rooms are cooled by ceiling fans and a breeze from the sea. An excellent buffet is served at the resort's Harbour Restaurant on Saturday nights. Scuba packages with Baskin' in the Sun. Winter rates are $990 for seven nights including accommodations and three boat dives; summer, $773. ☎ (800) 356-8937, (284) 494-3311. Winter room rates are from $147 per day. (17% tax/service charge included in rates.) Write Box 104, Road Town, Tortola, BVI.

Maria's By the Sea, Road Town, offers reef tours with Underwater Safaris. 20 rooms. Waterfront, but no beach. Room rates from $85 to $250 per day in winter, from $70 to $210 per day in summer.

Sugarmill, on the northwest shore of Tortola, is a village of hillside cottages built around the remains of a 360-year-old sugar mill. Its proprietors, Jeff and Jinx Morgan, are famous for their gourmet meals (they write for *Bon Apétit*). The old sugar mill houses the restaurant, where you may dine by candlelight on conch stew, grouper salad, grilled swordfish and salads with lettuce from the lodge's garden. Small beach. Their "Adventure Package" includes seven nights deluxe accommodation, six-day vehicle rental, four gourmet dinners at the Sugar Mill's restaurant, six one-tank dives with Baskin' in the Sun, a resort course, plus two shallow dives for beginners, gourmet picnic for two, full day sail to neighbouring islands with lunch and drinks, an autographed copy of *The Sugar Mill Caribbean Cookbook* by Jiff & Jinx Morgan, and a bottle of Sugar Mill rum. Winter rates (Dec 21-Apr 14) for the package are $1,514 with dives, $1,298 without dives; spring rates (Apr 15-May 31 and Nov 1-Dec 20) are $1,215 with dives, $999 without. Summer rates (June 1-Oct 31) are $1,127 with dives, $911 without. Rates are per person based on double occupancy (single rate not available). ☎ (800) 462-8834 or (284) 495-4355, fax (284) 495-4696. Write P.O. Box 425, Tortola, BVI.

Treasure Isle Hotel, Roadtown, has 40 air-conditioned rooms, pool, restaurant, bar. Dive packages with Underwater Safaris. Room rates are from $165 in winter, $90 in summer. ☎ (284) 494-2501. Write: P.O. Box 68, Road Town, Tortola, BVI. Dive packages are with Underwater Safaris. ☎ (800) 437-7880.

MARINA CAY

Marina Cay, a six-acre island off the northeast tip of Tortola, features Dive BVI's newest dive and water sports center offering daily dive and snorkeling trips, ocean kayaks, two new Hobie catamarans, Pusser's Fine Dining and a large Company Store.

Marina Cay Resort offers four one-bedroom units and two two-bedroom villas that accommodate up to 16 guests. All have been recently refurbished. Room rates are $95 for double occupancy room and $195 for a lagoon villa.

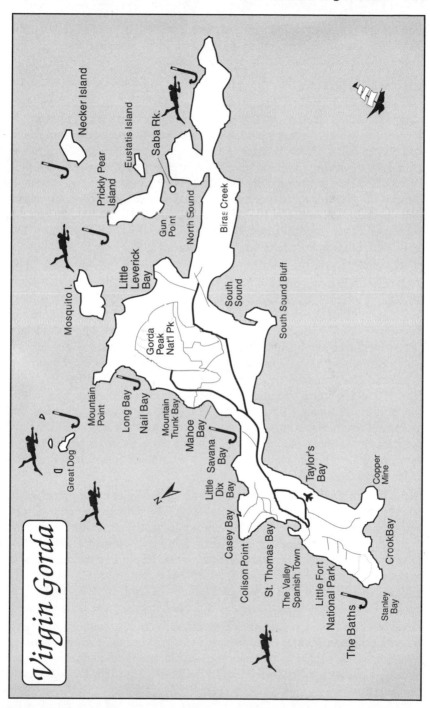

Virgin Gorda

Continental breakfast included. Taxes extra. ☎ (284) 494-2174 or fax (284) 494-4775. Dive/accommodation packages may be reserved through Dive BVI. ☎ (800) 848-7078.

VIRGIN GORDA

The Bitter End Yacht Club on Virgin Gorda's North Sound offers guest rooms in luxury villas along the shore and hillside or on a Freedom 30 live-aboard yacht. The club bar is *the* favorite story-swapping place for sailing and diving folk. Daily scuba trips, arranged through Kilbride's Underwater Tours, leave from the Bitter End Docks every morning. Rates are for couples. Deduct $100 per day for a single. Add $100 for an extra person. A suite in winter with all meals for two costs $570 per day or $3,990 for seven nights. Diving is extra. If you prefer to stay aboard a yacht, the same package costs $480 per day or $3,360 per seven nights. ☎ (800) 872-2392, (284) 494-2746, or write P.O. Box 46, Virgin Gorda, BVI.

Drake's Anchorage on Mosquito Island, just north of North Sound off Virgin Gorda, is a hideaway with 10 beachfront units and two deluxe villas. The island has four lovely beaches, with snorkeling offshore and moorings for cruising sailboats. Scuba diving is arranged with Kilbride's Underwater Tours or Dive BVI. The dive shops pick you up at the dock. Mosquito Island can be reached by flying into Virgin Gorda and taking a cab to Leverick Bay where a Drake's boat will pick you up. Room rates are from $218 per day in summer. Day rates for two in an oceanfront suite between Dec 16th and Mar 31 are $515 and include breakfast, lunch and dinner for two, use of windsurfers, snorkeling equipment, 19-ft sailboat, kayaks, bicycles and motorized dinghies; summer and fall package rates are from $405 for two per day. Seven-night packages with meals from $2,425 for two. Diving is extra. ☎ (800) 624-6651 or write Drake's Anchorage Resort Inn, P.O. Box 2510 Virgin Gorda, BVI.

Biras Creek Estate, located on a 140-acre peninsula, can be reached by scheduled ferry from Tortola. The resort has 34 luxury villas with garden and ocean views overlooking North Sound. Recently refurbished, the resort provides complimentary use of Boston Whalers, windsurfers and 25-ft sailboats. Diving, extra, is arranged at the desk. Rates for a room and three meals daily are from $495 in winter, $350 in summer. ☎ (800) 608-9661 or (284) 494-3555, fax (284) 494-3557. In the US, ☎ (800) 223-1108; from the UK, 0-800-894-057. Write: P.O. Box 54, Virgin Gorda, BVI.

Leverick Bay Hotel, on Leverick Bay, offers a variety of unique, affordable accommodations. Winter rates start at $119 per day for a room; summer, $96. Small beach. Diving, water-skiing, kayaking and small boat sailing are through Dive BVI. ☎ (800) 848-7078 or (284) 495-7328. E-mail: dbvi@ caribsurf.com.

Little Dix Bay features 90 luxury suites and guest rooms starting at $250 per day in summer (May - Nov), $450 per day during the high season (Dec 20 to Mar 31). The resort rests on a half-mile of pristine beach surrounded by tropical gardens. Paradise Watersports on premises offers scuba and snorkeling tours. One of Virgin Gorda's largest resorts with 90 rooms. ☎ (800) 928-3000 or book through your travel agent.

Peter Island Resort & Yacht Harbour offers luxurious beachfront rooms overlooking Sprat Bay and the Sir Francis Drake Channel. Excellent snorkeling off the beach. Dive BVI facility on site. Winter room rates are from $395 per day FAP; summer from $195 per day EP. ☎ (284) 495-2000, fax (284) 495-2500.

ANEGADA

Tiny Anegada, 12 miles northwest of Virgin Gorda, covers just 15 square miles. This off-the-beaten-track coral atoll, surrounded by uninterrupted beaches and gorgeous reefs, is home to 250 residents and a huge community of exotic Caribbean birds including a flamingo colony, herons, terns and ospreys. Shipwrecks and coral heads abound, a delight for divers and snorkelers, but sailors beware—approaching the island by boat can be treacherous without local knowledge and eyeball navigation. Snorkeling, diving and fly fishing, done from shore, is outstanding.

Much of the island's interior is a preserve for 2,000 wild goats, donkeys and cattle. Not for the average tourist, but a great spot if you want to get away from it all. Expect encounters with a ferocious mosquito population—carry as much repellent as you can. Fly in from Beef Island, Tortola or go by boat from any of the marinas.

Anegada Reef Hotel, on Setting Point, offers great beaches, snorkeling and fly fishing, 16 air-conditioned rooms, tackle shop, tank fills. Winter rates are from $165 per day, summer from $130. Rates include breakfast, lunch and dinner (surcharge for lobster). Informal restaurant. Jeep and bicycle rentals. A 15% service charge and 7% tax are added to the bill. Three-night deposit required. ☎ (284) 495-8002, fax (284) 495-9362.

Anegada Beach Campground offers 8 x 10-ft tents, a restaurant and snorkeling tours. Winter rates are $26 to $36. Bare site is under $10. ☎ (284) 495-9466 or write to Box 2710, Anegada, BVI.

Pristine Anchorages

Deadman's Bay, on the eastern tip of Peter Island, is a short sail out of Road Harbour that takes no more than an hour or two. Once there, you will find a long white sand beach at Peter Island Yacht Club. Yachtsmen are requested to anchor in the Bay's extreme southeastern corner and should be aware that the area is prone to a swell, especially in the winter months.

Salt Island. Heading upwind from Deadman's Bay is Salt Island, once a regular stopping-off point for ships requiring salt for food preservation on the trade routes. This is also the location of the BVI's famed wreck of the *Rhone*, which sank off the island in 1867. At Lee Bay, just north of the *Rhone*, moorings are provided for those diving the wreck in order to minimize anchor damage. Both Lee Bay and Salt Pond Bay off the settlement can be rough anchorages and are recommended for day use only.

Cooper Island's Machioneel Bay, located on the island's northwest shore, is a good lunch stop for those sailing upwind to Virgin Gorda. There is a dock for dinghies and a beach for swimming. The Cooper Island Beach Bar serves lunch, dinner and drinks.

The Virgin Gorda Baths, one of the BVI's most famous landmarks, lies on the southwestern shore of Virgin Gorda. Randomly placed large granite boulders form small grottoes and pools on the beach's edge, great for exploring and snorkeling. As with all these north shore anchorages, a swell can prevent overnight anchoring.

North Sound, Virgin Gorda, offers the yachtsman a wide array of overnight anchorages, and a variety of good dining spots. The harbor sits along the eastern tip of the island and is well protected by surrounding islands—Mosquito, Prickly Pear and Eustatia. Boats over five ft in draft should use the Sound's northern entrance at Calquhoun Reef; shallow drafts can use the Anguilla Point entrance in calm weather only.

The Dogs make a good stopping-off point for sailors on their way from North Sound to Jost Van Dyke; they are also a popular diving and snorkeling venue. On calm days the best anchorages are the bay to the west of Kitchen Point on George Dog, as well as on the south side of Great Dog.

Trellis Bay, Beef Island, is a well-protected anchorage fringed by a semicircular beach. It serves as the location for Boardsailing BVI, the Conch Shell Point Restaurant and The Loose Mongoose Beach Bar. At the Bay's center is The Last Resort, an English-style restaurant whose owner, Tony Snell, puts on a one-man cabaret act.

Marina Cay lies north of Trellis Bay and offers a restaurant, bar, small beach and moorings. It is fringed by coral and one should enter from the north.

Sandy Cay, located east of Little Jost Van Dyke, is uninhabited and offers a long stretch of white sandy beach. The water is deep almost until the shore; the area is prone to swells and not a good anchorage year-round.

Little Harbour, Jost Van Dyke, a quiet, easy-to-enter lagoon touts three restaurants, all with local food and atmosphere at the shore's edge.

Great Harbour, Jost Van Dyke (south coast), is the locale of Foxy's Tamarind Bar and several other good West Indian restaurants. A small settlement bordering a white sand beach fringes this picturesque harbor. The anchorage is fairly well protected and the holding good.

White Bay, Jost Van Dyke, lies west of Great Harbour and features a white sand beach, small hotel and a restaurant. A channel through the center of the reef allows entrance to the anchorage, which is subject to winter swells.

Norman Island's main anchorage is The Bight.

Pelican Island and the **Indians** are near The Bight and offer good snorkeling and excellent scuba diving.

Soper's Hole, one of Tortola's three main ports of entry, lies at the very west end of the island and is both deep and sheltered. Ferries to St. Thomas and St. John leave from here daily. There are several nearby restaurants and marinas.

Road Harbour, Tortola's largest harbor, skirts Road Town, capital of the BVI. Here one finds customs and immigration facilities, good supermarkets and shops, marinas, restaurants and a boat yard — all within walking distance of the harbor.

Brandywine Bay and **Maya Cove**, which also offer restaurants, are two more anchorages just beyond Road Harbour.

Other Activities and Sightseeing

Hiking and exploring are popular in the BVI. You will find deserted dungeons, sugar mills, pirate caves, rain forests and wooded trails. Tennis courts as well as horseback riding are provided by some of the hotels. Boardsailing and windsurfing equipment is available at many of the resorts.

TORTOLA

The 2.8-acre **J.R. O'Neal Botanic Gardens** in the centre of Road Town feature a beautiful waterfall, lily pond and exotic tropical plants and birds. Nearby, on Main Street, is the **Virgin Island Folk Museum** which displays many artifacts from the *Rhone* and from early plantations. Hikers and botanists will find huge elephant-ear plants, and lush ferns under a canopy of mahogany and manilkara trees at **Sage Mountain National Park**. Mt. Sage peaks at 1,780 ft.

If you are cruising the BVI, be sure to visit **Stanley's** in Cane Garden Bay on the weekend, where the steel band is reputed to be the best in the islands.

VIRGIN GORDA

Visitors will find the ruins of an 18th-century sugar mill at **Nail Bay** on Virgin Gorda's west coast. And just south of the Yacht Harbor at **Little Fort**

National Park is some masonry from an old Spanish fortress. Monster granite boulders are at the **Spring Bay** beach between Little Fort National Park and the Baths.

Gorda Peak is a 265-acre national park with a wealth of mahogany trees and exotic plants.

There are small shops (**not** duty free) around Road Town, Tortola and Spanish Town, Virgin Gorda, specializing in local crafts and gifts.

Dining

TORTOLA

Rhymer's Beach Bar and Restaurant at Cane Garden Bay, Tortola, is a favorite among the locals. Serving fresh fish and lobster, it has Buffet Night on Tuesday and Saturday. Open for breakfast, lunch and dinner. ☎ 54520.

Scatliffe's Tavern, another local favorite in Road Town, Tortola, specializes in local food such as fish soup made with coconut milk, conch fritters, ribs, and lobster dishes, followed by fresh lime pie. Near the high school. ☎ 42797.

Carib Casseroles, on Tortola, has a "Meals on Keels" service for bareboaters experienced with boil-a-bags as well as sit-down service. Food is a combination of Caribbean, French, Greek and Creole. Peanut Creole soup, curry and casseroles are featured here. Moderate.

VIRGIN GORDA

The Bath & Turtle is a patio tavern in the Yacht Harbour serving breakfast, lunch, and dinner. Burgers, sandwiches, and homemade soups. ☎ 55239.

Mad Dog near the Baths specializes in sandwiches all day. Spectacular view! ☎ 55830.

The Olde Yard Inn features a library and classical music. Homemade soups, local seafood, gourmet specialties. ☎ 55544. Reservations.

ANEGADA

The Anegada Reefs Hotel, Anegada serves lunch at their beach bar and specializes in barbecued lobster for dinner. Local fish or steak, chicken and ribs are also available. Moderate to expensive. ☎ 58002. VHF Ch 16.

MOSQUITO

Drake's Anchorage, on Mosquito, has been written up in *Gourmet* magazine for its fabulous Caribbean lobster and local fish dinners. Meals include fresh baked bread, soup, appetizer, salad, dessert and coffee. Moorings are available for a low overnight charge. ☎ 42254. VHF Ch 16.

JOST VAN DYKE

Sandcastle at White Bay on Jost Van Dyke serves gourmet fish dishes, lobster, orange-glazed duck, fresh breads and desserts for lunch and dinner in the open-air restaurant on the beach. The **Soggy Dollar Bar** offers the original "Painkiller." No credit cards. Reservations on channel 16 VHF. Prices are moderate to high.

Foxy's in Great Harbor (south coast) serves roti and sumptuous burgers for lunch, local lobster and steak for dinner. A favorite with the yachting crowd. ☎ 59258.

PETER ISLAND

Peter Island Hotel and Yacht Harbour offers lunch at the Beach Restaurant from 12:30 to 2:00 pm. Dinners are formal; men must wear a jacket and women, "cocktail" attire. ☎ 52000. Expensive.

Facts

Nearest Recompression Chamber: The nearest chamber is located on St. Thomas in the neighboring USVI.

Getting There: San Juan, Puerto Rico is the airline hub for the Caribbean, with frequent service to all parts of the US, Canada and Europe. Beef Island is the major airport of Tortola and the BVI. Flights to San Juan with connections to the BVI from the United States on American (☎ 800-433-7300), Delta and Continental Airlines. Atlantic Air BVI, Sunaire Express or American Eagle fly from San Juan to Beef Island. Gorda Aero Services (☎ 5-2271) flies to Anegada from Tortola on Mon, Wed, and Fri. Inter-island ferry service is also available from St. Thomas to St. John and Tortola. Ferries run from Tortola to Virgin Gorda, Peter Island, Jost Van Dyke. Baggage can sometimes be delayed by a day on the small airlines. Divers carrying a lot of equipment should fly direct to St. Thomas and take a water ferry, to avoid having to change planes.

Car rentals: *Tortola*: Hertz, ☎ 54405; Avis, ☎ 4-3322; Budget, ☎ 4-2639; International, ☎ 4-2516. *Virgin Gorda*: Speedy's, ☎ 4-5240.

Taxi Service: Available from Beef Island Airport, Road Town Jetty, West End Jetty and from the dock on Virgin Gorda. *Tortola:* BVI Taxi, ☎ 5-2378 or 4-2875; Andy's Taxi, ☎ 5-5252; Style's Taxi, ☎ 4-2260. *Virgin Gorda*: Mahogany Taxi, ☎ 5-5542.

Driving: Valid BVI driving license required. A temporary license may be obtained from the car rental agencies for $10. Driving is on the left-hand side of the road. Maximum speed is 30 mph. Bicycles must be registered at the Traffic Licensing Office in Road Town. Cost of registration is $5. License plate **must** be fixed to the bicycle.

Fishing: The removal of any marine organism from BVI waters is illegal for non-residents without a recreational fishing permit. ☎ 4-3429.

Documents: A valid passport is required to enter the BVI. For US and Canadian citizens an authenticated birth certificate or voter registration card with photo identification will suffice. Visitors may stay up to six months, provided they possess ongoing tickets, evidence of adequate means of support and pre-arranged accommodations. Visitors from some countries may need a visa. ☎ (284) 494-3701.

Currency: US Dollar. Personal checks not accepted.

Clothing: Casual, light clothing; some of the resorts require a jacket for dinner. Avoid exposed midriffs and bare chests in residential and commercial areas.

Nudity is punishable by law. A wetsuit top, shortie, or wetskin is recommended for night dives and winter diving. Snorkelers should have some protection from sunburn.

Time: Atlantic Standard (EST + 1 hr).

Language: English.

Climate: The BVI are in the tradewind belt and have a subtropical climate. Average temperatures are 75° to 85° F in winter and 80° to 90° F in summer. Nights are cooler. The hurricane season extends from July through September.

Taxes: There is a departure tax of $10 by air and $5 by sea. The hotel accommodation tax is 7%.

Religious Services: Methodist, Anglican, Roman Catholic, Seventh Day Adventist, Baptist, Jehovah's Witness, Pentecostal and Church of Christ.

For Additional Information and a list of all guesthouses, apartments, hotels, campgrounds, charter operators, and restaurants, contact the BVI Tourist Board. *In Tortola:* P.O. Box 134, Road Town, Tortola, British Virgin Islands, ☎ (284) 494-3134. *In New York:* BVI Tourist Board, 370 Lexington Avenue, Suite 1605, New York, NY 10017, ☎ (800) 835-8530 or 212-696-0400. *United Kingdom:* BVI Information Office, FCB Travel Marketing, 110 St. Martin's Lane, London WC2N 4DY, England, ☎ 171-240-4259. Web site: www.britishvirginislands. com/divebvi.

Cayman Islands

Grand Cayman, Cayman Brac & Little Cayman

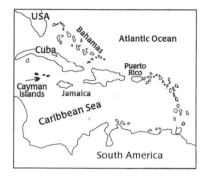

Dubbed "The Islands that Time Forgot" by the *Saturday Evening Post* in the early 1950s, the Caymans today have become one of the world's top dive-travel destinations. Some 480 miles, and an hour's flying time, south of Miami, this Caribbean trio entertains more than 200,000 visitors each year.

Physically beautiful, each island is blessed with an extraordinary fringing reef, superb marine life and sparkling, palm-lined beaches.

Underwater Cayman is a submerged mountain range complete with cliffs, drop-offs, gullies, caverns, sink holes and forests of coral. The islands are the visible above-the-sea portions of the mountains. At depth, the Cayman Trench drops off to more than 23,000 ft.

Grand Cayman, the largest and the most developed of the three, boasts world-class dive operations, restaurants and scores of luxury hotels and condominiums. The islands' no-tax status—granted by Britain in the 1700's because of the heroic action of Caymanians in saving the lives of passengers and crews of 10 sailing ships—has attracted numerous corporations and banks. Its capital, Georgetown, ranks as the fifth largest financial center in the world, with nearly 600 international banks.

Cayman Brac and Little Cayman lie 89 miles northeast of the big island and are separated by a seven-mile-wide channel. Both wildly beautiful, each has its own special personality.

Little Cayman is VERY QUIET—virtually untouched by developers. The smallest of the three islands—only 10 square miles—it has about 35 permanent residents. There are no shops, restaurants, movie theaters or traffic. Phones are few and far between. Small resorts cater almost exclusively to divers and fishermen.

Area Contributors: Christopher Lofting, Mike Emmanuel, Mina Heuslein, Bill Heuslein and Kenneth Liggett, and Diane Kegley, Red Sail Sports.

With daily direct flights from North America and easy access from many other parts of the globe, most divers head first for Grand Cayman. Its famed Seven Mile Beach is headquarters for dive activity. More adventurous divers seeking a unique wilderness experience flock to the Brac and Little Cayman for superlative wall dives. Little Cayman is also noted for unsurpassed flats fishing.

When To Go

Late summer and fall bring chance of a hurricane, but diving is possible year-round. Conditions are generally mild, although steady winds can kick up some chop. When this happens dive boats simply move to the leeward side of the island and calmer waters. Air temperature averages 77° F. Water temperature averages 80°.

History

As with many other Caribbean islands, the discovery of the Caymans is attributed to Christopher Columbus, who first saw them on his second voyage while en route from Panama to Cuba in 1503. Amazingly, his primitive ships were able to negotiate the coral reefs with little trouble. He named these islands "Las Tortugas" for the countless marine turtles who came to Cayman beaches to breed. The turtles, which lived in captivity for long periods, became a source of fresh meat for the sailors, and the Cayman Islands became a regular stop for exploring ships.

Marine Regulations

With a dramatic growth in tourism and an increase in cruiseship arrivals, the islands have enacted comprehensive legislation to protect the fragile marine environment. Marine areas are divided into three types: Marine Park Zones, Replenishment Zones and Environmental Zones.

The Marine Park Zones outlaw the taking of any marine life, living or dead, and only line fishing from shore and beyond the dropoff is permitted. Anchoring is allowed only at fixed moorings. (There are more than 200 permanent moorings around the islands.)

It is an offense for any vessel to cause reef damage with anchors or chains anywhere in Cayman waters.

In a Replenishment Zone, the taking of conch or lobster is prohibited, and spear guns, pole spears, fish traps and nets are prohibited. Line fishing and anchoring (at fixed moorings) are permitted. (Spearguns and Hawaiian slings may not be brought into the country.)

Environmental Zones are the most strictly regulated. There is an absolute ban on the taking of any kind of marine life, alive or dead; anchoring is prohibited and no in-water activities of any kind are tolerated. These areas

Seven Mile Beach, Grand Cayman.

are a breeding ground and nursery for the fish and other creatures which will later populate the reef and other waters.

The Marine Conservation Board employs full-time officers who may search any vessel or vehicle thought to contain marine life taken illegally. Penalties may include a maximum fine of CI $5,000 or imprisonment, or both.

Best Dive and Snorkeling Sites of Grand Cayman

Grand Cayman, noted for its fabulous wall-diving, has steep drop-offs on all sides. The West Wall, a drop-off that runs parallel to Seven Mile Beach, offers the most convenient diving on the island. Most dive operators are located in this area, and many hotels offer dive and snorkeling trips to the sites—all five- to 10-minute boat rides. Flat-bottom dive boats attest to the calm seas. Several beach dives are possible. More sites along the South Wall have recently opened, particularly for experienced divers and photographers. This area is defined by a barrier reef that breaks the surface and serves as a coral fence. Conditions here are more demanding.

The North Wall also lays claim to some of the most spectacular dive sites because of its unusual coral formations and frequent pelagic sightings.

Least explored is the East End Wall, often referred to as the last frontier.

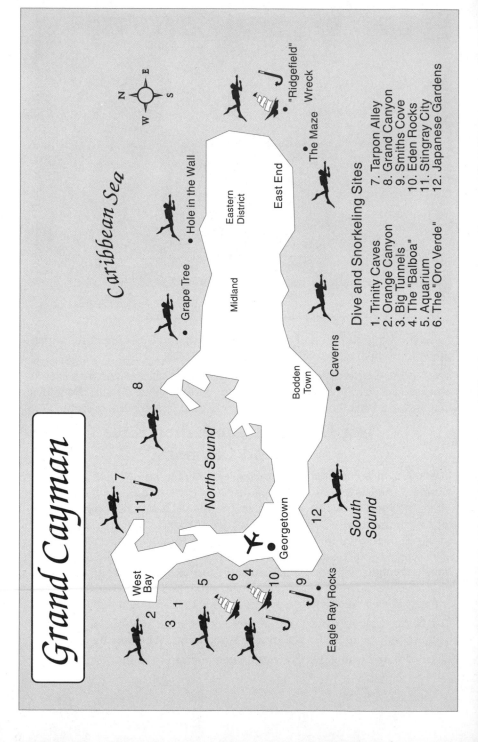

Grand Cayman

Caribbean Sea

N
E
W — S

"Ridgefield" Wreck

The Maze

Hole in the Wall

Eastern District

East End

Grape Tree

Midland

Caverns

Bodden Town

North Sound

8

Georgetown

South Sound

West Bay

7

11

5

6 4

2

1

3

10

9

12

Eagle Ray Rocks

Dive and Snorkeling Sites

1. Trinity Caves
2. Orange Canyon
3. Big Tunnels
4. The "Balboa"
5. Aquarium
6. The "Oro Verde"
7. Tarpon Alley
8. Grand Canyon
9. Smiths Cove
10. Eden Rocks
11. Stingray City
12. Japanese Gardens

Wreck of the Balboa *at night. "Lightning" is caused by a time exposure of a diver holding a light while swimming across the wreck.*

Water temperature holds steady at 82° F, visibility ranges from 100 to 150 ft. The coral reefs are exceptionally healthy, largely due to the conservancy measures enforced by the dive shops.

☆☆☆☆☆ **Stingray City** is the most photographed dive site in the Caymans, if not the entire Caribbean. Pictured in all the tourist board ads, the subject of endless travel articles and an Emmy-award film by Stan Waterman, this gathering of Southern stingrays in the shallow area of North Sound is a marine phenomenon which has thrilled scuba divers and snorkelers since their discovery by two dive instructors, Pat Kinney and Jay Ireland, early in 1986.

After observing the normally solitary and shy rays gathering regularly at a shallow site where boats cleaned their conch and fish, Kinney and Ireland began hand taming exercises—carefully avoiding the razor-sharp, venomous spine in their whip-like tails. When safe hand feeding became a predictable event, they invited small groups of divers and snorkelers out to watch.

Today, the 20-member cast of rays are big celebrities, luring curious visitors—as many as 150-200 per day—from across the globe. The location is shallow, 12-20 ft, ideal for snorkelers as well as divers. Feeding time occurs whenever a dive or snorkeling boat shows up.

☆☆☆☆☆ **Trinity Caves**, off the north end of Seven Mile Beach, winds into a maze of canyon trails between 60 and 100 ft. Reef features consist of gigantic barrel sponges, black coral, towering sea whips, sea fans, and a host of critters. Huge groupers and turtles, lobsters, squirrel fish, and schooling reef fish inhabit three cathedral-like caves for which the site is named. Their walls grasp clusters of pink anemones, vase sponges, and star corals. Sea conditions are generally calm, with an occasional light current. Exceptional visibility. Suggested for experienced divers.

☆☆☆☆ **Orange Canyon**, north of Trinity Caves, glows with vibrant orange elephant-ear sponges. The reef starts at 45 ft, the edge of a deep wall adorned with sea plumes, lavender sea fans and bushy corals—cover for shrimp, sea cucumbers, brittle stars, arrow crabs, file fish, turtles and small octopi. Calm seas.

☆☆☆☆ **Big Tunnels**, north of the Seven Mile Beach area, feature a 50-ft coral archway linked to several tunnels and ledges bursting with rainbow gorgonians, sea fans, basket sponges, tube sponges, and branching corals. Eagle rays drift by walls of sea urchins, anemones, grunts, puffer fish, bigeyes, and shrimp. Big morays peek from the ledges. An occasional nurse shark appears. Depths average 110 ft with excellent visibility. Experience recommended.

☆☆☆☆ **The Wreck of the *Balboa,*** a 375-ft freighter, rests at 30 ft in George Town Harbor—200 yards off the town pier. A favorite night dive, its twisted wreckage creates interesting video and still opportunities. Seas are calm with good visibility, though several divers visiting the wreck at one time may kick up silt. Schools of sergeant majors, grouper, queen and French angels mingle about the hull.

☆☆☆ **Aquarium** sits close to shore off the center of Seven Mile Beach. As the name implies, this spot serves as a grand meeting center for most every species of fish in the Caribbean. Count-and-name-the-fish is the favorite sport *du jour* at this 35-ft-deep coral grotto. Be sure to tote a waterproof fish ID card or book.

Spotted trunkfish, parrot fish, snappers, file fish, spotted morays, butterflyfish, queen angels, queen triggerfish, puffers and schooling barracuda inhabit Aquarium. Though hard to see through the crowds of fish, the reef is very pretty with nice stands of staghorn coral, sponges and soft corals. Visibility superb. Calm seas make this a good choice for new divers.

☆☆☆ **The Wreck of the *Oro Verde*** lies 30 to 50 ft beneath the surface, straight out from the Holiday Inn on Seven Mile Beach. After this 180-ft freighter ran aground in 1976, local dive operators scuttled the wreck to create an artificial reef. The hull, intact, is very photogenic. Divers are warmly

Photo courtesy Red Sail Watersports

Pool instruction by Red Sail Sports at the Hyatt Regency.

greeted by its inhabitants—Spanish hogfish, French angels, snappers, butterflyfish, blue tangs, rock beauties. Seas are calm.

☆☆☆ **Tarpon Alley,** a coral canyon, mirrors schools of giant silvery tarpon, mammoth grouper and sting rays. Large pelagics flash by too. The "alley," south of Orange Canyon, lies partially in the Seven Mile Beach replenishment zone. Top of the canyon walls are at 60 ft. Outside drop-offs plunge to several thousand ft. Surface conditions are occasionally choppy.

☆☆☆☆ **Grand Canyon**, an enormous channel enclosed by jagged, perpendicular mountains off Rum Point, is the favored north shore dive. The walls display a cornucopia of sponges, sea whips, sea fans, hard corals and critters. Depths start at 60 ft and drop off. Experience a must. Excellent visibility.

☆☆☆ **Japanese Gardens**, a series of long coral ridges off the island's south tip, blossom with elkhorn and antler corals, vase sponges and schooling fish. Depths start at 50 ft.

Snorkeling

Patch reefs and coral heads teeming with reef fish lie just a few yards off several of the island's swimming beaches. The best shore spots exist off West Bay Cemetery, Seven Mile Beach, the Eden Rock Dive Center in Georgetown, Smith Cove, Treasure Island Resort beach, Rum Point Club, Parrots Landing, Seaview Hotel, Coconut Harbour, Sunset House, Pirates Inn, Frank Sound Half Moon Bay, East End Diving Lodge and Morritt's Tortuga Club. Depths range from three to 20 ft. Clearer water and more dramatic coral formations are found farther offshore and may be reached by boat. Snorkeling cruises, some with dinner or lunch, are offered by the hotels and dive shops. Snorkelers are urged to inquire about currents and

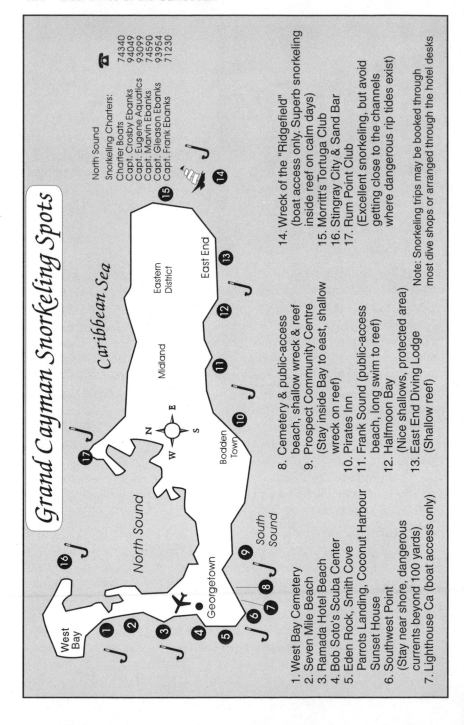

Grand Cayman Snorkeling Spots

Caribbean Sea

North Sound

South Sound

West Bay

Georgetown

Bodden Town

Midland

Eastern District

East End

North Sound
Snorkeling Charters:
Charter Boats   74340
Capt. Crosby Ebanks   94049
Capt. Eugene Aquatics   93099
Capt. Marvin Ebanks   74590
Capt. Gleason Ebanks   93954
Capt. Frank Ebanks   71230

1. West Bay Cemetery
2. Seven Mile Beach
3. Ramada Hotel Beach
4. Bob Soto's Scuba Center
5. Eden Rock, Smith Cove
   Parrots Landing, Coconut Harbour
   Sunset House
6. Southwest Point
   (Stay near shore, dangerous
   currents beyond 100 yards)
7. Lighthouse Ca (boat access only)

8. Cemetery & public-access
   beach, shallow wreck & reef
9. Prospect Community Centre
   (Stay inside Bay to east, shallow
   wreck on reef)
10. Pirates Inn
11. Frank Sound (public-access
    beach, long swim to reef)
12. Halfmoon Bay
    (Nice shallows, protected area)
13. East End Diving Lodge
    (Shallow reef)

14. Wreck of the "Ridgefield"
    (boat access only. Superb snorkeling
    inside reef on calm days)
15. Morritt's Tortuga Club
16. Stingray City & Sand Bar
17. Rum Point Club
    (Excellent snorkeling, but avoid
    getting close to the channels
    where dangerous rip tides exist)

Note: Snorkeling trips may be booked through
most dive shops or arranged through the hotel desks

local conditions in unfamiliar areas before attempting to explore on their own.

Swimmers off the Rum Point Club beach should stay clear of the channels, which have rip tides. Grand Cayman's Southwest Point shows a good variety of juvenile reef fish and invertebrates on a rocky bottom close to shore. Currents beyond 100 yds are dangerous.

A trail marked by a round blue and white sign with a swimmer outline denotes access through private property to the beach. All Cayman beaches are free for public use.

☆☆ **Smiths Cove,** south of George Town, shelters a shallow reef whiskered with pastel sea fans and plumes. Trumpet fish, squirrel fish, schools of grunts, sergeant majors, butterfly fish, parrot fish and angels offer constant entertainment. The reef sits 150 ft from the beach at Southwest Point. Depths are from 15 to 45 ft.

☆☆ **Eden Rocks,** favored by cruise ship groups, lies less than 200 yds offshore from the Eden Rock Diving Center. Depths range from five to 40 ft. The reef features beautiful coral grottoes, walls, caves and tunnels and tame fish. If you've yet to befriend a fish, this area offers the proper social climate. Good visibility and light currents are the norm here.

☆☆ **Sand Bar** at Stingray City in North Sound is home to several tame stingrays. Depths are shallow to 12 ft. Boat access. Trips departing from Georgetown or Seven Mile Beach are either a half- or full-day tour.

East End Diving

Grand Cayman's rural East End, 20 miles across the island from Seven Mile Beach, offers an entirely different dive-vacation setting. Devoid of shopping centers, traffic jams and commercial establishments, this wilderness region lures divers who relish a slower, laid back pace, uncrowded beaches and uncharted dive sites. Underwater terrain is similar to West Wall sites with fabulous walls, overhangs, caves, tunnels, grottos and remnants of ship-wrecks. There are no moorings.

Strong currents sometimes rule out a number of the sites in this area, but they greatly benefit the marine life by carrying nutrients that encourage the growth of gigantic, brilliant colored sponges and soft corals. Fish life is outstanding, with passing palegics, walls of tarpon, gigantic jewfish, eagle rays, green and hawksbill turtles. Whale sharks have been spotted here during winter.

Dive Operators

Costs for a two-tank dive average $60; one-tank dives, $45. Snorkeling trips range from $20 (Scuba Sensations) to $61 (Red Sail Watersports), with the average about $25. All the dive shops that offer boat tours have Stingray

City tours. These average $50 from the west coast. Most shops rent photo, video, dive and snorkeling gear. Trips include tanks and weights. Resort and certification courses are offered everywhere. Unless otherwise noted, shops accept American Express, MasterCard or Visa credit cards.

Ambassador Divers, a PADI shop located at Ambassadors Inn in George Town, specializes in computer diving. They offer one- and two-tank dives, certification and resort courses, snorkeling trips, gear rental, video rental, trips to Stingray City. Dive/accommodation packages. ☎ (800) 648-7748 or (345) 949-8839, fax (345) 949-8839. Write to P.O. Box 2396 GT, Grand Cayman, BWI.

Bob Soto's Diving Ltd. is a PADI five-star facility with Seven Mile Beach locations at the Treasure Island Hotel and the Scuba Centre, near to Soto's Reef. The operation offers dive and snorkeling trips, underwater photo and video services, camera and gear rentals, open water PADI certifications, completion dives, and comfortable custom dive boats. Complete dive/accommodation packages with Grand Cayman hotels and condominiums available. ☎ (800) 262-7686, (345) 949-2022, fax (345) 949-8731. Write to P.O. Box 1801, Grand Cayman, BWI.

Capitol's Surfside has been serving the Seven Mile Beach area for 28 years. Dive boats carry 20 divers. Courses and trips for scuba and snorkeling. All rentals. ☎ (800) 543-6828 or (345) 949-7330, fax (345) 949-8639.

Capt. Marvin's Aquatics' large boats carry 40 divers. Located in West Bay, this experienced dive operation offers scuba and snorkeling trips, Stingray City tours, courses and gear rental. ☎ (345) 945-4590, fax (345) 945-5673. Write to P.O. Box 413, West Bay, Grand Cayman, BWI.

Cayman Dive College specializes in teaching scuba. Courses are offered in English, German, French, Spanish or Japanese. Certification costs $375, resort course $94. ☎ (345) 949-4125, fax (345) 949-4125. Write to P.O. Box 30780, Seven Mile Beach, Grand Cayman, BWI.

Cayman Diving School offers courses ranging from Resort to Dive Master. ☎ (345) 949-4729, fax (345) 949-4729. Write to P.O. Box 1308, George Town, Grand Cayman, BWI.

Celebrity Divers in George Town features small, personalized tours with 10 or fewer divers on board. Snorkeling and Stingray City tours. ☎ (345) 949-3410. No credit cards.

Clint Ebanks Scuba Cayman Ltd. on West Bay Road offers certification and resort courses, one- and two-tank dive trips, Stingray City tours, and snorkeling trips. Gear rental. ☎ (345) 949-3873, fax (345) 949-6244.

Crosby Ebanks C & G Watersports at Coconut Place Tropic Center specializes in dive and snorkeling trips to Stingray City. ☎ (345) 945-4049, fax (345) 945-5994.

Dive Inn Ltd. greets divers and snorkelers with friendly, personalized service. Boats carry 12 passengers. Gear, photo and video rental. Certification and resort courses. ☎ (800) 322-0321 or (345) 949-4456, fax (345) 949-7125.

Dive 'N Stuff 's 12-passenger boats tour all the spots off Seven Mile Beach and offer special tours of Stingray City. PADI certification courses, gear rentals. ☎ (345) 949-6033, fax (345) 949-6033.

Divetech Ltd./Turtle Reef Divers features "the best shore dive at Turtle Reef" plus specialty and technical training. No boat trips. PADI and NAUI certification.

Dive Time Ltd. in Georgetown also has PADI and NAUI certification, one- and two-tank six-passenger boat dives, photo, video, snorkel and dive gear rental. ☎ (345) 947-2339, fax (345) 947-3308.

Divers Down, Georgetown, specializes in PADI nitrox certification courses ($250). Their custom, eight-passenger boat takes off for two one- or two-tank dive trips daily. Gear rentals. ☎ (345) 945-1611, fax 945-1611.

Don Foster's Dive Cayman, a full-service facility based at the Holiday Inn, Radisson Resort and Royal Palms on Seven Mile Beach, offers certification and resort courses, daily dives, rental and a photo center. Plus, snorkeling excursions, waverunners and sailboats. ☎ (800) 83-DIVER, or 972-722-2535, fax 972-722-6511 E-mail: dfdus@airmail.net.

Eden Rock Diving Center touts unlimited shore diving on GeorgeTown's waterfront, with guided tours of Eden Rocks Reef and Devil's Grotto. Certification with PADI, NAUI and SSI. Photo, video, dive and snorkel gear rentals. They sell underwater cameras, tropical T-shirts and gifts. ☎ (345) 949-7243, fax (345) 949-0842.

Fisheye of Cayman offers scuba tours aboard three custom dive boats to the north, west and south sides of the island, including Stingray City. Snorkelers may join dive trips to Stingray City and North Wall based on space availability. Trips include free use of underwater cameras. Accommodation packages. Web site: www.fisheye.com. E-mail: fisheye@candw.ky. ☎ (800) 887-8569, (345) 945-4209, fax (345) 945-4208.

Indies Divers at Indies Suites visits both North and West wall sites. Boats carry 12 divers. PADI certification and resort courses. Snorkelers welcome. Niceties include illustrated briefings, fresh fruit and towels.

Neptune's Realm Divers caters to small groups and individual divers with personalized tours and instruction. Boats carry a maximum of eight divers. PADI, NAUI, SSI and NASDS certification courses. ☎ (345) 945-2064.

Nitrox Divers, Georgetown, caters solely to Nitrox diving. Offering IANTD Nitrox certification courses ($250). Boat tours and dive gear rental. ☎ (345) 945-2064. Write to P.O. Box 959 GT, Grand Cayman, BWI.

Ocean Frontiers, Cayman's newest operation, offers East End diving. Snorkelers welcome on the 12-passenger boats. PADI courses. Gear and photo rentals. ☎ (345) 947-7500, fax (345) 947-7500.

Off the Wall Divers offer personalized dive/snorkeling tours. No credit cards. ☎ (345) 947-7790, fax (345) 947-7790.

Ollen Miller's Sun Divers on Seven Mile Beach features small groups, personalized service for divers and snorkelers. ☎ (345) 947-6606, fax (345) 947-6706.

Parrots Landing Watersports Park, a half-mile south of downtown Georgetown, has excellent shore diving on four beautiful, shallow reefs 30 yds from their dock and a wall dive 115 yds out. Seven 20-passenger dive boats visit the South Wall, West Wall and Northwest Point. A 60-ft sailing catamaran, *The Cockatoo*, sails from North Sound to Stingray City. Squid is provided for snorkelers to hand feed the rays. PADI and NAUI certifications. On shore, the park features picnic tables, sun deck and a half-dozen friendly Cayman parrots. Park shuttle boats and buses will pick you up anywhere along Seven Mile Beach. SSI and YMCA check-out dives. The park offers complete air/accommodation/dive packages with your choice of any hotel or condo on the island. ☎ (800) 448-0428 or (345) 949-7884. Write to P.O. Box 1995, Grand Cayman, BWI.

Peter Milburn's Dive Cayman Ltd. has been on the island for 18 years. Their 14-passenger boats make three dive/snorkel trips daily. Dive gear rental. No credit cards. ☎ (345) 945-5770, fax (345) 945-5786.

Quabbin Dives, located in Georgetown, offers a multilingual staff, PADI, NAUI and SSI courses. Large boats carry 30 divers and snorkelers. Gear and camera rentals. ☎ (345) 949-5597, fax (345) 949-4781.

Quabo Dives caters to small groups aboard their 20-passenger boats with personalized service for North Wall and West Wall dives.

Red Sail Sports, across from the Hyatt Regency and at the Westin Casuarina on Seven Mile Beach, offers dive and snorkeling trips, PADI certification courses and daily resort courses. Snorkel and dive trips, dinner sails and cocktail cruises. Waterskiing and parasailing. ☎ (800) 255-6425 or (345) 947-5965, fax (345) 947-5808.

Resort Sports Limited, at Beach Club colony and Spanish Bay Reef hotels, offers resort courses and PADI, NAUI or SSI certification. Camera and gear rentals for scuba and snorkeling. Night dives, Stingray City trips and snorkeling tours. ☎ (345) 949-8100, fax (345) 5167.

River Sport Divers Ltd. at the Coconut Place Shopping Center in West Bay, offers instruction and caters to all levels of divers. ☎ (345) 949-1181, fax (345) 949-1296.

Seasports picks up divers by boat at hotels and condos along Seven Mile Beach. Small groups. PADI, NAUI courses. Snorkelers welcome. ☎ (345) 949-3965.

Sunset Divers at Sunset House offers scuba instruction and dive packages, but is best known for its Underwater Photo Centre, operated by Cathy Church. The Centre offers 35mm and video camera rental, processing and photo instruction for all levels. Very informal and friendly with personalized service. ☎ (800) 854-4767 or (345) 949-7111, fax (345) 854-7101. Write to P.O. Box 479, Grand Cayman, BWI.

7-Mile Watersports tailors PADI courses to fit your needs. No boat trips. ☎ (345) 949-0332, fax (345) 949-0331.

Soto's Cruises, for advanced and certified divers, visits all the popular West Wall sites. ☎ (345) 945-4576, fax 945-1527. Write to P.O. Box 30192, Seven Mile Beach, Grand Cayman, BWI

Tortuga Divers Ltd., at the Morritt's Tortuga Club on the East End, operates two 34-foot custom dive boats that accommodate up to 14 passengers. The shop offers a nice range of services and courses for beginning divers and snorkelers. ☎ (345) 947-2097, fax (345) 947-9486.

Treasure Island Divers at the Treasure Island Resort, offers instruction, shore dives, snorkeling trips, sail cruises to all four sides of Grand Cayman. Their 45-foot boats have freshwater showers, marine heads and a sundeck that shades the bottom deck. Their first trip leaves at 8:00 am. ☎ (800) 872-7552 or (345) 949-4456, fax 954-351-9740. Write P.O. Box 30975 SMB, Grand Cayman, BWI.

Snorkel sails, glass-bottom boat rides, submarine rides, dinner cruises, fishing and more are booked through **Charter Boat Headquarters** in the Coconut Place Shopping Center on West Bay Road. ☎ (345) 947-4340.

Bayside Watersports is at Morgan's Harbour Marina, ☎ (345) 949-3200.

Atlantis Submarines takes up to 48 adventurous passengers wall diving in completely dry, air-conditioned, surface-pressure comfort. The 65-ft submarine plummets to depths of 150 ft as it explores the reef. Children must be at least four years old. Cost is $82 per person on trips with divers

Snorkeling, Sea Feather Bay, Cayman Brac.

outside that feed fish, $72 without divers. Half-price for children between four and 12 years old. ☎ (345) 949-7700.

Dive Resorts and Accommodations

Grand Cayman has accommodations and packages for every budget and every need. Every dive shop listed above offers a money-saving, dive accommodation package, some with air. For a complete list of guest houses, cottages and condos, contact the **Cayman Islands Department of Tourism**, 6100 Blue Lagoon Drive, Suite 150, Miami, FL 33126, ☎ (800) 346-3313 or (305) 266-2300, fax (305) 267-2932. *New York,* ☎ (212) 682-5582, fax (212) 986-5123. *United Kingdom,* ☎ 071-491-7771, fax 071-017-1409. *Canada,* ☎ (800) 263-5805 or (416) 485-1550, fax 416-485-7578. *Grand Cayman,* ☎ (345) 949-0623, fax (345) 949-4053. Web site: www.caymans .com.

Seven Mile Beach Resorts

Treasure Island Resort, a 25-acre beachfront luxury hotel, features 280 spacious air-conditioned rooms. All have ceiling fans, satellite TV, in-room safes and mini bars. Resort facilities include a well-equipped dive shop, gourmet restaurant, two freshwater pools, tennis and entertainment. Winter rates for a standard double room start at $220 per day. Summer, $155. ☎(800) 203-0775 or (345) 949-7777, fax (345) 949-8672. Call for current dive package rates.

Hyatt Regency offers 236 ultra-luxurious rooms, one- and two-bedroom villas, four pools, tropical gardens, adjacent golf course, gazebo-style swim-up bar. Winter rates start at $260 per day for a double. Summer, $185.

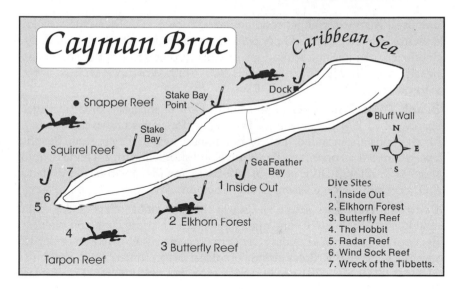

Red Sail Watersports is on the premises. Handicap accessible. ☎ (800) 233- 1234 or (345) 949-1234, fax (345) 949-8528. Major credit cards.

Holiday Inn allows children under 19 to stay free in a room with parents. Beachfront, dive shop on premises. Newly renovated. Handicap accessible. Winter $238, summer $178. Dive packages. ☎ (800) 421-9999 or (345) 945-4213. Major credit cards.

Radisson Resort, a huge 315-room luxury resort five minutes from town, features a pool, beach bar, restaurant and nightclub. Winter rates start at $215 per day for a double. Summer, $175. **Don Foster's Diving** on premises. All major credit cards. ☎ (800) 333-3333 or (345) 949-0088, fax (345) 949-0288.

Clarion Grand Pavilion Hotel features deluxe rooms starting at $160 in summer, $350 in winter. Resort amenities include two restaurants, two bars, a gym, jeep rentals, 24-hr room service. Dive shop nearby. Reef trips arranged at desk. ☎ (345) 945-5656, fax (345) 945-5353.

Westin Casuarina Resort offers 343 luxurious guest suites, all water sports—diving, snorkeling, fishing, windsurfing—restaurant, jacuzzi, pool, handicap access, tennis, photo centre, lush tropical grounds, and a lovely stretch of Seven Mile Beach. ☎ (800) 228-3000 or (345) 945-3800, fax (345) 949-5825. Write to P.O. Box 30620, Seven Mile Beach, Grand Cayman, BWI.

Georgetown Area

Ambassadors Inn, situated minutes from secluded Smith's Cove, has standard rooms for $80 in summer, $90 in winter. Ambassador Divers on premises. Rooms are all air conditioned with cable TV. Dive packages for a seven-night stay are $683 per person and include a two-tank dive daily. Snorkelers can join the scuba trips or walk 200 yds to a super snorkeling beach. ☎ (345) 949-7577, fax (345) 949-7050. Write to P.O. Box 1789, George Town, Grand Cayman, BWI.

Beach Club Colony, George Town, offers all-inclusive dive packages starting at $1,274 per person for five nights, four days of two-tank diving. Meals, transfers included. Lovely palm-lined beach. Restaurant. Resorts Sports Limited on premises offering dive and snorkeling trips. Tennis, photo shop. ☎ (800) 482-DIVE or (345) 949-8100, fax (345) 945-5167. Write to P.O. Box 903, George Town, Grand Cayman, BWI.

Coconut Harbour, south of Seven Mile Beach, offers suites with mini-kitchens, cabana bar and open air restaurant, shore diving on Waldo's Reef out front. Parrot's Landing Dive Shop on premises. Children under 12 stay free with parents. Rates include breakfast daily. Winter, $162. Summer, $135. ☎ (800) 552-6281 or (345) 949-7468, fax (345) 949-7117. Write to P.O. Box 2086 GT, Grand Cayman, BWI.

Indies Suites, a beachfront 41-suite hotel, features a pool, jacuzzi, bar, and handicap access. Apartments rent from $170 per day in summer, $225 in winter. Indies Divers on premises offers dive and snorkeling trips to Stingray City, the North and West Walls, gear rental. ☎ (800) 654-3130 or (345) 947-5025, fax (345) 947-5024.

Spanish Bay Reef Resort, an all-inclusive resort, includes room, meals, beverages, bicycles, scuba/snorkel lesson, snorkeling equipment, airport transfers, taxes and gratuities. Winter rates for three nights, two days of diving, double occupancy, are $684 per person. ☎ (800) 482-DIVE or (345) 949-3765, fax (345) 9491842. Write to P.O. Box 903, George Town, Grand Cayman, BWI.

Sleep Inn Hotel features standard and deluxe guest suites from $105 in summer, $175 in winter. Watersports can be arranged. ☎ (800) SLEEP-INN or (345) 949-9111, fax (345) 949-6699.

Sunset House, a 59-room resort owned and operated by divers for divers, sits south of Seven Mile Beach. Good diving from the beach! Room rates for a standard start at $110 in summer, $135 in winter. Packages for five nights, four days of two-tank diving and unlimited shore diving start at $662.50. ☎ (800) 854-4767 or (345) 949-7111, fax (345) 949-7101. Write to P.O. Box 479, George Town, Grand Cayman, BWI.

North Side

Cayman Kai Resort Ltd. features luxurious cottages, villas, and town houses, some air-conditioned, on the north side of Grand Cayman. Lodges have a living-dining area, kitchen and patio. One bedroom with one bath

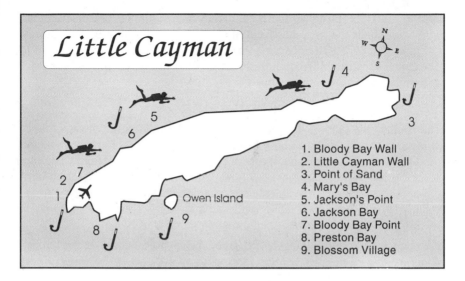

for two divers rents for $190 per day in winter, $150 in summer. Two bedrooms are $240 in winter, $190 in summer. A dive shop on the premises offers gear rentals and reef trips to the North Walls sites. ☎ (800) 223-5427 or (345) 947-7722.

East End

Cayman Diving Lodge offers 14 guest rooms, a club-like atmosphere, and all-inclusive dive or snorkeling packages. For divers, a five-night stay with three two-tank dives, three meals a day and accommodations runs $775 in summer, $840 in winter. Snorkelers join the dive trips, but may choose to explore the shallow reef in a protected lagoon off the resort's beach. Dive trips are more adventurous than in the Seven Mile Beach area. Expect some current, but with it comes a host of marine life and robust corals and sponges. Super for divers who prefer off-the-beaten-track vacations. ☎ (800) TLC-DIVE or (345) 947-7555, fax (345) 947-7560.

Morritt's Tortuga Club caters to those seeking luxurious oceanfront accommodations in a very private setting. The 121 air-conditioned suites feature kitchenettes, TV and phones. Pool, jacuzzi, restaurant, bar, laundry facilities and Tortugas Divers shop on premises offers five days of diving for $225. Room rates start at $145 in summer, $175 in winter. ☎ (800) 447-0309 or (345) 947-7449, fax (345) 947-7669. Write to P.O. Box 496-GT, East End, Grand Cayman, BWI.

Other Activities

Fishing, windsurfing, parasailing, and tennis are offered at most condos and resorts. An 18-hole, a nine-hole and a special Cayman course are located next to the Hyatt Regency Grand Cayman. On the latter, you use special lightweight balls that travel about half the distance of a normal ball. Grand Cayman's night clubs and larger hotels offer live entertainment and dancing. The Cayman National Theater presents live performances of drama, comedy and musicals.

Sightseeing

The capital city, George Town, has a well scrubbed look not always found in the Caribbean. Visitors can tour the area by foot, taxi, moped or rental car. Courtesy phones at the airport connect to the car rental dealers. Driving is on the left. Along George Town's waterfront several historic clapboard buildings have been lovingly restored and converted into souvenir shops, galleries and boutiques. Native crafts such as black coral and turtle shell jewelry along with imported goods may be purchased here.

Heading north along the famed Seven Mile Beach you come to the largest congregation of hotels, condos, shopping malls and restaurants. Each morning dive boats line up here and offer door-to-reef service to resort and condo guests.

A side trip to the Cayman Turtle Farm is always fun, as is a visit to Hell, the town where visitors delight in having mail postmarked to send back home.

Dining

Grand Cayman offers visitors an enormous variety of choices in dining. Shopping centers along West Bay Road house several fast food eateries such as **Burger King, Pizza Hut, Kentucky Fried Chicken** and **TCBY Yogurt.** For superb local specialties such as conch stew, curried chicken and native fish try the **Cracked Conch** by the sea on West Bay Road, **Myrtles** on N. Church St. or the **Almond Tree** on N. Church St. near George Town.

For more formal dining—all seafood—try the **Wharf**, waterfront on West Bay Road, ☎ 949-2231, **Seaharvest Restaurant** in front of Sunset House, ☎ 945-1383, **The Lobster Pot**, above Bob Soto's Dive shop, or **Ristorante Pappagallo** on West Bay Road, located in an exotic, modern thatched-hut-style building.

CAYMAN BRAC

Often called the loveliest of the islands, this 12-mile strip of land is rumored to be the resting place of pirates' treasure. Lying some 87 miles east of Grand Cayman, Cayman Brac's (*brac* is Gaelic for bluff) most striking feature is a 140-foot-high limestone formation covered by unusual foliage, including flowering cactus, orchids and tropical fruits such as mango and papaya. Rare species of birds, including the endangered green, blue and red

Caymanian parrot, inhabit the island, which is a major flyway for migratory birds. Resident brown booby birds soar the cliffs. Cayman Brac is also known for its many caves where pirates, in earlier centuries, took refuge and, according to legend, buried their treasures. In fact, a peg-legged turtle pirate is the country's national symbol. Native fir, palm and papaya trees shade the narrow streets. Fragrant thickets of bougainvilleas, hibiscus, periwinkle, and oleander surround the islanders' houses, many of which were built with wood salvaged from the wreckage of ships that crashed on the reefs. A visit to the Cayman Brac Museum in Stake Bay offers a look at the history of ship building on the island.

Activities other than diving and snorkeling are limited. There are a few restaurants scattered along the main road that also feature elevated caves with ladders for the tourists; Nims gift shop which offers fabulous hand-made woven bags, local crafts and post cards; and the main town area which has a convenience store, post office, gift shops and the island museum.

Best Dive and Snorkeling Sites of Cayman Brac

☆☆☆☆ **Wreck of the *Tibbetts*,** a 330-ft Russian destroyer built for the Cuban Navy, was renamed the Captain Keith Tibbets and deliberately sunk off the northwest coast of Cayman Brac on September 17, 1996. The vessel, the most exciting new dive attraction in the Cayman Islands, is easily accessible from shore, if you don't mind a 200-yd swim, but favored as a boat dive. All levels of divers may explore several swim-throughs, including the bridge and upper deck. Fore and aft cannons, missile launcher and machine gun turrets remain on the ship. Snorkelers may easily view the top of the radar tower at 12 feet and the bridge at 32 feet below the surface.

☆☆☆☆ **The Hobbit,** off the Brac's southeast tip, presents divers with a fairy tale setting of giant barrel sponges and dazzling corals inhabited by chubs, turtles, queen angels, octopi, grunts and queen triggerfish. Average depth runs 70 ft. Suggested for intermediate to advanced divers. Excellent visibility. Boat access.

☆☆☆☆ **Radar Reef** encompasses a series of coral pinnacles and canyons, each home to a splendid variety of elkhorn, star, and brain corals, lavender sea fans, tube and barrel sponges, feather dusters, and sea whips. Inhabitants of this lively community include turtles, sting rays, octopi, and swirls of tropicals. A normally calm surface and shallow depths—from 30 to 60 ft—make this a good choice for new divers. Boat access or swim out from the beach adjacent to Island Dock.

Cayman Brac Snorkeling

Several excellent shore-entry points exist off the north and south shores. Wind conditions determine which area is calm. Usually, if the north shore

Wreck of the Tibbetts.

spots are choppy, the south shore is calm. Check with area dive shops for daily conditions.

North Shore

☆☆☆☆ **WindSock Reef and the Wreck of the *Tibbetts*,** in White Bay off the northwest coast is the Brac's most popular snorkeling spot. The reef, which lies close to the shoreline, shelters elkhorn and brain coral patches while providing haven for a good variety of juveniles and tropicals. This spur and groove reef encircles gardens of elkhorn, pillar corals, sea fans, orange sponges and gorgonians. Angels, barracuda, butterfly fish, file fish, trumpet fish and critters hide in the ledges and crevices. Expect good visibility and usually calm seas. Typical inhabitants are stoplight parrot fish, blue tangs, midnight parrot fish, sergeant majors, turtles, grey angels, grunts, trumpet fish and triggerfish. Shore area depths range from four to 20 ft.

The mast of the *Tibbetts'* wreck breaks the surface and is easily spotted from the beach. Some prefer snorkeling the wreck, which lies 200 yds offshore, from a boat; but if you're in good shape, you can swim out. The top of the wreck lies 12 ft below the surface. See scuba section for details. Check with area dive shops before venturing out. Visibility usually 100 ft or better.

To reach White Bay, travel the North Shore Rd (A6) west from the airport to Promise Lane. Turn left. The beach entry point is behind the closed Buccaneer Inn Hotel.

☆☆ **Stake Bay**. Find this spot by turning off the North Shore Rd at the Cayman Brac Museum. Reef terrain, depths and fish life are similar to White Bay. Sea conditions usually calm, but will kick up when the wind is out of the North.

☆☆ **Creek** lies off the north shore. A turn towards the shore from Cliff's Store on the North Shore Rd (A6) will lead to the Island Dock. Enter from the beach area left of the dock, facing seaward. Dense patches of elkhorn predominate. Depths are shallow to 30 ft. Angels, small turtles, and sergeant majors swarm the reef. Wind speed and direction determines the conditions, though seas are usually calm with a light current.

Additional entry points are found at the boat launching areas where cuts through the dense coral have been blasted. Parking is available along the north road.

South Shore

☆☆ **Sea Feather Bay**, located off the South Shore Rd at the Bluff Rd crossing, provides haven for pretty wrasses, turtles, blue parrot fish, grouper, indigo hamlets, squirrelfish, porkfish, blue tangs, and rockfish. Reef terrain comprises long stretches of dense elkhorn interspersed with tube sponges, fire coral, rose coral and gorgonians. After a big storm, this area becomes a wash-up zone for some strange cargo such as rubber doll parts and unusual bottles which may come from Cuba. Expect some surge and shallow breakers. Visibility good, though silt may churn up the shallows following a storm.

Experienced snorkelers may want to dive the barrier reef at the south western tip of the island. Water entry is best by boat, but if you enjoy a long swim you can get out to the reef from either the public beach or one of the hotel beaches.

Cayman Brac Dive Operators and Accommodations

Brac Aquatics offers courses, reef tours and gear rentals. ☎ (345) 948-1429, fax (345) 948-1527.

Brac Reef Beach Resort and Reef Divers has comfortable air conditioned rooms with satellite TV, a great beach, fresh water pool, whirlpool, beach bar and restaurant. Complete dive/accommodation packages start at $888 in summer, $1,246 in winter, for five nights, three meals daily, three one-tank dives per day, ground transfers and bicycles. Unlimited beach dives. ☎ (800) 327-3835 or (813) 323-8727, fax (345) 948-1207. Dive shop (345) 948-1323, fax 948-1207. E-mail: refz79a@ prodigy.com. Write to P.O. Box 56, Cayman Brac, BWI.

Brac Caribbean Beach Village offers 16 condo units from $143 per day. Each unit has two bedrooms, air conditioning, ceiling fan and telephone. Beachfront. ☎ (800) 791-7911 or (345) 948-2265, fax (345) 948-2206.

Brac Haven Villas has six, one-bedroom condos that rent from $180 per day. ☎ (345) 948-2478, fax (345) 948-2329. Write to P.O. Box 89, Stake Bay, Cayman Brac, BWI.

Divi Tiara Beach Hotel and Peter Hughes Dive Tiara cater almost exclusively to divers and snorkelers. This first-class resort features a freshwater pool, jacuzzi, tennis, 71 spacious, air-conditioned rooms, auto rentals, sailboards, bicycles and paddleboats. Snorkeling and diving are found right off the resort's palm-lined beach. Dive Tiara spares no effort to make every dive trip relaxing, safe and fun aboard any one of six custom-designed dive boats. The shop offers tours to the best dives of Cayman Brac as well as Little Cayman daily. A seasoned boat crew readily assists divers with gear set-ups and getting in and out of the water. There's no need to lug your gear back and forth to your room; it stays overnight in a gear storage room on Tiara's dive pier. Room rates based on a double are $95 in summer, $125 in winter. One-tank dives are $25, two-tank, $50. Package rates available. ☎ (800) 367-3484 or (919) 419-3484, fax (919) 419-2075. Write to Divi Resorts, 6340 Quadrangle Drive, Suite 300, Chapel Hill, NC 27514.

La Esperanza offers two-bedroom condos and three-bedroom condos from $70 in summer, $110 in winter.

There are other facilities such as "**Soon Come**," a charming modern two-bedroom, beachfront, reef-front house for rent on the isolated south shore. ☎ (212) 447-0337, fax (212) 447-0335.

LITTLE CAYMAN

Populated by fewer than 70 people, Little Cayman retains a rural and unhurried ambiance. Its grass runway, unpaved roads and limited phone service attest to its long-standing reputation as a great get-away vacation spot. Activities include diving, snorkeling, fly fishing and counting iguanas. When you visit Little Cayman, keep in mind that there are no stores. Items such as aspirin, mosquito repellent, decongestants, and suntan lotion should be packed from home. Few accommodations offer air conditioning.

Best Dives of Little Cayman

☆☆☆☆☆ **Bloody Bay Wall** is one of the top five dives in all the Caymans. The "Wall" peaks as a shallow reef at 15 ft and drops off to an unfathomed bottom. Bright orange and lavender tube sponges, pastel gorgonians and soft corals flourish in the shallows. An extremely friendly six-foot barracuda named Snort may join your dive—flashing his pearly whites while cheerfully posing for videos and still photos. Eagle rays blast by the wall along with slow-moving turtles and huge parrot fish. Spotted morays peek from the walls. Sea conditions are usually calm, although a stiff wind will churn the surface. Divers of all levels will enjoy diving Bloody Bay Wall. Super snorkeling in the shallows. Boat access.

☆☆☆☆ **Little Cayman Wall**, off the island's west end, starts shallow with a blaze of yellow, orange and blue sponges at 15 ft, then drops off to unknown depths. Soft corals, big barrel sponges decorate the wall. Great for snorkeling and diving. Boat access.

Snorkeling

Little Cayman offers several superb snorkeling spots with visibility often exceeding 100 ft. Ground transportation to beach-access sites is easily arranged through the dive operators. For the ultimate in free diving head out to Bloody Bay and Spot Bay off the north shore, where the seas are calm and the marine life spectacular. The boat ride takes about 25 minutes. Average depth on top of the North Wall is 25 ft.

Note: The Western half of the wall is called the "Bloody Bay Wall" and the eastern half "Jackson Wall."

☆☆☆ **Point of Sand,** off the southeast end of Little Cayman, is excellent for experienced and beginning snorkelers. A gentle current flowing from west to east maintains very good visibility. The bottom is sandy with many coral heads scattered about. Marine life is fine and the site is accessible from the shore. Ground transportation can be arranged from the resorts.

☆☆☆ Good snorkeling for beginners at **Mary's Bay** starts 50 yds from the beach—inside the barrier reef. There is no current and visibility runs about 30 to 50 ft. A host of fish and invertebrates are found in the shallows. Depth averages three to eight ft. The bottom is turtle grass, requiring booties or other submersible footwear. An old shack on an otherwise deserted shore marks the spot.

☆☆ **Jackson Point**, aka School Bus, is for experienced snorkelers only. Swim out about 75 yds from the beach, where you'll see a small wall towering from a sandy bottom at 40 ft to 15 ft. Hundreds of fish, rays and turtles congregate in the shallows. Corals and sponges carpet the area. Swimming another 50 to 60 ft brings you to a much larger wall that drops off to extraordinary depths.

☆☆ **Jackson Bay** resembles Jackson Point except for the bottom of the mini-wall, which drops off to a depth of 50 to 60 ft. Beach access.

☆☆☆ **Bloody Bay Point,** recommended for seasoned snorkelers, requires a 100-yd swim out to the reef. The bottom eases down to about

30 ft before the drop-off to The Great Wall begins. Well worth a visit for the spectacular coral and marine life.

☆ **Preston Bay**, just east of the lighthouse, provides another good shore-entry choice for beginning snorkelers. Maximum shoreline depth is six ft and visibility 30 to 50 ft. Swarming fish and a white sandy bottom offer endless photo opportunities.

☆☆ **Blossom Village,** a lovely, shallow reef, displays crowds of reef fish and critters amidst staghorn and brain corals at depths from four to eight ft. Boat access. A light current maintains 50-100 ft visibility.

Little Cayman Dive Operators and Accommodations

Little Cayman dive operations are smaller than those on Cayman Brac and Grand Cayman.

Little Cayman Beach Resort features air-conditioned rooms, fresh water pool, jacuzzi, cabana bar, tennis, restaurant, and a full-service dive/photo operation. Windsurfers, sailboats and bicycles. Rates per person for a double, including three meals and three one-tank dives daily, are $1,179 in summer, $1,288 winter. Lower rates for non-divers. ☎ (800) 327-3835 or (813) 323-8727, fax (813) 323-8827.

Southern Cross Club, a fishing and diving resort comprised of five double cottages, warmly welcomes divers. Divemasters will take you to all the top dive and snorkel sites on Bloody Bay Wall or South Shore. Snorkelers mix with scuba groups. IANTD Nitrox facility. Resort courses are available. ☎(800) 899-2582 or (345) 948-1098 or in the United States (317) 636-9501. Write to Southern Cross Club, Little Cayman, Cayman Islands, BWI. E-mail: scc@candw.ky. Web site http://scubacentral.com/scc.html.

Sam McCoy's Diving and Fishing Lodge, on the north shore, offers rustic accommodations for up to 14 divers (seven rooms). Rooms in the main lodge are air-conditioned with private bath. Twenty-ft fiberglass runabouts are used for reef trips. Shore diving from Jackson's Point. Rates per day start at $159 per person and include all diving, three meals per day, all transportation. Dive packages available. ☎ (800) 626-0496 or (345) 948-0026, fax (345) 948-0057. Or write to Carl McCoy, P.O. Box 711, Georgetown, Grand Cayman, BWI.

Pirates Point Resort features rustic guest cottages and a guest house on seven acres of secluded white beach. Owner Gladys Howard offers friendly service, all-inclusive dive packages from $195 per person summer, $215 winter, per day. ☎ (800) 327-8777 or (345) 948-1010, fax (345) 948-1011.

Cayman Live-Aboards

The Cayman Aggressor III. Based in George Town, this luxury yacht features double staterooms and one quad which holds 18 passengers, along with a salon, carpeting, E-6 film processing, air-conditioning, TV, video equipment and hot showers. Nitrox, rebreather rentals and courses. Enjoyable meals, including soups and salads, chicken, turkey, native fish and snacks, are prepared on board. Packages cover transfers, meals, diving, tanks, backpacks and weights. Prices are commensurate with those of Cayman land resorts. Write to Aggressor Fleet, PO Drawer 1470, Morgan City, LA 70381. Week-long tours range from $1,495 to $1,695. ☎ (800) 348-2628, fax (504) 384-0817. E-mail: divboat@aol.com or 103261.1275 @compuserve.com. Web site: www.aggressor.com.

Little Cayman Diver II offers week-long tours to the reefs and walls surrounding Little Cayman. All-inclusive rates range from $1,395 to $1,595 with occasional specials as low as $1,295. The yacht is 90 ft long and accommodates from 10 to 12 passengers in five cabins. Each cabin is the width of the boat, has air-conditioning and sits above the water line. Offers unlimited, unstructured 24-hour diving. ☎ (800) 458-2722 or (813) 932-1993. Write to P.O. Box 280058, Tampa, FL 33682.

Facts

Nearest Recompression Chamber: George Town. This chamber is operated and staffed 24 hours a day by the British Sub-Aqua Club. ☎ 555 for help.

Getting There: Cayman Airways provides scheduled flights from Miami, Houston, Atlanta, Tampa and Orlando to Grand Cayman with connecting flights to Cayman Brac and Little Cayman. Northwest, United, American and Air Jamaica fly nonstop from gateway cities into Grand Cayman. During peak season (Dec 15-April 15) charter flights direct from many major snowbelt cities to Grand Cayman are available from Cayman Airways. Flight time from Miami is 1½ hrs. Grand Cayman is a regular stop on many cruise lines as well.

Island Transportation: Rental cars, motorbikes, and bicycles are available on Grand Cayman and Cayman Brac. Friendly and informative taxi drivers are stationed at hotels and other convenient locations.

Driving: As in England, driving in the Cayman Islands is on the left. A temporary license is issued for a few dollars to persons holding US, Canadian or international licenses.

Documents: Proof of citizenship and an outbound ticket (birth certificate, voter's registration certificate) are required from US, British, or Canadian citizens. No vaccinations are required unless you are coming from an epidemic area.

Customs: The penalties for trying to bring drugs into the Cayman Islands are stiff fines and, frequently, prison terms. No spearguns or Hawaiian slings permitted into the country.

Currency: The Cayman Island Dollar, equal to US $1.20.

Climate: Temperatures average about 80° F year-round. The islands are subject to some rainy periods, but generally sunny and diveable.

Clothing: Casual, lightweight clothing. Some nightclubs require that men wear a jacket. Wetskins or shorty wetsuits are useful to avoid abrasions, as are light gloves for protection against the stinging corals. Snorkelers should wear protective clothing against sunburn.

Electricity: 110 volts AC, 60 cycles. Same as US.

Time: Eastern Standard Time year-round.

Tax: There is a 6% government tax on accommodations. A service charge of 10-15% is added to hotel and restaurant bills. Departure tax is US $10.

Religious Services: Catholic, Protestant, Baptist, Mormon and non-denominational churches are found on Grand Cayman.

Additional Information: *United States*: The Cayman Islands Department of Tourism, 6100 Blue Lagoon Drive, Suite 150, Miami, FL 33126-2085. ☎ (800) G-CAYMAN, (305) 266-2300, fax (305) 267-2932. *New York*: 420 Lexington Ave, Suite 2733, New York, NY. ☎ (212) 682-5582, fax (212) 986-5123. *United Kingdom:* 6 Arlington Street, London, SW1A 1RE United Kingdom. ☎ 171-491-7771, fax 0171-409-7773. *The Cayman Islands: Box 67, Grand Cayman, Cayman Islands, BWI.* ☎ (345) 949-0623, fax (345) 949-4053. Web site: www.caymans.com.

Cozumel & Akumal

COZUMEL

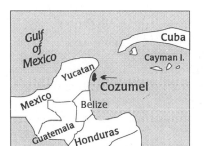

Cozumel, Mexico's largest island and top Caribbean dive destination, lies 12 miles off the Yucatán Peninsula, separated by a 3,000-ft-deep channel. Dense jungle foliage covers most of this island's interior, but its surrounding coast welcomes visitors with miles of luxuriant, white sand beaches.

Topside tourist activity centers around San Miguel, the island's cultural and commercial center, which boasts an impressive seaside maze of shops, cantinas and restaurants. An ultra-modern cruise-ship terminal accom- modates daily-arriving ocean liners and ferries from the mainland. Most dive resorts are scattered along the west coast where calm waters prevail.

A 1961 visit by Jacques Cousteau first brought attention to Cozumel's spectacular diving and its incredible water clarity. Its fringing reef system is fed by warm, fast-moving Yucatán currents (a part of the Gulf Stream) as they sweep through the deep channel on the west side of the island. These currents bring a constant wash of plankton and other nutrients that support thousands of exotic fish. Immense rays, and jewfish populate the spectacular drop-offs and wrecks on the outer reefs; sea turtles nest along the beaches from May to September. And, visibility remains a constant 100 to 150 ft year-round, except during and after major storms.

Despite an onslaught of divers, Cozumel's reefs and marine life are better than ever. Once a mecca for spear fishermen, all of the reefs surrounding the island are now protected as a marine park. Those of you who may remember the dive operators' requests for qualifications being "You dive before?" will now be asked for C cards. A functional, free-to-divers recompression chamber is now in operation.

When to Go

The best time to visit Cozumel is from Dec to June. Water and air temperatures average 80° F year-round with hotter conditions in summer. Summer and fall often bring heavy rains or hurricanes.

History

Cozumel was first inhabited by the Maya Indians, who settled as early as 300 AD. They named it "Ah-Cuzamil-Peten," place of the swallows. Remains of their temples and shrines still can be found.

During the 1800's Cozumel was a busy seaport stopover for ships carrying chicle (used to make gum) from Central America to North America.

Best Dives of Cozumel

Most tours include a shallow dive on the inner reef and a drift dive along the outer wall. Currents on the drift dives vary with the weather from very mild to too-strong-to-stop-for-a-photograph. The dive boat drops you off at one end of the reef, then follows your bubbles as you drift with the current to a predetermined point where you surface to rendezvous with the boat. Note: a maximum depth of 120 ft is enforced by the dive operators. Novice divers may wish to avoid the strong currents associated with drift diving and stick to the inner reefs.

☆☆☆☆☆ The **Palancar National Park Reef** complex, off the southwestern tip of the island, encompasses more than three miles of winding tunnels and coral canyons. Its most prominent feature is a 12-ft bronze statue of Christ, created by sculptor Enrique Miralda to commemorate the first Catholic Mass said on the island. The statue stands in 40 ft of water at the north end of the reef known as Big Horseshoe. Depths on the inner reef range from 30 to 60 ft. Visibility exceeds 100 ft. The drop-off on the reef's outer wall is laced with immense coral arches and tunnels—shelter to huge crabs, lobster and all types of morays. Vibrant growths of tree-sized sea fans, yellow and lavender tube sponges, barrel sponges, giant sea whips and pink-tipped anemones adorn the walls.

Huge towering coral pinnacles on the south end of Palancar provide excellent photo and video opportunities. Fish are abundant, with gigantic parrot fish and groupers, schools of pork fish and grunts everywhere. Many of the groupers are tame and may be hand fed. At depth you'll find a profusion of black coral.

☆☆☆☆ **San Francisco Reef** offers underwater photographers a kaleidoscope of seascapes with an array of pastel gorgonians and sea fans, vase and barrel sponges, coral arches, caves and tunnels. Usually a drift dive, with huge angels, rays, groupers, and sea turtles greeting you along the way. Depths along the reef ledge are from 20 ft to 70 ft. The wall then drops off to channel depths. Visibility is excellent—usually 150 ft.

☆☆☆ **Paraiso Reef North** is a popular shallow dive just north of the cruise ship pier in San Miguel. The reef is accessible by swimming straight out 200 yds from the beach at the Hotel Sol Caribe or by dive boat. The

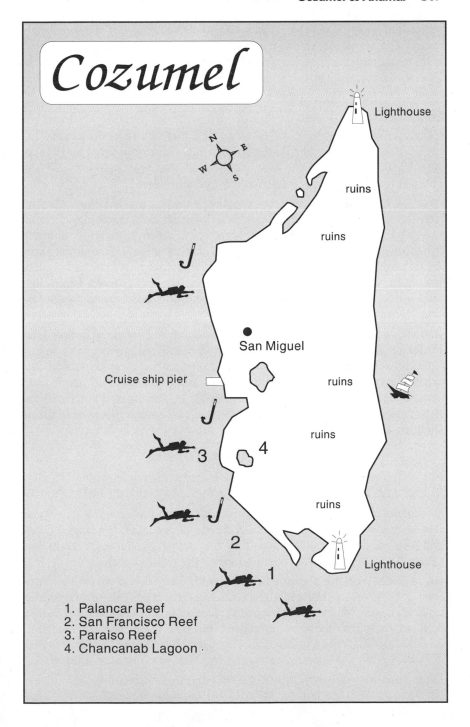

Cozumel

Lighthouse

ruins

ruins

San Miguel

Cruise ship pier

ruins

ruins

3

4

ruins

2

1

Lighthouse

1. Palancar Reef
2. San Francisco Reef
3. Paraiso Reef
4. Chancanab Lagoon

remains of a twin engine airplane, sunk intentionally as part of a movie set, rest at 30 ft, creating a home for a vast array of fish life. Huge green morays, eagle rays, turtles, yellowtail, French angels, schools of pork fish, butterfly fish, and queen trigger fish may be found. The reef is a good choice for novice divers.

Snorkeling

Good snorkeling may be found all along Cozumel's east coast beaches. The reefs off the beaches at both the **Scuba Club Galapago Resort** and **Playa San Francisco** have some nice stands of elkhorn and brain coral with a constant show of juvenile tropicals and invertebrates.

☆☆☆ **Chancanab Lagoon**, south of the cruise ship pier at Laguna Beach, is protected from wind and waves. Ideal for snorkeling, depths range from very shallow to about 30 ft. Schools of grunts, angel fish, damsel fish, trumpet fish, turtles, and snapper dart between the clumps of coral. Seafans and soft corals adorn the reef. Visibility runs about 75 ft, sometimes better. Snorkeling gear may be rented from shops on the beach. Changing rooms, freshwater showers and lockers are available. Small admission fee. A botanical garden and restaurant are on the premises.

A pretty snorkeling-depth reef aprons the south end of neighboring **Isla Mujeres**. Enter from the shore at Playa Garrafon, four miles from town. This spot—El Garrafon ("the carafe")—is one of the most populated (by fish and swimmers) in the Caribbean. Just wade out from the beach with some cracker crumbs and you'll immediately be surrounded by crowds of friendly fish. Ideal for first-time snorkelers. The beach has a dive shop, showers, refreshment stands & shops.

Dive Operators

NOTE: To telephone or fax any of the Mexican listings from the US, dial 011 52 + 987 + the five digit number. In Mexico just dial the last five digits.

Most of the dive shops offer three- to seven-day, reduced-rate dive packages. Before forking over your money, ask if refunds are given for missed dives and whether you can get that in writing. Some divers prefer to pay each day rather than risk missing the boat and losing the price of a trip.

Aqua Safari, on the ocean at 5th St. South, offers drift dives on Palancar Reef, night dives, rentals and repairs. Custom dive boats can accommodate up to 20 divers. Multilingual dive guides. Expect to dive with a crowd during high season and to carry your own gear. ☎ (011) 52-987-20101, fax (011) 52-987-20661. Write to: P.O. Box 41, Cozumel, Quintana Roo, Mexico 77600. E-mail: dive@aquasafari.com. Web site: www.aquasafari.com.

Blue Bubble Divers offers sunset dives, wreck and reef dives. Dive/accommodation packages from $400. Guides are friendly and helpful.

Photo by Jon Huber

Drift Dive, Palancar Reef.

Good briefings. Punctual. ☎ (800) 878-8853, (011) 52-987-21865, fax (011) 52-987-21865. Write to 5th Ave. South, Cozumel Quintana Roo, Mexico 77600. E-mail: bubbles@cozunet.finred.com.mx. Web site:www.gssolutions.com/bluebubble.

Caribbean Divers International visits Palancar, Santa Rosa and Maracaibo reefs. Dive as a group. No computers. NAUI, PADI and PDIC courses. Bilingual staff. ☎ (800) 874-7312, (011) 52-987-21080, fax (011) 52-987-21426. Packages through Pied Piper. ☎ (800) 874-7312. E-mail: caridive@cozumel.czm.com.mx. Write to Box 191, Cozumel, Quintana Roo, Mexico 77600.

Del Mar Aquatics offers courses, trips, services. Dive/accommodation packages offered. Two boats carry 30 divers each. Expect crowds. ☎ (800) 877-4383, (011) 52-987-21833, fax (011) 52-987-21833. Write to P.O. Box 129, Cozumel, Quintana Roo, Mexico 77600.

DIMI Educational Dive Center features all the best reef dives plus cave and cavern diving. Nitrox. Boats carry eight divers. Four night hotel/dive packages from $175 per person. ☎ (011) 52-987-22915, fax (011) 52-987-23964. E-mail: dimidive@cozumel.czm.com.mx. Write to Av. Rafael Melgar #45-B, Cozumel, Quintana Roo, Mexico.

Dive Palancar at the Diamond Resort has trips aboard a 44-ft custom dive boat to Palancar and Santa Rosa plus inland cenote (cave and cavern) dives.

Beach diving tours. Dive and snorkeling courses. Seven-night hotel/dive packages from $1,000. English-speaking guides. Boats on time. Fine service. ☎ (800) 247-3483, (011) 52-987-23443, ext. 895.

Dive Paradise offers personalized tours for divers and snorkelers. Boats carry a maximum of seven divers. Nitrox available. Computers are required if you want to join their "experienced diver program." Snorkelers may join trips for $30. Shaded boats. ☎ (011) 52-987-21007, fax (011) 52-987-21061. E-mail: applep@cozumel.czm.com.mx. Web site: www.dparadise.com. Write to 601 Melgar, Cozumel, Quintana Roo, Mexico 77600. Hotel/dive packages from $1,099 for seven nights are offered by Landfall Productions. ☎ (800) 525-3833. E-mail: lndfall@aol.com.

Dive With Martin offers punctual, personalized tours to sites around the entire island perimeter. Small groups on fast boats plus excellent service makes this operation very popular. Write to 601 Melgar, Cozumel, Quintana Roo, Mexico 77600. ☎ (281) 859-0700, (011) 52-987-22610, fax (281) 859-7720, (011) 52-987-21340. Three days diving for $150. E-mail: dwm@flash.nte. Web site: www.flash.net/~dwm.

Diving Adventures tours the reefs from San Miguel down to Santa Rosa. Packages for three nights with two days of diving from $250. ☎ (888) 338-0388, (011) 52-987-23009. E-mail: diventur@cozumel.czm.com.mx. Write to Calle 5 #2 Cozumel, Quintana Roo, Mexico 77600.

Marine Sports offers hotel/dive packages with the Fiesta Inn from $247 for three nights, two days diving. Boats tour Palancar Underwater Park. ☎ (800) FIESTA-1, (011) 52-98722899, fax (011) 52-987-22154.

Nitrox Solutions offers IANTD and PADI Nitrox certifications to all levels. Their spacious training facility and Nitrox fill station is equipped with the latest in training materials and the DNAx Membrane System from Undersea Breathing Systems in Florida. (DNAx is considered by many to be the most advanced system to date.) In-town, Calle 3 and the Waterfront—two doors from the Bahia Hotel. ☎ (800) 967-1333 or (011) 52-967-5666. E-mail: nitrox@cozumel.czm.com.mx. Web site:www.islacozumel.net/diving/ nitrox.

Papa Hogs Scuba Emporium, San Miguel, visits the southern sites, Barracuda Reef. ☎ (800) 780-3949, (011) 52-987-21651, fax (011) 52-987-21651. E-mail: diving@papahogs.com. Web site: www.papahogs.com.

Scuba Cozumel, a five-star PADI Dive Center and first-class operation, visits Palancar National Park aboard comfortable custom boats carrying four to 12 divers. Forty-three-ft catamarans carry bigger groups. No crowds. Dive/hotel packages with Scuba Club Dive Resort (formerly the Galapagos Inn) through Landfall Productions are from $739 for seven nights including five, two-tank boat trips, all meals and unlimited beach dives. ☎ (800) 525-3833 or (800) 847-5708. E-mail: lndfall@aol.com.

Scuba Du at the Hotel Stouffer Presidente offers personalized dive tours, small groups, Nitrox and fast, custom boats. Dive-hotel packages. ☎ (011) 52-987-21379, fax (011) 52-987-24130. Write to P.O. Box 137, Cozumel, Quintana Roo, Mexico 77600.

Cozumel Accommodations

NOTE: To telephone or fax any of the Mexican listings from the US, dial 01152 + 987 + the five digit number.

Hotel Presidente Inter-Continental, two miles south of town at the Chancanab Lagoon, features a large pool, tennis, restaurants, entertainment and dive packages with Scuba Du. Rates for hotel and diving for two start at $233 per person, per day, for hotel, breakfast buffet, daily two-tank dive. Good snorkeling off the beach. ☎ (800) 346-6116 or (800) 298-9009.

Casa Del Mar an affordable dive resort across the street from the beach, offers 196 air-conditioned rooms, telephones, on-site dive shop, snorkeling reef in front of hotel, sand beach, shopping arcade, gardens, pool, and restaurant. The hotel's bar is built from salvaged shipwrecks. Accommodation rates start at under $60 per night for a single or a double. ☎ (800) 435-3240 or (011) 52-987-21900. Web site: www.iminet.com/mexico/coz202.html.

Diamond Resort, located 10 minutes from the best reefs, is a first-class, all-inclusive dive resort. On site, Dive Palancar provides PADI five-star services and a choice of five daily dive-trip departure times. Resort features 350 deluxe rooms, children's program, good restaurants, pool and a variety of watersports and activities for adults and kids. Per-person rates for seven nights and five days of diving are from $994 off-season. In-season rates are from $744 for three nights. All rates includes three meals per day. ☎ (800) 433-0885, (011) 52-987-23443, fax (011) 52-987-24508 or (713)-680-2306. E-mail: divetours@aol.com. Web site: www.dsi-divetours.com.

Fiesta Inn Cozumel offers 180 clean, air-conditioned deluxe rooms—all with satellite color TV, telephones, balconies, purified drinking water, large swimming pool, jacuzzi, tennis court, karaoke bar and Cafe La Fiesta, which serves delicious Mexican and international dishes. Snorkeling is available off the resort beach. High-season dive packages through Landfall Productions start at $619 per diver, ($375 for non-diver) and include seven nights accommodations, five two-tank boat dives with Dive Paradise, complimentary welcome beach tank on day of arrival, snacks and beverages on dive days. ☎ (800) 525-3833. E-mail: lndfall@aol.com. Direct ☎ (800) FIESTA-1 or (011) 52-987-22899, fax (011) 52-987-22154.

Fiesta Americana Cozumel Reef features 172 deluxe ocean- and reef-view rooms and four parlor suites with color, satellite TV, private terraces, room service. On-site scuba shop, Dive House Cozumel, visits all the best southwest sites. Amenities include two lighted tennis courts, fax service, equipment storage lockers, custom charters, gym and jogging trail, two restaurants, gift shop, poolside snack bar car, bike and moped rentals and purified water. Night dives and snorkeling trips. Money-saving dive-hotel packages through Landfall. ☎ (800) 525-3833, E-mail lndfall@aol.com. Hotel direct, ☎ (800) FIESTA-1 or (011) 52-987-22622, fax (011) 52-987-22666. Web site: www.fiestamexico.com.

Paradisus Cozumel (formerly known as the Melia Mayan Paradisus) sits on Cozumel's longest stretch of natural beach. Located 2½ miles from town on the northeast side of the island, this all-inclusive hotel offers air-conditioned deluxe ocean-view and garden-view rooms with terraces, remote control satellite TV, telephone with international dialing. King-size or two double beds. For diving and snorkeling trips, guests must travel to the Paradisus Beach & Dive Club on the southern side of the island. Beach Club features restaurants, dive shop, training pool, changing rooms, lockers, showers and a variety of non-motorized and motorized water sports, plus horseback riding. Hotel guests receive complimentary use of non-motorized sports equipment—kayaks, Sailfish, wind surfers and "spyaks." Lunch for guests is no charge. ☎ 888-341-5993, (011) 52-987-20411, fax (011) 52-987-21599. E-mail: paradisu@cancun.rce. com.mx.

Plaza Las Glorias, within walking distance of San Miguel, is a charming four-story, pueblo-style 170-room resort. Air-conditioned rooms have balconies or patios. Features include a dive shop, boutique, two restaurants, pool and ocean views. Room rates are from $120 to $175. ☎ (800) 342-AMIGO or (011) 52-987-22000, fax (011) 52-987-21937.

Scuba Club Galapago (formerly the Galapago Inn) is both casual and elegant, with thatch-roofed huts lining the beach, a pool with three mosaic sea turtles, air-conditioned rooms (each with a refrigerator and spacious closet), gourmet dining and an on-site dive shop. Just offshore is a nice snorkeling reef. The inn operates five roomy dive boats, and offers photography and scuba courses, E-6 film processing and professional service. Write to Aqua-Sub Tours, PO Box 630608, Houston, TX 77263. ☎ (800) 847-5708; fax 713-783-3305. Good dive-hotel packages through Landfall ☎ (800) 525-3833. Web site: www.galapago.com.

Villablanca Garden Beach Hotel, located in front of Paradise Reef, features 50 air-conditioned rooms and suites with phones, sunken tubs, ceiling fans and refrigerators. Pool, white sand beach. Divers picked up at hotel's private pier. Dive/hotel packages from $490 include seven nights accommodations, five two-tank dives with Dive Paradise, complimentary

snacks and beverages on dive trips. ☎ (800) 525-3833 or 510-794-1599.
E-mail: lndfall@aol.com.

Sightseeing and Other Activities

Diving and sport fishing are the main activities on Cozumel, followed by
wind surfing, jetskiing, and water-skiing, which are offered by the resorts.
The widest range of watersports rentals are at **Playa San Francisco**.

San Miguel's main tourist areas are **Plaza del Sol**—where you'll find cafés,
craft shops, jewelry stores, restaurants and fast food joints—and the
malecon, Cozumel's seaside boardwalk. While touring the town stop in
at the **Museum of the Island of Cozumel**, a two-story former
turn-of-the-century hotel that features displays of island wildlife and
anthropological and cultural history. Between May and September the
museum offers marine-biologist-led tours to witness the sea turtles lay eggs
on the eastern shore.

The **Chankanab Lagoon Botanical Gardens**, two miles south of town,
has 300 species of tropical plants and trees and an interesting Mayan
museum.

Further south you'll come to the **Celarain Lighthouse**, which you may
climb for a spectacular view of the area. Be sure to clear your visit first with
the resident caretaker.

Rent a jeep to explore the windward east coast of Cozumel. You'll find
pounding surf and marvelous stretches of uninhabited beaches lined with
mangroves and coconut palms. It may be wise to avoid swimming here
because of the dangerous currents and strong undertow, except at **Playa
Chiquero**, a protected crescent-shaped cove, and **Playa Chen Rio,** which
is protected by a rock breakwater.

Remains of Mayan temples and pyramids can be found at the northern end
of the island. Guided tours to explore **San Gervasio** (once the Mayan
capital), also on the north end, may be booked through most large hotels.
Ferry trips to the larger, more impressive Mayan ruins on the mainland can
be booked in town at the International Pier. Most dive packages include a
side trip to **Tulum**, a Mayan walled city built in the late 13th century, or to
Isla Mujeres, a fabulous nearby snorkeling island.

Sightseeing flights around Cozumel, to neighboring islands, or the mainland
can be arranged at the airport.

Dining

Local lobster, native grilled fish and a variety of Mexican dishes such as
tacos, enchiladas or caracol (a giant conch) predominate at Cozumel's
restaurants and roadside stands. Several superb native eateries within a few

blocks of the pier offer island specialties such as grilled turtle, grilled fish in banana leaves, conch cocktail and spicy steak strips. All in all, dining is quite good in Cozumel whether you choose romantic garden dining with strolling serenaders or a fast snack at one of the many stands.

Music is featured at most restaurants and hotel bars on Cozumel, and the island has a number of discos, including Scaramouche and Neptuno.

Pepe's Grill on Ave. Rafael Melgar features savory steaks, lobster and seafood. ☎ 2-02-13.

Cafe Del Puerto at the plaza is one of Cozumel's best spots for lobster and crab. You'll be entertained with live guitar music. ☎ 2-03-16.

El Portal offers fabulous Mexican-style spicy breakfasts. ☎ 2-03-16.

Carlos' N Charlies and Jimmy's Kitchen, on Ave. Rafael Melgar 11, is a divers' favorite for Mexican steaks and seafood. ☎ 2-01-91.

La Palmeras, at the pier (27 Rafael Melgar), is a good spot for breakfast and lunch. ☎ 2-05-32.

La Laguna, on the beach at Chankanab National Park, serves up tasty shrimp, crabs and fish. ☎ 2-05-84.

Pizza Rolandi, on Ave. Melgar 22, specializes in Italian favorites.

AKUMAL

Akumal ("place of the turtle") lies 60 miles south of Cancun on Mexico's Yucatán Peninsula in an area known as the Tulum Corridor. Laid back and off the beaten track, this tiny resort community originated as a section of a large coconut plantation. It wasn't until 1958 that Mexican treasure divers salvaging a sunken Spanish galleon discovered great sport diving opportunities along the off-shore barrier reef. Pristine corals and sponges, frequent turtle sightings, silky white, sand beaches and terrific beach snorkeling have popularized Akumal with local divers and a discriminating group of visitors. Three dive operators serve the area.

Drawbacks exist for those who like "pampered" diving—Akumal dive guides are friendly and helpful, but they do **not** carry, store or wash your gear. The diving is **not** "easy" in terms of services. Divers "schlep" their own tanks, weights and equipment to and from the boats. The boats are open, with ladders—no platforms, no sun canopies. On the other hand, most sites lie close to shore, a five- to 10-minute boat ride. Spear fishing is prohibited.

Akumal dive operators also offer divers and snorkelers freshwater tours to jungle pools or "cenotes," which are sunken limestone caverns with dazzling stalagmites and stalactites. These inland adventures include a jungle trek through nature's most exotic gardens.

When to Go

The best time to dive Akumal is Oct through April. Weather is very hot in May and June and rain is heavy during July, Aug and Sept.

Best Dives of Akumal

Akumal's ocean scuba sites are gentle drift dives with easy pickups along a barrier reef that parallels the shoreline of Akumal Bay, neighboring Half Moon Bay and nearby Yalku Lagoon. Snorkeling opportunities exist all along the coast.

The reef structure comprises three distinct systems running parallel to one another at progressively greater depths. The inner reef, a network of patch reefs, ranges from three to 35 ft, with huge stands of elkhorn and formations of boulder, brain and plate corals. An expanse of white sand separates the inner reef from the middle reef which is three miles long at depths from 40 to 55 ft. Several reef areas are shot through with coral caves and tunnels. Further out, a well-developed outer reef from 60 to 125 ft features more outstanding caverns and canyons. Abundant tropicals inhabit the patch reefs and the middle reef. Larger fish and turtles roam the outer reef.

Frequent sightings of loggerhead, green and hawksbill turtles that nest along Yucatán beaches highlight many dives. Currents normally run less than one knot.

Snorkelers exploring from the beach can swim up to the breakers on the reef. Conditions inside are normally calm, with depths from three to 20 ft.

☆☆☆ **Akumal Shark Caves**, at 40 ft, shelter six or more nurse sharks and walls of porkfish, grunts, and snapper. Cavern walls blossom with rose gorgonians, lettuce corals, yellow seafans, flower and brush corals. Orange vase sponges and soft corals proliferate in the gently moving current. Drift dive. Expect some surge. Experience suggested.

☆☆☆☆ **La Tortuga**, named for the big turtles that paddle by, slopes from 70 to 80 ft. Located outside the reef, this site offers a slightly more challenging current. Surface can get rough at times. Good to excellent visibility.

☆☆☆ **The Nets**, at 45 ft depths, and El Mero, at 75 ft, both adjacent to Shark Caves, offer normally excellent visibility, vibrant red sponges, star corals, sea feathers, and soft corals. Terrain slopes into a labyrinth of canyons, tunnels and overhangs. Both spots provide habitat to arrow crabs, sea cucumbers, lobster and shrimp. Lots of tunnels and small caves. French and queen angels, sergeant majors, trigger and parrot fish bob with the current. Gentle drift dive.

THE CENOTES

Cenotes are freshwater pools with submerged limestone caverns. "Gin clear" best describes the visibility, though you may pass through a thermal layer of "soup" as you drop down to more crystal clear water. Scuba depths average 40 to 60 ft. You'll see fish, but the magnificence of these limestone caverns lies in the fantastic stalagmites and stalactites. Lights make the colors stand out and your dive more exciting.

Akumal, Cozumel and Cancun dive shops offer guided cenote (cavern) tours to certified divers. Unlike cave diving, you stay within close sight of the entrance. No special certification required. Before signing up for a cenote trip make sure your guide is cave-certified by one of the national associations—National Association for Cave Diving (NACD), National Speleological Society Cave Diving Section (NSS CDS) or International Assocation of Nitrox and Technical Divers (IANTD). The guide should also be wearing doubles with octopus rigs and using a continuous guideline (a rope to lead you back to the surface should one of you kick up the silt and decrease the visibility to zero). Groups should be very small. A thorough briefing on emergency procedures should precede the dive.

Be sure to maintain neutral bouyancy to avoid kicking up the silty bottoms and smashing the flowstones. Keep a close watch on your air supply. Don't explore passageways on your own. You'll need a wet suit; water temperatures in the cenotes average 70° F. Cenote dives cost about $45 per tank.

☆☆☆ **The Car Wash, Gran Cenote, Temple of Doom** and **Dos Ojos** are favorite cavern dives in Akumal. All average 50 to 60 ft depths. Temple of Doom requires jumping from a ledge 15 ft above the pool.

Some of these caverns are partially above water and shallow enough for snorkelers, who are offered specialty tours.

☆☆☆☆ **Nohoch Nah Chich**, listed in the *Guinness Book of World Records* as the world's longest underwater cave system, was also featured in the PBS TV series, *The New Explorers*, as one of Yucatán's most exciting caverns. Visitors snorkel in the shallow fresh water amidst brilliant white stalactites and stalagmites. Unlimited visibility and an openness to the caverns offer breathtaking views.

Joining a jungle walk and snorkeling expedition to Nohoch Nah Chich involves a mile-and-a-half trek through impressive flora. Horses or donkeys carry your gear. Be sure to apply sun protective lotions and bug repellent and wear a hat that will shade your face. Not suitable for young children or people with severe disabilities or medical problems.

Akumal Snorkeling Sites

Uncrowded beaches, secluded bays and a healthy marine population make Akumal delightful for family snorkeling vacations.

☆☆☆ **Akumal Bay's** best snorkeling is off the beach in front of the Club Akumal Caribe. Depths range from three ft to 20 ft with coral heads leading out to the breakers at the barrier reef. A variety of corals, sea fans, sponges, reef fish, occasional moray eels, barracudas, jacks, grouper, sting rays, parrot fish and turtles inhabit the bay. Bottom terrain is sandy, with coral heads scattered about. Bay conditions inside the barrier reef are almost always tranquil.

☆☆☆ **Half Moon Bay**, about three minutes down the interior road from Akumal Bay, resembles Akumal Bay in terrain and marine life. This is a residential area, but anyone can use the beach.

☆☆☆☆ **Yalcu Lagoon**, at the end of the interior road, a short drive from Half Moon Bay, features partially submerged caves, throngs of fish and crystal clear, tranquil water. Fresh water mixing with seawater provides nutrients and aquatic plants that attract rich marine life. Big parrot fish, angels, Spanish hogfish, rays, juvenile turtles and spotted eels nibble on the plants around the rocks. A natural entrance from the sea ensures a constant mix of nutrients. The outlying barrier reef protects this magnificent natural aquarium from wind-driven waves and rough seas. Enter the lagoon from the head of the bay or climb down the big rocks anywhere along the shore. Guided boat and beach-entry snorkeling tours are offered by the dive shop at Club Akumal Caribe.

Snorkeling up and down the coast. . .

Several sheltered bays and secluded beaches with good shore-entry snorkeling exist along the coast. About six miles south of Akumal, the dirt road turn off at KM 249 leads to ☆☆ **Chemuyil**, a quiet, horseshoe-shaped cove of tranquil water edged by a lovely, powder-white beach. A shallow snorkeling reef crosses the mouth of the bay. A small beach bar (the Marco Polo) serves fresh seafood, cold beer and soft drinks. Full camping facilities and a few tented "palapas" for overnight rental are available.

About 20 miles south of Akumal lies ☆☆ **Xel-Ha** (pronounced shell ha), the world's largest natural aquarium, covering 10 acres of lagoons, coves and inlets teeming with exotic fish. Platforms above the rocky limestone shore provide sea life viewing for non-swimmers. Unlike Akumal, this spot is packed with tourists. Busloads mobbed with avid snorkelers arrive regularly in season.

A small admission fee is charged. On-site showers, shops, a maritime museum, seafood restaurant and Subway sandwich shop serve visitors. Snorkeling gear is available for rent. Despite the crowds, most snorkelers, especially those touring with children, immensely enjoy this spot. Venture across highway 307 to visit some small ruins.

☆☆ **Xcaret** (Scaret), Mayan for "little inlet," about 40 miles north of Akumal, is a private ranch turned aquatic theme park. Once a Mayan port, this novel playground now features dolphin swims and snorkeling through "the underground river," which flows through a series of open-ended caves. A mix of fresh and saltwater nourishes sea plants, which in turn feed armies of fish that entertain between 400 and 500 snorkelers per day. The effect is like drifting through a very big, very pretty, shaded pool stocked with fish. Holes in the "roof" of the river caves filter light into a spectrum of colors.

Topside features include a wild-bird aviary, butterfly pavilion, saltwater aquarium, botanical garden, a couple of Mayan temple ruins, and the Museum of Mayan Archaeological Sites with scale models of 26 Mayan ceremonial sites found on the Yucatán peninsula. There are three restaurants, two snack bars, one cafeteria, showers, lockers, photo center, horse shows, gift shops and a sundeck with spectacular ocean views. Crowded, but very user friendly.

The open-air restaurant, **La Peninsula**, offers a good selection of entreés and remains open at night. **La Caleta**, another alfresco restaurant near the inlet, specializes in spicy seafood.

The Maya prized Xcaret, believing that its waters could purify bodies and souls. Thus it became important as a place to take a "sacred bath" before crossing the sea to Cozumel to worship Ixchel, Goddess of Fertility.

We can't guarantee the soul-purifying properties, but most snorkelers find Xcaret a fun day or half-day diversion. One of our snorkeling researchers returning from Xcaret claims relief from back pain!

Akumal Accommodations

Hotel Club Akumal Caribe features a variety of air-conditioned accommodations and an on-site dive shop. On the main beach choose from spacious Maya bungalows with garden views or first class hotel rooms facing the pool and ocean. All are clean and modern with full baths, air-conditioning, ceiling fans and compact refrigerators. Also on the main beach is the Cannon House Suite, with two bedrooms, two baths, living room and kitchen.

Two bedroom condos on Half Moon Bay have one king-size bed, two twins, kitchens and living rooms. Winter rates range from $81 per night for a bungalow, from $99 for a hotel room, and from $355 for a three-bedroom villa.

Contact the reservation office for additional accommodation rates and information. In the US, ☎ (800) 351-1622; in Canada, ☎ (800) 343-1440; in Texas, ☎ (915) 584-3552; in Mexico, ☎ (800) 351-1622. E-mail: club aku-mal@aol.com.

Akumal Dive Operators

Akumal Dive Center at Club Akumal offers cenote, jungle, cave and open-water diving with top-notch dive masters. Groups are small and tours are personalized. Guides are environmentally aware and enforce local marine sanctuary regulations. C-cards a must. Cave dives only to certifirfed cave divers. ☎ (800) 351-1622, (011) 52-987-59025, fax (915) 581-6709. E-mail: clubakumal@aol.com.

Aquatech Villas DeRosa in Aventuras Akumal features technical training, Nitrox, rebreathers, cave and cavern diving. ☎ (011) 52-987-59020, fax (011) 52-987-59020. E-mail: 105107.2445@compuserve.com.

Mike Madden's Cedam Dive Centers are at four locations—Club Oasis Puerto Aventuras, Beach Club Hotel Puerto Aventuras, Robinson Club Tulum and Club Oasis Aventuras Akumal. Tours include reef diving, cavern diving, day trips to Cozumel and cave diving for certified cave divers. Snorkeling trips offered to Nohoch, the world's longest underwater cave (the Indiana Jones Jungle Adventure). All levels of certification are offered from Open Water Diver through Scuba Instructor, with special courses in night diving, deep diving and photography. Cavern and Cave certifications are available with NACD, NSS-CDS and IANTD instructors. Technical certifications such as Nitrox, Deep Air and Trimix are also offered. ☎ (011) 52-987-35147, fax (011) 52-987-35129. E-mail: mmaden@cancun. rce.com.mx. Web site: www.cedamdive.com.

Note: The trip from Cancun to Cozumel by boat takes 40-60 minutes.

Facts

Helpful Phone Numbers: Police (Cozume), ☎ 20092; hospital (Cozumel), ☎ 20140.

Nearest Recompression Chamber: On the mainland there is a recompression chamber run by doctors trained in hyperbaric medicine in Playa del Carmen. In Cozumel there is a chamber in San Miguel, ☎ 22387.

Getting There: Direct flights to Cozumel and Cancun from the US are offered by American Airlines, ☎ (800) 733-4300, Continental, United, Northwest, Mexicana and Aero Mexico. There are additional domestic flights from Acapulco, Cancun, Guadalajara, Mexico City, Merida, Monterey, and Veracruz. Cruise ships from Miami: Norwegian Caribbean Lines, Holland America, Carnival. Cozumel island also can be reached by bus ferry, car ferry and hydrofoil from Cancun. Isla Mujeres is reached by bus ferry, car ferry and air taxi from Cancun. AeroCozumel and Aerocaribe fly between the islands. Cozumel is a 40- to 60-minute boat trip from Cancun.

Island Transportation: Taxi service is inexpensive and readily available. Mopeds, cars and Jeeps may be rented in town or at the airport. Book rental cars in advance of your trip.

Departure tax: $12.

Driving: On the right.

Documents: US and Canadian citizens need a tourist card. To obtain one, you must show a valid passport or birth certificate with raised seal. Citizens of other countries should contact their nearest Mexican consulate for regulations. The tourist card is necessary to leave the country as well and may be obtained from the Mexican consulate or your airline prior to departure.

Customs: Plants, flowers and fruits may not be brought into Cozumel. Persons carrying illegal drugs will be jailed. You may bring three bottles of liquor and one carton of cigarettes. Dogs and cats should have a current vaccination certificate. Divers carrying a lot of electronic or camera gear, especially video equipment, should register it with US Customs in advance of the trip.

Water: Drink only bottled or filtered water to avoid diarrheal intestinal ailment. Also avoid raw vegetables and the skin of fruit and foods that sit out for any length of time.

Currency: The exchange rate of the Mexican peso fluctuates a great deal. At this writing US $1=5.5 nuevos pesos. Banks are open weekday mornings. Major credit cards and traveler's checks are widely accepted in Akumal, Cancun and Cozumel.

Climate: Temperatures range from the low 70's in winter to the high 90's in summer, with an average of about 80° F. Winter months bring cooler weather; summer and fall, chance of heavy rain.

Clothing: Lightweight, casual. Wetsuits are not needed, but lightweight (1/8") short suits or wetskins are comfortable on deep wall dives.

Electricity: 110 volts; 60 cycles (same as US).

Time: Central Standard Time.

Language: Spanish; English widely spoken.

For Additional Information: *In New York,* Mexican Government Tourist Office, 405 Park Avenue, Suite 1400, NY, NY 10022. ☎ (800) 446-3942 or (212) 421-6655, fax (212) 753-2874. *In California,* 10100 Santa Monica Blvd., Los Angeles, CA 90067. ☎ (310) 203-0821. *In Florida,* 128 Aragon Avenue, Coral Gables, FL 33134 ☎ (305) 443-9160. *In Canada,* Mexican Government Tourist Office, Suite 1526, One Place Ville Marie, Montreal, Quebec, Canada H3B 2B5. ☎ (514) 871-1052, fax (514) 871-1052. *In the UK,* Mexican Government Tourism Office, 60/61 Trafalgar Square, 3rd Floor, London, England WC2N 5DS. ☎ 44-71-734-1058, fax 44-71-930-9202. Web site: www.mexico-travel.com\.

Curaçao

Curaçao, the largest of five islands that make up the Netherlands Antilles, which include Bonaire, Saba, Saint Maarten and St. Eustatius, is a dry and hilly island completely surrounded with rich coral reefs—many within a stone's throw of shore. Its coastline sparkles with beautiful sand beaches, secluded lagoons and snorkeling coves.

Willemstad, its capital, is delightfully Dutch, with open-air markets, narrow streets and rows of shops offering imports from all over the world. It is best known for its colorful Dutch-colonial architecture. According to legend, the first governor of Curaçao suffered from migraine headaches due to glare from the white houses and ordered all residents to paint their homes pastel. The rows of pastel-colored town houses with gabled roofs, red tile and rococo-style facades in downtown Willemstad probably are the most photographed sights on the island.

St. Anna Bay, like an Amsterdam canal, divides the capital city in two parts—the Punda and the Otrabanda. A pontoon walking bridge, which opens several times a day to allow cruise ships to dock in town, connects the two sides of the city.

Christoffel Park in the northwestern sector of Curaçao is marked by the island's highest peak. The volcanic crest of Mt. Christoffel dominates the landscape, rising 1,250 ft above the sea. Undulating hills are punctuated with the evergreen wayaca and cacti, reaching as much as 10 ft from the parched land like outstretched fingers.

History

Curaçao's heritage and history is long and multi-faceted. The Caiquetio Indians, a tribe of which were the "Indios Curaçao," were the original inhabitants of Curaçao. In 1499, when Alonso de Ojeda, a Spanish navigator who sailed with Columbus, discovered the island and the Indians, he named it for them.

Later, in 1634, the Dutch captured Curaçao, forcing evacuation by the Spaniards and the Indian natives. By 1635, only 50 of the 462 inhabitants were native Indians and approximately 350 of the rest were Dutch soldiers. The island became one of the leading slave and salt trade centers for the Dutch West Indies Company.

For many years, England and France tried to conquer the island. The English were successful in 1800, but were defeated two years later by the Dutch. England eventually recaptured the island, only to give it back as a result of the Treaty of Paris in 1815.

By the mid-1800s, Curaçao's population was as varied as any in the world. One-time soldiers married Curaçaoan women and established a livelihood on the island. Merchants from Europe stayed. Others were freed slaves who chose to remain on the island. All carried a part of their culture and tradition to this tropical paradise.

Curaçao's harbor became the site of one of the world's largest oil refineries in 1914, following the discovery of oil in Venezuela.

Best Dive and Snorkeling Sites

Like its sister islands, Aruba and Bonaire, Curaçao lies far south of the hurricane belt and offers clear skies and good diving year-round. Most dives require a boat. The reefs and wrecks are "a stone's throw from shore," but the "shore" adjacent to the best reefs is often formed of jagged, razor-like, ironshore cliffs. Seas along the south coast—locale of the underwater park—are usually dead calm in the morning, but may kick up a three- or four-ft surge in mid-afternoon.

The Curaçao Underwater Park, established in 1983 by the Netherlands Antilles National Park Foundation (STINAPA), stretches 12½ miles from the Princess Beach Hotel to East Point and features 20 dive sites marked by numbered mooring buoys and another 10 unmarked sites. Within the park, divers and snorkelers find crystal-clear water and spectacular subsea land-scapes. The reefs are in pristine condition, with many yet to be explored. Diving did not become popular in Curaçao until the 1980s when officials realized the potential for additional tourist growth. Before then, the island was promoted solely for honeymoons, sport fishing and sailing.

Although the park's terrain features dramatic coral walls with deep drop-offs, there is excellent diving in the shallow waters, with 50-foot brain coral, gigantic sponges, huge, perfectly formed trees of elkhorn and enormous, lush seafan gardens. Visibility is a dependable 100 ft.

To the west is the (not yet official) Banda Abao Underwater Park, with more than 21 outstanding dive and snorkeling sites.

For the very adventurous, the westernmost dive site, **Wata Mula**, features a sloping reef and cave frequented by huge moray eels, groupers, nurse sharks and rays. This area is diveable only on very calm days and only with an experienced dive guide. Seas at this end of the island are often very

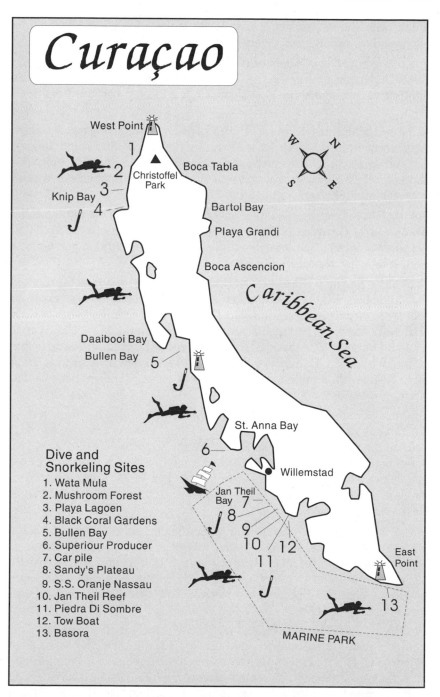

Curaçao

West Point

1

2

Christoffel Park ▲

3

Knip Bay

4

Boca Tabla

Bartol Bay

Playa Grandi

Boca Ascencion

Caribbean Sea

Daaibooi Bay

Bullen Bay   5

St. Anna Bay

6

Dive and Snorkeling Sites

1. Wata Mula
2. Mushroom Forest
3. Playa Lagoen
4. Black Coral Gardens
5. Bullen Bay
6. Superiour Producer
7. Car pile
8. Sandy's Plateau
9. S.S. Oranje Nassau
10. Jan Theil Reef
11. Piedra Di Sombre
12. Tow Boat
13. Basora

Jan Theil Bay

Willemstad

7

8

9

10   12

11

East Point

13

MARINE PARK

rough, with strong currents. Yet, visibility and marine life is outstanding. Suggested for experienced divers in top physical condition.

South of Wata Mula is **Mushroom Forest**, the most beautiful of the Banda Abao Underwater Park. This gently sloping reef is highlighted by giant mushroom-shaped elkhorn corals at 50 ft. It is located offshore from Sanu Pretu.

At the end of Mushroom Forest is **Playa Lagoen,** a snorkeling beach nestled between two massive rock formations. Snorkelers will find some juvenile fish and small coral heads along the rocks. Be sure to tote a floating dive flag as small fishing boats weave in and out of the area. Energetic divers can swim out about 150 yds to the drop-off.

South of Playa Lagoen, sea turtles and occasional mantas are sighted at the **Black Coral Gardens** off Boca St. Martha. Steep drop-offs, 60 to 130 ft, support a colossal black coral forest. Nearby is **Mike's Place**, known for a giant sponge locally called the "double bed."

☆☆☆☆ **Sandy's Plateau** (aka *Boka Di Sorsaka*), is part of the marked trail. It can be reached by swimming out from Jan Thiel Bay. It is an excellent spot for novice divers and snorkelers. The terrain is a combination of walls and steep slopes colored with lavender and pink star corals, yellow pencil corals and orange tube sponges. Lush stands of elkhorn coral grow to within 10 ft of the surface. Dense coral flows around an undercut ledge from 10 to 30 ft. Soldierfish, trumpetfish and schools of sergeant majors hover at the ledge.

Offshore from the Curaçao Seaquarium in Jan Thiel Bay lies the wreck of the ☆☆☆☆ **S.S. Oranje Nassau**, a Dutch steamer that ran aground here on the Koraal Specht over 80 years ago. Also known as *Bopor Kibra,* Papiamento for broken ship, this is a shallow dive and a favorite spot for free diving. The seas are always choppy over the wreck. Entry is best from the diveshop docks adjacent to the seaquarium. Check with the divemaster for the day's conditions.

This area is known for outstanding corals. Depths start shallow with large pillar and star corals, seafans, huge brain coral, and gorgeous stands of elkhorn. It then terraces off to a wall starting at 50 ft. Fish life includes swarms of blue chromis and creole wrasses, French angels, barracuda and jacks. Sea conditions are choppy and recommended for divers and snorkelers with some ocean experience.

☆☆☆☆ **Jan Thiel Reef**, just outside of Jan Thiel Bay is a fabulous snorkeling site. Lush, shallow gardens at 15 ft are alive with a mass of gorgonians, two-foot lavender sea anemones, seafans, long, purple tube sponges, pastel star, leaf, fire, pencil and brain corals. Fishlife is superb, with walls of grunts, trumpetfish, parrot fish, angels and small rays. Added

Tugboat wreck off Curaçao.

buoyancy from a snorkeling vest or shorty wetsuit will help you to stay clear of the fire coral. You can swim from Playa Jan Thiel, just east of the Princess Beach Hotel. The beach has changing facilities and is a favorite for picnics. Admission fee.

☆☆☆ **Piedra Di Sombre** is located between Caracas Bay and Jan Thiel Bay. Ideal for snorkeling and diving, the site is a steep wall covered with abundant seafans, seawhips, wire coral, star coral, club finger coral, seafans and rows of gorgonians. Depths are from 30 ft to 125 ft. Numerous black corals grow on the wall. Reef residents are lizardfish, black durgons, angelfish and barracuda.

☆☆☆☆ The ***Superior Producer*** is Curaçao's favorite wreck dive. The 100-ft freighter sank in 1977 when her heavy cargo of clothing shifted. The ship is intact and stands upright on a sandy plain at the foot of a steep, coral-covered slope. The wreck is encrusted with orange, red, purple, green and yellow corals and sponges. Clouds of silversides command the wheelhouse; rays and porpoises are frequently sighted. The site has a mooring buoy and is most conveniently reached from a boat, but can also be reached by a rugged swim from shore. The closest water-entry point is from the Curaçao public swimming pool at the Rif recreation area. Top of the wreck is at 90 ft with sections of the mainmast reaching up to within 40 ft of the surface. Divers are advised to watch the tables or dive computer as several bounty hunters have ended up in the island's recompression chamber.

The mooring for ☆☆☆ **PBH** is in front of the Princess Beach Hotel. This reef starts shallow enough for snorkeling and drops off at 40 ft. Arrow crabs, octopi, and hordes of juvenile fish swim the shallow terrace. Black corals and large grouper are found at depth.

☆☆☆ **Car Pile**, by the Princess Beach Hotel, is an artificial reef constructed from piles of old car and truck wrecks. Depth is 60 to 125 ft. Watch out for jagged pieces of metal and avoid getting under the heaps as the mass is not dependably stable. The wrecks are completely covered over with corals, algae and sponges with resident lobster, crabs and fish. You can reach it by swimming out from the hotel beach. Expect a light to moderate current.

☆☆☆ **Tow Boat**, the favorite shallow dive in the Curaçao Underwater Park, is intact, sitting upright on a sandy shelf, and can be explored at 15 ft. Tube corals, Christmas trees worms, sponges and sheet corals cover the wheelhouse. Schools of reef fish frolic around the bow. Great for wide-angle photography. Divers can continue down a steep drop-off to explore black corals, vase and basket sponges. The wreck is accessible only by boat, a short ride from Caracas Bay.

Choppy seas are usually encountered enroute to ☆☆☆☆ **Piedra Pretu**, near the easternmost corner of the coast, but the effort is paid back with exposure to one of the most spectacular reefs in the Caribbean. Massive black-coral trees, huge barrel sponges and dense beds of staghorn and elkhorn adorn a shallow terrace which drops off to a vertical wall. Depths are from 20 to 150 ft. Boat access only.

☆☆☆☆ **Basora** is the easternmost dive site on Curaçao. Much like Piedra Pretu, the area is rich with huge brain and star corals and towering pillar formations. Sheets of star corals drape the wall. Fish include monster grouper, sting rays and morays.

☆☆☆ **Bullen Bay**, just north of the park, is an outstanding dive with a protected shallow area for snorkeling and a nice drop-off for diving. Yellow pencil corals and pretty white sea plumes highlight the reef. Average depth is 40 ft.

☆☆☆☆☆ **Klein Curaçao** (little Curaçao) is an uninhabited island about a two-hour boat ride east of Curaçao. It is a rugged strip of desolate volcanic rock which plunges into a most spectacular reef. A constant parade of scorpion fish, red-legged hermit crabs, yellow stingrays, spotted morays, yellow frogfish, eagle rays and huge turtles whistle by the wall.

The shelf drops 100 ft into a blaze of orange elephant-ear sponges, purple tube and rope sponges, black corals, huge seafans and massive boulder corals.

Dive BVI's catamaran Sea Lion *over reef dive (facing)* Bret Gilliam

Sunset, Bonaire (above) Jon Huber

Frogfish, Dominica (above) Karen Sabo, Landfall Productions

Squirrelfish, Dominica (above) Karen Sabo, Landfall Productions

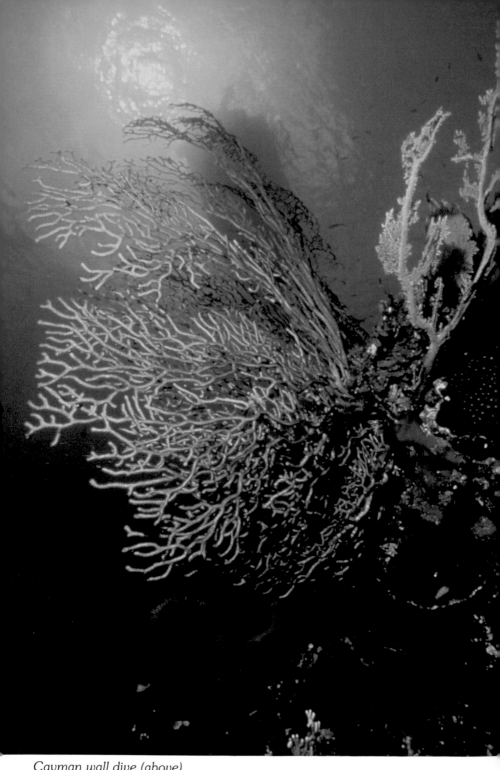

Cayman wall dive (above)

Reef scene, St. Lucia (above) Denis Sabo, Landfall Productions

Blue Hole, Belize (above)

Bigeye (above) Jon Huber

Yacht Promenade *(above)* Fiona Dugdale

The Old Pier, Bonaire (above) Jon Huber

Sea turtle (above)

Trunk Bay, St. John, USVI (above)

First dive, Humacao, Puerto Rico (above) Rick Ockelmann

Moray eel (above) Karen Sabo, Landfall Productions

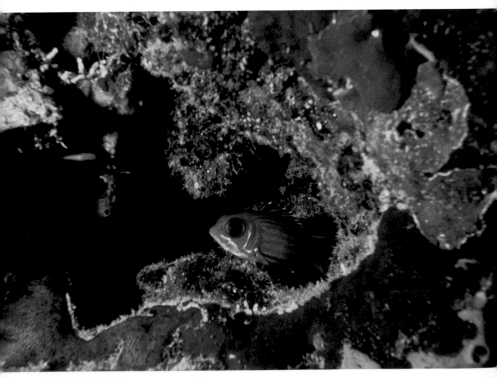

Squirrelfish in coral (above) Jon Huber

Yellow pencil coral, Bullen Bay, Curaçao (above) Jon Huber

Vase sponge, Pigeon Island, Guadeloupe (above) Rick Ockelmann

Off St. Vincent (above) Karen Sabo, Landfall Productions

Snorkeling Malmok, Aruba (above) Jon Huber

Stingray City, Grand Cayman (above) Redsail Watersports

Diamond Rock, Saba (above) Joan Borque

French angelfish, Bonaire (above) Jon Huber

Nisbet Plantation Beach, Nevis (above) Jon Huber

Seal pond at Curaçao Seaquarium. To the left, protruding from the water's surface, is the top of the shipwreck, S.S. Oranje Nassau.

Beaches

Curaçao is surrounded by beautiful beaches, from popular hotel beaches to intimate secluded coves. Along the southern coast, there are free public beaches at West Point Bay, Knip Bay, Klein Knip, Santa Cruz, Jeremi Bay and Daaibooi Bay. Knip Bay is the largest and loveliest swimming beach on the island. Snorkeling is good along the adjacent cliffs.

The main private beaches, which charge a small fee per car, are Blauw Bay, Jan Thiel, Cas Abao, Barbara Beach and Port Marie.

Be careful of the tree with small green apples that borders some beaches. This is the manzanilla and its sap will cause burns and blisters on wet exposed skin. Its fruit is poisonous.

Dive Operators

Reef and wreck diving and snorkeling trips may be booked through the following operators. Most offer certification courses.

All West Diving & Adventures Curaçao at West Point Beach. Contact Hans & Bernardien v/d Eeden. ☎ 5999-8640102, fax 8640107.

Aqua Diving, Grote Berg. Contact Arjan v/d Meule. ☎ (011) 5999-8649700, fax 8649288.

Atlantis Diving, Drielstraat 6. Roland de Kneg, Manager. ☎ (011) 5999-4658288, fax 4658288.

Reef scene, St. Vincent (facing) Karen Sabo, Landfall Productions

Big Blue Diving, Club Seru Coral, Koral Partier 10. Manager, Tom Zeck. ☎ (011) 5999-5605454, fax 4624188.

Coral Cliff Divers, Coral Cliff Hotel at Santa Martha Bay. Owner/Manager Marlies Feijts. ☎ (011) 5999-8642822, fax 8642237.

Curaçao Seascape, on the beach at the Curaçao Caribbean Hotel, has fast, comfortable, custom dive boats and friendly service. Snorkelers welcome. Manager, Eva Van Dalen. ☎ (011) 5999-4625000, fax 4625846.

Diving School Wederfoort/Sami Scuba Center, at Marine Beach Club St. Michiel Bay z/n. Eric & Yolander Wederfoort owners. ☎ (011) 5999-8684414, fax 8692062.

Eden Roc Diving Center, Holiday Beach Hotel, Patereeuwensweg. Contact Gerlinde Seupel. ☎ (011) 5999-8648400, fax 8648400.

Habitat Curaçao Dive Resort, Rif St. Marie. Albert Romijn, Manager. ☎ 5999-8648800, fax 8648464.

Holland Diving Curaçao, Hotel Holland, F.D. Rooseveltweg #534. ☎ 5999-8697060, fax 8697060.

Ocean Divers Curaçao, Socratesstraar 15b. Shirley Pikeur, Manager. ☎ (011) 5999-4657254, fax 4657254.

Peter Hughes/Princess Dive Facility, at the Princess Beach Resort & Casino, Holiday Inn Crowne Plaza Hotel, offers reef trips and certification courses. Lex Kleine, Manager. In US ☎ (800) 932-6237; Curaçao (011) 5999-4658991, fax 4655756. E-Mail: dancer@winnet.net.

Red Sail Sports, at Sonesta Beach Hotel, Piscadera Bay. Staff carries gear and tanks. Towels provided. In US ☎ (800) 255-6425; Curaçao (011) 5999-7368800, fax 4627502.

Scuba Do Dive Center, at Jan Thiel Beach & Sports Resorts. Contact H. Ferwerda. ☎ 5999-7679300, fax 7679300.

Toucan Diving, Valk Plaza Hotel, Plaza Piar. Bibi Rutten, Manager. ☎ (011) 5999-4612500, fax 4616543.

The Ultimate Dive Store, at Orionweg 23. Robby v/d Heuvel, Manager. ☎ (011) 5999-5608713, fax 4654431.

Underwater Curaçao, adjacent to the Seaquarium, at the Lion's Dive Hotel, is a PADI five-star facility. Their double-decker dive boats can easily accommodate large groups. Underwater Curaçao's services include round-trip mini-van service from your hotel or cruise ship. ☎ (011) 5999-4618100, fax 4618200.

Travel Packages

Diving is just starting to take off in Curaçao, with new watersports facilities and dive resorts in the planning stage. A wide range of accommodations are available. Some hotels offer villa-style arrangements and apartments, and there are a wide variety of smaller, more intimate guest houses and inns. Dive/vacation packages, including mid-week air fare from the US, start at $538. Packages can be booked through the resorts, travel agents, or dive tour operators: **Landfall Productions**, Newark, CA, ☎ (800) 525-3833, fax (510) 794-1617, Web site http://ecotravel.com/landfall; **Scuba Tours**, Little Falls, NJ, ☎ 800 526-1394, fax (201) 256-0591; **Sea Safaris**, Manhattan Beach, CA, ☎ (800) 262-6670, fax (310) 545-1672; **Ocean Connections,** Houston, TX, ☎ (800) 331-2458/(800) 364-6232, fax (713) 486-8362; **Blue Bonnett Tours**, Miami, FL, ☎ (800) 334-8582, fax (305) 256-9389; **Caribbean Adventure Tours**, Atlanta, GA, ☎ (800) 377-6344, fax (404) 952-0656; **Paradise Expeditions**, Lincoln Park, NJ, ☎ (800) 332-4846, fax (201) 696-2335; **Go Diving**, Minnetonka, MN, ☎ (800) 328-5285; **Caribbean Dive Tours**, Marietta, GA, ☎ (800) 786-3483, fax (404) 565-0129.

Accommodations

All prices in US dollars.

Airport Hotel Holland & Casino offers casino, dining, kitchens, pool, satellite TV and scuba. AC. Children's rates available. Rates: $70-$130. ☎ (011) 5999-688044, fax (011) 5999-688114.

Coral Cliff Resort & Beach Club is nestled in the Santa Marta cliffs on its own private beach. Each unit has a fully-equipped kitchenette and panoramic vistas. Casino, restaurant, meeting room, satellite TV, tennis court and watersports. Reserve through your travel agent. Summer, $145-$210; winter, $180-$240. ☎ (011) 5999-641610, fax 641781.

Curaçao Caribbean Hotel & Casino is a huge beachfront hotel with watersports, casino, shopping gallery, tennis, five restaurants, beach bar. Dive packages with Seascape Diving. Five minutes from town. Winter rates for four days/three nights, with four dives for a double, start at $468 per person. For eight days/seven nights, $938 per person. Includes room, airport transfers, discount booklet, free shuttle bus to and from town, tax and service charge, diving, tanks, backpack, weights, belts, unlimited air for shore diving, lockers, T-shirt, service charge on diving. Reserve through your travel agent or ☎ (800) 545-9376 or (203) 831-0682, fax (203) 831-0817. Write to P.O. Box 2133, Curaçao, NA.

Habitat Curaçao, on the southwest coast in St. Marie, offers restaurant, pool, satellite TV, tennis courts and a variety of watersports. Twenty-four-

Beach at Curaçao Caribbean Resort.

hour-a-day unlimited diving with all-inclusive packages for eight days/seven nights starting at $649. In the US, ☎ (800) 327-6709, fax (305) 438-4220. Curaçao, (011) 5999-8648800, fax 8648464. E-mail: maduro@netpoint.net.

Holiday Beach Hotel & Casino is located on Coconut Beach facing the Curaçao Underwater Park. The 200-room hotel has a complete dive shop, beach, casino, two restaurants, open-air bar, pool, satellite TV, tennis courts and meeting rooms. Handicapped facilities. Rooms are spacious and modern. AC, visitor information hot-line in rooms and children's rates available. Summer $110-$115; winter, $147-163, PO Box 2178, Curaçao, N.A. US & Canada, ☎ (800) 444-5244. Curaçao, (011) 5999-4625400, fax 4625409.

Kadushi Cliffs Resort, beachfront location with 12 rooms. Restaurant kitchens, meeting facilities, pool, satellite TV. Rates for summer and winter, $295. ☎ (011) 5999-8640200, fax 8640282.

Lions Dive Hotel & Marina is a luxurious 72-room, oceanfront dive complex adjacent to the Curaçao Seaquarium. Rooms overlook the Curaçao Marine Park and the *Orange Nassau*. Rooms are air-conditioned and have an ocean-view balcony or terrace. The resort features three restaurants, fitness center and dive shop, **Underwater Curaçao**. Resort and certification courses are available. Summer, $105-$125; winter, $120-$145. ☎ (800) 451-9376 (US) or (800) 468-0023 (Canada). In Curaçao, (011) 5999-4618100, fax 4618200. Write to International Travel and Resort Dive Desk, 25 West 39th Street, NY, NY 10018.

Plaza Hotel & Casino, oceanfront with 235 rooms, has a casino, restaurants, dining, meeting facilities, pool, watersports and satellite TV. IDD diving school on premises. Summer, $100-$140; winter, $100-$140. Write to PO Box 813, Willemstad, Curaçao, N.A. ☎ (US) (800) 766-6016. Curaçao, (011) 5999-4612500, fax 4618347.

The **Princess Beach Resort & Casino, a Holiday Inn Crown Plaza Resort** overlooks the ocean on a long white-sand beach. Luxury accommodations, swim-up bar, shopping arcade, restaurant and casino. Dive and snorkeling sites off the beach. Packages. Diving with Peter Hughes. ☎ (800) 332-8266. In Curaçao, (011) 5999-7367888, fax 4614131.   Or book through your travel agent.

Sonesta Beach Resort & Casino has a beachfront location with 248 rooms. Casino, three restaurants, fitness center, facilities for handicapped, pool, satellite TV, tennis courts and watersports. Summer, $160-$220; winter, $230-$335. ☎ (011) 5999-7368800 or fax (011) 5999-4627502.

Other Activities

Wherever there is wind and water you are sure to find windsurfing—a cross between sailing and surfing. The area of the Spanish Water Bay at the southeast end of the island is **the** spot for testing your board skills. If you haven't tried it before take a lesson from a pro. The basics can be learned within a few hours from a certified instructor. Experienced boardsailors should head for the Marie Pompoen Area near the Seaquarium. The winds average 12-18 knots, and blow from left to right when facing the water. Check with your hotel's front desk for more information. Sailboards, Sunfish sailboats, and jetskis are rented at most of the hotels' watersports centers.

The **Curaçao Golf & Squash Club,** near the office for the refinery, offers a nine-hole, oiled-sand course. Stiff trade winds add to the challenge. There are two squash courts which are open all week. ☎ 873590 for reservations.

Horseback riding the beach trails or through the *Kunucu* (countryside) can be arranged through the **Ashari Ranch** (☎ 8690315) or **Rancho Alegre** (☎ 8681181).

In addition to horseback riding, active travelers can jog along the special paved path at the **Rif Recreation Area *Koredor***, a two-mile stretch of palm-lined beachfront about a mile from Willemstad's pontoon bridge.

Deep-sea fishing charters complete with bait and tackle can be arranged for about $50 an hour for a party of four through the marinas at Spanish Water Bay or through the hotel watersports centers. Sport fishing is for marlin, tuna, wahoo and sailfish. Hook and line fishing is allowed in the underwater parks.

Sightseeing

Architecture is the big topside attraction in Curaçao. Walking tours of Willemstad and the surrounding countryside are offered by **Old City Tours**. Scheduled departures are on Tuesdays and Saturday at 9 am, with pickup by jeep at your hotel. A variety of escorted tours for groups of four or more are offered by **Casper Tours, Blenchi Tours** and **Taber Tours**. Arrangements may be booked through most hotels. Taxi tours are about $15 per hour and take up to four passengers.

Many of the hotels offer a free shuttle van to and from Willemstad every half-hour until evening. Traffic in town is busy and walking is the best way to see the town. The main town area (Punda) is safe for tourists, but there are occasional robberies. Avoid the long, narrow streets on the outskirts of

Slave hut at Christoffel National Park.

town. One area is a government-sanctioned red-light district established to serve transient seamen and is best left unexplored.

In the 1700s, lavish homes and plantations, known as *landhuisen* or landhouses, were built in the countryside. Government and private funds have assisted in the restoration of many of these homes, which now serve as museums, shops, restaurants and even the famous **Seniour Curaçao Liqueur Factory.**

Landhuis Jan Kock, built in 1650, on the road to Westpunt (near Daaibooi Bay), is one of the oldest buildings on the island. Said to be haunted, the *landhuis* was restored as a museum in 1960. On Sundays from 11 am to 6 pm, Dutch-style pancakes and local specialties are served. Nice gift shop.

Landhuis Brievengat, a Dutch version of the 18th-century West Indian plantation, was torn down and rebuilt. It now operates as a museum and cultural center, open daily from 9:30 am to 12:30 pm. It is located just north of Willemstad.

The beautifully restored 1700 *Landhuis Ascension*, originally a plantation house, is a recreation center for Dutch marines stationed on the island. An open house featuring local music, handicrafts and refreshments is held on the first Sunday of the month.

Landhuis Habaai is the only remaining "Jewish Quarter" home built by early Sephardic settlers. Located in Otrobanda (St. Helena), the plantation home has an authentic cobbled courtyard.

Landhuis Chobolobo is home to the Senior Cubaçao Liqueur Factory which distills and distributes the world-famous Curaçao liqueur using the original recipe and distilling equipment from the early 1900s.

The popular drink is the result of an agricultural mistake. When Spaniards landed on the island in the early 1500s, they planted hundreds of orange trees. The arid climate and sparse rainfall did not provide appropriate growing conditions for the citrus crop, and inedible, bitter fruit was produced. The settlers were not dismayed. They discovered the orange peel, when dried in the sun, produced an aromatic oil which could be used to prepare a variety of drinks and foods. Today, the fruit is used to produce Curaçao liqueur. Visitors can tour the factory weekdays from 8 am to noon and 1 to 5 pm to view the process and sample the liqueur.

The island's **Amstel Brewery** manufactures Amstel Beer—the only beer in the world brewed from distilled sea water. Tours available on Tuesday and Thursday at 10 am.

In downtown Willemstad, just a few minutes walk from the pontoon bridge, is a colorful floating market. Scores of schooners tie up alongside the canal offering fresh fish, tropical fruits, produce, and spices. Docked vessels arrive daily from Venezuela, Colombia and other West Indian islands. Park where you can and walk, as traffic is heavy and stopping on the narrow street is tough.

At the western end of the island is **Christoffel National Park** and Mt. Christoffel. A protected wildlife preserve and garden covering 4,500 acres of land, the park has been open to the public since 1978 and features 20 miles of one-way trails through fields of cactus, divi divi trees and exotic flowers. Wild iguanas, rabbits, donkeys, deer and more than 100 species of birds inhabit the preserve. If you love roller coasters, you will love the big rolling hills of this park. Drive slowly. Hiking trails are very rugged and should be traveled in the cool morning hours. The park is open Monday through Saturday. Admission is US $9; a guide can be hired for about US $14.

Walking tours are popular and may be arranged, in advance, through most hotels. Jeeps and four-wheel-drive vehicles are available for rent.

Boca Tabla is the site of a wonderful cave which opens to the sea. You walk the sand path to the cave entrance (signs lead the way) and climb down a path of huge boulders for a spectacular view of crashing waves into the cave entrance. Very photogenic! Because Curaçaons believe women make the ocean angry or more active, a woman may be asked to stay in the cave to liven up the attraction.

So strong is this belief that during a rescue operation off the north shore in 1992, a woman reporter was asked to leave the area so that male divers might do their job more easily.

Cave at Boca Tabla opens to the sea.

An even more spectacular natural wonder is **Wata Mula,** a 30-ft-wide crater that tunnels to the open sea. Huge waves crash and recede rhythmically while spewing fountains of froth and rainbows high into the air. Both dramatic and mesmerising, it is a photo buff's delight. Take care if you are driving. The ground is sharp ironshore. The land meets the sea quite abruptly and without warning shoots straight down jagged cliffs into crashing waves. Plus, the area is badly littered with broken beer bottles.

You'll see 20-ft sharks, turtles as big as manhole covers, giant moray eels and more than 400 species of fish, crabs, turtles, anemones, sponges, corals and marine life at the **Curaçao Seaquarium.** A "Touch Tank" allows children to pick up starfish, sea urchins and other small sea animals. All species in the 75 hexagonal aquariums are native to the surrounding waters.

The Seaquarium complex also has two restaurants, a magnificent beach and gift shop. It's open daily from 10 am to 10 pm. Admission fee.

Other attractions include the **Arawak Clay Factory,** the **Curaçao Museum,** the **Hato Caves** near the Hotel Holland, the **Botanical Garden and Zoo**, and numerous old fortresses such as **Rif Fort, Fort Amsterdam** and **Fort Nassau.**

Dining

With culinary influences from more than 40 countries, Curaçao offers a wide and wonderful variety of restaurant choices, including Dutch, Indonesian,

Creole, Swiss, Chinese, French, South American, Indian, Italian and American cuisine. They range from casual eateries to gourmet restaurants, many with spectacular views. Popular fast-food eateries are scattered about the island. Local food is usually chicken, fish or meat in a thin sauce made of onions, peppers and tomatoes, with French fries or a biscuit-like pancake.

The **Golden Star Bar and Restaurant**, in town at Socratesstraat 2, is **the** place for goat stew and fungi or other local cuisine at low prices. Hamburgers, sate (skewered meat or fish), bacon and egg sandwiches, sailfish cakes, and fried chicken are on the menu too. Open for lunch and dinner. ☎ 54795 or 54865.

La Pergola, at Waterfort arches in the Punda section of Willemstad, is a fine Italian restaurant with lovely views and excellent food. Local seafood, pasta, and steaks. Expensive, but a definite memorable treat. Reservations a must. ☎ 4613482. Ask for Simone.

Rumours at the Lion's Dive Hotel is open daily for breakfast, lunch and dinner and features meat dishes and fresh catches of the day. ☎ 4617555.

For the charm of a typical Dutch coffee house with Creole and international dishes, try the **Bon Appetit Lunchroom** in the heart of Willemstad's shopping center, at Hanchi Snoa. ☎ 4616916.

The *Landuis Groot Davelaar* houses the 18th-century **De Taveerne Restaurant & Wine Cellar**. An international lunch and dinner menu also features fine wine and cheeses. Closed Sunday. Reservations. ☎ 7370669.

History buffs and romantics will love candlelight dining at the **Fort Nassau Restaurant**. The fort sits high over Willemstad with a 360° panoramic view of St. Anna Bay. Both the food and view are spectacular! Open daily from 7 to 11 pm and for lunch Monday to Friday from noon to 2 pm. Prices for lunch average $15 per person. Dinner entrées (à la carte) are from $22. ☎ 4613086 or 4613450.

Fine seafood, from Creole red snapper to Spanish specialties, such as paella mariner, are offered by **El Marinero Seafood** in Biesheuvel, at Schottergatweg Noord 87B. Reservations, ☎ 79833.

Fort Waakzaamheid Bistro is known for its BBQ salad bar and fresh seafood. In Otrobanda, at Berg Domi. ☎ 4623633.

For downhome Antillean dishes, there is the **March**—an open-air restaurant where you can choose your lunch from dozens of Curaçaoan delicacies cooked up in giant pots. Low, low prices.

In West Punt, stop in at **Jaanchie's Restaurant** for conch stew, goat stew and fried or broiled fish. Located at Westpunt 15. ☎ 8640126. This is a beautiful, open-air restaurant with a garden atmosphere. Local folk artists' work decorate the columns. Very casual, very charming, very special. Excellent local dishes. Average prices.

Fincamar at Lagoen K-27 at West Point is marked by a huge horse sculpture outside. This seafood restaurant is one of Curaçao's finest. The back wall is open to scenic views of West Point's towering cliffs. European atmosphere. Prices for dinner entrées start at $18 sans service charges. ☎ 8641377.

Fast food fans will find their fill at Breedestraate in Willemstad.

Facts

Helpful Phone Numbers: Police, ☎ 114. Taxi Service, ☎ 616711. Island Bus Service, ☎ 684733.

Nearest Recompression Chamber: St. Elisabeth Hospital, ☎ 624900 or 625100.

Getting There: ALM Airlines flies from Atlanta four times a week (Thursday, Friday, Saturday and Sunday), and daily from Miami. Connecting flights are available from most major cities on Air Aruba, American Airlines and Guyana Airways..

Driving: Traffic moves on the right. A US driver's license is accepted. Car rentals: Budget, ☎ 683198; National, ☎ 683489 or 611644; Jeep Car Rental, ☎ 379044; Love Car Rental, ☎ 690444; 24-Hour Car Rental, ☎ 689410 or 617568. Curaçao also has an excellent bus system to transport visitors around the island.

Language: The official language is Dutch, but English and Spanish are spoken as well. Most residents speak Papiamento, a blend of Portuguese, Dutch, African, English, French and some Arawak Indian.

Documents: Passports are not required for US and Canadian Citizens. Travelers will need proof of citizenship and a return or continuing ticket. A passport or birth certificate is necessary for reentering the US.

Customs: Arriving passengers may bring in 400 cigarettes, 50 cigars, 100 cigarillos, 2 liters of liquor. There is a duty-free shop at the airport.

US residents may bring home, free of duty, $400 worth of articles, including 200 cigarettes, and 1 quart liquor per person over 21 years of age plus $25 worth of Edam or Gouda cheese for personal use.

Airport Tax: For international flights, $10; for inter-island flights, $5.65.

Currency: The guilder, or florin, is the Netherlands Antilles' unit of money. The official rate of exchange is US $1 = 1.77 NA florin. However, US dollars and major credit cards are accepted throughout the island.

Climate: Curaçao's tropical climate remains fairly constant year round. The average temperature is 80° F and less than 23 inches of rain fall annually. The island is outside of the hurricane belt and its cooling trade winds average 15 mph.

Clothing: Snorkelers should bring wetskins or long-sleeve shirts to protect from the sun. Wetsuits are comfortable when making several deep dives, but warm ocean temperatures make them unnecessary baggage for the average sport diver. Topside dress is casual, lightweight. Topless sunbathing is practiced on some beaches. Jackets are required for a few restaurants.

Electricity: 110-128 volts, AC (50 HZ), which is compatible with American electric razors and blow dryers. Adaptors are not needed. The Lions Dive Hotel has 220 volts.

Religious Services: Protestant, Catholic, Jewish, Episcopal, Seventh Day Adventist.

Additional Information: Curaçao Tourist Board, 475 Park Avenue South, Suite 2000, NY, NY 10016, ☎ (800) 332-8266 or (212) 683-7660, fax (212) 683-9337. *In Miami*: 330 Biscayne Boulevard, Suite 808, Miami, FL 333132, ☎ (305) 374-5811, fax (305) 374-6741.

In Curaçao: The Curaçao Tourism Development Foundation, 19 Willemstad, Netherlands Antilles; ☎ (011) 5999-4616000, fax (011) 5999-4612305. E-mail: Curaçao @ix.netcom.com. Web site: www. interknowledge.com/Curaçao/index/html.

Dominica

Dominica, covering 290 square miles, is the largest island in the Windward chain. Situated between Martinique and Guadeloupe, it is a mountainous island with sheer cliffs on the coasts and volcanic peaks inland. Narrow strips of grey sand skirt much of its perimeter. It is ideal for the diver who craves a wilderness adventure—there are no casinos, and no duty-free shopping.

Intrepid travelers are lured by the island's sensuous environment and dramatic scenery, both topside and beneath the sea. Its mountainside trails throb with the colors and scents of wild orchids and teas, heliconias, giant ferns, and fruit trees. Cascading waterfalls and wild rivers harmonize with the sounds of exotic parrots and sea birds. Mountain pools simmer from the volcanos seething beneath them. Hillsides, dotted with tiny villages and the ruins of forts and former plantations, climb toward Morne Diablotin, the island's tallest peak, with an elevation of 4,747 ft.

Subsea terrain, too, is spectacular, with hot springs bubbling up through the sea floor, and shallow wrecks, caves, ledges and walls of critters. Black coral "trees" thrive as shallow as 50 ft.

The island's economic mainstay is agriculture, with abundant banana and coconut crops. But the island's most outstanding feature is water. There are more than 365 rivers, thermal springs, pools, and waterfalls fed by 350 inches of rainfall per year in the interior and 50 inches on the drier west coast. Thankfully, all of the resorts and dive sites lie off the "dry" western shores.

Most of the 84,000 inhabitants live on the coasts, but 3,700 acres in the northeastern section of Dominica are set aside for the Carib Indian, the island's original inhabitants. The Caribs are fishermen and farmers, canoe builders, basket makers and carvers.

Roseau, the capital and main city, is built on a flat plain of the Roseau River. It is a busy area which may be seen in its entirety by way of a half-hour

---

Dive Contributors: Karen & Dennis Sabo, dive instructors and operators of Landfall Productions; Derek Perryman, Dive Dominica.

walk. Most interesting are some old French Colonial buildings, botanical gardens at the south end and the Old Market on the waterfront where island crafts are offered.

Visitors arriving by cruise ship at the Cabrits National Park, on the northwest tip of Dominica, step off the 300-ft pier and are immediately surrounded by twin waterfalls and a lush garden.

When to Go
The best time to dive Dominica is during the driest season, Feb through April, though expect the possibility of "liquid sunshine" (rain) all year. Whenever you go, plan on doing combat with a ferocious mosquito population, especially at dawn and dusk.

History
Dominica means Sunday in Latin (*Dies Dominica*, day of the Lord). It was named by Columbus for the Sunday he discovered it, Nov 3, 1493. The island is also called *Waitukubuli* by the Carib Indians, which is translated by some to mean "tall is her body," and by others to mean "land of many battles."

The island was first assigned to the Carib Indians in 1660 by an Anglo-French treaty, but later French settlers moved in and established sugar plantations worked by imported black labor, which stirred friction between the Caribs, the Brits and the French. Hence, possession passed back and forth between France and Britain during the 18th century. The island gained independence in 1978.

Best Dives and Snorkeling Sites
☆☆☆☆ **Soufriere Pinnacle** rises from the depths of Soufriere Bay to within five ft of the surface. A favorite of macro-photographers, the pinnacle is a cornucopia of crabs, shrimp, lobster, octopi, anemones, starfish, tree worms, and gorgonians. Calm seas and light currents invite all levels of diver and snorkeler. The site is four miles off the southwest shore—a 15-minute boat ride.

☆☆☆☆ **Coral Gardens**, a short trip from Castaways Beach, is a shallow reef ranging in depth from 15 to 90 ft. Good for diving and snorkeling, the reef is vibrant with corkscrew and pink anemones, arrow crabs, violet Peterson shrimp, flourescent crinoids and flamingo tongue snails. Spotted and green moray eels, sting rays and scorpion fish hide in the shadows.

☆☆☆☆ **Scotts Head Pinnacle,** off the southwest tip of the island, is a kaleidoscope of brilliant finger sponges, nudibranches, bushy wire corals, sea plumes, crinoids, anemones, and gorgonians over a vertical maze of arches, caves, walls, and ledges. Beware the stinging hydroids!

Fish life is abundant with queen, French and gray angels, mackerel, kingfish, spotted drums, black-bar soldier fish, eels and octopus. The reef starts at 15 ft and drops to great depths. Sea conditions are usually moderate, occasionally rough. Suggested for experienced divers.

☆☆☆ **Scotts Head Drop-Off** lies five miles off Scotts Head, a fishing village at the southern tip of the island. Divers and snorkelers will find large sponges and lavish soft corals along the reef's shallow ledge. The ledge, which starts at five ft, runs along a wall that drops to 140 ft. Conditions are light to moderate. Good visibility.

☆☆ **Champagne** is a shallow site highlighted by sub-aquatic freshwater hot springs that emit a continuous profusion of hot bubbles. A fun dive, it's like jumping into a giant glass of club soda. Near shore with dependably calm conditions, the site covers an area of about 300 square ft. Depths range from near the surface to 80 ft, with 10 ft the average. The bottom is uninspiring brown weeds ruffled by schools of tiny sprat, reef fish and lobster. Dive or snorkel.

☆☆☆ **Canefield Tug** is a 60-ft wreck lying upright on a sandy bottom. The wreck is intact and acts as an artificial reef attracting colonies of hydroids, anemones, schools of squirrel fish, soldier fish and sergeant majors. The site is four miles from shore at Rivermouth. Visibility and sea conditions vary. Depths are from 55 to 90 ft.

☆☆☆ **Canefield Barge** is an overturned barge over patches of shallow reef. Depths of five to 40 ft and calm seas make this a good choice for snorkelers and divers. A bevy of small reef fish hover about the wreck. The bottom is vibrant with basket stars, anemones, hydroids and iridescent sponges.

☆☆☆ **Point Guinard Caves**, an area of shallow reefs, grottoes and caves, are fun for all level divers and snorkelers. The Caves at 50 ft may be penetrated at 30 ft, but there is rich coral growth in the shallows. It is a great spot for night dives and macro-photography, with sea horses, blood stars, octopi, crabs, lobster and hordes of sponges.

☆☆☆☆ **Danglebens Reef**, named for one of the divemaster's ancestors, is a complex of small pinnacles and canyons ending in a deep wall. Average reef depths are 40 to 120 ft. Large barrel and tube sponges, healthy corals, black coral bushes, big grouper and morays delight all level of divers. Excellent visibility. Sea conditions are light.

Shore Snorkeling

The best shore-entry snorkeling spots are Scotts Head on Sourfriere Bay in the southwest and Douglas Bay in the northwest, which has a reef less than 200 ft from the shore. Point Guignard off the southwest coast is another popular spot. On the north and northeast coasts try Woodford Hill Bay, Hodges Bay, Grand Baptiste Bay and Hampstead Beach. Check with dive shops for wind and water conditions before snorkeling.

Dive Operators

Dive Dominica at Castle Comfort Lodge is a full-service dive center. Boats depart at 9:30 for a two-tank trip. Refreshments on board. Friendly staff will wash, rinse and store all of your gear and return it to the boat for the next dive. Shore diving in front of the lodge. ☎ (888) 262-6611 or (809) 448-2188, fax (809) 448-6088. E-mail: dive@tod.dm. Web site: www.delphis.dm/dive. html.

Anchorage Dive Centres offers courses, reef, wreck and whale watching aboard two fast boats. Dive-hotel packages. ☎ (809) 448-2638; Fax: (809) 448-5680. Write to PO Box 34, Roseau, Dominica.

Dive Castaways features personal tours to their own special sites. ☎ (800) 223-9815 or (809) 449-6244, fax (809) 449-6246. Dive-hotel packages from $925. Write to PO Box 5, Roseau, Dominica. E-mail: castaways@mail. tod.dm. Web site: www.delphis.dm/castaways.htm.

East Carib Dive has day trips to the north and south. ☎ (809) 449-6575, fax (809) 449-6575. Write to: PO Box 375, Roseau, Dominica. Dive-hotel packages for groups and individuals. ☎ (800) 525-3833.

Nature Island Dive caters to small groups with a variety of water and landsports including kayaking and mountain biking. Dive boats visit Soufriere, Scotts Head Reserve and local reefs. ☎ (809) 449-8181, fax (809) 449-8182. E-mail: walshs@tod.dm. Website: www.delphis.dm/nid. htm.

Tours

Landfall Productions, run by dive instructors and underwater photo pros, Karen and Dennis Sabo, offer all-inclusive group and individual dive and snorkeling tours to Dominica from $675 for a diver, from $455 for a non-diver. ☎ (800) 525-3833 or (510) 794-1599, fax (510) 794-1617. E-mail: lndfall@aol.com. Write to 39675 Cedar Boulevard, Suite 295B, Newark, CA 94560.

Paradise Expedition & Trading Co. Ltd packages air, hotel and diving vacations from the US. Write to 6 Lincoln Park Plaza, Lincoln Park, NJ 07035. ☎ (800) 468-4748, fax 201-696-2335.

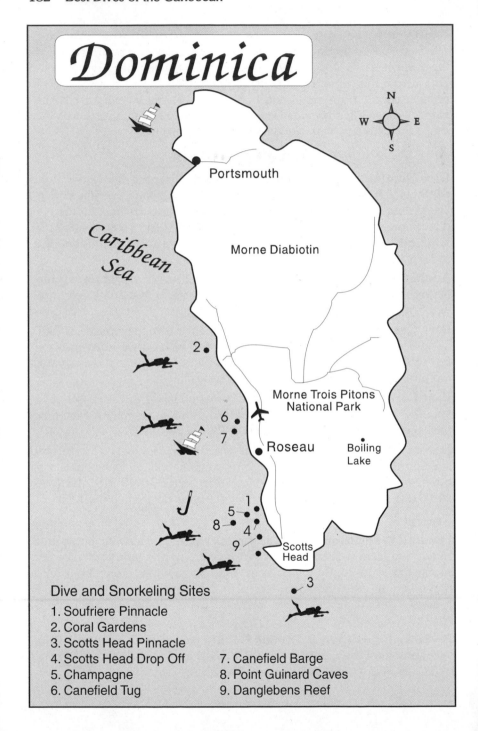

Dominica

Caribbean Sea

Portsmouth

Morne Diabiotin

Morne Trois Pitons
National Park

Roseau

Boiling
Lake

2

6
7

1
5
8
4
9

Scotts
Head

3

Dive and Snorkeling Sites

1. Soufriere Pinnacle
2. Coral Gardens
3. Scotts Head Pinnacle
4. Scotts Head Drop Off
5. Champagne
6. Canefield Tug

7. Canefield Barge
8. Point Guinard Caves
9. Danglebens Reef

Island Trails offers guided hiking/snorkeling/scuba tours. ☎ (800) 233-4366.

Accommodations

Anchorage Hotel & Dive Center, one-mile south of Roseau, features 32 air-conditioned, clean, modern rooms, cable TV, phones, squash court, pool, bar, restaurant, and full-service PADI dive center. ☎ (809) 448-2638, fax (809) 448-5680. E-mail: anchorage@mail.tod.dm.

Castle Comfort Diving Lodge is a cozy 10-room inn. Five rooms have ocean-view balconies. All are air-conditioned and have ceiling fans. Great meals! Friendly service. Dive-hotel packages with Dive Dominica from $899 per week include breakfast and dinner, six boat dives, unlimited air for shore diving. Sites are about 25 minutes from the lodge. Boats depart at 9:30 am. In the US reserve through Landfall, ☎ (800) 525-3833. Hotel direct, ☎ (809) 448-2188, fax (809) 448-6088. E-mail: dive@tod.dm.

The **Fort Young Hotel** is a newly rebuilt and refurbished hotel within the walls of the original fort built in 1770. High on a cliff overlooking the Caribbean, the 33-room, ocean-front hotel features cable TV, pool, walking proximity to the city, direct overseas dial telephones, restaurant and bar. Neat atmosphere. Dive packages are offered with Dive Dominica from $989 for seven nights, breakfast, 10 dives, transfers. ☎ (800) 525-3833 or (809) 448-5000, fax (809) 448-5006.

The Castaways Beach Hotel, a charming 27-room waterfront resort surrounded by botanical gardens, features modern, spacious guest rooms with ceiling fans and air-conditioning. A beachfront terrace looks out over the sea. Adjacent dive shop. Creole and international cuisine is served at the resort's Almond Tree Restaurant. Casual and quiet. Package tours through Landfall Productions and Caradonna Caribbean Tours from $925 per person. ☎ (888) CASTAWAYS or (809) 449-6244/5, fax (809) 449-6246. E-mail: castaways@mail.tod.dm. Web site: www.delphis.dm/castaways.htm.

Lauro Club, on the midwest coast, is a group of cottages situated on a cliff over the sea. A good choice for a dive honeymoon, each of 10 cottages features a living room that opens onto a private balcony overlooking the Caribbean. Swimming pool, bar, restaurant, entertainment. Diving with East Carib Dive. Packages from $925 include seven nights accommodations, breakfast and dinner daily, 10 boat dives, east coast tour, river trip, taxes. ☎ (800) 525-3833, (809) 449-6602, fax (809) 449-6603.

Dining

Local specialties include frog legs (mountain chicken), stuffed land crab backs, callaloo soup—made from dasheen leaves and coconut crea—and spicy freshwater shrimps. Manicou, a rodent similar to an opossum, is a local favorite that sometimes turns up on restaurant menus. Restaurants in Roseau serve more familiar dishes too.

Try local specialties at **Falls View Guest House Restaurant** on the outskirts of Roseau. ☎ 448-0064 ($15-$20) or **La Tropical** at Wykies Guesthouse in the heart of Roseau, ☎ 448-8015 ($8-$10). Stop by the Ocean Breeze Restaurant at the Lauro Club Resort for sumptuous lobster and steak barbecue on Wednesday and Saturday nights, ☎ 448-2638 ($15-$23). **Al's Ice Cream**, 11 Cork Street, Roseau, serves 25 flavors, snacks and drinks.

The Sutton Place Grille on Old Street, Roseau, offers West Indian dining in the courtyard of a 100-year-old stone house ($10-$30). ☎ 449-8700.

Other Activities and Sightseeing

As in all high-altitude areas, be sure to figure strenuous and high-altitude climbs into your dive tables. More than one person has suffered decompression sickness from the combination.

Besides diving there is hiking, canoeing, guided, jungle-river tours and rainforest tours. A new coastal road rings the island. Resorts offer windsurfing, water skiing, sailing and tennis.

The favorite topside wonder is **Trafalgar Falls**, just north of Roseau. You can drive to within a 15-minute walk of the 100-ft falls, which converge into a lovely pool of granite boulders.

Scotts Head at the southwest tip of the island is a picturesque fishing village offering scenic views of the Atlantic Ocean and Caribbean Sea. It is also the site of the region's first aloe farm.

Heading north, turn left at the village of Soufriere to reach Sulfur Springs, where you can see bubbling hot springs of grey mud. Or if you enjoy long hikes, head for **Valley of Desolation** and **Boiling Lake**, east of Roseau, where the scenery is absolutely intoxicating.

Emerald Pool in the Central Forest Reserve is a short hike from the road on the northeast side of **Morne Trois Pitons National Park.** Located in the rainforest, the pool is fed by a lovely waterfall.

Boat tours of **Indian River** will bring you close up to exotic birds and plants. Or take the cross-island road to the **Carib Reserve** on the central eastern coast. Native craft shops pave the way. Tours in this region take off from **The Floral Gardens**, (☎ 445-7636) situated at the base of the tropical rain forest bordering the Carib Reserve.

Souvenir shoppers seeking island crafts should head for the craft stalls in Roseau's Old Market, located in the courtyard behind the post office.

Facts

Helpful Phone Numbers: Police, ☎ 999; ambulance, ☎ 999; Tourist Board, ☎ (809) 448-2351/82186; Canefield Airport, ☎ 449-1199; American Eagle, ☎ 445-7204; Liat, ☎ 448-2421; Air Guadaloupe, ☎ 448-2181; Cardinal Airlines, ☎ 449-0322/8922.

Nearest Recompression Chamber: None within a reasonable distance.

Airlines: Reaching Dominica requires a stop in San Juan, Antigua, St. Lucia, St. Maartin or Guadeloupe. From most European and North American cities, it can be reached in a day's journey without an overnight stay. Liat, Air Guadaloupe, Air Martinique and Nature Island Airways are the carriers from the larger islands into Dominica. Gateway islands are served by American Airlines (☎ (800) 433-7300).

Island Transportation: All areas may be reached via bus and taxi services.

Baggage: Only one carry-on bag is permitted and it must fit under your seat. International baggage allowances prevail on flights to Dominica and may not exceed a total of 44 pounds. Baggage in excess of 44 pounds will be charged (depending upon the carrier) around US $1 per pound and flown on a "space available" basis.

Driving: On the left. A local license is required and may be obtained from the airports or at the Traffic Department, High Street, Roseau (Mon to Fri). Must be aged 25 to 65 and show a valid driver's license with at least two years experience.

Documents: US and Canadian citizens need a passport or proof of citizenship bearing a photograph. A return or onward ticket is also required.

Customs: Banana, coconut, plants and straw materials cannot be brought in. Citrus, coffee, avocado, plants and soil are forbidden.

Currency: The Eastern Caribbean Dollar exchange rate is approximately $2.67 to US $1. Major credit cards are accepted at some hotels and restaurants, but most purchases and tours require cash in EC dollars. Businesses exchange at EC $2.60 for US $1.

Language: English is the official language. Creole or French patois is widely spoken.

Climate: Temperatures drop and the chance of showers rises with the elevation. Temperatures range from 75° to 90° F. The coolest months are Dec through March.

Clothing: Lightweight casual cottons are best. Visitors should **not** wear swim suits or short shorts in the streets or stores. A light sweater is suggested for cooler evenings. Pack light, the island is not dressy.

For hiking, bring comfortable hiking shoes, light weight raincoat, camera and film, knapsack and shoulder bag, bottled water, hat, sunglasses, sun screen and mosquito repellent.

The water temperature on a deep dive may drop as low as 72° F. Baggage permitting, a shorty or wetsuit jacket is recommended.

Electricity: 220/240 volts, 50 cycles. A converter is necessary for US appliances.

Time: Atlantic Standard Time, one hour ahead of Eastern Standard Time and four hours behind GMT.

Valuables: Lock everything up as you would at home. Avoid taking valuables to the beach.

Departure Tax: US $12.

Religious Services: Roman Catholic, Anglican, Methodist, Pentecostal, Berean Bible, Baptist, Seventh Day Adventist and Baha'i Faith.

Additional Information: *US:* Caribbean Tourism Organization, 20 East 46th St., NY, NY 10017-2452, ☎ (212) 475-7542, fax (212) 697-4258. London: Dominica Tourist Office, 1 Collingham Gardens, London SW5 OHW, ☎ 071 835-1937, fax 071 373-8743. Dominica: National Development Corp., PO Box 73, Roseau, Commonwealth of Dominica, WI, ☎ 809-448-2351/82186, fax (809) 448-5840. Web site: frenchcaribbean.com/DominicaActivSports.html.

Dominican Republic

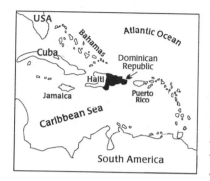

The Dominican Republic shares the Caribbean's second largest island, Hispaniola (between Cuba and Puerto Rico), with Haiti. Located on the eastern half of the island, the Dominican Republic, with an area of 19,376 square miles, is flanked by the Atlantic Ocean to the north and the Caribbean Sea to the south. Its central portion is sculpted by four great mountain ranges with peaks over 10,000 ft. Its coastline varies from rocky cliffs to sandy beaches. Reefs and ancient wrecks surround much of the shoreline.

Santo Domingo, on the south Caribbean coast and eastern bank of the Ozama River, is the main port and capital city. Home to more than one million people, it is the oldest city of the New World and professed burial place of its founder, Christopher Columbus. Built in the early 1500s, the city was the first hub of Spanish culture and commerce in the western hemisphere.

One section, about 15 city blocks, has been restored as "Old Santo Domingo" and includes the castle of Diego Colon, Columbus' son and the island's first viceroy. The 22-room castle has been tastefully refurbished with paintings and tapestries to reflect the 16th century. Colonial-style shops, galleries and restaurants surround the old city's central plaza.

The main city area is very cosmopolitan and tourist-oriented, with 3,498 hotel rooms, several casinos, shopping malls, nightclubs and restaurants. The city boasts the New World's first cathedral, first university (Santo Thomas de Aquino), first hospital (San Nicolas de Bari), the Monastery of San Francisco, the Ozama Fortress and the world's largest open-air discotheque along its shoreline drive, the Malecon.

When touring Santo Domingo expect solicitations from countless beggars and youthful entrepreneurs pushing shoeshines and other services.

Boca Chica, 31 miles east of Santo Domingo, La Romana, 110 miles east of Santo Domingo and Bayahibe, 125 miles east of Santo Domingo, are

Dive-material contributor: Walter Frischbutter, Treasure Divers.

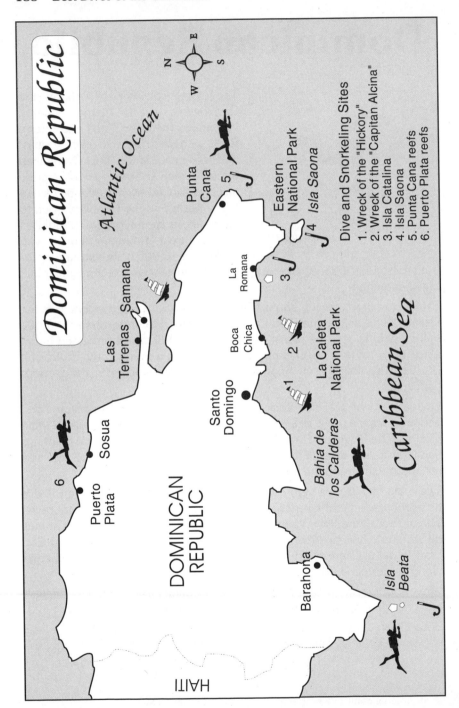

Dominican Republic

Atlantic Ocean

Caribbean Sea

HAITI

DOMINICAN REPUBLIC

Puerto Plata

Sosua

Las Terrenas

Samana

Punta Cana

Santo Domingo

Boca Chica

La Caleta National Park

Bahia de los Calderas

Barahona

Isla Beata

La Romana

Eastern National Park

Isla Saona

Dive and Snorkeling Sites
1. Wreck of the "Hickory"
2. Wreck of the "Capitan Alcina"
3. Isla Catalina
4. Isla Saona
5. Punta Cana reefs
6. Puerto Plata reefs

the jump-off points for the country's best Caribbean dive and snorkeling sites, including La Caleta National Park and the Eastern National Park (Parque Nacional del Este), which encompasses the islands of Saona and Catalina. The marine portion of the parks is a sanctuary for manatees, turtles and waves of passing dolphins. Dependably calm seas and miles of virgin reefs prevail.

Costa Caribe, just west of Boca Chica, is the chief weekend playground for Santo Domingo's million residents. Formerly known as the fishing villages of Juan Dolio and Guayacanes, this beautiful stretch has more than 15 miles of uninterrupted beaches shaded by coconut palms and serviced by first class hotels. It is a half-hour drive from the Las Americas International Airport and under an hour from Santo Domingo, the capital city. Given the close proximity to the capital this area draws crowds on weekends.

On the north coast, the main tourist area stretches from Puerto Plata, a large city and deep-water port, to Cabrera, where impressive beaches and coconut groves have lured Europeans for more than 500 years. This area is also a prime whale-watching spot. During winter months (December to March) thousands of humpback whales migrate to an offshore breeding ground. The breeding ground is 50 miles north of the coast, but the herds are spotted en route as they pass the Samana Peninsula, which forms the northeast corner of the Dominican Republic. Reefs and wrecks dot the northern shores, but rough seas frequently rule out diving except during summer. Large, modern, upscale resorts skyline the area.

The country's southwest region is the least developed. It is the locale of the largest lake in the Caribbean, Lake Enriquillo, which has water three times more saline than the ocean, and where the largest American crocodile colony of the New World resides.

Mosquitos readily announce their presence throughout the coastal areas. Bring and use repellent. We find Autan (sold in the Caribbean) and Off Deep Woods useful. Autan, if you can find it, is the best defense against the tiny gnats or no-see-ums that come out after a rainfall.

The best weather and the fewest mosquitos exist from mid-Dec through April, but divers may prefer the summer months when the water is warmer and calmer seas prevail on the north and east coasts. When the skies cooperate, diving along the Caribbean's southeast coast is good year-round.

History

Christopher Columbus discovered the island of Hispaniola in December, 1492 when his flagship, *Santa Maria*, ran aground on what is now Haiti's north coast. Thirty-nine crewmen who were left behind started the first Spanish settlement in the New World, La Navidad. But, when Columbus returned a year later, the settlement had been destroyed and all the crewmen killed.

Late in 1493, Columbus established a new colony at Isabela, near Puerto Plata, but abandoned the site for a better harbor on the south coast, now known as Santo Domingo (originally Santiago de Guzman). Columbus' son Diego was appointed viceroy, and Hispaniola became the hub of Spanish culture and commerce in the New World. From there the Spanish colonizers moved on to exploit Mexico and Peru.

French, Dutch and English explorers settled various parts of Hispaniola during the 1500s and 1600s. As the Spanish settlers congregated around Santo Domingo, the north and west coasts were left to buccaneers and foreign settlers who eventually came under the protection of France. In 1697 Spain recognized France's claims to the western third of the island.

The French colony first known as Saint Domingue, and later as Haiti, prospered while the Spanish colony declined. By 1795, Spanish Hispaniola was ceded to France. By 1844, Juan Pablo Duarte established the Dominican Republic as an independent nation, but the nation, under constant Haitian threat, asked Spain to reinstate its sovereignty. Fighting between Spain and Haiti continued until 1865 when a strong-willed military dictator, Ulises Heureaux, took over. Heureaux was in power until 1897 when he was assassinated.

The early 1900s brought intercession by the US. US occupation brought military rule and economic exploitation by US businesses. The Dominicans resented the US military troops and forced their evacuation in 1924.

From 1930 to 1961, the island was ruled by Dominican military dictator Rafael Leonidas Trujillo Molina. Trujillo's corrupt form of government left no citizen safe from arrest or degradation by his secret police. Despite the misery he brought upon the people, Trujillo modernized and rebuilt highways, sugar, coffee and cocoa plantations, and by 1947, paid off all of the nation's foreign debts. On May 30, 1961, he was assassinated by his army.

With Trujillo's death, the Dominican Republic attempted to establish a democracy. In 1962, the country held its first free election in 38 years and elected Juan Bosch, a writer and professor. The new government, plagued by unrest and agitation from the upper class and military, fell to national unrest in a bloodless coup. The US, alarmed at reports of communist influence, stepped in. Military command was then turned over to an Inter-American Peace Force.

Since then, the Dominican Republic struggled through the 1970s' worldwide recession, which touched off a crisis in the sugar industry; then a 1979 hurricane, which devastated much of the island; and social unrest fueled by crowded cities. The 1980's brought rising foreign debt and inflation.

With its continued struggle for a better quality of life, the Dominican Republic remains at peace; its golden beaches flaunt the promise of a new era of tourism.

Best Dive and Snorkeling Sites

The best dive and snorkeling sights are off Boca Chica, 30 miles east of Santa Domingo, and the marine portion of the Eastern National Park off La Romana, 110 miles east of Santo Domingo. Both marine parks, less than a mile from the shore, display healthy corals in all but the extreme shallows. Large fish are rare, as sport fishing is big and reef preservation is new to Santo Domingo. New laws prohibiting spearfishing and coral collecting in the sanctuary have brought back a decent population of tropicals.

There are several good dive sites in La Caleta and along the reefs that start 1½ miles out from La Romana and follow the coast past Bayahibe to Isla Catalina and Isla Saona. Reef depths range from the shallows to 150 ft. Dive and snorkeling boats leave from the marinas at Boca Chica, La Romana and Bayahibe.

☆☆☆☆ **Isla Catalina** is an uninhabited islet, 2½ miles off La Romana, which was once used as a zoo. Exotic wild birds and monkeys are often sighted along its beaches. The island, surrounded by beautiful reefs that start at 15 ft and drop to 110, is ideal for snorkelers and all levels of divers. The reef, protected from spearfishing and coral collecting, flourishes with walls of tropicals, lobster, sea fans, sea rods, big barrel sponges and black corals at depth. Seas are calm with an occasional light current. Visibility is excellent, though the shallows get kicked up when several snorkeling boats anchor at the same time.

There are no facilities or fresh water on the island but, for the adventurous among you, camping is possible if permission is obtained from La Romana Naval Station in advance. You need to bring everything with you. At dusk you will be joined by a ferocious mosquito population. Wear and carry as much bug repellent as you can.

☆☆☆ **The Hickory** is a 140-ft wreck intentionally scuttled in the shallows of La Caleta National Marine Park off La Caleta Beach. Remains of the wreck are found between three ft and 60 ft. The wreck is covered with anemones and hydroids and lots of reef fish—squirrel fish, sergeant majors, and spotted drums. It is surrounded by a pretty reef. Calm seas and 100-ft-plus visibility make this spot good for divers and snorkelers.

☆☆☆ **Wreck of the _Capitan Alcina_** is another ship purposely sunk in La Caleta National Park to attract fish. The wreck sits in a ravine between canyons of the reef. You can reach the top at 75 ft, the bottom at 126 ft. Expect a good reef-fish population, pillar corals, big brain corals, sea rods, plumes, sea fans and deep-water gorgonians. The sea is always fairly calm and currents are mild. Suggested for experienced divers.

When the Atlantic seas are calm (usually in summer for a short period) there is additional diving off Isla Punta Cana on the southeast coast, and off Sosua and Cabrera on the north coast. Sport fishing and spearfishing in the northern coastal areas have taken a toll on the fish population, but some of the underwater terrain is pretty. Numerous dive shops are found around Puerto Plata.

Punta Cana Dive Sites

Pristine coral reefs and mini-walls off Bavaro and Punta Cana on the East Coast are subject to wind and current patterns. When seas are calm this is a super diving area.

☆☆ **Pepe** features massive hard coral formations, groupers, rays and nurse sharks. Depths range from 45 to 60 ft. Good photo opportunities. Conditions vary with the wind.

☆☆ **Entrada de Las Cuevas**, from seven to 50 ft, starts inside of the barrier reef which is formed of caverns and overhangs covered with hard corals. Huge schools of silversides, lobsters and rays inhabit the caverns. Conditions vary.

☆ **El Acuario**, from seven to 35 ft, is a horseshoe-shaped area within the inner reef. Chutes, passages, overhangs and caverns shelter hordes of tropicals. On calm days this area is good for all level divers.

☆ **La Choza**, part of the barrier section of the reef, extends out to form high coral channels, and is a habitat for schooling fish and several stingrays. This spot is often calm with depths from 35 to 50 ft.

☆ **El Tiburon**, from 60- to 70-ft depths, is part of the outer reef, which is a series of eroded spur and groove formations and large coral heads. Reef sharks, large groupers and large schools of fish are often sighted around the coral heads. Conditions vary. Expect some surge on most days.

Dive Operators

Stick with the dive shops associated with the resorts, as most of the Dominican dive shops cater to locals. Certification cards are required to dive in the Dominican Republic.

Treasure Divers at the Don Juan Beach Resort in Boca Chica has one of the finest English-speaking operations in the Dominican Republic. Instructor Walter Frischbutter offers reef and wreck trips and cave diving (experienced and properly equipped cave divers only) off Boca Chica and La Caleta. PADI certification courses. ☎ (809) 523-5320, fax (809) 523-4444.

Diver's Cove Dominicano, a PADI training center in San Pedro, sits halfway between Boca Chica and La Romana. Trips and courses. ☎ (809) 556-5350 or (809) 529-8225.

Punta Cana Dive Center, at the Punta Cana Resort, visits reefs off Punta Cana on the east coast. Cost for a one-tank dive is $45; three dives for $115. Includes BCD, regulator, tank, weights, snorkel and mask. Resort course is $80. Resort, ☎ (800) 972-2139, (809) 541-2714, fax (809) 541-2286.

If you are staying on the north coast, try **Caribbean Marine Puerto Plata**. This PADI center visits the northern wrecks and reefs. ☎ (809) 320-2249, fax (809) 320-2262.

The resorts listed below either have dive shops or can arrange for dive and snorkeling trips.

Accommodations

A complete list of resorts and rates is available from the Dominican Republic tourist office, PO Box 497, Santo Domingo, Dominican Republic. ☎ (800) 752-1151 or (809) 689-3657, fax (809) 682-3806.

Hamaca Beach Hotel, beachfront, Boca Chica, features 460 deluxe rooms and suites. Pools, jacuzzi, sauna, water sports, tennis, horseback riding, gym, four restaurants, five bars, children's playground. All rooms have AC, cable TV, private bathroom, Rates for garden view are $125 per night, per person, based on double occupancy, $140 for ocean-front. Costs includes all meals and snacks, activities and taxes. Scuba and snorkeling boat trips are not included. ☎ (800) 945-0792, (809) 523-4611, fax (809) 523-6767.

Don Juan Beach Resort in Boca Chica offers 124 air-conditioned suites, snackbar, restaurant, pool, disco, tennis, dive shop, sand beach, entertainment, baby sitting service, and free parking. Rates start at $100 per day in winter. Book through your travel agent or ☎ (809) 687-9157, fax (809) 688-5271.

Club Dominicus Beach Resort in Bayahibe is a stone's throw from the reef. This Italian-run beachfront resort offers 340 rooms and all-inclusive packages that include diving, Sunfish sailboats, sailboards, three meals daily and nightly calypso shows. Winter room rates are from $110 to $145 in winter, $85 to $120 in summer. ☎ (809) 565-6591, fax (809) 567-4710 or (809) 687-8583.

Casa De Campo, a huge 7,000-acre resort complex in La Romana, has its own airport and marina, 750 rooms or villas and a variety of sports. The resort appeals more to South Americans and Europeans than Americans and is geared to snorkelers more than divers. But if you are a snorkeler who is also a trap or skeet shooter, tennis player, horseback rider, polo player, artist or golfer, curiosity alone will lure you here. This place has it all, including a 16th-century replica of a Mediterranean artist village, Altos de Chavon, and its acclaimed School of Design. For watersports there are glass-bottom boats, snorkeling, picnic cruises to Catalina Island, 14 swimming pools, miles of beaches, snorkeling off their Minitas Beach, paddleboats and windsurfing. ☎ (800) 877-3643, (305) 856-7083 or (809) 523-3333, fax (809) 523-8394 or (305) 858-4677.

Punta Cana Beach Resort offers a wide choice of accommodations from villas, studios and suites. All are air-conditioned, with cable TV. Punta Cana Dive PADI Center on premises. Other sports offered are horseback riding, bicycling, tennis and pool swimming. Features include a beautiful palm-lined beach, disco and outdoor restaurant that offers grilled seafood for lunch. Franco's Pizzeria serves pizza, salads and ice cream. Pool bar and beach bar. Good fish-watch snorkeling off the beach. Children seven and over may join daily snorkeling tours at no charge. Winter rates are from $115 to $135 per person, per day, meals included. Children 2-12 years when sharing a room with two adults pay $15 per day. ☎ (800) 972-2139 or (809) 541-2714, fax 541-2286.

Club Med, Punta Cana, features traditional Club Med amenities—water skiing, windsurfing, sailing, and lounging. Good for families. Gorgeous, palm-studded beaches. No dive shop, but scuba and snorkeling trips are easily arranged. Rates for seven nights are $798 per adult, including three meals daily with wine and beer for lunch and dinner. ☎ 1-(800) CLUB-MED.

Dining

Don't drink the water or eat the skins of raw fruit or vegetables! You might suffer Caonabo's revenge, aka "the tourist's disease." The cure, even worse to some than the disease, is *mangu*, a purée of green plantains.

Note: Menu prices are often in Dominican pesos. D$12.50=US $1.

Italian, Spanish, French and Jamaican restaurants are plastered along the beach roads and the cities. Full-course dinners in the tourist areas are about US $20. Much lower prices prevail in the small local restaurants. Several good restaurants and wonderful street vendors are found along the beach road (the Malecon) in Santo Domingo. The vendors' carts steam with sizzling fried pork rinds (chicharones) and meat-filled pastries (pastelitos). American sandwiches, snacks, pizza, and salads are offered at the Sheraton's coffee shop. Beer afficionados will enjoy a cold Presidente.

In La Romana you'll find a wide range of restaurants in the Casa de Campo complex. For super views and fresh seafood try **Casa del Rio** in Altos.

Dominican menus typically offer a version of *La Bandera,* a compote of white rice, red beans and stewed meat, usually served with a salad and fried plantains. Regional dishes include fish in coconut milk in Samana and goat meat in Azua, where the goats are fed a daily dish of wild oregano. In Puerto Plata and the south coast, crabs are the favored menu item. A breakfast favorite is *tortilla de jamon*—a hot ham omelet. *Sancocho* is a Dominican stew prepared differently in each region. *Sancocho Prieto* is a black stew made with seven different meats (don't ask which seven meats).

Other Activities and Sightseeing

If you plan to tour Old Santo Domingo, include a stop at **El Alcazar,** Diego Columbus' Castle; **Casa del Cordon,** the first residential house built in Santo Domingo; the **Dominican Monastery;** and the ruins of **St. Nicolas De Bari Hospital.** The remains of Christopher Columbus are believed to be in the **Cathedral of Santa Maria la Menor,** the oldest cathedral in the New World.

In La Romana there is the **Museum of Archaeology** at Altos de Chavon, which features exhibits of the Taino Indians, Hispaniola's first inhabitants.

City and mountain excursions are offered from Santo Domingo tour companies. Try **Metro Tours, ☎** 544-4580 or **Palm Tours, ☎** 682-3407.

Facts

Helpful Phone Numbers: Police or ambulance, ☎ 911. Doctor: *Santo Domingo,* Clinica Gomez Patino, Independencia, ☎ (701) 685-9131; *La Romana,* Centro Medico Oriental, Sta. Rosa, ☎ 556-2555. Tourist board, ☎ 689-3657. International Airports: *Las Americas,* Santo Domingo, ☎ 549-0450/80; *Herrera,* Santo Domingo, ☎ 567-3900; *Punta Aguila,* La Romana, ☎ 556-5565; *Punta Cana,* Higuey, ☎ 686-8790; *La Union,* Puerto Plata, ☎ 586-0219; *Cibao,* Santiago, ☎ 582-4894.

Nearest Recompression Chamber: Santo Domingo.

Airlines: Direct service is available from US gateway cities and most Canadian and European travel centers. American, ☎ (800) 433-7300; American Eagle, ☎ (800) 433-7300; Continental, ☎ 562-6688; Air Canada, ☎ 567-2236; Air Aruba, ☎ 541-8766; ALM, Iberia, Lufthansa, Varig, Viasa, Aeropostal, Air France.

Driving: On the right.

Rental Cars: Avis, ☎ (809) 535-7191, fax (809) 535-1747; ☎ Budget (800) 472-3325.

Documents: Citizens of the US, Canada and the Caribbean must have a valid passport and a Tourist Card, which costs $10 and may be purchased upon arrival at one of the international airports. Maximum stay is 60 days. Citizens of the United Kingdom may stay up to 90 days with a valid passport.

Customs: You may bring in a liter of alcohol, 200 cigarettes and gift articles with a value of no more than $100. Anyone entering the country with opium, cocaine, coca, cannabis or related drug-making herbs will be fined or imprisoned without bail. You **may not leave** with more than US $5,000 in cash or travelers checks.

Currency: The Dominican Peso. US $1=D $14.02. The US dollar is not accepted. Change only as much as you think you'll need as most banks won't change it back to US currency. It is easiest to change currency at the airport. Banks are closed on weekends. Major credit cards are accepted at large establishments; however, a surcharge of 3-5% is added on.

Language: Spanish is the official language. People linked to tourism usually also speak English.

Climate: Temperatures along the south coast are approximately 82° F in winter, slightly higher in summer with highs in the 90s.

Clothing: Lightweight. Carry a sweater or jacket for winter evenings. The seashore resorts are informal. Shorts and bare chests are not welcome in the churches. Divers should bring a shorty wetsuit, lightweight wetsuit or wetsuit jacket during winter months. In summer a wetskin or T-shirt suffices.

Electricity: 110-120 volts, 60 cycles, as in the US.

Time: Atlantic Standard (Eastern Standard + 1 hour)

Departure Tax: US $10.

Religious Services: Catholic, Evangelical Protestant, Assembly of God, Protestant Episcopal, Seventh-Day Adventist.

Additional Information: *In the US,* ☎ (800) 752-1151; *in Canada,* ☎ (800) 563-1 611, fax (514) 499-1393. Web site: www.codetel.net.do; news and information, www.drl.com.

Grenada

Nestled in the eastern Caribbean, Grenada—the largest of a three-island nation that also includes Carriacou and Petit Martinique—is the most southerly of the Windward Islands and is the gateway to the Grenadines.

Renowned for its deep, sheltered harbors, the island has long been a favorite stopover for yachts and cruise ships. St. George's, the capital city, boasts a superb harbor, shaped like a horseshoe, that was formed partially out of the crater of an extinct volcano.

The island's perimeter is blessed with 80 miles of white sand beaches. Its coastline stretches out in hundreds of small peninsulas that form numerous sheltered bays and lagoons. Offshore coral reefs provide home to huge turtles, stingrays, and tropicals. Shipwrecks abound.

Intriguing, too, is Grenada's mountainous terrain. Volcanic in origin, it is thickly wooded, and wildly tropical, with towering thickets of bamboo, banana plantations, orchids, bubbling hot springs and waterfalls—home to butterflies, armadillos, monkeys and exotic cuckoo birds. Fertile soils produce a fragrant bounty of tropical fruits, cocoa, nutmeg, mace, ginger root, thyme, tonka bean, tamarind, turmeric, cinnamon and cloves. Red-roofed houses pepper the hillside.

Carriacou and Petit Martinique retain the idyllic character of early life in the Caribbean. In Carriacou, boat builders still construct and launch sturdy, wooden schooners as they have for generations. The brightly-colored boats ply between the islands, carrying passengers and cargo, their huge white sails billowing in the trade wind. Carriacou has great diving and snorkeling reefs off her south and west coasts around White, Mabouya and Sandy Islands.

History

History records Christopher Columbus as the first to sight Grenada in 1498. He named the egg-shaped island Concepcion. Peaceful tribes of Ciboneys and Arawaks first inhabited the island, followed by the more war-like Caribs, who named the island Camerhogne.

Contributor: David Macnaghten, Dive Grenada.

St. George's, horseshoe-shaped harbor.

The Caribs were driven by the French to mass suicide in 1651 at the famous "Carib's Leap," located at the northern end of the island where the town of Sauteurs (named after the event—French for "jumpers") now stands.

During the dynastic wars of the 18th century, Grenada changed hands several times between the British and French, until it was finally ceded to the British in 1783. Grenada became independent on February 7, 1974.

The late 1970s brought the reign of a Marxist government, which endorsed the establishment of a Cuban military runway and submarine base on Grenada. Tropical fields were being devastated, the tourist population dwindled and the deteriorating island was crawling with Soviet operatives. In 1984, terrorists took over an American medical school. President Reagan responded by sending in troops and replanting the seeds of democracy. Today, peace and tranquility reign and the island is rebuilding a healthy tourist trade.

Nicknamed the "Isle of Spice," Grenada is one of the last Caribbean islands that actively exports spices. Many of the islanders' homes are constructed of the ballast stones off-loaded by early merchant ships when they took on spices.

Best Dive and Snorkeling Sites

Grenada dive and snorkeling sites are off shore from Grand Anse Beach, Molinere Point and Dragon Bay, all on the west (leeward) coast.

Diving and snorkeling is weather dependent. During dry periods the visibility exceeds 100 ft. After a heavy rainfall, runoff from the rivers can lower visibility to 25 ft. Decompression dives are not recommended as there are no chambers in the area.

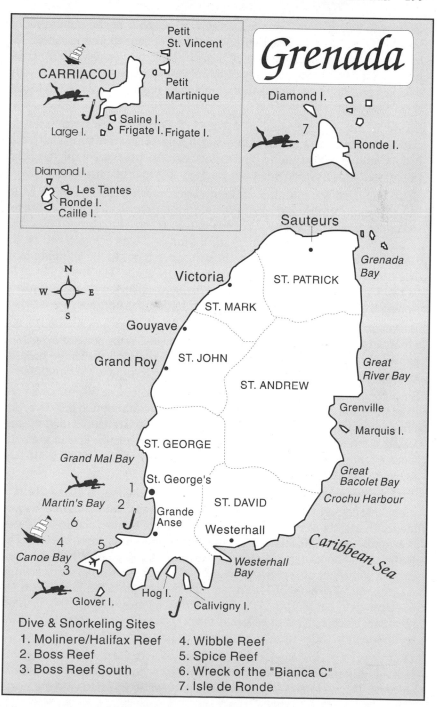

CARRIACOU

Petit
St. Vincent

Petit
Martinique

Saline I.

Large I.   Frigate I. Frigate I.

Diamond I.

Les Tantes
Ronde I.
Caille I.

Diamond I.

7

Ronde I.

Grenada
Bay

Sauteurs

Victoria

ST. PATRICK

ST. MARK

Gouyave

ST. JOHN

Grand Roy

ST. ANDREW

Great
River Bay

Grenville

Marquis I.

ST. GEORGE

Grand Mal Bay

St. George's

Great
Bacolet Bay

Crochu Harbour

ST. DAVID

Martin's Bay

1

2

6

Grande
Anse

Westerhall

4

5

Canoe Bay

3

Westerhall
Bay

Caribbean Sea

Glover I.

Hog I.

Calivigny I.

N
W   E
S

Dive & Snorkeling Sites
1. Molinere/Halifax Reef
2. Boss Reef
3. Boss Reef South
4. Wibble Reef
5. Spice Reef
6. Wreck of the "Bianca C"
7. Isle de Ronde

Good snorkeling from Grenada's shore is possible at the southernmost headland of Morne Rouge Bay and the reef system of Grand Anse. The innermost reef has been destroyed, but a 100-200 ft swim will take you over huge sea fans and nice coral heads teaming with tropicals. Bring a floating dive flag and stay near to it as many small craft are in the area. A light surge should be expected.

Sandy Island, off the southwest coast of Carriacou, is surrounded by outstanding reefs and gorgeous beaches. It is one of the best snorkeling spots in the Caribbean. You need a boat to get there. Anchorage is south (leeward) of the island (yachtsmen need two anchors to avoid being washed ashore)

☆☆ The most adventurous scuba trip is to the **Bianca C**, a 600-ft cruise ship that sank October 24, 1961. Possibly the largest wreck in the Caribbean, the cruise liner, crippled by a boiler explosion, was at anchor for two days outside St. George's while it burned. It sank as it was being towed by the *HMS Londonderry* during an attempt to move it out of the shipping lane. The bottom rests on a sandy plain in 167 ft of water. The top decks at 90 to 120 ft are encrusted with hydroids and have collapsed since the sinking. Remains of the internal walls are badly rusted and crumble to the touch.

Because of the depth you are down just 15-17 minutes. Most dives proceed around the stern of the boat, where you can "swim" in the pools with resident barracuda. Eagle rays, an occasional shark, hawkbill turtles or grouper shadow by. A scattering of corals are beginning to grow on the hull.

Strong currents do occur on the *Bianca*, but die out at 50 feet or so. All divers should have open-water experience before attempting this dive, and then only with a qualified, local, dive guide. Dive Grenada's dive master, David Macnaghten, fastens a safety line from the anchor line to the ship. Once everyone is back on the line, it is cast off and you begin your slow ascent to the surface.

☆☆☆ An easier dive, and also good for snorkeling, is **Boss Reef**, a six-mile-long reef that stretches from Grande Anse Bay to Canoe Bay off the southwest tip of the island. Just a five-minute boat ride from the shore, it extends some 100 feet across and offers three main dive sites — **The Hole**, a fish hangout that slopes down to 50 ft; **Valleys of Whales**, a coral canyon with walls of grunts, yellow tail and parrot fish named for one whale sighting; and **Forests of Dean**, an area dense with branching corals. All three range in depth from 20 to 40 ft with some drop-offs to 60 ft. Fish are abundant, with schools of sergeant majors, goat fish, rays, grouper, turtles and barracuda. Seas usually run a one- to two-ft chop.

☆☆☆ West of Boss Reef is **Wibble Reef**. Most of the dives here are gentle (1 knot) drift dives that take you through vast schools of creole wrasse and chromis. The reef starts at 40 ft and slopes down to 167 ft toward the north,

Grand Anse beach.

and gently to the south. Groves of black coral and gigantic sea fans adorn the wall, which displays a constantly changing panorama of fish. The bottom is sandy, with soft corals, lobsters and small critters.

☆☆ **Spice Island Reef,** just off Pt. Salines, the southwest tip of Grenada, is one of the best spots for snorkeling and shallow dives. The reef drops gradually from 20 to 80 ft. The shallows are home to a vast of array of juvenile fish, octopi, parrot fish, sea fans and finger corals.

☆☆☆ **Isle de Ronde,** a group of tiny, picturesque islands off the north coast of Grenada, drop off to pristine fringing reefs vibrant with soft corals, sea fans and gorgonians. Trips to these islands take about 1½ hours from St. George's. For experienced divers.

☆☆ The **Halifax-Molinere Wall** is close to shore, making it a favorite night dive. The reef starts at 20 ft and drops down to a sandy bottom at 90 ft. Marine life is decent, with large vase sponges, sea whips, gorgonians, sea fans, finger corals, spotted morays, Spanish hogfish, large French angels, sergeant majors, turtles and rock beauties. Visibility varies with the weather. A day of rough seas and winds may kick up the silt and reduce visibility. Expect a light current. Previous open-water experience is suggested.

Dive Operators

Dive Grenada, at Cot Bam on Grand Anse Beach and at the Calabash Hotel in Lance aux Épines, offers dive trips at 10 am and 2 pm. Night dives at 6:30 pm, snorkeling at Molinere at 2 pm. PADI courses for all levels of experience. One-tank dives cost $32, five for $150, 10 for $280. Trips to the *Bianca C* cost $45. Trips to Ilse De Ronde for diving and snorkeling cost $110 (minimum four people). Dive Grenada also offers water skiing, windsurfing, cruises, offshore fishing, underwater video and a wide choice of motorized watersports equipment. ☎ (800) 843-8362, (809) 444-1092, fax 444-6699. E-mail: diveg'da@caribsurf.com. Web site: www.divegrenada.com.

Grand Anse Aquatics Ltd. features diving, snorkeling and other watersports at Coyaba Beach Resort, Spice Island Inn, and Blue Horizons, St. George's. Dive packages with the Coyaba Beach Hotel. ☎ (809) 444-4129, fax (809) 444-4808.

Sanvics Watersports at the Grenada Renaissance Resort, Grand Anse Beach, tours the reefs aboard their 32-ft custom dive/snorkeling boat, *Catch the Spirit.* Trips to offshore islands include beverages, barbecues and snorkeling equipment. ☎ (809) 444-4371, ext 638, fax (809) 444-5227.

Scuba Express, at the True Blue Inn, True Blue, Grenada, offers PADI courses, trips to the *Bianca C*, reefs and offshore islands. Boats take a maximum of 10 divers. ☎ (809) 444-2133.

Scuba World, a PADI Resort Centre at The Rex Grenadian Resort and Secret Harbour/The Moorings, visits all the best dive sites and offers courses for beginners and experienced divers. ☎ (809) 444-3333, ext 584, fax (809) 444-1111.

Carriacou Silver Diving Ltd, in Hillsborough, Carriacou, visits approximately 30 diving sites in the immediate vicinity and offers PADI, SSI, CMAS/DSTA certifcation courses. Dive Paradise rents snorkel gear and underwater cameras. ☎ (809) 443-7882 or (809) 443-7337.

Tanki's Watersport Paradise, Ltd., L'Esterre Bay, Carriacou, offers dive trips to Carriacou's best sites, PADI courses, modern equipment. ☎ (809) 443-8406, fax (809)443-8391.

Sailing

Day- and week-long scuba and snorkeling trips to secluded bays, to Carriacou and the Grenadines may be arranged through **Starwind** ☎ (809) 440-3678 or 440-2508.

Crewed or bareboat vacation charters may be booked through the **Moorings,** ☎ (800) 437-7880, or write to The Moorings, Ltd., 1305 US # 19 South, Suite 402, Clearwater, FL 34624.

Grenada Yacht Services at St. George's Harbour, has complete marina facilities and charters for week-long or shorter excursions. There are no port dues or fees for visiting yachts. ☎ (809) 440-2508.

Accommodations

GRENADA

Grenada is one of the Caribbean's best bargains. Guesthouse rooms rent for as low as $40 in summer and $50 in winter. More luxurious cottages are offered for $90 a night. Hotels average $150 for a double. Web site: www.interknowledge.com/grenada. E-mail: gbt@caribsurf.com.

The **Grenada Renaissance Resort** sits on the famous two-mile-long Grand Anse Beach surrounded by tropical gardens. The 186-room resort offers deluxe accommodations—king-sized or extra-large twin beds, air conditioning, balconies, direct-dial telephones, color TV, conference facilities. Beachfront open-air restaurant, snack bar, dive shop, pool and beach bar. Winter rates, from $186-$246. Sanvics Watersports on premises provides scuba, snorkeling and fishing trips plus jet skiing, banana boats, donut rides and out-island barbecues. Major credit cards accepted. ☎ (800) 228-9898 or (809) 444-4371, fax (809) 444-4800. Write, PO Box 441, St. George's, Grenada, West Indies. E-mail: higrenada@carbisurf.com.

Coyaba Beach Resort on Grand Anse Beach, a low-rise, 70-room resort, offers a sea view from all rooms, balconies, air conditioning, tennis, palm-lined beach, phones, dive shop, two restaurants. Walking distance from shopping and restaurants. Winter room rates range from $125 for a single, $175 for a double. Summer from $80. Grand Anse Aquatics dive shop on premises. ☎ (809) 444-4129, fax (809) 444-4808. Write PO Box 336, St. George's, Grenada, West Indies.

Siesta Hotel, St. Georges, Grenada consists of 37 new, studio, one- and two-bedroom luxury apartments 200 yds from Grand Anse Beach. All have air-conditioning, ceiling fan, kitchen, telephone, TV, balcony, ocean views. Pool and poolside restaurant. Minutes from the airport, golf course and St. Georges. Dive shop in walking distance. Winter room rates from $105 to $135. ☎ (809) 444-4646, fax (809) 444-4647, or write PO Box 27, St. George's, Grenada, West Indies.

Secret Harbour Hotel, L'Anse aux Épines, Grenada, features 20 deluxe suites with large balconies and living areas, antique four-poster beds and tiled baths. The resort is owned by The Moorings Inc., the world's largest yacht charter operation. A romantic restaurant overlooks Mount Hartman Bay. Summer rates start at $135 per night, winter rates at $225. ☎ (800) 437-7880, (813) 538-8760 or direct (809) 444-4439, fax (809) 444-4819. Write PO Box 11, St. George's, Grenada, West Indies.

Spice Island Inn, on Grand Anse Beach, offers ultra-luxurious beachfront suites with whirlpool bath, spa, or private pool. Dine on your own patio or enjoy sumptuous buffets in the beachside restaurant. All-inclusive rates range from $260 to $385 per day, per person in summer; from $290 to $430 in winter. ☎ (809) 444-4258/4423, fax (809) 444-4807. Or write PO Box 6, St. George's, Grenada.

Lance Aux Épines Cottages, on the south end of Grenada—about two miles south of Grand Anse beach—has, clean, modern, one- and two-bedroom cottages that are fully equipped and designed for self-catering. Daily maid service. The cottages are on the beach and within walking distance of restaurants and a mini-market. Rates for a double are from $85 in summer and $115 in winter. ☎ (809) 444-4565, PO Box 187, St. George's Grenada, West Indies.

Roydon's Guest House, in Grand Anse, offers singles (EP) for $40 per night and $50 for a double. ☎ (809) 444-4476.

CARRIACOU

Note: Boats leave from the Carenage, St. George's and Hillsborough, Carriacou. Travel time is three to four hours.

Silver Beach Resort is centrally located for watersports on Carriacou. Ocean-front rooms or cottages are between $85 and $105 per night in winter, from $60 to $95 in summer. Dive shop (Karibik) on premises visits over 20 Carriacou sights. ☎ (809) 443-7337, fax (809) 443-7165, or write Silver Beach Resort, Hillsborough, Carriacou, Grenada, West Indies.

Other Activities on Grenada

Sunfish sailing, water skiing, jet skiing and board sailing can be arranged through your hotel. Or for information call the tourist board at ☎ (809) 444-1353.

The *Rhum Runner*, based in St. George's harbor, offers water tours for reef viewing, harbor tours, moonlight cruises with barbecues, sails up Grenada's coast, and all-you-can-drink rum-punch cruises complete with live, electronic or steel band music.

Tennis, golf and spectator sports are also on the island. **Secret Harbour, Twelve Degrees North, Calabash, Coyaba, Spice Island Inn** and the **Renaissance Grenada Resort** all have tennis courts. Visitors may also play on the **Richmond Hill** and **Tanteen Tennis Club** courts.

The **Grenada Golf and Country Club** has a nine-hole golf course. Concentration is key for this course, as the view of both the Atlantic and Caribbean waters can be distracting. Cricket, one of the most popular sports on the island, is played at 10 am on Saturday mornings from January to May near St. Georges.

A less formal sport in Grenada is known as hashing. The sport is a run or walk—whichever one chooses. Participants are guided by special markers through the course, sometimes through Grenada's hilliest areas. Participants must be on the lookout for markers that are purposely put in place to take them off course. Those who make it to the end—and everyone does—enjoy a lighthearted celebration. It is held by the **Hash House Harriers' Club** in various parts of the island every other weekend.

Touring St. George's

Most island tours include and take off from historic St. George's. It is known as one of the most picturesque and truly West-Indian towns in the Caribbean.

The center of activity in St. George's is the *Carenage*, or inner harbor. Fishing boats of all sizes and descriptions pull in and out continuously. The adventurous among you may wish to bargain for a trip on one of the fishing boats out to Glover's or Hog island for a day of snorkeling.

At the center of the Carenage stands **Christ of the Deep**, a statue given to Grenada by the Costa Cruise Line in remembrance of the hospitality shown the passengers of the *Bianca C* when it burned in the harbor in 1961. Also at the harbor are the post office, public library and small shops selling perfumes, lotions, potpourri, and teas made from local flowers, spices and herbs. Nearby is the **Grenada National Museum**, which houses archaeological finds, Josephine Bonaparte's marble bathtub, the first telegraph installed on the island in 1871, a rum still, and memorabilia depicting the Indian cultures of Grenada.

The Sendall Tunnel takes you to the other side of St. George's, the *Esplanade,* the outer harbor with the fish and meat markets. In back is **Market Square**, where vendors sell brooms, baskets, fruits and vegetables. Early Saturday morning is the best time to see the market when it overflows with exotic fruits, vegetables and spices.

Stop by **St. George's Anglican Church**, built on the site of a church originally constructed by monks. Its walls are lined with plaques relating the 18th- and 19th-century history of Grenada.

Forts surround the city. **Fort George**, which is the oldest, was built by the French in 1705 and **Fort Matthew** and **Fort Frederick** were started by the French and completed by the British in 1783. All can be visited. St. George's also has a zoo, botanical gardens, Bay Gardens, and Tower House—the great house of a 1916 plantation filled with island relics, prints, paintings and historic family photos.

Island Tours

Grenada is small enough to be toured in one day. Leaving St. George's to the south coast is **Westerhall**, a stunning peninsula known for its magnificent homes and gardens. Next, down a dirt road is **Bacolet Bay**, a wild peninsula on the Atlantic where high surf pounds against miles of uninhabited beaches. Continuing on, **La Sagesse Nature Center** offers hiking trails, wild birds, a banana plantation with guided nature walks, an extensive beach and café. Next is Marquis Village, the center of a handicraft industry. Nearby, also on the eastern shore, is the town of Grenville, Grenada's second city, which is the perfect spot to try the local seafood. Try a bit of barracuda or lambi (conch) at the Seahaven, washed down with mauby—a local drink made from tree bark.

If you tour on a Saturday, be sure to stop by Grenville's large open-air market. This island "bread basket" offers fresh fish, fruits, vegetables, breads, pastries, spices and Grenadian delicacies prepared on the spot. While mingling with the Grenadians doing their weekly marketing, you can stop and watch the expert weavers from Marquis as they ply strips of wild palm into hats, baskets, bags and placemats.

Before leaving the east coast, you can glimpse the old Pearls Airport, which was replaced by the Point Salines International Airport in 1984.

The half-hour ride back through the Grand Etang district zigs and zags through the **Grand Etang National Park.** Dense tropical foliage, including bamboo, tree ferns, cocoa, bananas and elephant ears, mixed with vistas of the sea, make it one of the most beautiful drives in the Caribbean. Stop at the Grand Etang Visitors Center in the Forest Reserve, which houses exhibits of the area's flora and fauna and videotapes of the island. Nearby is Grand Etang Lake, the crater of an extinct volcano and, above that, the summit of Mt. Qua Qua (2,372 ft). There are boats for rowing and picnic facilities. Also in this area are hiking trails of varying degrees of difficulty, which wind through the tropical vegetation. Bring pants and a long-sleeved shirt.

The west coast ride north from St. George's takes you past colorful fishing villages set at the foot of the mountains, where papaya and breadfruit trees abound. Not far up the coast, a turnoff leads to spectacular **Concord Falls.** For the adventurous, a half-hour hike into the interior tropical forest through spice and fruit plantations takes you to a more remote second falls, where the reward is a refreshing swim.

Continuing north along the coast road is **Dougaldston Estate**, where cloves, cinnamon, mace, nutmeg and cocoa are prepared and sorted. The employees will explain how the spices grow, their uses, and show you the large trays where the spices are set to dry before separating.

Close by is **Gouyave**, a fishing village and the center of the nutmeg industry.

At the northernmost tip are the great cliffs of **Sauteurs**. Nearby is **Levera Beach**, a deserted beach ringed by sea grapes and palm trees and the meeting place of the Atlantic and the Caribbean. From here you can see the Grenadines.

If time permits, take a detour from the coast road to the **River Antoine Rum Distillery**, dating from the 18th century and one of the last enterprises still powered by a water wheel.

Tours encircling the island run six hours and hit all the high points. City tours run two hours. A special tour for photographers is Photo Safari which includes a professional photographer guide who will tailor a trip for you.

Tour Operators

Island tours can be arranged through the following companies:

Carib Tours/Carin Travel, Grand Anse, ☎ 444-4363; **Henry Safari Tours** offers a variety of mini-bus sightseeing safaris and hikes, ☎ 444-5313; **Caribbean Horizons** offers cruises and rain forest tours, fishing, sailing and day trips to the Tobago Cays in the Grenadines, ☎ 444-1555, fax 444-2899; **Island Tours Ltd,** ☎ 440-2906; **National Taxi Association** tours with air-conditioned taxis and mini buses, ☎ 440-6850, after hours 440-5286, 4070, or 1617.

Ferry between Carriacou and Grenada

From Grenada: The *Alexia II* and the *Adelaide B* depart Grenada Wed 9:30 am and Sat 9:30 am. The *Alexia III* departs Grenada Tues 9:30 am, Fri 11 am and Sun 7 am. **From Carriacou to Grenada:** *Alexia III* departs Carriacou Wed 1 pm, Sat 1 pm and Sun 8:30 pm. The *Alexia II* and *Adelaide B* depart Carriacou Thurs 10 am and Mon 10 am. Fares: $7.50 one way, US $12 return. Both the *Adelaide B* and the mail boat take passengers to Petit Martinique.

Dining

Dining in Grenada is West Indian informal, characterized by open settings and a view of the sea. In St. George's proper, **Delicious Landing** on the Carenage offers great views, seafood and island drinks. Also on the Carenage, **Rudolf's** (☎ 440-2241) offers a pub-like setting for fish and chips and lobster "as-you-like-it." **The Nutmeg** (☎ 440-2539), with its second floor harbor view has delicious turtle soup and curried lambi.

In Belmont, a five-minute drive south from St. George's, internationally praised **Mama's** (☎ 440-1459) serves some 21 to 25 dishes "family style." There is no menu—just the best and freshest offerings bought and prepared in the small kitchen. From lobster and callaloo soup to fresh fish, chicken, manicou or tatou (armadillo)—and other entrées—to a wide variety of salads and vegetables. Exotic ice cream finishes the meal.

Spice Island Inn (☎ 444-4258) holds weekly Grenadian buffets to the sounds of a steel band. The chef at **Secret Harbour Hotel** (☎ 444- 4819) serves his delicacies amid island antiques—a giant marble chess set and Empire-style chaise lounges. For those wanting a different ethnic cuisine, try **Coconuts Beach Restaurant** (☎ 444-4644), a French Creole restaurant on Grand Anse Beach. For Chinese food, there's the **Bird's**

Nest (☎ 444-4264). Or try **Tropicana** (☎ 440-1586) on Lagoon Road for Grenadian/Chinese dishes.

Grenada's spice baskets filled with everything from whole nutmegs and cloves to saffron or bay leaves make an ideal souvenir for as little as US $5. You might even find a recipe book tucked among the spices so you can recreate a fete of your own.

Fast food can be found at **Kentucky Fried Chicken** on Granby St. and Grand Anse, St. George's, ☎ 440-3821, or **Rick's Café** at the Grand Anse Shopping Centre.

CARRIACOU

The Caribbee Inn, Prospect (☎ 443-7380), serves French Creole favorites by candlelight. **Cassada Bay's** open-air dining room offers views of five islands. Menu features include Caribbean and international cuisine featuring lobster, seafood, chicken and steak.

Facts

Helpful Phone Numbers: Police, ☎ 911/440-2244/3999; hospital, ☎ 440-2052; Coast Guard, ☎ 440-2852, stands by on Marine channel 16 VHF.

Nearest Recompression Chamber: Barbados, Trinidad. **Avoid decompression dives**—no chambers are close enough for an emergency.

Airlines: American Airlines (☎ 800-433-7300), flies from US gateway cities. BWIA flies from Grenada to Aruba, Canada, Caracas, Curacao, Frankfurt, London, New York, Miami (daily), Stockholm and other European cities. LIAT connects with international airlines—British Airways, BWIA, Air Canada, American Airlines, Air France, Lufthansa, in Barbados, St. Lucia, Trinidad, Martinique and Antigua. American Airlines flies from America through Puerto Rico. ALM flies between Curacao and Grenada. LIAT has daily flights to Carriacou and other islands in the Caribbean.

Airport: Point Salines International Airport is located on the southwest tip of Grenada.

Driving: On the left. You must produce a bona fide drivers license for the local traffic department.

Documents: British, American and Canadian citizens do not need passports for visits not exceeding three months, provided they have two documents proving citizenship (one with a photograph—i.e., an expired passport or drivers license with photo) plus a birth certificate or voter's registration card, and an onward or return ticket. For all other nationalities, a valid passport is required. However, any traveler in Trinidad en route to or from Grenada requires a valid passport for their transit stop.

Customs: There is no restriction on the amount of foreign currency brought into Grenada. Clothing and dive gear are also admitted freely, as long as they are for personal use.

Currency: East Caribbean Dollar (EC $) at a rate of EC $2.68 to US $1.

Credit Cards: Major credit cards are accepted by most tourist-oriented businesses. Traveler's checks and US currency are accepted almost everywhere.

Language: English.

Climate: The year-round average temperature is 80° F and annual rainfall averages 78 inches. Peak rainfall is in summer and late fall.

Clothing: Bring a wetskin or shorty wetsuit in winter. For land, casual lightweight clothing. For hiking the rainforest, bring sturdy shoes with nonslip soles, a long-sleeved shirt and long pants—cotton or a coolweave fabric. Swimwear and very short shorts are not welcome in the city streets, stores or hotel restaurants.

Electricity: 220 volts, 50 cycles. AC transformers and adapters are needed.

Time: Eastern Standard.

Tax: A departure tax of US $14 for adults; US $6.50 for children over 5. There is a US $4 departure tax from Carriacou.

Religious Services: Catholic, Anglican, Presbyterian, Methodist, Scots Kirk, Seventh Day Adventist, Jehovah's Witness, Christian Scientist, Baha'i Faith.

Additional Information: Grenada Board of Tourism, Suite 900 D, 820 Second Avenue, NY, NY 10017. *In the US:* ☎ (800) 927-9554 or 212-687-9554. *In Grenada:* ☎ (809) 440-2279. E-mail: gbt@caribsurf.com or grenada@panther.netmani.co.uk. Web site: www.interknowledge.com/grenada.

Guadeloupe

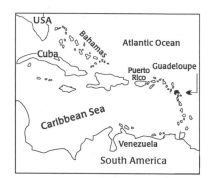

Touted by Jacques Cousteau as "one of the world's 10 best diving spots," Guadeloupe combines the cultural and cosmopolitan charm of a European vacation with fabulous diving on reefs untouched by all but a minimal group of discriminating dive-travelers. Named for Our Lady of Guadeloupe by Christopher Columbus in 1493, this charming French island is blessed with miles of beautiful white-sand beaches and spectacular sub-sea attractions. Guadeloupe is actually two main islands connected by a bridge across the River Salée and several out islands. From the air it resembles the wings of a butterfly. Basse Terre, the western wing, is mountainous, highlighted by the still-active volcano, Mt. Soufrière. Travelers touring this portion of the islands will find tropical rain forests, bamboo trees, hot springs, postcard waterfalls, and a profusion of tropical flowers, fruits, almond and palm trees. Grande Terre, the eastern wing of Guadeloupe, is flat, dry, and home to modern resorts, beautiful swimming beaches, fields of sugar cane and unlimited topside tourist attractions.

The prime dive-vacation attraction is Pigeon Island, located just off the central western coast of Basse Terre. Pigeon Island, a mountain in the sea surrounded by miles of dense coral reefs, was the site for the film, *The Silent World*.

Residents of Guadeloupe are extremely friendly and kind to tourists. Still, non-French-speaking divers visiting Guadeloupe should pick up a French phrase book and familiarize themselves with the language. English is **not** widely spoken; even the grunts grunt with a French accent. Also, divers and snorkelers must bring their own equipment, except for tanks and weights. European adapters, if needed, are widely available for a few dollars at any dive shop.

Area contributors: Richard Ockelmann and Beth Ann Molino, BDC; Myron Clement, French West Indies Department of Tourism, Guy Genin of Chez Guy Diving; Raphael Legrand, Directeur, Auberge de la Distillerie Hotel; Florence Marie, Relais du Moulin Hotel.

Topless sunbathing, snorkeling, scuba and swimming are *de rigueur* on Guadeloupe.

Best Dive and Snorkeling Sites

Pigeon Island, composed of volcanic stone and scrub trees, lies off the western coast of Basse Terre, the western wing of Guadeloupe. The area consists of two land masses, North Pigeon and South Pigeon. The waters surrounding it come under French Government protection as an Underwater Natural Park—the Cousteau Marine Sanctuary.

☆☆☆☆☆ **North East Reef.** The northeast side of North Pigeon Island is a superb wall dive. Beginning at the surface, the wall drops 40 ft to a shelf, then slopes down to 70 ft and finally plunges steeply to 140 ft. The wall is carpeted with lacy soft corals, tube sponges, plate corals, and large pillar-coral formations. Residents include huge groupers, puffers, lobsters, big French angels and throngs of small critters—arrow crabs, feather dusters and tube sponges. The seas are usually calm, visibility more than 100 ft. Recommended for both novice and experienced divers.

☆☆☆☆☆**North Side Reef.** You'll find superb seascapes for photography on the north side of North Pigeon Island. Huge clusters of tube sponges, some six feet tall, and enormous green and purple sea fans grow on the ledges and outcrops of the wall. The reef begins in the shallows and drops off to a maze of small canyons and outcrops. Divers are befriended by large gray snappers. They are tame and may be handfed. Large curious barracuda circle overhead; trumpet fish and damsels adorn the lush thickets of coral. Star and brain corals abound. North Side Reef is a super dive for novices as well as experienced divers. Seas are calm, visibility excellent.

☆☆☆☆ **West Side Reef,** off North Pigeon Island, is everyone's favorite. The wall begins at the surface, drops to a shelf at 25 ft, slopes down to 40 ft, then drops off sharply to the bottom at 140 ft. As in all of the Cousteau Marine Sanctuary, the corals here are vibrantly alive with color and create a dramatic landscape. Large brain coral heads and gardens of soft corals thrive. Fish life is abundant. Inhabitants of the reef include large hog snappers, trumpet fish, and parrotfish. Photo enthusiasts are drawn to the gigantic orange sponges and teal sea fans. Calm seas invite divers of all experience levels to this site.

☆☆☆ **Rock Canyons**, located off Iles des Saintes, a small group of islands just south of Basse Terre, is a large maze of narrow rocky coral alleys and caves. Its walls, riddled with endless nooks and crannies, provide shelter for sea cumbers, bristle worms, tree worms, arrow crabs, sea horses, octopi, lobster, eels and an ever-present mob of grunts. Huge formations of rare pink corals color the area. The canyon entrance starts at 10 ft then drops to

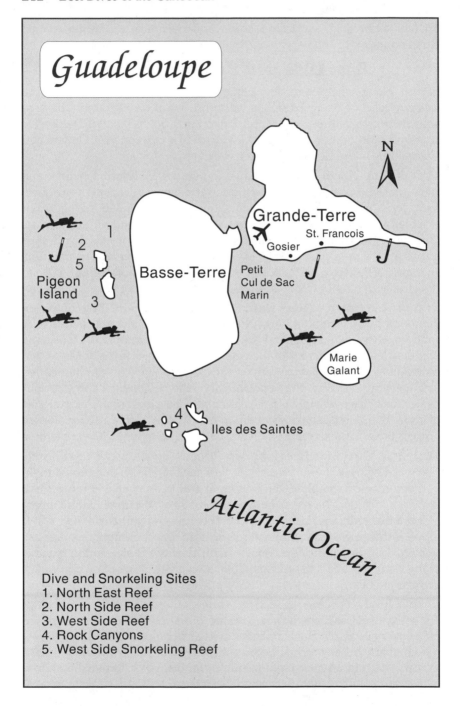

Guadeloupe

N

Grande-Terre

St. Francois

Gosier

Basse-Terre

Petit
Cul de Sac
Marin

Pigeon
Island

Marie
Galant

Iles des Saintes

Atlantic Ocean

Dive and Snorkeling Sites
1. North East Reef
2. North Side Reef
3. West Side Reef
4. Rock Canyons
5. West Side Snorkeling Reef

a sandy bottom at 45 ft. Tricky surface surges and currents make this a site for experienced divers.

☆☆☆☆☆ **Pigeon Island's West Side Reef** is the best snorkeling area in the Cousteau Marine Sanctuary. Its shallow walls ruffle with enormous feather dusters, sea plumes, sea rods, huge sea fans and sponges. Barrel sponges (large enough to camp in) thrive among clumps of elkhorn and enormous brain corals. Puffer fish and unusual golden moray eels are inhabitants. Expect calm seas and exceptional visibility.

Additional snorkeling and diving sites are found among the lagoons and bays of Les Saintes, the east coast of BasseTerre, and off-shore Gosier (the south coast of Grande Terre). Check out Mouton Vert, Mouchoir Carré, and Cay Ismini. They are close by the hotels in the bay of Petit Cul de Sac Marin, near Rivière Salée, the river separating the two halves of Guadeloupe. North of Salée is another bay, Grand Cul de Sac Marin, where the small islets of Fajou and Caret also offer decent diving. St. Francois Reef on the eastern end of the south shore of Grande Terre is a good snorkeling reef, as is Ilet de Gosier, off Gosier. Diving is a young sport on Guadeloupe and every dive-explorer has a unique opportunity to find a new "best dive" of his/her own. New sites are discovered every day.

Dive Operators

Chez Guy is directly opposite Pigeon Island on Malendure Beach in Bouillante on Basse Terre, with a branch on Les Saintes. Operator and master diver Guy Genin has three fast, comfortable boats for daily dive and snorkeling excursions to Pigeon Island. The boats have wide hydroplanes that double as diving platforms. This operation boasts 60 complete sets of equipment. Rates: $30 per dive, including transfer from hotel. Chez Guy also offers a one-week, all-inclusive package for $590, which includes two dives per day, equipment and accommodations with breakfast and dinner at Guy's guest house, the Auberge de la Plongée. ☎ (590) 98-8172, fax (590) 98-8358.

The Nautilus Club, which faces Pigeon Island from the beach at Malendure, specializes in diving excursions. The shop's four boats carry 14 passengers. ☎ (590) 98-8569, fax (590) 90-2187.

Les Heures Saines is a modern PADI and NAUI dive center facing Pigeon from Rocher de Malendure. Five instructors, Dominique Derame, Francois Aubry, Pascale Estripeau, Frederic Aragones and Louis Galbiati escort daily dives and night dives. Single dives are $50. Les Heures Saines also has two dive lodges: Le Paradis Créole, with one week at $900 for meals, accommodations and 10 dives, and Les Bungalow-Villas at $780 for the same. ☎ (590) 98-8663, fax (590) 95-5090.

Aqua-fari Club is based at La Créole Beach Hotel in Gosier, a bustling resort area 15 miles east of Point-à-Pitre, Guadeloupe's largest city. Divemaster Alain Verdonck offers guided wreck dives and excursions to nearby coral reefs and Pigeon Island (a one-hour drive). Prices range from $36 to $64 depending on the dive site. A 10-dive package is available; it includes airport-to-hotel transfer, welcome cocktail, bus trip to Pigeon, two dives a day, one night dive, and cocktail party. ☎ (011) (590) 84-2626.

Another well-organized watersports center is **Nauticase** at the Hotel Salako, ☎ (590) 84-2222.

Accommodations

Rates are US $.

If your tongue doesn't curl comfortably around conversational French, head for one of the bigger hotels where English is spoken. Or if getting to know people is one of the reasons you travel, stay at a Relais Créole, a small family-owned inn. Most of the hotels are situated on Grande Terre (one-hour drive to Malendure). Among the small hotels close to Pigeon Island on Basse Terre are Raphael Legrand's charming 12-room **Auberge De La Distillerie** at Tabanon near Petit-Bourg. This fully air-conditioned inn is a short ride from Pigeon Island dive operators. ☎ (590) 94-2591, fax (590) 94-1191. The adjacent restaurant, Le Bitaco, is popular with the locals and noted for Creole dishes. Freshwater pool.

Hotel Paradis Créole is a small dive lodge operated by Les Heures Saines divers. One week's accommodations, including meals and 10 guided dives, are available for $900 per person; in bungalow-studios, $780 per person. ☎ (590) 98-7162 or (590) 98-8663, fax (590) 98-7776.

La Sucrerie du Comte has opened on the site of an old rum distillery. With 26 comfortable bungalow rooms, La Sucrerie is by the sea at Sainte Rose in the north of the western wing of Basse Terre. Rates are $134 for two people in a bungalow with breakfast; lower from January 6 to April 12. ☎ (590) 28-6017. Write to Comte de Loheac, Sainte-Rose 97115, Guadeloupe, FWI.

Le Domaine de Malendure, on Basse Terre overlooking Cousteau's Reserve, offers 50 deluxe, air-conditioned, hillside cottages with TV, telephone and 1½ baths. Restaurant, pool and swim-up bar. Dive and snorkeling tours to Pigeon Island. ☎ (800) 742-4276.

Relais du Moulin, near Sainte Anne on Grande Terre, is marked by a sugar-mill tower which serves as the office. This small resort features 40 air-conditioned bungalows set in a bougainvillea garden, a tennis court and pool. The beach is a half-mile away. The hotel has a fabulous West Indian restaurant and a snack bar at the pool. Entertainment. Combination hotel and sailing vacations are offered. Relais du Moulin is about an hour's drive from Pigeon Island. Rates are $145 to $178 for a double. ☎ (590) 88-2396. Reservations through your travel agent.

La Créole Beach Hotel, located on the beach at Gosier, offers large, well appointed rooms. Aqua-Fari Dive Shop on premises offers tours to the coral reef surrounding Gosier Island as well as excursions to Pigeon Island. Introductory dives. Rates for a double are $130 to $500. Dive Packages available with Aqua-Fari Club. ☎ (590) 90-4646, fax (590) 90-1666. In the US, ☎ (800) 742-4276.

Meridien Guadeloupe, just east of Gosier at St. Francois, features 265 four-star beachfront rooms. Despite the boom in tourism, the town of St. Francois manages to retain its fishing village look. On the road east of it are any number of beachside bistros serving lobster and seafood. Rates are $136 to $340 for a double. Dive shops here offer daily trips to the offshore reefs of Grande Terre and excursions to Pigeon Island. ☎ (590) 88-5100, fax (590) 88-40-71.

Other Activities

Sailboats, crewed or bareboat, are plentiful. For rentals or tours try **Vacances Yachting Antilles** at Marina Bas-du-Fort, Pointe-A-Pitre. ☎ 90-8295. Full-day picnic sails on the trimaran, *La Grande Voile* (☎ 84-4642), or catamaran, *Papyrus*, can be arranged through your hotel. ☎ 90-9298.

Sightseeing

Hiking through Basse Terre's Parc Naturel takes you along well-marked trails through tropical rain forests to waterfalls, mountain pools, and La Soufrière, a 4,813-ft volcano and the park's most famous site. You'll also find exhibits on the volcano, coffee, the sea, and the forest. Hiking brochures are available from the Guadeloupe Tourist Office (address below). Those who can dive all day and still party all night will find the cities of Guadeloupe alive with lights and loud with dancing and entertainment.

Local craft items, such as dolls, jewelry, furniture or souvenirs are made from fruit, wood, sea-shells, stone, and leather and are widely available in the town shops.

Dining

Guadeloupe is a gourmet's delight. Top restaurants and hotel dining rooms offer classic French and Caribbean cuisine. Though the island is French, it is also decidedly Creole, and Creole eateries are gaining enormously in popularity. Some are beachside cafés, some are in-town bistros, and several are little more than the front porch of the cook's home. On Malendure Beach, Basse Terre, check out **Chez Loulouse**, noted for Chef Loulouse's crayfish sauce Américaine. This is a small native seafood eatery in a simple setting. ☎ 98-7034. In Gosier, try **Le Bassignac** on the Beach Road (*Route de la Plage*). Seafood specialties in a comfortable beachside setting.

Facts

Nearest Recompression Chamber: Located in Pointe-à-Pitre, Grande Terre.

Getting There: Connections from Miami on Air France and from San Juan, take American Eagle (☎ 800-433-7300). Inter-island flights can be arranged at Le Raizet Airport. Water ferries to Iles des Saintes are available from the city of Pointe-à-Pitre, Basse Terre, or Trois Rivieres on the south coast.

Island Transportation: All major car rental agencies are at the airport. Reservations should be made before arriving in Guadeloupe to insure getting a car. Bus service in Mercedes vans is available between cities. The cities are clearly marked on the outside.

Driving: Right side of the road. The main roads between major cities are clearly marked. A wonderful tourist map is available from the tourist office in Pointe-à-Pitre.

Documents: For stays of up to three months Canadian and US citizens require a return ticket and two forms of ID—either a passport or proof of citizenship such as a birth certificate or voter's registration card with some type of photo. A passport is recommended. British citizens require a passport.

Currency: French franc. 5 FF=US $1.

Climate: Temperatures range from 75 to 85° F. Water temperatures are warm year-round so you won't need a wetsuit, although a wetskin or $^1/_8$ - inch shortie wetsuit is comfortable in mid-winter.

Clothing: Casual light clothing. Most beaches are topless.

Equipment Required: Bring all of your own scuba gear except for tanks and weights. Most operators have Scubapro tanks, which do not require any special regulator adaptor.

Electricity: European adaptors required.

Time: Atlantic Standard (EST + 1 hr).

Language: French, local Creole dialect.

Tax: A service charge of 10 to 15% is included on most hotel and restaurant tabs.

Religious Services: Catholic, Protestant, Jewish.

Additional Information: French West Indies Tourist Board, 444 Madison Avenue, NY, NY 10022. ☎ (900) 990-0040 (95¢ per minute). Web site: www. guadeloupe.com

The Bay Islands

Honduras

Located between 12 and 40 miles off the coast of Honduras, the Bay Islands (Las Islas de la Bahia) serve as a remote outpost set in the middle of the world's second largest barrier reef. Geographically, the islands form the visible portion of the Bonacca Ridge, a subsea mountain range borne of volcanic activity centuries ago. The islands, all mountainous jungle, slope down to postcard-perfect white sand beaches shaded by coconut palms. Inland, fragrant almond, mango, cashew, mandarin orange and breadfruit trees shade the cliffs and provide food and shelter to iguanas, parrots, snakes, deer and wild boar.

Roatan, the largest of the 70-island chain, is the most populated, with 30,000 residents, and the most developed. It is where you'll find the most dive resorts and creature comforts. Guanaja, next in size, is surrounded by its own barrier reef. Third in size, and a newcomer to this "dedicated-dive-resort" group, is Utila. The Cayos Cochinos, a mini-cluster of small fishing-village islands boasts one dive resort on their biggest island, Cochino Grande.

The smaller islands are uninhabited or sparsely populated. Most do not have roads. Phones, faxes and e-mail are newcomers. Surrounding reefs are impressive, with brilliantly colored sponges and corals, towering pinnacles, walls, tunnels, wrecks and caves. Visibility and water clarity are superb. Big turtles, grouper, rays, eels, and pelagics proliferate despite an active fishing industry. And snorkelers discover their own special paradise in the small patch reefs that dot the shallow bays throughout the area.

Contributors: Alvin Jackson, Roatan; Linda Fouke, Bayman Bay Club, Guanaja; Ray Jones, Coco View Resort.

And, while everyone in the Bay Islands speaks "dive" fluently, the predominant language is English. On the mainland, however, Spanish is spoken.

Plan on an entire day to reach the Bay Islands from the US. The islands are close to Honduras' coastline, but the mainland airport at San Pedro Sula is 160 miles away. Some flights depart La Ceiba, which is closer. Connections are often erratic. Luggage sometimes arrives late. Sand fleas and no-see-ums are a nuisance and make their presence known as soon as you arrive. Apply repellent beforehand.

History

Evidence from shreds of pottery and pre-Columbian remains indicate the early presence of Lanca, Maya and Payan Indians on the Bay Islands. Columbus is credited with their latter-day discovery in 1502.

During the early 1500's, the Spaniards, in their manic quest for gold and precious gems, brutally attacked and enslaved the Bay Island Indians. Finally, during the mid-1500's, the Indians revolted. One chief, Lempira, put up such a fierce offensive, it took thousands of Spanish troops to kill him. Lempira has since been declared a national hero and the currency of Honduras is named for him.

Following that conquest, word of Spanish treasure ships lured pirates from Jamaica and the Caymans to set up a base at Port Royal, Roatan. Tales of jewels and stashed treasures hidden on the island abound.

Best Dive and Snorkeling Sites

Roatan

☆☆☆☆☆ **West End Wall**, which encompasses **Peter's Place** and **Herbie's Place,** is great for diving and snorkeling. The reef starts at the shore and extends out 20 yds, where the wall drops off sharply from a ledge at 15 ft. Visibility often exceeds 100 ft. Fishlife is superb, with schools of horse-eye jacks, permits, and schoolmaster. Seas are calm, with an occasional light current. No spearfishing.

Guanaja

☆☆☆☆☆ **The Bayman Drop and Pinnacle** are wall dives off the north shore. The top of the wall is between 10 and 40 ft. The Pinnacle rises from 135 to 50 ft at the top, where you'll find large barrel sponges, azure vase sponges, gorgonia and black coral. **Do not enter the crack at 70 ft**. Large black coral trees are found at 80 ft. Good for diving and snorkeling. No collecting or spearfishing.

☆☆☆☆ **Pavilions** is a series of blind tunnels, pillar corals and outcroppings between 30 and 60 ft. Soft corals and sponges dominate the

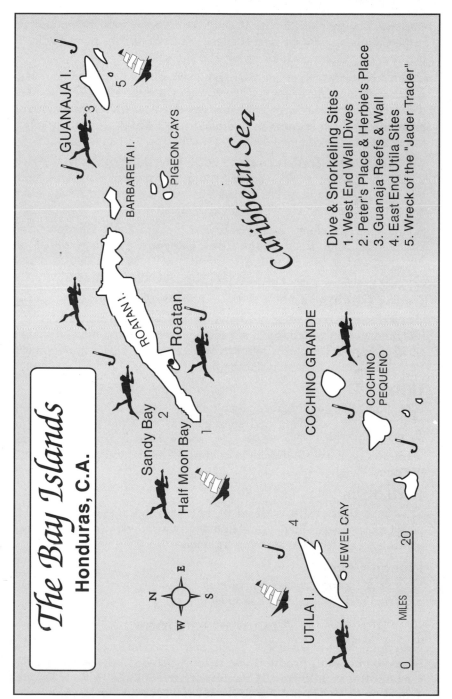

The Bay Islands
Honduras, C.A.

GUANAJA I.

BARBARETA I.

PIGEON CAYS

Caribbean Sea

ROATAN I.

Roatan

Sandy Bay
2

Half Moon Bay
1

COCHINO GRANDE

COCHINO PEQUENO

JEWEL CAY

UTILA I.

Dive & Snorkeling Sites
1. West End Wall Dives
2. Peter's Place & Herbie's Place
3. Guanaja Reefs & Wall
4. East End Utila Sites
5. Wreck of the "Jader Trader"

N
E
S
W

0   20
MILES

shallows. Beware of the fire coral which seems hotter here than other parts of the Caribbean. The site is off Michael's Rock around the point next to the Bayman Bay Club. Good for diving and snorkeling.

☆☆☆ **Waterfall Reef**, the site of a huge black coral tree growing off the wall at 45 ft (top of the dive is five ft), takes its name from a series of overhangs with soft bushy corals which appear to cascade down the slope. Numerous anemones, big vase sponges and lots of fish make Waterfall a photographers' favorite. Good visibility.

☆☆☆☆ *Jader Trader* is a 200-ft wreck lying on its right side at 90 ft off the southwest side of Guanaja. Big morays, schools of silversides, turtles and barracuda are in residence. Seas average two to four ft with a light current. Always good visibility. For experienced divers.

Additional dives along Guanaja's barrier reef are **Eel's Garden** off the Bayman Bay Club shore, **Black Rock Canyons**, a maze of tunnels and canyons, **Jim's Silverlode,** a sheer wall off southwest cay with huge sponges and soft corals. **The Cut** branches out into caverns and tunnels.

Cayos Cochinos

Cayos Cochinos are a group of 13 small islands deemed a Biological Reserve and managed, in part, by the Smithsonian Institution to conduct a scientific study of the reef. The park is patrolled by park rangers. Diving and snorkeling from the shore or by boat is outstanding.

Utila

Utila, fringed by yet-unnamed virgin reefs, caves and canyons, offers some of the best shore diving and snorkeling in the Caribbean. Wildlife is exceptional, with turtles, eagle rays, southern sting rays and tropicals. Offshore sites are a 15-45-minute boat ride. The shore dives lie about 150 yds out.

Barbaretta

☆☆☆☆ **Barbaretta Wall** off Barbaretta island, a favorite snorkeling-picnic spot between Guanaja and Roatan, is a wonderland of barrel sponges and soft corals. The wall stretches for a mile.

Pigeon Cays

☆☆☆☆ Pigeon Cays are a small cluster of islands surrounded by shallow protected reefs, all perfect for snorkeling.

Accommodations

Each resort offers dive services. Group and individual tours from the US are offered by **Landfall Productions**, ☎ (800) 525-3833. E-mail: lndfall@aol. com. Also **Rothschild Travel Consultants,** ☎ (800) 359-0747 and **Tropical Travel**, ☎ (800) 451-8017 or (281) 367-3386, (281) 298-2335.

Roatan

Anthony's Key Resort was the first dedicated dive resort in the Bay Islands. The resort features beachside and reefside rustic cabins. Packages offered from $750 to $825 per person, per week, include three meals daily, three boat dives daily, unlimited shore dives, and horseback riding. The **Institute for Marine Sciences** is on the grounds of the resort and features dolphin swims. ☎ (800) 227-DIVE, or (305) 666-1997, fax (305) 666-2292. E-mail: ark @gate.net. Web site: www. aventuras.com/anthony.key. Dive-hotel package tours are offered by Dive Safaris, ☎ (800) 359-0747, and Landfall Productions, ☎ (800) 525-3833.

Coco View Resort, on the southside peninsula, is a group of oceanside bungalows, two-story cottages and cabanas built over the water. Standard rooms each have one double and one twin bed. Bungalows have two rooms, each with a kingsize bed.

Rates for a winter dive package are $800 per person, double occupancy, for seven nights in either a cottage or cabana and include three meals daily, beach barbecues, taxes, transfers from the airport, two two-tank boat dives daily, unlimited shore diving and night diving. Non-divers pay $725. Great wall dives are a stone's throw from the beach bar. Nearby is a 140-ft tanker wreck, *Prince Albert*, in 25 ft of water. Disabled access. ☎ (800) 282-8932, (800) 525-3833 or (352) 588-4158, fax (352) 588-4158. Web site: roatan.com/honduras.htm.

Fantasy Island Beach Resort sprawls across its own 15-acre island off Roatan's south coast. A small bridge connects the resort to the main island. Built in 1989 by local entrepreneur, Albert Jackson, the resort's 73 guest rooms are luxurious, with air-conditioning, phones, refrigerators, full baths and cable TV. There is a full-service dive operation on premises with a fleet of 42-ft custom dive boats. Excellent shore diving and snorkeling. Package rates for seven nights in a standard room with six days of diving, three meals daily, service charges, airport transfers in Roatan and use of kayaks, sailboats and Hobie Cats are $895 per person, double occupancy. Non-divers pay $795. Rates drop between Sept 15 and Dec 15 (hurricane season). ☎ (800) 676-2826 or (011) 504-455191, fax (813) 835-4569. Packages: ☎ (800) 525-3833.

Inn of Last Resort, Roatan's newest dedicated dive resort, features 30 large guest rooms built of natural woods and decorated with tropical accents. All rooms are air-conditioned. Restaurant. Good shore diving and snorkeling off the resort's beach. Packages from $695 include seven nights, three meals daily, three boat dives daily, unlimited shore diving day and night, airport transfers. ☎ (800) 374-8181, (011) 504-45-1838, fax (011) 504-45-1828. Pack-ages from the US, ☎ (800) 525-3833. E-mail: lastresort@globalnet.hn. Web site: www.dive.com/innlast.html.

The Reef House Resort touts 11 lovely cottages in two wings. All are furnished in tropical decor. Two are air-conditioned, the rest have ceiling fans and the trade winds for cooling. Great shore diving and fine snorkeling off the jetty in front of the resort. Snorkeling trips to neighboring islands. Side trips to explore mainland Honduras Maya sites and hot springs are offered. Dive packages with round-trip transportation from the airport cost from $550 for five nights, $725 for seven nights, including room (double), welcome drink, three meals per day, unlimited shore diving, two boat dives per day with an experienced guide, one night dive, tanks, air, weight belts and weights. Non-divers pay $450 for five nights, $575 for seven nights. Nice wall dive from the pier. Dive shop offers equipment, still camera and housing rentals for disposable cameras. ☎ (800) 328-8897 or (210) 681-2888, fax (210) 733-7889, in Roatan (504) 45-2142.

Romeo's Dive & Yacht Club is at the south end of Roatan on Brick Bay. Standard rooms, some air-conditioned, have porches facing the sea. Restaurant and lounge. The dive shop has a fleet of 40-ft custom boats. Winter rates for a dive package for seven nights from $525 summer, $715 winter, per person, double occupancy. Includes three boat dives daily, three meals per day, transfers, two night dives, use of kayaks and paddle boats. Pool. ☎ (800) 535-DIVE or (305) 559-0511, fax (305) 559-0558. E-mail: brick bay@aol.com. Packages with air from the US, ☎ (800) 525-3833.

Roatan Beach House Rentals are offered at $505 to $938 per week for a two-bedroom, four-guest, modern home. Dive packages available. ☎ (800) 525-3833. E-mail: lndfall@aol.com.

Guanaja

Bayman Bay Club is a beautiful waterfront lodge. Guests stay in cottages on a hillside overlooking the reef. The resort features a dive shop, restaurant, gameroom and clubhouse. Spacious rooms are cooled by ceiling fans and sea breezes. Sea-kayak dive adventures and guided hikes to the island's lovely waterfall are offered. Great snorkeling is right off the resort's 300-ft dock. Dive packages are $899 ($799 for non-divers) and include three meals daily, two boat dives daily, unlimited shore dives, one night dive, hiking tips and use of kayaks. ☎ (800) 524-1823, fax (954) 572-1907, or (011) 504-454179. Write to Terra Firma 11750 NW 19th Street, Fort Lauderdale, FL 33323. E-mail: reservations@baymanbayclub.com or info@baymanbay club.com. Web site: www.baymanbayclub.com.

Nautilus Beach Resort is a charming, Georgian-style, six-room resort on a 1,000-ft beach. Some rooms are air-conditioned. A full-service PADI dive shop on premises offers basic and advanced courses and operates a 27-ft Delta dive boat. Oxygen. Dive packages are $560 per week, per person, for a double, including a two-tank morning boat dive and one-tank afternoon boat dive daily, three meals per day, airport transfers, unlimited fills for shore dives. ☎ (800) 566-6143 or (206) 937-7484, fax (206) 933-8075. E-mail: dive trav@aa.net. Web site: www.seattleweb.com/divetravel/r-honduras-nautilus. html.

Posada Del Sol is a luxurious Spanish villa resort on 72 acres of oceanfront greenery and, except for two small villages, is the only developed area on the southeast shore. It has an excellent restaurant, bar, pool and tennis court. Rooms are luxurious and spacious. Three 42-ft dive boats whisk guests to 50 moored dive sites. Packages at $900 per diver, double, include three meals daily, two boat dives daily, one night dive, unlimited shore diving, round-the-island cruise, weights, beach barbecue, and airport transfers on Guanaja. Handicapped access. ☎ (800) 642-3483 or (561) 624-3483, fax (561) 624-3225. E-mail: posadadel@aol.com. Web site: www.posada delsol. com.

Casa Sobre El Mar is a small family-run hotel built on concrete piers over the reef one-half mile from Guanaja. The effect is like staying on a live-aboard that doesn't rock. Comfortable rooms have private baths and are cooled by sea breezes. No sand flies or mosquitos! Free launch to Guanaja any time. Week-long packages are $595 per person year-round and include three boat dives daily, unlimited 24-hour front-door or back-porch diving with three meals daily—fresh lobster, fish, shrimp, crab, fruits and vegetables. ☎ (800) 869-7295 or direct (011) 504-45-4269. Write to Casa Sobre el Mar, Pond Cay, Islas de la Bahia, Honduras, Central America.

Utila

Utila Lodge is a two-story, eight-room inn. Rooms are air-conditioned and overlook the sea. Dive shop on premises. Packages for seven nights, six days of diving are $750 per person. Included are three meals daily, three

Dolphins are frequently spotted off the Bay Islands.

boat dives per day, two night dives, tanks and weights, belts, unlimited fills for shore dives and airport transfers. ☎ (504) 45-3143.

Laguna Beach Resort, the newest and most luxurious dive resort on Utila, has air-conditioned bungalows perched at the water's edge. Full-service dive operation offers three dives daily, night dives and unlimited beach diving on the spectacular fringing coral reef that lies about 150 yds offshore. Snorkelers find lots of fish in the turtle grass on the way out. The dock takes you half-way there. Kayaks for guests' use. Rates for a week with diving average $850, $750 for a non-diver. ☎ (800) 66-UTILA (88452) or (318) 893-0013, fax (318) 893-5024. Direct (011) 504-45-3239. E-mail: awhite @utila.com. Web site: http://www.utila.com.

Cayos Cochinos

Plantation Beach Resort, formerly a pineapple plantation, on Cochinos Grand is a delightful 10-room beachfront resort. Guests stay in chalets crafted of solid Honduran mahogany, each with private bath, ceiling fans, and either one king or two twin beds. Rooms are clean and simple. Great diving and snorkeling is a giant stride off the beach. All-inclusive, seven-night packages are $895 per person. Transfers not included. ☎ (800) 628-3723 or (011) 504-42-0974, fax (011) 504-42-0974. Write to 8582 Katy Freeway, Suite 118, Houston TX 77024. E-mail: hkinett@hondutel.hn. Web site: www.tnt group.com/di,ve/index.html.

Note: If your flight arrives after 4 pm on day of arrival or departs before 8 am on day of departure, an overnight on the mainland will be necessary at a cost of approximately $50 per room.

Live-Aboard

The **Bay Islands Aggressor** is a seven-cabin, 18-passenger, air-conditioned luxury yacht that visits all the best dive sights off the Bay Islands. A week stay costs $1,295 per person. Pick-up is from Roatan. ☎ (800) 348-2628 or write to PO Drawer K, Morgan City, LA 70381. E-mail: divboat@aol.com. Web site: www.aggressor.com.

Sightseeing and Other Activities

Some resorts offer water-taxi service or have kayaks for getting around the bays. The main après-dive activities are fishing, bird watching, and hiking.

Facts

Nearest Recompression Chamber: Roatan. Bay Islands Air evacuation is possible from some other areas.

Getting There: The best days to travel are Friday and Saturday. Isleña Airlines flies to the Bay Islands every day but Sunday from Tegucigalpa, San Pedro Sula and La Ceiba to Guanaja. *From Miami:* American Airlines, ☎ (800) 433-7300, has daily flights to San Pedro Sula, Honduras. *From Houston:* Continental Airlines to San Pedro Sula with a stop in Tegucigalpa. Direct flights to Roatan from Miami, Houston and New Orleans are provided by TACA weekly. Water taxis are sent by the island resorts to pick you up.

Precautions: Register your cameras and electronic gear with customs before visiting Honduras. Do not bring drugs, plants or flowers into or out of the country.

Language: English on the Bay Islands, Spanish on mainland Honduras.

Documents: A passport, visa, and onward ticket is required to enter Honduras.

Departure tax: US $15-$20 depending on the exchange rate.

Health: Vaccinations are not required. Check with your own doctor for health precautions. On the islands, drinking water comes from mountain wells. Ask about the water before drinking. Pack a diver's first-aid kit for sea stings and bug bites. Buy all your sundries and cosmetics before you leave home.

Currency: The lempira (L). L 9.22=US $1.

Climate: Hot and humid. March and April are the hottest months. Rain clouds crop up most afternoons during summer and fall. Coolest months are January and February. Water temperature averages 80° F year-round.

Clothing: Shorts and T-shirts, jeans and sneakers. Long-sleeve shirts and long pants are good for mountain hikes and protection from bugs or sunburn. Snorkelers should wear protective clothing for the hot sun. Divers will find a lycra suit comfortable for deep wall dives.

Electricity: Most resorts have 110 volts, but some have 220. Carry an adaptor to be sure.

For Additional Information: Contact the resorts directly, the tour operators listed under "Dive Resorts," or the Honduras Institute of Tourism, ☎ (800) 410-9608. Web site: www.islands.com/coral/roatan/roatan.html#how.

Jamaica

Jamaica's first tourists arrived in the late 1800's by banana boat, the result of a brainstorm by New England sea captain Lorenzo Down Baker, who fell in love with this mountainous island of delights. By the turn of the century banana exports had grown and Jamaica had become one of the trendiest vacation spots in the world.

Today most tourists arrive by jet and cruise ship. In all, 1.3 million tourists arrive each year to experience Jamaica's watersports, mountain vistas, night life and duty-free shopping.

At 4,411 square miles, it is the third largest island in the Caribbean after Cuba and Puerto Rico. Geographically, it is a cornucopia of scenic wonders. Miles of soft sand beaches and lush greenery line the coasts, and high mountains loom inland. Overall, the terrain is very mountainous, with half of the land rising above 1,000 ft. The highest point, Blue Mountain Peak, soars to 7,402 ft—higher than any in the eastern half of North America. Hundreds of wild rivers and plunging waterfalls crisscross the mountains and moisten the fertile valleys, which produce some of the world's best coffee, fruits, flowers and vegetables. The flatter southern coast can look like the African savanna or the Indian plains and has alternating black and white sand beaches as well as mineral springs.

Offshore reef tracts provide a bounty of dive and snorkeling sites. Many are a short swim from the beach. Wall dives predominate as Jamaica's north stretch of reef edges the Great Cayman Trench. A ledge of shallow reefs stretches around the island's perimeter. Depths range from extreme shallows to awesome depths.

Almost everything imaginable grows in Jamaica's sensuous environment. Marine scientists have identified more than 50 species of sponges on the surrounding reefs. In the heyday of the British Empire, flowering and fruit trees were brought from Asia, the Pacific and Africa, evergreens from Canada, roses and nasturtiums from England. The breadfruit was sent from Tahiti, first by Captain Bligh on the *Bounty*. In return, Jamaica's native pineapple was sent to Hawaii and its mahogany to Central America. There are varieties of orchids, bromeliads and ferns in Jamaica that are native nowhere else and fruits like the Bombay mango that flourish only here.

The island's 2.4 million permanent residents are a mix of African, European, Afro-European, East Indian, Afro-East Indian, Chinese, Afro-Chinese—and seemingly every other combination of races. Most are black; many are shades of brown. Together they blend into a unique culture steeped in magical rituals, legends and customs.

Religion is an important force. The vast majority are Christian, but there are communities of Jews, Hindus and Moslems. The Church of Jamaica, formerly the Church of England, has the largest membership. Rastafarianism commands a large following.

Jamaicans speak English and speak it eloquently, but with their own musical lilt and some words which are a survival from West African languages.

When Jamaicans speak Patois, a blend of English and African, the discussion may be almost incomprehensible to the visitor at first, but after awhile you catch the rhythm and pick up some expressions—*Weh yuh ben deh (Where've you been)? Minuh hab nutten* (I don't have anything). *Yeh-mon (Yes, man).*

Proverbs and place names express the vitality of Jamaica talk. For "mind your own business," there is "Cockroach no business inna fowl-yard"; for being corrupted by bad companions, "You lay down wid dawg, you get up wid fleas"; and for the pretentious, "The higher monkey climb, the more him expose."

Jamaica also boasts a broad variety of birds, both native and migratory, from the tiny bee hummingbird and its cousin the "doctor bird' (whose longer-tailed profile is the logo of Air Jamaica) to the mysterious solitaire with its mournful cry. Divers visiting the north coast will meet the kling-kling—a shiny black Antillian grackle who shares breakfast toast. A hike through the highest mountains may be rewarded by a sight of *papillio homerus*, one of the world's largest butterflies, also a native.

History

When Columbus sighted Jamaica on his second voyage in 1494, he recorded in his log: *"The fairest land ever eyes beheld... the mountains touch the sky."*

The Spanish never fully settled Jamaica, but they stayed long enough to kill off the peaceful resident Arawak Indians through forced labor, mass executions and European diseases.

Spanish colonists raised cattle on Jamaica and shipped lard, *manteca,* from a north coast port today called Montego Bay. Jamaica became a provisions stop for ships headed to Central America in search of gold. In the century and a half of their rule, the Spaniards made two introductions that became pivotal to Jamaica's future. They brought in sugar cane and slaves from Africa to cultivate it.

In 1509 the Spaniards established New Seville as the capital, near the modern town of Ocho Rios. Today, the foundations of New Seville are being excavated and a search continues for the remains of two ships Columbus left beached nearby.

By 1655, the British conquered the island, driving the Spaniards from their new capital of St. Jago de la Vega (now Spanish Town) to Cuba.

For nearly 200 years fortunes were built on sugar plantations with slave labor. Corruption became commonplace. Buccaneers were encouraged to operate from Jamaica, attack the treasure ships of Spain and France and capture territory. A young indentured laborer from Wales called Henry Morgan rose to become Jamaica's Lieutenant Governor and prospered as one of history's best-known pirates. His home base, Port Royal, on a peninsula outside today's capital, Kingston, was considered "the richest, wickedest city in Christendom," until one hot afternoon in 1692 when an earthquake tumbled most of it beneath the sea. Today, Port Royal and her treasures are covered by a dense reef. When winds are calm the site makes an interesting dive.

Magnificent plantation houses like Rose Hall and Greenwood rose above the cane fields. A spirit of independence among the planters and slaves took root during the early 1700's. There was the presence of the Maroons, descendants of slaves that had escaped from the Spaniards. They called them "cimarrones" (runaways). The Maroons lived in the mountains, defied the British troops, served as a magnet for other runaways and periodically staged rebellions, until a treaty in 1739 gave them some measure of local autonomy, which they still retain today.

The planters, too, were rebellious. When the 13 American colonies declared independence from Britain, the Jamaica House of Assembly voted to join them.

Slavery ended in 1834. Economic chaos followed and Jamaica's Assembly voted away its traditional independence and became a full colony of England. Jamaica remained a British colony until August 6, 1962 when the Union Jack was lowered and the black, green and gold flag of the independent nation of Jamaica was raised.

Despite the loss of slave labor, Jamaica's rich farmlands prospered and indirectly launched its tourism industry when the banana boat captains began carrying North American vacationers.

Jamaica also expanded citrus exports, including new hybrids like the ortanique and the "ugly fruit." Rum became the principal export and a new overseas market was found for Jamaican ginger in a product called ginger ale. Pimento was exported under the name "allspice" and Jamaica Blue Mountain coffee became a premium brand worldwide.

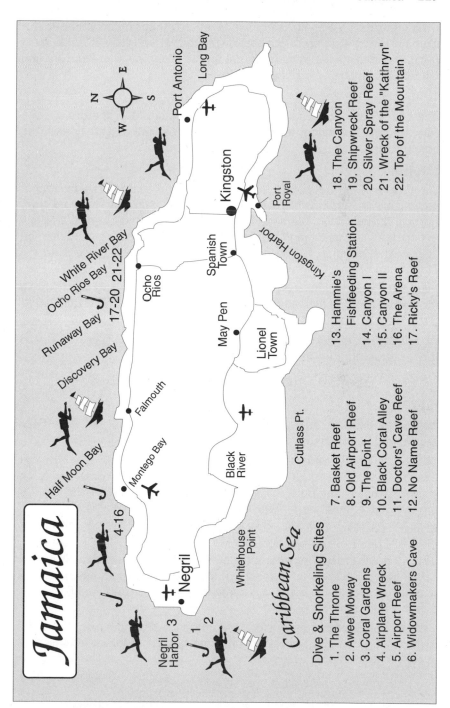

Jamaica

Caribbean Sea

Port Antonio

Long Bay

Kingston

Port Royal

Spanish Town

Kingston Harbor

May Pen

Lionel Town

Ocho Rios

White River Bay

Ocho Rios Bay 21-22

17-20

Runaway Bay

Discovery Bay

Falmouth

Montego Bay

Black River

Cutlass Pt.

Half Moon Bay

4-16

Whitehouse Point

Negril

Negril Harbor 3

1 2

Dive & Snorkeling Sites

1. The Throne
2. Awee Moway
3. Coral Gardens
4. Airplane Wreck
5. Airport Reef
6. Widowmakers Cave
7. Basket Reef
8. Old Airport Reef
9. The Point
10. Black Coral Alley
11. Doctors' Cave Reef
12. No Name Reef
13. Hammie's Fishfeeding Station
14. Canyon I
15. Canyon II
16. The Arena
17. Ricky's Reef
18. The Canyon
19. Shipwreck Reef
20. Silver Spray Reef
21. Wreck of the "Kathryn"
22. Top of the Mountain

During the 1970's Jamaica supplied nearly two-thirds of the US needs for aluminum from the island's rich bauxite (alumina) deposits. With the current collapse of that market, Jamaica is building an economy where tourism and modern agriculture take a bigger place.

When to Go
The best months to dive Jamaica are Dec through May, the dry season. June through Nov brings the chance of a hurricane, though July and Aug are often dry.

Diving
Offshore diving is most popular along the north and west coasts of the island, particularly in Negril on the leeward western tip, which is sheltered from high winds and waves. Montego Bay, Runaway Bay and Ocho Rios follow in popularity. Despite many sites being a short swim from shore, diving on your own is prohibited. You must be accompanied by a guide from the Association of Dive Operators.

Marine Park regulations are as follows: 1) Always stay at least two ft above the reef. 2) Don't touch or stand on the coral and don't take souvenirs. 3) Don't wear gloves.

Also, it is illegal to buy or possess coral and turtle products. There is a closed lobster season from April till June 30.

Best Dive and Snorkeling Sites

NEGRIL
Negril has three reef areas, with most interest between 50 and 70 ft. Seas are dependably calm and the visibility often exceeds 100 ft.

☆☆☆☆ **The Throne** is a 50-ft-wide cave at a depth of 65 ft, which you enter from the top at 40 ft. Its walls are carpeted with soft corals and huge yellow sponges hang from ceiling to floor. There is a chute at the back of the cave, 12 ft by three ft, with fine growths of black coral. Eels, octopi, turtles, sting rays, barracuda, reef fish, and an occasional nurse shark inhabit the cave.

☆☆☆ South of The Throne is a shallow reef area known as **Awee Moway.** Local dive guides have tamed resident stingrays, which you may pet if you approach them slowly. Eagle rays come by at night. Depths are 20 to 50 ft. Seas are calm.

☆☆ **Coral Gardens** is a shallow dive and snorkeling area near the shore. Elkhorn, staghorn, brain and star coral form the reef. Fish life includes filefish, angels, triggerfish and fairy basslets. Starfish and anemones are along the base.

☆☆ **Airplane Wreck** at 70 ft is in Bloody Bay off the Sandals resort beach. The wreck, an intentionally sunk Cessna, attracts numerous fish and is beginning to cover over with sponges and corals.

MONTEGO BAY

Montego Bay is Jamaica's first marine park. Depths vary from waist deep to a ledge at 30 ft to vertical drops of 100 ft. The shallow reefs show signs of wear from storms and crowds of snorkelers, but the deeper scuba sites are fairly lush, with big tube sponges, sea whips and good sized fish. Seas are usually calmest in the morning.

☆☆ **Airport Reef** has expansive coral fingers and gullies at depths of 25 to 35 ft. The reef is in Montego Bay. Throngs of small fish, blue chromis, trumpet fish, tangs and parrot fish inhabit the area. Visibility varies from 60 to 80 ft.

☆☆☆ **Widowmakers Cave** is named after the cave in James Jones' novel, *Go to the Widowmaker*. The wall starts at 40 ft and slopes down to a cave at 80 ft. You swim into the cave till you reach a wide chimney which exits up onto a beautiful shallow reef.

Copper sweepers crowd the cave, as do parrot fish, king fish, Creole wrasses and barracuda. Black corals, sea feathers, sponges and long gorgonians cover the wall. Seas vary. Currents are usually light. Boat dive.

☆☆☆☆ **Basket Reef** starts in 50 ft with a sheer drop to 150 ft. Named for huge barrel sponges that adorn the ledge, the reef is extremely photogenic. Expect a light current. A short boat trip.

☆ **Old Airport Reef** is a shallow reef with lots of fish and corals at 15 ft and small caves and crevasses at 35 ft. A good second dive. A boat dive. Good for snorkeling and diving.

☆☆☆ **The Point** is a drift dive with an average current of two knots. Bermuda chub, rays, occasional hammerhead sharks, barracuda, big angelfish, and parrot fish seem to fly by a static display of crimson sponges, long lacy corals, slender gorgonians and anemones growing on the wall. Depths go to 3,000 ft.

☆☆☆ **Black Coral Alley** is a narrow canyon landscaped with bushy black coral trees. The canyon starts at the base of a coral-covered seamount. Swim around the pinnacle to spot crabs, tubeworms, sea cucumbers, urchins and octopi hiding in the ledges and crevices. Depths are from 40 to 65 ft. Visibility about 80 ft.

☆☆ **Doctors Cave Reef** is a shallow dive opposite Doctors Cave Beach. Depths average 25 ft. This spot is ideal for beginners—completely sheltered from the afternoon wind and waves. The reef is mostly elkhorn clumps with some brain and star coral heads. Small, friendly reef fish scurry about. Visibility varies from 40 to 60 ft. Boat access

☆☆☆☆ **No Name Reef** is straight out from Doctors Cave. The reef is pretty, with yellow and purple seafans, tube and barrel sponges, lacy corals, gorgonians and patches of finger coral.

Shore Dives

The following sites are accessible from the jetty at Chalet Caribe, just west of Montego Bay. Currents are normally very light though winter storms blowing from the north will make entry difficult or impossible. Before entering the water check with the dive shop for rules on diving the Marine Park. Cave and tunnel dives should be attempted only by experienced cave divers.

☆ **Hammie's Fishfeeding Station** came about in 1981 when dive shop owners, Theo and Hammie Smit started a private marine sanctuary. The site is now part of the Montego Bay Marine Park. Friendly fish will pose for pictures. Check with dive guide for appropriate fish rewards. Depth is 25 ft.

☆☆ **Canyon I** is a cave/tunnel dive out past the fish feeding station. There is an entrance to the cave at the edge of the reef 30 ft down. Exit at 70 ft. Rare orange sponges grow in the tunnel. Next to Canyon I is **Canyon II**, a hangout for spiny and rock lobsters, schoolmaster snappers and an occasional nurse shark.

☆☆**The Arena** is about 250 yds from the jetty. This shallow reef is bowl-shaped, resembling an amphitheater with walls of coral. The walls slope to 70 ft, where two tunnels lead to more caverns with abundant black coral and big barrel sponges. There is a neat old anchor at the top of the reef. Turtles and eagle rays are common dive buddies.

RUNAWAY BAY

☆☆☆**Ricky's Reef** is a huge reef complex with gigantic lavender and yellow tube sponges, thick growths of lacy soft corals, bush corals, orange tube corals, cactus corals, lettuce corals, and stony corals. Most interest is at 90 ft. For experienced divers.

☆☆ **The Canyon** cuts between two walls covered with dense growths of sea rods, sea plumes, sea whips, tube sponges, feather corals, bush corals, and mesh sea fans. Depths are from 35 to 100 ft. Expect a rendezvous with curious angel fish, sergeant majors, trumpet fish, barracuda and an occasional nurse shark. For experienced divers.

☆☆ **Shipwreck Reef** is a shallow reef shot through with caves and crevices. The dive is in front of the Ambience Jamaica resort. An old freighter at 15 ft houses spotted morays, schooling fish and barracuda. An occasional visit by a turtle adds interest. Average depth is 30 ft. Nice for snorkeling or diving.

☆☆ **Silver Spray Reef** is another shallow garden with a good many of fish and nice soft corals.

OCHO RIOS

☆☆☆ **Wreck of *The Kathryn*** was a Canadian mine sweeper acquired by Jamaica many years ago and used as a cargo vessel and later as a fishing vessel. In 1991 it was acquired by Fantasy Divers and Water Sports, who sank it to create a new dive and fish breeding spot. The ship sits in 50 ft of water. It's located a mile east of the mouth of the White River off the coast of St. Mary.

☆☆☆ **Top of the Mountain** is a sea mount at 60 ft, decorated with orange sponges, bushy corals, and gorgonians. At 75 ft a cave leads inside the pinnacle. Visibility averages 70 ft.

Dive Operators

NEGRIL

Negril Scuba Centre offers reef trips, night dives, cave dives and underwater photography rentals. Repairs. ☎ (809) 957-4425, fax (809) 957-4425. Write to PO Box 49, Negril, Jamaica.

Sundivers Negril Ltd. is a PADI five-star center at the Poinciana Beach Hotel offering reef trips and specialty courses, custom underwater videos. ☎ (809) 957-4069, fax (809) 957-4069.

Blue Whale Divers offers boat and shore dives. ☎ (809) 957-4438.

MONTEGO BAY

Poseidon Divers is a PADI facility with two locations. One at Marguerites' Restaurant near Doctor's Cave Beach offers boat dives and courses. Videos and guided snorkel trips can be arranged. At Chalet Caribe Hotel all diving is done from shore. Courses available. ☎ (809) 952-3624, fax (809) 952-3079. E-mail: poseidon@infochan.com.

Scuba and snorkeling reef tours are offered by **Jamaica Scuba Divers**, located at the Half Moon Hotel. ☎ (809) 953-9266 (fax/phone). E-mail: northmarine@montego-bay-jamaica.com.

Scuba diving in Montego Bay is also available from: **North Coast Marine Sports,** at ☎ (809) 953-9266, fax (809) 953-9266, and **Reef Keeper Divers**, also a PADI Dive Center, ☎ (809) 979-0103, fax (809) 979-0101.

Tango Divers specializes in 35 mm photo courses and drive-and-dive trips for divers and snorkelers. They also operate an 18-ft boat. ☎ (809) 952-2452, fax (809) 952-6271. Write to Suite M81, 17 Humber Ave., Montego Bay, Jamaica.

Fisherman's Inn watersports center offers diving, snorkeling, fishing and sailing plus dockage for visiting yachts. It is located in Falmouth, a few miles east of Montego Bay. Handicapped divers program. ☎ (809) 954-3427, fax (809) 954-3427.

OCHO RIOS

Fantasea Divers, located at the Sans Souci Hotel & Spa, is a PADI international training facility. The shop has a certified Handicapped Scuba Association instructor on staff. Several instructors are trained in American Sign Language for communication with the hearing-impaired. Trips range from shallow reefs and caves to deep walls and drop-offs and to the *Katharine* described above. Most sites are 10 minutes by boat. ☎ (809) 974-5344. Dive/hotel packages.

Sea and Dive Jamaica has three dive boats and offers morning and afternoon dives, snorkeling trips, hotel packages, rentals, repairs, oxygen. ☎ (809) 974-5762, fax (809) 974-5762. Write to 74 Main Street, Ocho Rios, Jamaica.

Resort Divers Ltd. offers PADI specialty courses, reef trips, night diving and wreck diving aboard four dive boats. Underwater camera rental, gear rental. ☎ (809) 974-5338, fax (809) 974-0577.

Princess of the Sea Water Sports Ltd. take divers and snorkelers out on two fast boats. Specialties include underwater video service, resort courses. ☎ (809) 974-1480, fax (809) 974-0574.

Barlovento is a 72-ft sailing yacht which explores remote reef and hidden beaches. Dive or snorkel. Day sails only. Compressor on board. ☎ (800) 562-7273 or (809) 974-1518, fax, (809) 974-5362.

Accommodations

The all-inclusive resorts following usually include airport transfers, all meals, drinks, dive trips, equipment, and tips. Scuba courses are extra and require a medical certificate from home. Rates subject to change. All prices in US dollars based on double occupancy.

Wholesale and retail dive/hotel tours are offered by **Dive Safaris,** ☎ (800) 359-0747 and **ICS Scuba and Travel,** ☎ (800) 722-0205 or (516) 797-2132.

NEGRIL

Poinciana Beach Hotel spreads across 1,000 ft of Negril's seven mile beach. This 130-room, all-inclusive resort offers air-conditioned rooms with private balconies, good facilities for children, entertainment, selected free watersports, tennis, gym, pool, jacuzzi, satellite TV. Dive packages with Sundivers are from $750 in winter for five nights/six days and include tanks, air, weights, guide and boat trip. Add $15 per day for BC's and regulators. Add $130 for unlimited day diving. Non-divers pay $622. Summer rates drop to $626 for a diver and $498 for a non-diver. ☎ (800) 468-6728 or (809) 957-4069, fax (305) 749-6794. Write to PO Box 16003, Plantation, FL 33318.

Negril Scuba Center offers low-priced accommodations from $290 for seven days and six nights. ☎ (800) 848-DIVE or (809) 957-4425.

Rock Cliff Hotel is a charming resort with shore diving from the dock and Sundivers on premises. Packages. ☎ (809) 957-4069 or (800) 359-0747. Write to Sundivers, Lighthouse Road, Negril, Jamaica.

Hedonism II is an all-inclusive resort for couples and singles only. Features are luxurious rooms and suites, five bars, a clothing-optional island with swim-up pool bar, laser karaoke, indoor game room with satellite TV, sauna, arts and crafts centers. Sports include scuba, water skiing, snorkeling, windsurfing, sailing, kayaking, water trikes, tennis, fitness center, squash, bicycles, golf and horseback riding. Rates for three nights start at $690 per person in winter, $625 in summer. ☎ (800) 859-SUPER. *In the UK:* ☎ 01992 447420.

Grand Lido is another adults-only, all-inclusive resort scattered over 22 acres in Negril. Features include nine bars, clothing-optional beach, games room, tennis, 24-hr food and drink Club Houses. Sports include scuba, snorkeling, kayaking, Sunfish sailing, windsurfing, and water skiing. Rates per person, for three nights, start from $950 winter, $830 summer. ☎ (800) 859-7873 or (809) 957-4010, fax (809) 957-4317.

Sandals Negril is yet another all-inclusive resort that caters to couples only. Facilities include two pools, swim bar, scuba center, satellite TV and disco. Rates for two for six nights range from $2,530. ☎ (800) SANDALS, fax (305) 667-8996. Write to Unique Vacations, 7610, SW 61st Ave., Miami, FL 33143.

Negril Inn is a smaller, 46-room, all-inclusive resort open to anyone 13 years or older. Rates of $160 winter, $130 summer, per person, per day, include one dive per day, transfers from Montego Bay, meals, accommodations, most drinks, entertainment, sports. ☎ 800-NEGRIL N or (516) 261-1800, fax (516) 261-9606.

Those who prefer sleeping under the stars may pitch a tent at Lighthouse Park on the beach. Contact the Jamaica Tourist Board for details. ☎ (800) 233-4582.

MONTEGO BAY

Bariblue Beach Hotel is a bed & breakfast inn offering three nights and five dives from $200. ☎ (809) 953-2022, fax (809) 953-2250 or write PO Box 610, Montego Bay, Jamaica.

Sandals Montego Bay is an all-inclusive resort for couples. See *Sandals Negril* for details.

FALMOUTH

Braco Village Resort is an all-inclusive resort 38 miles east of Montego Bay in the village of Braco. Rates include deluxe air-conditioned rooms with gazebo or balcony, transfers between Montego Bay Airport and hotel, breakfast, lunch and dinner daily, beer, soft drinks and bar drinks (premium brands), pool, three bars, three restaurants and a sidewalk café. The hotel has 2,000 ft of white sand beach with a clothing-optional section. Winter $190-$300, summer $163-$255. ☎ (800) 654-1337, fax (516) 223-4815. E-mail: sales@fdrholidays.com

Fisherman's Inn & Dive Resort, a 30-minute drive east of Montego Bay, is a dedicated dive resort on a phosphorescent lagoon at Oyster Bay. Designed and built by divers for divers, the resort features modern, spacious, air-conditioned, waterfront rooms, a good restaurant, poolside bar. Their dive boat, the *Jamaica Queen*, a 42-ft custom yacht, is fast and comfortable. Dive sites are a five-minute ride from the resort dock. Rates for seven nights, eight days in winter are $711 per person for a double (non-diver pays $435) and includes room, one two-tank dive plus one one-tank dive daily, including tank and weight belt, breakfast and dinner daily, airport transfer, beach shuttle, lounges and beach towers. Summer rates drop to $611 for a diver and $365 for a non-diver. ☎ (800) 247-0475 or (809) 954-3427.

Trelawny Beach Hotel is a beachfront family resort. With the exception of lunch and liquor, moderate rates include meals and watersports. Book through your travel agent or direct. ☎ (809) 954-2450, fax (809) 954-2173. Write Box 54, Falmouth, Jamaica.

OCHOS RIOS

Boscobel Beach is an all-inclusive resort for families that offers scuba and snorkeling as part of the price. One child under 14 per adult (in parents' suite) can stay for free. Additional children under 14 stay for $50 per day. A Super Nanny program teaches kids to reggae, tie-dye a T-shirt, play with animals in the petting zoo, work in the computer lab, snorkel, play tennis, video games, collect shells and build sand castles. There is even a "Kiddy cocktail" party. Rooms and suites are luxurious. Rates per person start at $795 for three nights in winter, $690 in summer. ☎ 800-859-SUPER.

Dining

Credit cards are accepted at most resorts and large restaurants, but expect to pay cash at the smaller establishments. Inexpensive, under $20; moderate, $20 to $35; expensive, $35+.

NEGRIL

You'll find "Rasta Pasta" and other Jamaican specialties at low prices in Negril at **Paradise Yard**, ☎ 957-4006, **Cosmo's, Pamela's Country Restaurant, Miss Nellie's Chicken Lavish,** and **De Buss**. For French cooking, **Cafe au Lait** is a must, ☎ 957-4471. **The Negril Yacht Club** serves excellent Chinese food.

Be sure to spend one night at **Rick's Café** for sunset watching, light meals and drinks. It's on the tip of Negril's West End. ☎ 957-4335. No credit cards.

MONTEGO BAY

Great seafood, steaks and rum punches are served at **Pier 1**, off Howard Cook Blvd. Moderate to expensive. Or for more casual dining, try **Marguerite's** (dinner only) on Gloucester Avenue. Specials include fried fish, lobster and cheeseburgers. ☎ 952-2452.

Stop at the **Pork Pit** on Gloucester Avenue for spicy hot jerk pork and Red Stripe beer. Inexpensive. Cash only.

For very elegant dining with a spectacular view of the town and harbor try **Richmond Hill**, ☎ 952-2835, or **Calabash Restaurant**, ☎ 940-0657. Expensive.

OCHO RIOS

Jamaican-Italian (really) cuisine has found the perfect home at **Evita's** in Ocho Rios, where the "Rasta Pasta" is a must try. The menu offers 15 other pasta specials, excellent fish, steak or pork dishes. Evita's is set in an old plantation house overlooking the bay. Moderate. ☎ 974-2333.

Jungle Hut complements its lobster dishes with a rustic ambiance.

Almond Tree offers excellent native cuisine and atmosphere. Overlooks the sea at 83 Main St. Moderate to expensive. ☎ 974-2813.

Sightseeing and Other Activities

NEGRIL

Negril is the quietest area of Jamaica and one of the loveliest. Building codes have kept the highest structure "no higher than the highest palm tree." Most activities are water-related and can be arranged through the dive shops.

Getting around Negril is easy. You can rent a car, bicycle, or canoe, or just stroll along the beautiful seven-mile beach. Among the interesting buildings to visit is the 19th-century **Courthouse of Lucea**, and the **clock tower** modeled after the helmet once worn by the German Royal Guard. The clock itself was made in 1817; it keeps perfect time, and is tended by a family that has had the job for over a hundred years.

MONTEGO BAY

This second largest city in Jamaica offers many attractions, from architecture and museums to natural scenic beauty. **The Cage**, an 18th-century jail for slaves and runaway seamen, is in the center of the city and houses a small museum. **St. James Parish Church**, built in 1775-1782, is regarded as one of the finest churches in Jamaica. **The Bird Sanctuary** at Anchovy features "Doctor Bird" hummingbirds, one of 24 species found only in Jamaica. A trip into the interior on the **Hilton High Day Tour** gives a taste of country farm life and exposure to a different Jamaica: the mysterious cockpit country, and blond Jamaicans whose ancestors came long ago from Germany.

Montego Bay offers duty-free shopping for liquor, china, glassware, perfumes, cigars, English cashmeres and a variety of crafts. There are also several art galleries, including the **Gallery of West Indian Art**. that are worth a browse.

Montego Bay's nightlife is varied. A once-a-week event deserving special consideration is **An Evening on the Great River**—a torchlight ride in dugout canoes followed by dinner, dancing and entertainment.

Discos throughout the city play reggae and rock.

OCHOS RIOS

Ocho Rios is the central point of a magnificent region that includes both deserted and developed beaches, fern-clad cliffs and breathtaking waterfalls. Tranquil, yet stimulating, it evolved from a center of Spanish cultural influence to a region of lush sugar and colorful fishing villages and finally to a modern Caribbean resort area.

Ocho Rios may well be the most photographed area in the West Indies. **Shaw Park Gardens** on the high ground affords spectacular vistas of the coast. **Dunn's River Falls**, over 600 ft high and cascading in tiers onto the beach, is considered the Niagara of the Caribbean. **Fern Gully** offers a spectacular, curving three-mile journey through a world of tropical ferns, including the 30-ft-tall Fern Tree and more than 550 other native varieties.

Several excellent plantation tours give an introduction to Caribbean farming, and to strange and exotic vegetation. **"Firefly,"** the mountaintop house where Noel Coward lived and is buried, is open to visitors. There are the 16th-century Spanish ruins of **New Seville**, and, of course, there is Discovery Bay, which today features historic **Columbus Park**. The **Chukka Cove Equestrian Center** offers several scenic horseback trails as well as polo and dressage lessons (dressage refers to precision movements of a trained horse in response to barely perceptible signals from its rider).

PORT ANTONIO

Port Antonio is a playground of the world's elite—from royalty and movie stars to captains of industry, commerce and politics. It has also been the backdrop for several feature films. For many years, Port Antonio was a well-kept secret hideaway of Clara Bow, Bette Davis, Errol Flynn, Ginger Rogers and J.P. Morgan.

Orchids, bananas, tree-ferns and palms grow along the roadside around this quiet port town. Elegant villas nestled in the hills and along the seacoast are a contrast to old abandoned mansions, historic forts, waterfalls, and caves.

Sightseeing in Port Antonio is relaxing. There is **Fort George,** overlooking the two harbors, with 10-ft-thick walls and cannons pointed out to sea. The once glorious **Folly Mansion** is now a legendary ruin. In contrast, the **Errol Flynn Plantation** is well-tended and prosperous.

Water-lovers can choose between an icy-cold dip in **Somerset Falls** and snorkeling, scuba diving and swimming in the "bottomless" **Blue Lagoon** (actually 180 ft deep). Or they can get carried away down the Rio Grande in a two-passenger 30-ft bamboo raft, guided by a licensed Jamaican raftsman. For those who like to explore, there are **Nonsuch Caves** with fossils, coral formations and remnants of an early Arawak Indian community. East of Port Antonio is **Reach Falls**, one of the most spectacular waterfalls in Jamaica.

KINGSTON

Kingston, Jamaica's capital, is the largest English-speaking city south of Miami.

Set against a backdrop of the Blue Mountain range, Kingston is a busy, well-populated, cosmopolitan city. It is the cultural center as well. The **National Gallery of Jamaica** and the **Institute of Jamaica** offer an exciting view of Jamaican culture, including the most complete collection of the country's art to be found anywhere.

MANDEVILLE

The inland town of Mandeville is considered the most English town in Jamaica; many of its original buildings of early 1800's vintage remain. Outside Mandeville are bauxite mines and a production facility, which are open for touring. Nearby is the famous **Picakapeppa factory,** where the popular Jamaican hot sauce is produced. **Marshall's Pen**, located on a 300-acre cattle farm, is a well-kept 18th-century great house with a hiking trail and bird sanctuary.

On the way from Mandeville to the south coast, **Bamboo Avenue** is a lovely two-mile drive covered by giant bamboos over a century old.

Facts

Helpful Phone Numbers: Police, ☎ 119; ambulance, ☎ 110. Hospital, *Montego Bay*, Cornwall Regional Hospital, ☎ 952-5100; *Ocho Rios*, St. Ann's Bay Hospital, ☎ 972-2272. Pharmacy, Montego Bay, McKenzie's, 16 Strand St., ☎ 952-2467. US Embassy, ☎ 929-4850.

Nearest Recompression Chamber: The Marine Lab at Discovery Bay.

Getting There: Donald Sangster International Airport in Montego Bay is the best entry point for the dive-resort areas. American Airlines, ☎ (800) 433-7300, offers direct service from New York. Air Jamaica, ☎ (800) 523-5585, flies from Atlanta, Baltimore, Chicago, Fort Lauderdale, Miami, Los Angeles, New York, Orlando and Philadelphia. Continental, ☎ (800) 231-0856, flies from Newark; BWIA from San Juan; Northwest, ☎ (800) 447-4747, has daily flights from Minneapolis and Tampa; US Air from Baltimore and Charlotte.

Precautions: Avoid touring the off-the-beaten-track areas of the cities, especially at night. The dive-resort areas listed are fairly quiet, but ragged natives pandering *ganja* (marijuana) may approach you.

Driving: On the left. Rental cars are scarce in season. Be sure to arrange for a rental car in advance of your trip.

Language: English and "Patois" (Jamaican Creole words and speech patterns used by most of the population).

Documents: Visitors from the US or Canada must show proof of citizenship such as a birth certificate with raised seal or a passport and a return ticket. British visitors must have a passport and a return ticket.

Customs: Visitors are prohibited from bringing in drugs, fresh fruit, flowers, meat or rum. Firearms or ammunition are prohibited.

Airport Tax: US $15.

Currency: The Jamaican dollar. The exchange rate fluctuates daily, depending on the foreign exchange markets. The current rate stands at US $1=JA $35.

Climate: Average temperature is 82° F. Water temperature ranges from 80° to 90°. Wetsuits are not necessary, but a lycra suit is comfortable in winter.

Clothing: Lightweight, casual. Hiking shoes for visiting the "mist forests."

Electricity: Varies with the hotel. Some have 110 volts/60 cycles and others 220. To be safe, carry a converter for your appliances.

Religious Services: Protestant, Catholic, Jewish, Rastafarian.

For Additional Information: The Jamaica Tourist Board, ☎ (800) 233-4582. *In New York:* 801 Second Avenue, 20th Floor, NY, NY 10017, ☎ (212) 856- 9727, fax (212) 856-9730. *In Miami:* 1320 S. Dixie Highway, Suite 1100, Coral Gables, FL 33146, ☎ (305) 665-0557. *In Los Angeles*: 3440 Wilshire Boulevard, Suite 1207, Los Angeles, CA 90010, ☎ (800) 421-8206 or (213) 384-1123. *In Canada:* 1 Eglinton Avenue, #616, Toronto, Ontario M4P 3A1, ☎ (416) 482-7850, fax 482-1730. *In the UK:* 1-2 Prince Consort Road, London, England SW7 2B2, ☎ 44-171-224-0505, fax 44-171-224-0551.

Puerto Rico

Puerto Rico's beautiful beaches, cosmopolitan cities and abundant man-made attractions pale in comparison to the pristine reefs that surround three fourths of its coastline. Coupled with first-class hotels, easy access from the US, affordable dive accommodation packages, and a choice of rural or urban settings, it is gaining popularity as an all-around vacation spot for Caribbean divers. At the eastern end of the Greater Antilles chain, this 110-by-35-mile island has the Atlantic Ocean to the north and the Caribbean to the south. Vieques and Culebra islands lie to the east, and Mona Island is to the west. There are 3½ million residents of Puerto Rico, with about one million in the San Juan metropolitan area.

The island's terrain ranges from palm-lined beaches on four coastlines, to rugged mountain ranges, gently rolling hills and deserts. There are 20 designated forest reserves in Puerto Rico and an additional six proposed. The most notable include the 28,000-acre El Yunque rain forest near San Juan, part of the Caribbean National Forest and the only tropical rainforest in the US Forest Service; the Guajataca Forest, with 25 miles of trails through karst reserves—an area of huge, moonscape craters and caves; and the Guanica Forest Reserve, a dry forest with the largest number of bird species on the island. There are also two Phosphorescent Bays, one off La Parguera on the southwest coast and one off the island of Vieques.

Diving and snorkeling is along the Continental Shelf, which surrounds the island on the east, south and west coasts. Underwater terrain is diverse, with shallow reefs off Humacao on the east coast, caves and wrecks off Aguadilla on the west coast, and dramatic walls at The Great Trench, which starts in the Virgin Islands, stretches the entire length of Puerto Rico's south coast and winds up at Cabo Rojo on the west coast. Marine life is exciting, with manatees in the brackish mangrove areas, pelagics at Mona Island (50 miles southwest), and all species of sea turtles at Culebra. In winter, migrating humpback whales travel the Mona Passage off the west coast. Dolphins frequent the eastern shores. Towering soft corals grow to 20 ft in some spots.

Contributors: Gareth Edmondson-Jones; James Abbott, Coral Head Divers; Cathy Rothschild, Dive Safaris; Jose E. Rafols, Aquatica Underwater Adventures; Efra Figueroa, Parguera Divers; Rick & Lisa Ockelmann.

History

Cave drawings indicate that people lived on Puerto Rico for more than 2,000 years before Christopher Columbus claimed it for Spain in 1493. Back then, it was known as Borinquen and inhabited by several Indian tribes, including the Taino Indians. The Spaniards renamed it San Juan for St. John the Baptist, but later changed it to Puerto Rico, which means "Rich Port."

Ponce de Léon, seeker of the Fountain of Youth, was the first governor in 1508. During the next three centuries, settlers defended the island from the French, the Dutch and English—traditional enemies of the Spanish empire. Following the Spanish-American War in 1898, Spain ceded the island to the United States. Puerto Ricans became US citizens in 1917, held their first gubernatorial elections in 1948, and adopted Commonwealth status in 1952.

The Caribbean's most industrially developed island is a major producer and exporter of manufactured goods, pharmaceuticals and high technology equipment. Since the 19th century, Puerto Rico has been a major exporter of rum and today 83% of the rum sold in the US comes from Puerto Rico.

Best East Coast Dive and Snorkeling Sites

Diving off Puerto Rico's east coast centers around Fajardo, Humacao and the offshore islands of Icacos, Palominos, Palminitos, Monkey Island, Vieques and Culebra. Outstanding features are towering soft corals, walls, dramatic overhangs and abundance of fish. Many of the mainland dive sites are close to shore, but the best are about a 20-minute boat ride. Depths are from 35 to 100 ft. Shore diving and snorkeling is possible off Fajardo, but freshwater runoff near the shore clouds the water and lowers visibility. Spearfishing and coral collecting are prohibited.

☆☆☆☆**The Reserve**, a 20-minute boat ride from Humacao, appears like rivers of white sand between coral canyons. The spur and groove formations shelter towering pillar coral, large star and brain coral heads ruffled with sea rods, spiny sea fans and slender tube sponges. Nurse sharks, stingrays, spotted and green morays and tropicals inhabit the reef's ledges and overhangs. Seas average two to four ft. Depths average 50 to 80 ft. Water temperature ranges from 82° to 90° F. Divers should have some experience.

☆☆☆☆**Basslet Reef**, one mile from Humacao, is a small wall with overhangs, caves and swim-throughs. It is frequented by hawksbill turtles, nurse sharks, and enormous angelfish. Most of the reef is formed of mushrooming pillar corals rippled by a healthy display of sea plumes and sea rods. Dolphin visit the area during early summer and spring. Top of the wall is at 60 ft. Usually no current, but expect three- to five-ft surface swells. Basslet Reef is a 15-minute boat ride from Palmas Del Mar docks.

Seafan at The Reserve, Humacao.

⭐⭐⭐⭐⭐**The Cracks** is a section of subsea cliffs ripped apart by an earthquake. The result is an intriguing maze of chasms and fissures where throngs of fish and lobster hide out. Small caves and coral buttresses drop down to a sandy bottom. Dramatic photo opportunities. Depths are from 50 to 80 ft. For novice and experienced divers only. Seas run three to five ft.

⭐⭐⭐⭐**Monkey Reef** is a 25-minute boat trip from Palmas Del Mar docks. The reef is an expanse of sloping hills covered over with acres of soft corals and sponges. One area slopes to a sandy bottom where you will find large, friendly southern sting rays, spotted eagle rays and thousands of shells. The other side is ledges and overhangs where you never know what to expect. Depths range from 20 to 50 ft. Excellent for novice and experienced divers.

⭐⭐⭐ **La Jolla Ridge** is a small coral wall one mile from shore. A healthy display of soft corals, sea whips, sea fans and throngs of schooling fish starts at 40 ft and plunges down to 80 ft. Ledges, overhangs and swim-throughs are home to every imaginable sea creature. A spectacular dive at night, when the area becomes a ballet of basket stars. Recommended for novice and experienced divers. Seas average two to four ft.

⭐⭐⭐ **The Grotto**, a spur and groove reef four miles from Palmas Del Mar docks, is a memorable dive experience. Small caves, overhangs and swim-thoughs are inhabited by crowds of copper sweepers, fairy tailed basslets and blue chromis. Good for all level divers.

Photo by Rick Cckelmann

☆☆☆ **The Drift** is a gently sloping hill covered on one side with giant sponges, sea rods and whips. As you glide over the top you approach a valley of swim-throughs and ledges frequented by moray eels, lobsters, queen and French angels, and nurse sharks.

CULEBRA AND VIEQUES

Trips to out islands, Culebra and Vieques, take off from Humacao or Puerto del Rey Marina at Fajardo, north of Humacao. Puerto del Rey is the largest marina in the Caribbean, with 700 deepwater slips and service facilities. For ferry schedules, ☎ (787) 863-0705. If you wish to ferry an automobile you must reserve space a week in advance.

Culebra is a mini-archipelago with 23 offshore islands situated mid-point between Puerto Rico and St. Thomas. Shallow coral reefs surround the entire area. A favorite snorkeling and photo spot is Culebrita where there is also a lighthouse. The main five-mile-long island, home to 2,000 people, is a National Wildlife Refuge known for its white sand beaches, sea bird colonies—boobies, frigates, and gulls—and as a nesting ground for all species of Caribbean sea turtles—leatherback, green, hawksbill and loggerhead. The turtles nest from April through July. (National Wildlife Refuge, ☎ 787-742-3291). Expeditions for turtle watching are conducted by Earthwatch, a non-profit organization.

Vieques

Vieques is a popular camping island for locals and a day trip for east coast divers and snorkelers. Known for its beautiful beaches, two thirds of the island is owned by the US Navy, with a small section still used for military operations and maneuvers. The rest is rural. At presstime, plans to build Vieques' first resort were in the works.

Shallow reefs and drop-offs lie within one mile of the shoreline. Many are at less than 50-ft depth, with some very shallow areas. Sea conditions, sometimes rough, vary with the wind. Swells on the leeward side average two to three ft. Vieques subsea highlights are walls, caves, giant barrel sponges, healthy fish populations, and a magnificent phosphorescent bay. Beach dives are possible off the West end at Green Beach, with reef depths from 10 to 25 ft.

Two towns, Esperanza and Isabel Segunda, serve Vieques' 8,000 residents. Accommodations are available at **Casa Del Frances** near Espernaza, ☎ (787) 741-3751.

Vieques is a one-hour boat trip from Fajardo or Humacao. Or get there by air via Sunaire Express from San Juan's international airport (about $50 round trip).

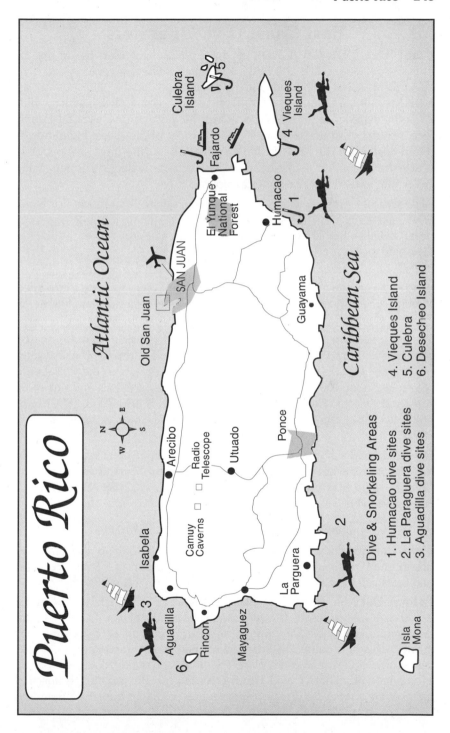

Puerto Rico

Atlantic Ocean

Caribbean Sea

Old San Juan

SAN JUAN

El Yunque National Forest

Humacao

Fajardo

Culebra Island

Vieques Island

Guayama

Ponce

Arecibo

Radio Telescope

Utuado

Camuy Caverns

Isabela

Aguadilla

Rincon

Mayaguez

La Parguera

Isla Mona

Dive & Snorkeling Areas

1. Humacao dive sites
2. La Paraguera dive sites
3. Aguadilla dive sites
4. Vieques Island
5. Culebra
6. Desecheo Island

N E
W   S

East Coast Dive Operators

Coral Head Divers (CHD) at the Palmas Del Mar Resort, is an English-speaking, PADI and NAUI Pro Facility offering personalized dive adventures. CHD is owned and operated by Captain Jim Abbott, an award-winning (Platinum Pro 5000) and accomplished dive instructor with 20 years experience. Jim has pioneered the pristine dive sites off Puerto Rico's south coast and personally escorts most of the dives. Hundreds of return customers can attest to Jim's reputation as "the most gracious dive host in the Caribbean"—dive boats are never overcrowded and he personally looks after each diver's safety and enjoyment.

CHD visits 24 sites, all within five to 30 minutes from the dock. For those of you whose favorite après-dive activity is more diving, the shop also rents ocean kayaks suitable for carrying a tank out to a nearby islet for additional diving or snorkeling.

CHD carries state-of-the-art equipment including dive computers provided at no extra charge to divers who don't have their own. Pure air is provided through an electric-powered fill station with water separators and filters—all well maintained.

The shop has two dive boats: a six-passenger, 26-ft dive boat, for nearby sites, and a 48-ft custom dive boat, *Cool Change,* for trips to Monkey Island or Vieques. CHD is one of the best-equipped operators in the Caribbean, with more than 100 sets of hypoallergenic masks, snorkels and fins of all sizes and designs. Reservations required. ☎ (787) 850-7208, (800) 635-4529, fax (787) 285-8507. Write to PO Box 0246, Humacao, Puerto Rico 00792.

Dive and snorkeling tours aboard the *Fiesta,* a 48-ft trimaran, and weekly live-aboard charters are offered by **Caribbean Marine Services** on Culebra. ☎ (800) 635-4529 or (787) 850-7208, fax (787) 285-8507. E-mail: coralheaddivers@worldnet.att.net.

East Coast Accommodations

Note: Paradores are country inns that offer quality lodging near places of great natural beauty, historical monuments and points of interest. For a list and rates call the central booking number, ☎ (800) 443-0266.

Palmas del Mar, located 40 miles southeast of San Juan, is a beautiful 2,700-acre luxury resort with three miles of sandy beach. Rooms feature air-conditioning, cable TV, phones, and Caribbean decor. Sports facilities include 20 tennis courts, 18-hole golf course, five swimming pools, fitness center, and equestrian center. Water sports include sailing, deep-sea fishing, snorkeling and diving. **Coral Head Divers** is on the grounds. Rothschild travel offers discounted dive/accommodation packages from the US starting at $260 for three nights (double), four boat dives, transfers, taxes and service charges. ☎ (800) 359-0747. Contact the hotel at (787) 852-6111, fax (787) 852-2230. Write to PO Box 2020, Humacao, Puerto Rico 00792.

Best South Coast Dive and Snorkeling Sites

Dive trips off the south coast originate in Ponce, Puerto Rico's second largest city or La Parguera, a sleepy fishing village known for its famed Phosphorescent Bay—one of four bio-luminescent bodies of water in the world. It is also home to the University of Puerto Rico's Marine Science Facility.

A 2½-hour drive from San Juan airport, La Parguera is not yet heavily populated by tourists. Accommodations are modest, local attractions and other activities are limited.

☆☆ **Ponce Caja de Muertos** (Coffin Island), **Cayo Ratones, Cayo Caribe** and **Cayo Cardon** form a crescent barrier reef from Ponce west to Tallaboa. All are a 20-minute boat ride from Ponce. Shore dives are possible off Coffin Island, a park administered by the Department of Natural Resources. Depths range from 15 to 40 ft.

☆☆☆ **LA PARGUERA WALL DIVES**

There are no shore dives. The best sites are along a 20-mile wall that edges the Great Trench from La Parguera to Ponce. Recommended for advanced divers, depths on the wall vary from 50 to over 100 ft. Visibility exceeds 150 ft. Currents, if any, are light. Seas average one to two ft. Boat trips are all 45 minutes to an hour long.

Black Wall is a vertical wall that starts at 60 ft and drops down to great depths. Divers encounter lots of schooling fish, green morays, big crabs, deep-water black gorgonians, and good coral heads.

Hole in the Wall at 120 ft, as the name implies, is a hole where divers can swim through and come up in 100 ft of water.

Hai Lite is a group of deep-water trenches with valleys of schooling grunts and squirrel fish. Beautiful barrel and giant tube sponges. Lavender trumpetfish.

Grunts Valley, like Hai Lite, is a hangout for myriads of grunts, yellowtail, snapper, squirrel fish.

Cylinders is a sharp sloping wall named for huge gas cylinders dropped by a cargo ship 20 years ago. The cylinders are covered with corals and sponges.

Fallen Rock is an enormous rock in the middle of a Y-shaped trench. The walls are sheer, with lots of schooling fish, big barrel sponges and gorgonians. The adjacent trench is so conjested with traveling fish the locals nicknamed it "L.A. Highway." Expect the unexpected!

☆☆ LA PARGUERA INNER-REEF DIVES

The Playground is the site of the Parguera Divers Bubble Bell. You fill the bell with fresh air from your tank and experience an underwater habitat for two. You can talk, kiss, eat or just hang out under it. Two big French angelfish will hover close and play in your bubbles.

Barracuda City, at 50 ft, is a dense forest of staghorn and elkhorn corals packed with clouds of the silvery fish for which it was named. While encountering one or two barracuda on any Caribbean reef is scarcely noteworthy, this spot can be downright unnerving. Exciting photo possibilities for those who dare!

Hog Heaven I, II, III is a newly discovered, triple-site reef off La Parguera with a fascinating complex of coral caves, holes and canyons. It was named by local divemaster, Efra Figueroa. Upon first diving the area, he met a colossal hogfish. The big hogfish is gone, but sightings of nurse sharks are common.

The Pinnacles are coral formations estimated to be 5,000 years old. They appear like giant mushrooms with holes and caves. This is a spot for marine invertebrates—octopi, sea horses, arrow crabs, basket sponges and more.

The Forest is a mass of towering soft corals growing across rocky canyons. Many critters and fish. Expect a light surge.

Additional similar dive and snorkeling sites off the south coast are **1990, The Star, Aquarium, Manhattan, Coral Garden, Sponge Garden, The Chinmey** and others.

South Coast Dive Operators

Paraguera Divers Training Center, a PADI and NAUI instruction facility, offers basic certification, dive master, rescue and medic courses. Snorkeling, jet skis, windsurfing, mangrove-trail tours, Phosphorescent Bay trips, fishing and boat rentals can be arranged. Open water referrals accepted for PADI and NAUI. Major credit cards and travelers checks accepted.

This English-, Spanish- and German-speaking dive center is owned and operated by Captain Efra Figueroa, who personally escorts most dives. His background is impressive, with 23 years of diving all over the world as a US Navy diver, a University of Puerto Rico Marine Sciences instructor and recompression chamber operator, Sea Grant Program consultant for marine advisory services, co-director for seven NAUI ITC's (Instructor Training Courses), and certified instructor for PADI, NAUI, CMAS, SSI, ARC, and MEDIC-FIRST AID since 1976. Efra also has a degree in zoology and animal science. ☎ (787) 899-4171, fax (787) 899-5558. Write to Parguera Divers, PO Box 514, Lajas, Puerto Rico 00667.

Marine Sports & Dive Shop, in Ponce, visits Coffin Island. ☎ (787) 844-6175.

South Coast Accommodations

Copamarina Beach Resort in Guanica, a new resort halfway between Ponce and La Parguera, offers 70 deluxe, air-conditioned rooms, tennis court, cable TV, direct dial telephone, restaurant and pool. Diving and snorkeling off Gilligan's Island, less than a mile away, and along the offshore wall. ☎ (800) 468-4553 or (787) 821-0505, fax (787) 821-0070. Dive packages for five nights, eight dives in the high season (Dec 18-Apr 14) are $673; for non-divers, $393. In summer (Apr 15-May 23 and Sep 4-Dec 17) for five nights, eight dives, it's $620; $340 for the non-diver. Rates include daily continental breakfast and all hotel taxes. Book packages through Dive Safaris, ☎ (800) 359-0474, fax (212) 749-6172. E-mail: rothschild@ divesafaris.com.

Parador Posada Porlamar has 19 air-conditioned rooms with kitchen facilities, TV, pool and charming gardens. The dive dock for Parguera Divers is directly in front of the hotel. Dive/accommodation packages start at $259 per person for three nights, four dives, breakfast buffet and lunch aboard the dive boat. ☎ (800) 359-0747 or (212) 662-4858. Write to 900 West End Ave., Suite 1B, NY, NY 10025, or ☎ (800) 899-4015. E-mail: rothschild @divesafaris.com.

Parador Villa Parguera faces Phosphorescent Bay and is next door to the dive dock. This parador (small hotel) features waterfront rooms with private terraces. There are 52 rooms, a fine restaurant and bar, plus pool. Dive/accommodation packages start at $257 per person (double occupancy) for three nights and four dive trips. ☎ (800) 359-0747 or (212) 662-4858. Write to 900 West End Ave., Suite 1B, NY, NY 10025. Hotel direct: ☎ (787) 899-7777. Route 304, La Parguera, Lajas, PR 00667.

Best West Coast Dive and Snorkeling Sites

The hub of west coast diving is Aguadilla, named for a natural spring which for centuries served as a watering place for Spanish sailors. Pretty beaches shaded by coconut palms stretch from Rincon, south of Aguadilla, to Crash Boat Beach, north of Aguadilla. Visibility and water temperature along Puerto Rico's west coast sites are best during spring and summer—March through November. Sea conditions are rough and suggested for advanced divers only. Beach dives are possible at Crash Boat Beach, though visibility is often clouded by freshwater runoff.

☆☆☆ **Yellow Reef** is a pyramid-shaped sea mount that starts at 15 ft and drops to 85 ft. Coral caverns, arches and a 10-ton anchor make it uniquely interesting. Average depth is 60 ft. The bottom is sandy and dotted with other pinnacles. Big schools of amberjacks (200+) are always about, as are queen angels, rock beauties and nurse sharks. Big star coral heads, orange cups and big barrel sponges prevail. This area is wind-dependent—wiped out for diving if swells exceed four ft.

☆☆☆☆☆ **South Gardens—Desecheo Island**, 13 miles offshore, is being considered for a marine sanctuary. This popular west-coast dive features a huge fish population, immense barrel sponges, giant sea fans (six ft across) and shallow depths. Sting rays and turtles are frequently sighted. Dives are off the protected southwest tip of the island, where you can explore an unknown wreck or a cave at 25 ft. Snorkelers will be encircled by curious fish along the rocky shore. Star, brain and staghorn corals form the shallow reef.

☆☆☆ **Airplane Wreck** is a B-29 bomber that went down in 1949. Huge grouper patrol its coral-encrusted wings, propellers and landing gear. The wreck sits at 115 ft, on a sandy bottom surrounded by rocky ledges. Visibility is around 80 ft. Possible strong surface currents make line descent and ascents a must. Hordes of lobster hide in the surrounding rock ledges. This is a decompression dive with a mandatory (by the dive operator) stop at 15 ft. For advanced divers only.

MONA ISLAND, a remote, uninhabited island 50 miles off the southwest tip of Puerto Rico, is a six-hour boat trip from the mainland across rough water or a half-hour flight from Mayaguez. The trip and stay are a rugged adventure, but intrepid nature lovers are rewarded with colonies of sea birds, colorful marine life, 200-foot cliffs and dazzling white beaches. Virgin dive sites average 80-ft depths. Camping overnight is permitted, but most visitors arrive by boat for day visits. Contact the Department of Natural Resources, ☎ (787) 724-3724.

West Coast Dive Operator

Aquatica Underwater Adventures is a PADI/NAUI instruction center offering referrals, open water, advanced and rescue courses; dive and snorkeling trips. C card and log book requested. Repairs and rentals. English-speaking dive master and captain, Jose E. Rafols, is Coast Guard certified to operate a 100-ton vessel. Dive boats depart from Aguadilla or Joyuda Beach. Trips to Desecheo Island and shore dives off Aguadila and Isabella. ☎/fax (787) 890-6071. Write to: PO Box 250350, Ramey, Aguadilla, PR 00604. E-mail: aquatica@caribene.

West Coast Accommodations

Tours below may be booked by your travel agent.

Joyuda Beach Hotel is a beachfront property offering 52 tastefully decorated guest rooms. The dive-boat pier is a short walk away. Joyuda

Beach on Cabo Rojo is a quaint fishing and resort community with more than 20 great seafood restaurants. Dive packages for three nights start at $249 per person, including four dives. Book through your travel agent or write to PO Box 250350, Ramey, Puerto Rico 00604.

Mayaguez Hilton, at Mayaguez, just north of Cabo Rojo, has 145 luxurious guest rooms and suites with full amenities. Two fine restaurants, bar, dance club, casino, olympic pool, and three tennis courts. Dive packages available. Book through your travel agent or ☎ (787) 831-7575.

Dining

Puerto Rico boasts some of the finest restaurants in the Caribbean, offering international dishes from Spain, France, Italy, Germany, Mexico, Argentina, and the Orient. Traditional Puerto Rican cuisine offers an interesting mix of Spanish, Creole and native Indian influences. Some of the island's best restaurants are *mesones gastronomicos* (gastronomic inns), located outside the San Juan urban area and featuring local cuisine at reasonable prices.

EAST COAST

Anchor's Inn in Fajardo serves steaks and seafood. Located on Route 987, Km 2.7, ☎ 863-7200. For French and international cuisine try **DuPort** on Route 3, Km 51.3, ☎ 860-4260, major credit cards. In Humacao, fish and lobster dinners are offered by **Daniel Seafood** at 7 Marina, ☎ 852-1784, major credit cards; and **Paradise Seafood** on Route 3 at Km 75, ☎ 852-1180.

SOUTH COAST

For steaks and seafood in Ponce, stop in at **Lydia's** on Ramal 52, Km 255, ☎ 844-3933, major credit cards; or **Pito's** on Route 2, Cucharas, ☎ 841-4977, major credit cards.

WEST COAST

Cabo Rojo has an abundance of good seafood restaurants. Try **Perichi's** on Route 102, Km 14.3, ☎ 851-3131, credit cards accepted; or **Brisas del Mar** on Route 308, Pto. Real, ☎ 851-1264, major credit cards accepted.

Caracol in Aguadilla offers international and seafood favorites. It's on Route 107, Km 2, ☎ 882-8000.

Sightseeing

Visitors to Puerto Rico will find many attractions, especially in the capital city of San Juan. The seven-square-block area of Old San Juan, named a National Historic Zone in the 1950s, is chock-a-block with interesting museums, churches, forts, restored homes, restaurants, boutiques, art galleries, sidewalk cafés and some of the most authentic examples of 16th- and 17th-century Spanish colonial architecture in the western hemisphere. The peaceful countryside "out on the island" offers Spanish colonial towns,

15 picturesque country inns (*paradores puertorriquenos*), great seaside restaurants, beautiful beaches, and dramatic mountain scenery.

OLD SAN JUAN. Founded in 1521, Old San Juan is the oldest capital city under the US flag. Among the many landmark sites are **El Morro,** constructed by the Spanish from 1540-1586 to protect the San Juan harbor from invasion by Sir Francis Drake; **La Fortaleza,** the official home and office of the governor of Puerto Rico, built in 1540 and the oldest executive mansion in continuous use in the New World; **Casa Blanca,** built in 1523 as the residence of the family of Ponce de Léon, the first governor of the island and today housing a Taino Indian museum and a Ponce de Léon family museum; the **Pablo Casals Museum,** which houses memorabilia of the famous cellist who lived in Puerto Rico for the last 20 years of his life; and the **San Juan Cathedral,** one of the oldest places of Christian worship in the Western Hemisphere.

PONCE. Puerto Rico's second largest city is just 90 minutes by car south of San Juan. Since 1988, more than 500 historic buildings dating from the mid-1800s to the 1930s have been meticulously restored. The **Ponce Art Museum**, designed by Edward Durell Stone, is the most extensive in the Caribbean. Founded by former Governor Luis A. Ferre, the museum houses more than 1,000 paintings and 400 sculptures, and is noted for its late Renaissance and Baroque works. Ponce is also well known for its 1883 red and black firehouse, traditional town square, and pre-Columbian **Tibes Indian Ceremonial Park,** the oldest Indian burial ground in the Antilles. Nearby is **Hacienda Buena Vista,** a recently restored 19th-century coffee plantation and grain mill, now open to the public as a museum.

SAN GERMAN. This quaint Spanish town's **Porta Coeli Church,** built in 1606, is the oldest church still intact under the US flag. The town itself, located in the southwest corner of the island, still retains much of its original Spanish colonial architecture and charm.

ARECIBO OBSERVATORY. Two hours from San Juan on the north coast in the town of Arecibo, which dates to 1556, is the world's largest radio telescope, equal to the size of 13 football fields. Here scientists from Cornell University and the National Science Foundation study the planets and distant galaxies by gathering radio waves from space.

THE RIO CAMUY CAVE PARK. Opened in Dec 1986, this 300-acre park is one of Puerto Rico's most fascinating sightseeing attractions and is located near the Arecibo Observatory. The caves have been hailed by experts as one of the world's most spectacular cave systems with one of the largest underground rivers known.

EL YUNQUE, 35 miles east of San Juan, is a vast 28,000-acre rainforest in the Luquillo Mountains. Some 100 billion gallons of rain fall each year on over 240 varieties of trees and flowers. It is the only tropical rain forest in the US Forest Service.

LAS CABEZAS DE SAN JUAN NATURE RESERVE. Opened in March 1991, this 316-acre nature reserve encompasses seven different ecological systems, including: forest, mangroves, lagoons, beaches, cliffs, offshore islets and coral reefs. Visitors may tour the reserve's nature center and 19th-century working lighthouse, *El Faro*, which offers views of distant Caribbean islands. Contact The Conservation Trust, ☎ (787) 722-5834. Las Cabezas is a 45-minute drive from San Juan.

INDIAN CEREMONIAL PARKS. Two sites on the island showcase Puerto Rico's Indian heritage. Located near Ponce, **Tibes Indian Ceremonial Park** is the oldest Indian burial ground uncovered in the Antilles. The site has seven ceremonial ball courts, two dance grounds and a re-created Taino Indian village. A museum displays Indian ceremonial objects, jewelry and pottery.

FESTIVALS. Each town honors its patron saint during the year. Catholic in origin, the festivities have combined many African and Spanish customs. The fiestas usually take place at the town's central square and can last up to 10 days. They include processions, games, local food, music and dance. Folkloric festivals are held year-round in many of Puerto Rico's cities and towns. Some celebrate the coffee harvest. Others showcase flower exhibitions, musical competitions and local crafts displays.

Other Activities

Fishing. Puerto Rico hosts many deep-sea fishing tournaments, in which 30 world records have been broken. The island's annual Billfish Tournament is the world's largest consecutively held tournament of its kind. Deep sea fishing boats can be chartered in San Juan, Fajardo, Humacao, Mayaguez and other towns. Lake fishing for largemouth bass, peacock bass, sunfish, catfish and tilapia is also popular. For more details, contact the Department of Natural Resources at ☎ (787) 722-5938.

Camping. There are several camping facilities on the island. For information, contact the Parks Association in San Juan at ☎ (787) 721-2800.

Tennis courts and **golf** courses proliferate.

Shopping

Puerto Rico has duty-free shopping at the Luis Munoz Marin International Airport and several factory outlets in Old San Juan.

Facts

Nearest Recompression Chamber: Roosevelt Roads US Navy Base, ☎ (787) 865-2000. The base is on the easternmost point off Ceiba between Fajardo and Humacao.

Getting There: Major airlines including American, ☎ (800) 433-7300, United and USAir fly into San Juan from most major US cities. American has service to Aguadilla from Miami. American has made the Luis Munoz Marin International Airport its hub for all flights from the US to other Caribbean destinations, Europe and Latin America. International carriers include Air Portugal, British Airways, BWIA, Iberia, LACSA, LIAT, Lufthansa and Mexicana.

Island Transportation: *By Road*—Taxis, buses and rental cars are available at the airport and major hotels. All taxi cabs are metered, but they may be rented unmetered for an hourly rate. "Publicos" (public cars) run on frequent schedules to all island towns (usually during daytime hours) and depart from main squares. They have fixed rates. The "Ruta Panoramica" is a scenic road meandering across the island and offering stunning vistas.

By Ferry and Boat Service—Ferries shuttle passengers to and from Culebra and Vieques at reasonable rates. Car transport is available on some. San Juan's harbor can also be crossed by the Catano ferry to the Bacardi Rum plant's free tours.

Driving: On the right. Distance markers are in kilometers.

Customs: US citizens do not need to clear customs or immigration (other citizens do). On departure, luggage must be inspected by the US Agriculture Department, as laws prohibit taking certain fruits and plants out of the country.

Entry Requirements: Since Puerto Rico is a Commonwealth of the United States, no passports are required for US citizens. Visitors do need a valid driver's license to rent a car. If you are a citizen of any other country, a visa is required. Vaccinations are not necessary.

Pets: Dogs and cats may be brought to Puerto Rico from the US with two documents: a health certificate dated not more than 10 days prior to departure showing that the animal is disease-free and certified by an official or registered veterinarian; a certificate of rabies vaccination, dated not more than 30 days prior to departure, authenticated by the proper authorities.

Currency: The US $ is legal tender and credit cards are widely accepted. Several foreign exchange offices are available in San Juan and at the airport for the benefit of international travelers.

Climate: Temperatures average mid-80's on land and underwater. During winter and on deep dives a light wetsuit is recommended. The rainy season is April to Nov, but most days have some sunshine. The south coast receives much less rainfall than the north.

Clothing: Lightweight, casual. Bring a light jacket for mountain hikes in winter.

Electricity: 110 volts, AC 60 cycles, same as US.

Time: Puerto Rico operates on Atlantic Standard Time, which is one hour ahead of Eastern Standard Time and the same as Eastern Daylight Savings Time.

Language: Spanish is the official language, although many people speak English, which is taught from kindergarten through high school.

Taxes: The airport departure tax is included in the price of the airline ticket, and there's a 7% government tax at all hotels. Gratuities in restaurants are not included in the bill but 15% is the usual tip.

Religious Services: The majority of Puerto Ricans are Catholic, but religious freedom for all faiths is guaranteed by the Commonwealth Constitution. Catholic services are conducted throughout the island in both English and Spanish. There is a Jewish Community Center in Miramar and a Jewish Reform Congregation in Santurce. There are English-speaking Protestant services for Baptists, Episcopalians, Lutherans, Presbyterians and inter-denominational services.

For Additional Information:

Puerto Rico Tourism Company Offices: *In New York*—575 Fifth Avenue, NY, NY 10017, ☎ (212) 599-6262, toll free (800) 223-6530. *In California*—3575 West Cahuenga Blvd., Suite 560, Los Angeles, CA 90068, ☎ (213) 874-5991. *In Florida* —200 SE First St., Suite 700, Miami, FL 33131, ☎ (305) 381-8915. *In the UK* —67-69 Whitfield St., London WIP 5RL United Kingdom, ☎ (011) 44-171-436-4060. *In Canada*—☎ (416) 969-9025. *In Puerto Rico*—Paseo de la Princesa Old San Juan, PR 00901, ☎ (787) 721-2400.

Saba

Located 30 miles off the coast of St. Maarten, Saba is a tiny, five-mile-square mountain that rises almost vertically to 3,000 ft. Once an active volcano, it is an island of paradoxes—a Caribbean hideaway without a single beach, with a road that engineers insisted couldn't be built, and with a capital called "The Bottom" that's on top of a mountain. The smallest of the Netherlands Antilles, Saba rises from the sea like the nose of a friendly dolphin breaking the water's surface. Its cliffs rise sharply from the blue Caribbean, culminating in mist-shrouded 2,855-foot Mount Scenery.

Tiny white villages cling to the sides of the mountain—Hell's Gate, Windwardside, St. John's, The Bottom—linked by a road that dips and soars, curves and backtracks like a giant roller coaster. Visitors arrive at one end of the road or the other, since it begins at the airport and ends at the pier.

Diving is superb, and most reefs, walls, ledges and pinnacles are within 100 yds of shore—five or six minutes by boat. With little fishing, less than 1,000 divers per year and a government long-active in marine management, fish life is spectacular. Water clarity is too. The sea floor is a dense, heavy, black sand—not prone to silting or clouding the water. A constant wash of open-ocean currents supports a rich growth of soft and hard corals on submerged lava rocks and pinnacles. And it is one of the few destinations left in the Caribbean where you can still find huge turtles and grouper.

If arriving by air, the first sight of Saba may surprise you as your Windward Airways' STOL (Short Take-Off and Landing) aircraft swoops down to Juancho E. Yrausquin Airport's mini-runway. You may at first think it is a matter of visual perspective; that, perhaps, you are still quite high. But, indeed, the runway measures just 1,312 feet. Nonetheless, touchdown is gentle. The airstrip stretches along Flat Point, one of the few level areas on the island. From here, the road rises in 20 serpentine curves to the village of Hell's Gate which, despite its name, nestles in the shadow of the island's largest church.

Contributors: Joan Borque, Sea Saba; Bill Wilson McQueen, Mike Meyers, Saba Deep; Gail Knopfler.

Swinging through groves of feathery tree ferns and past terraced banana plantations, the road continues on to Windwardside, a toylike village astride a saddle of land connecting Mount Scenery and Booby Hill. Its tiny houses, sparkling white under bright red roofs, are laced with wooden gingerbread. The narrow streets meander between stone walls enclosing miniscule yards that frequently contain the graves of previous owners. It is not unusual to find a doorside gravestone draped with the family's laundry drying in the sun. With level space so limited, the ingenious Sabans have converted every available square inch to some use.

Mini-shops with such eye-catching names as "Around the Bend" and "Green Shutters," are tucked in among the cottages. Most carry Saba's unique "Spanish Work," a form of airy linen drawnwork created by generations of Saban wives awaiting the return of their sailor husbands.

Leaving Windwardside, the highway snakes its way past Kate's Hill, Peter Simon's Hill and Big Rendezvous to the village of St. John's. From this point, you can see St. Eustatius floating on the southern horizon.

The road continues climbing, then swoops down to The Bottom, Saba's capital and, with 350 of the island's 950 inhabitants, her largest town. The village did not get its name, as is often stated, because it is set in the bottom of a volcanic crater—it isn't. The name is a corruption of the Dutch words "De Botte," meaning "The Bowl." A look at the surrounding hills tells why.

From The Bottom, the road makes its final descent, corkscrewing down to Fort Bay and the cruise ship pier.

When to Go

The best visibility is during winter, though seas can be rough outside the leeward side of the island. Summertime brings warmer 80° water with plankton blooms and lowered visibility, but a tremendous amount of fish life. Water temperature varies from 76° in Feb to 82° in Oct. Sea conditions vary. The island is round, with no natural harbors and a very small leeward side. Seas are usually calm, but tropical storms can rule out many dive sites.

History

Saba's discovery is credited to Christopher Columbus, who first sighted the island in 1493. It remained sparsely inhabited by the Caribs until a group of Englishmen shipwrecked on Saban shores in the early 1600's. Later, in the 1640's, the Dutch built a community at Tent Bay. With nearby bountiful fishing grounds, Saba became a desirable property to several nations. Overall, the island changed hands 12 times, being claimed by the British, Spaniards, French, and, lastly, in 1816, the Dutch. St. Maarten and St. Eustatius changed hands even more times, but the Sabans, taking advantage of the unique topography, fought off invaders by pelting them from above with rocks and boulders. Saba has always been English speaking—influenced by early English missionaries and settlers.

Because of the island's largely vertical terrain and unapproachable coastline, roads, taxis, airports and even electricity are recent innovations on the Saban scene.

Until 1934, Saba had no telephones. Work on "the road" began in 1938, but the first automobile did not arrive until 1947. The Leo A. Chane Pier at Fort Bay was built in 1972. Approaching the island in Saba's early days meant riding the crest of a wave onto a rocky beach at Ladder Bay. Flights of steps carved by hand from volcanic rock connected one village to another. Two hundred steps rose from the small landing stage at Fort Bay to The Bottom; 900 more linked the capital to Windwardside, the island's second largest village.

Everything, from pianos to prelates, was hoisted up these stairs. Twelve men were needed to manhandle a Steinway from the Bay to the Bottom; four men and a sedan chair to tote a visiting bishop up the steep stairs.

Without roads, wheeled vehicles were, of course, useless; Sabans walked or rode tiny donkeys. During World War II, tales of the wondrous "jeep" reached local ears and thoughts that, perhaps, here at last was a vehicle that could conquer the precipitous Saban landscape. Officials were prompted to construct a road from Fort Bay to The Bottom... just in case.

Even not-so-old timers reminisce about the arrival of the island's first car—a second-hand jeep—in March, 1947. The novelty was swung over the side of a freighter that arrived every month from Curacao, eased onto two longboats, hauled through the surf and finally deposited at the foot of the Fort Bay Road.

When the ignition key was turned, however, nothing happened; the shipper had forgotten to have the engine overhauled. Hurried consultations were held and the ship's engineer was summoned ashore. A few adjustments, a couple of stout whacks with a wrench and the engine sprang to life. Minutes later, the jeep roared into the capital, pursued by the entire junior population, shouting "donkey on wheels!" Today, about 200 cars negotiate "the road."

When electricity finally reached the island in 1963, it was a sometime thing—from 6 pm till midnight. Not until 1970 was electric service extended to 24 hours a day.

SABA MARINE PARK

The Saba Marine Park (SMP) was established in 1987 "to preserve Saba's Marine resources for the benefit and enjoyment of the people, in perpetuity." The project was funded by World Wildlife Fund-Netherlands, the Prince Bernhard Fund, and the Dutch and Saban Governments.

The park encompasses the entire island and includes the waters and the seabed from the highwater mark down to 200 ft and two offshore seamounts. It was set up by Dutch marine biologist, Tom van't Hof, who also established successful marine parks in Bonaire and Curacao.

Park officials maintain a system of mooring buoys and administer the Saba Marine Park Hyperbaric Facility, a four-person recompression chamber operated by a staff of trained volunteers.

Visitors to the marine park are charged a "dollar-a-dive" to help maintain the park and facilities. Spearfishing and collecting of any marine animals are prohibited. Divers must use proper bouyancy control and must not sit or stand on the corals. Anchoring on corals is prohibited. Vessels entering the park are advised to contact the marine park office on VHF channel 16 for directions on anchoring. For additional information Write to **Saba Marine Park**, Fort Bay, PO Box 18, The Bottom, Saba, Netherlands Antilles.

STAY SAFE

Saba's altitude and any strenuous climbing—even from the dock back to your hotel room—must be considered when calculating the diving tables. Some of the new dive computers will figure in the altitude for you. Without careful planning, both the altitude and strenuous activity may bring on decompression sickness.

Dr. John Buchanan, co-author of *Guide to the Saba Marine Park* suggests divers climb Mt. Scenery "only if their dive tables or dive computers say that it is OK for them to fly."

Saba dive guides will help you plan each dive safely. All dive sites have permanent moorings with submerged lines for descents, ascents and safety stops. It is further suggested that, after making a decompression dive, divers **without** decompression sickness symptoms allow 48 hours before flying.

Best Dive and Snorkeling Sites

☆☆☆☆☆ **Tent Reef** is a shelf between 30 and 40 ft which becomes **Tent Wall** as the bottom drops quickly from 40 ft to over 100 ft. A series of overhangs on the slope make interesting photo frames. Currents around this southwest corner of the island nurture a multitude of delicate gorgonians, iridescent tube sponges and large barrel sponges—home to small shrimp and feeding polyps. From the dark sand, fields of garden eels emerge, playing hide and seek with legions of razorfish. Resident French angels patrol thickets of black coral bushes. At depth, the wall becomes a brilliant blue and red tapestry of encrusting sponges and long, velvet-like wire corals. Residents include black margates, horse-eye jacks, sergeant majors, tiger grouper and butterflyfish with occasional sightings of manta rays, spotted eagle rays, nurse sharks and seahorses.

☆☆☆ **Ladder Labyrinth** is an erratic maze of coral-covered mounds off Saba's western, leeward coast. Depths are from 30 to 60 ft. The reef is vibrant with enormous lavender sea fans, swaying sea plumes and a carpet of star corals. Within the labyrinth are hundreds of crevices teeming with banded coral shrimp and lobsters. Schools of curious barracuda circle the area. Seas are usually calm. Good for diving and snorkeling.

☆☆☆☆ **Diamond Rock** is a white-rock monolith astir with frigate birds and brown notty terns. Below the surface, between 35 and 80 ft, are hundreds of pink-tipped anemones, stinging corals and yellow tube sponges. Stingrays nap on the sandy bottom at 80 ft. Frequent sightings of hawksbill turtles, bigeyes, permits, spadefish, frogfish, rare orange filefish, flying gurnards, yellow jawfish, sailfin blennies and bull sharks make this an exciting dive. Light current. Outstanding visibility. Fifteen-minute boat ride. Recommended for novice and experienced divers. Photo opportunities abound.

☆☆☆☆ **Third Encounter**, off Saba's west coast, is a plateau on top of a submerged mountain range. Located a mile from shore, average depth is 100 ft. Explosions of creole wrasses and brown chromis adorn the seamounts amidst huge clusters of orange elephant ear sponges. Black tip sharks guard a monument of coral named the "Eye of the Needle"—a 200-ft column that tops at 90 ft. Experienced divers only. Superb visibility. Current.

☆☆☆ **Torrents Point** off the island's northwest corner is the start of the Edward S. Arnold marked Snorkeling Trail. An outstanding shallow dive spot, depths range from five to 30 ft as you swim from marker one through 11. Black volcanic rocks, small caves and ledges swarm with fish and invertebrates. Pink sponges and lace corals grow in the crevices. Light pouring through the tunnels creates dramatic photo opportunities. This spot is weather-dependent. Ocean swells from the north, usually during winter months, make exploring the open caves hazardous, especially the areas known as #10 (The Rocks) and #9 (Into The Alley). Check with a local divemaster before entering the water.

Snorkeling

Saba's entire coastline is excellent for snorkeling. There are three locations for easily entering the water: the Fort Bay Harbor area, Well's Bay/Torrens Point area, and Cove Bay, near the airport. Snorkel boat trips can be arranged through the dive shops. A snorkel trail is located at Torrens Point.

Dive Operators

Rates for diving in Saba average: $45 for a single tank; $80 for a two-tank dive; $60 to $90 for a resort course; $350 for a C-course. Packages available (see *Accommodations*). All Saba shops require a C-card to join the dive trips. Courses and open-water check-outs available. Snorkelers join the dive boats or go in off the shore at Torrens Point. Sites are five to 15 minutes from the pier.

Sea Saba is a PADI training facility with two 40-ft custom dive boats. Dive trips are tailored to visitors' requests, usually making a deep dive at 10 am and a shallow dive at noon. C-cards required. Owners, Joan and Lou Bourque, have been on Saba for more than 10 years and offer a variety of dive and accommodation packages. E-6 processing, equipment sales and rentals. Joan is an expert underwater photographer and entertains visitors with a weekly slide show. ☎ (011) 599-4-62246 or fax (011) 599-4-62362. Write PO Box 530, Windwardside, Saba, NA. E-mail: brqswks@sedona. net or seasaba@aol.com.

Saba Deep at Fort Bay Harbor, on the southwest side of the island, offers guided scuba and snorkeling tours. The shop is part of a dive complex in the now-restored old harbor master's building with a restaurant, sundeck and dive boutique upstairs. Dive and accommodation packages. Resort and certification courses. Owner Mike Myers is a NAUI and PADI certified instructor. Toll free, ☎ (888) DIVE SABA, (011) 599-4-63347, fax (011) 599-4-63397. Write to PO Box 22, Fort Bay, Saba, NA. E-mail: diving@ sabadeep.com. Web site: www.sabadeep.com/-diving.

Saba Reef Divers (formerly Wilson's) offers PADI certifications through Master Instructor and ANDI certification in both Nitrox ($250) and rebreather technologies. Experienced dive guides visit the best sites aboard the shop's 40-ft boat. One nicety of this operation is the use of a surface-air-equipped hang bar with regulator at 15 ft. New rental gear includes "safety sausages" and Dive Alerts. The shop has two locations—Fort Bay at the Pier and Windwardside. Scuba and snorkeling equipment rentals. Nitrox fills cost $10 more than air. Dive accommodations packages available. ☎ (011) 599-4-62541, fax (011) 599-4-62653. E-mail: sabareef@aol.com. Web site: www.divetravel.net/sabadive.

Accommodations

Accommodations may be reserved through your travel agent, direct or packaged through the dive shops listed above. A government room tax of 5% and a service charge of 10% or 15% is added to your bill.

Island Trails offers combination hiking and snorkeling or scuba tours from the US. ☎ (800) 233-4366.

Captain's Quarters, a former sea captain's home, is set into the hillside at the base of Mt. Scenery in Windwardside. Its 10 rooms are clustered around a pool and outdoor bar, all overlooking the Caribbean. Each room has private bath and balcony, some with unusual antiques. Island cuisine

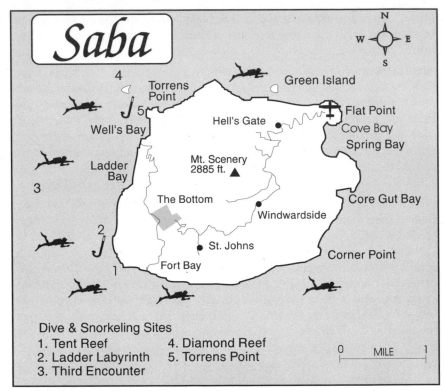

Saba

N
W—◇—E
S

4   Torrens
    Point   Green Island

5   Well's Bay   Flat Point
                 Hell's Gate   Cove Bay
                                Spring Bay

    Ladder   Mt. Scenery
3   Bay   2885 ft. ▲

                              Core Gut Bay
    The Bottom
               Windwardside

2
    St. Johns   Corner Point
1   Fort Bay

Dive & Snorkeling Sites
1. Tent Reef   4. Diamond Reef
2. Ladder Labyrinth   5. Torrens Point
3. Third Encounter

0   MILE   1

is served in the indoor/outdoor dining area. Winter rates, per-person, double occupancy for accommodations and diving: five nights/10 dives, $831 to $900. Room only costs $125 for a double. A 10-15% service charge is tacked on at checkout. Reservations for a package may be made with Sea Saba or Saba Deep or through your local travel agent. ☎ (212) 289-6031, (011) 599-4-62201, fax (011) 599-4-62377. Write Captain's Quarters, Windwardside, Saba, NA. E-mail: sabacq@megatropic.com. Additional packages available through Caradonna tours, ☎ (800) 328-2288. E-mail: caradonna @aol.com.

Julianas is a group of eight one-bedroom units, one apartment and a separate two-bedroom cottage built in 1989. Owners, Franklin and Juliana Johnson, are local residents who maintain the property. Grounds are landscaped with tropical flowers and plants. Pool, café open for breakfast and lunch. Each room has an ocean view. Room rates are $115 for a double in winter, $90 in summer; $135 for a cottage in winter, $115 in summer. Packages (double occupancy) with Saba Deep cost $560 for five nights/six dives in winter (Dec 16-Apr 15), $320 for non-divers. Summer rates drop to $525 for a diver, $282 for a non-diver. ☎ (800) 223-9815 or direct (011)

599-4-62269, fax (011) 599-4-62389. Write Juliana's, Windwardside, Saba, NA.

The Cottage Club, a group of 10 Saban cottages with full kitchens, bath, cable TV, phone, fax and two beds, is a new favorite spot for divers and snorkelers. Winter rates for five nights, six dives, per person, for a double are $539 ($831 for a single). Packages are available with all three dive shops or book through your travel agent. Rooms are $136.50 plus tax, and $20 per additional person. ☎ (011) 599-4-62386, fax (011) 599-4-62476.

The Gate House, located in Hell's Gate, high on the mountain, features six double rooms tastefully furnished in island decor. All have private baths and two include kitchen. The cafe offers breakfast and dinner. Room rates are $80 for a double, $70 for a single in winter. Dive packages for five nights, six dives are (winter) $475, non-diver $240; (summer) $435, non-diver $200. ☎ (708) 354-9641, fax (708) 352-1390, or direct (011) 599-4-62416, fax (011) 599-4-62529.

Scout's Place, in Windwardside is a cheerful, low-budget, 10-room property with pool and restaurant. Packages with Saba Deep. ☎ (011) 599-4-62205 or (212) 545-8469. Write Scout's Place, Windwardside, Saba, NA.

Private homes with dive packages are available through Saba Real Estate, PO Box 17, Saba, NA. ☎ (011) 599-4-62299, fax 599-4-62415.

Queen's Garden Resort, at 1,200 feet above sea level, offers cool tradewinds and spectacular views. The resort complex encompasses 12 one- and two-bedroom luxury units with spacious living rooms, bedrooms, bathrooms, fully equipped kitchens with microwave oven, electric range, refrigerator, coffee maker, cable TV, phone and ceiling fans. Some have private jacuzzis.

Weekly summer rates are $1,070 for a double. Winter rates start at $150 per night (two persons) for a studio apartment, one-bedroom $200, two-bedroom $300. Dive packages may be arranged by the dive shops. With diving, rates start at $895 for five nights/six dives. ☎ (800) 599-9407, direct (011) 599-4-63494.

Saba Cottages and Private Villas' dive packages are offered by Sea Saba. Rates per person for seven nights, 10 dives, vary from $625 to $655. Some cottages are close to everything, others a short walk away. ☎ (011) 599-4-62246, fax (011) 599-4-62362.

Other Activities and Sightseeing

Saba nightlife is limited to star gazing and swapping dive stories. Restaurants serve as the town meeting places. Diving, hiking and birdwatching are the mainstay of daytime activities. Hiking, though strenuous, is exceptionally pleasant as there are no mosquitoes or biting insects. If your dive computer says it's all right to fly and you are in excellent physical condition you may want to climb Mt. Scenery. The hike takes about 90 minutes. On the climb you'll pass through several types of tropical vegetation. At 1,600, feet the rain forest is enveloped in clouds. Wildlife includes lizards, iguanas, hummingbirds and tree frogs.

Directional signs and interpretive signboards have been placed along many of Saba's trails. Pick up a copy of the *Saba Nature Trails* brochure at the Tourist Office to help you plan your hikes.

There are a few craft and souvenir shops in Windwardside and The Bottom offering local Saban threadwork, a lacy embroidery applied to linens, hand-woven fabrics, silk-screened clothing and Saba Spice—a 151-proof rum.

Dining

In Two Deep Restaurant, upstairs at Saba Deep complex in Fort Bay, is open for breakfast, brunch, lunch and dinner. Menu offers "New England" style omelettes, chowders, salads and sandwiches.

The Captain's Quarters Hotel Restaurant in Windwardside offers three meals daily, American and West Indian. ☎ 62201.

Cantonese culinary creations are at **Saba Chinese Restaurant,** ☎ 62268, and **Chinese Family Restaurant**, which also features satellite TV—both in Windwardside.

Pizza and burgers are served at **Guido's**, ☎ 62230, in Windwardside.

Fresh rolls, cakes, pizzas, deli sandwiches, and lunch special under $6 are found over at the **Caribake Bakery & Deli** in Windwardside, ☎ 62539.

Local delights, including curried goat and soursop ice cream, are served at the **Sunset Restaurant**, ☎ 62205, in The Bottom, or the **Brigadoon Restaurant** in Windwardside, ☎ 62380.

Facts

Nearest Recompression Chamber: Saba Marine Park Hyperbaric Facility at Fort Bay. ☎ 599-4-63295, fax 599-4-63435.

Airlines: International flights connect through St. Maarten via Windward Island Airways (WINAIR), ☎ (800) 634-4907. There are also connecting flights between Saba and St. Eustatius.

Ferry: *Style*, a 52-ft, luxury commuter craft, departs Great Bay Marina in St. Maarten on Wed, Fri and Sun for Saba. Returns to St. Maarten at 3 pm. *Voyager I*, a mono-hull ferry holds up to 150 passengers and departs from Bobby's Marina in Philipsburg, St. Maarten on Thurs and Sat at 8:30 am and arrives at Fort Bay, Saba at 10. Cost for adults is US $60 round-trip, $40 one-way; half-price for children under 12. The ride takes 45-60 minutes.

Driving: On the right. Rentals are available through Johnson's Rent A Car or your hotel. Beware of hairpin turns, potholes and bumps along "the road."

Seaport: A deep-water pier accommodates ships at Fort Bay. Anchorage for yachts at Ladder Bay and Wells Bay.

Documents: US and Canadian citizens require official proof of citizenship (passport, voter registration card, or birth certificate) and a return or onward ticket.

Customs: No customs.

Currency: Netherlands Antilles Guilder. US $ accepted everywhere. Credit cards are widely accepted. NAfl 1.80=US $1.

Language: Dutch is the official language, but English is widely spoken.

Climate: Air temperature ranges from 78° to 82° F year-round. Winter evenings may cool to 60°. Rainfall averages 42 inches per year.

Clothing: Casual, lightweight. Sweater or light jacket suggested for winter evenings. Wetsuit needed for winter diving, when water temperatures drop to 75°. A light wetsuit or lycra wet skin is recommended for summer.

Electricity: 110 volts, 60 cycles (220 volts on request).

Time: Atlantic Standard (Eastern Standard + 1 hr).

Departure Tax: US $5 within NA, US $10 elsewhere.

Religious Services: Limited.

Additional Information: Saba Tourist Bureau, PO Box 6322, Boca Raton, FL 33427, ☎ (800) 722-2394, (800) SABA-DWI or (561) 394-8580, fax (561) 394-8588. Web site: www.turq.com/saba.

St. Eustatius (Statia)

St. Eustatius is a speck of land about 38 miles south of St. Maarten, six miles north of St. Kitts, and 17 miles southeast of Saba. It is one of the lesser-known islands in the eastern Caribbean—so small and with a name so long that it is often deleted from maps. A part of the Netherlands Antilles, this eight-square-mile territory is home to a population of 1,800.

Statia's profile is distinct, with a flat plain in the center, sharp, green hills at the north end, and The Quill, a 2,000-ft extinct volcano, covering most of the south end. The Quill is noted by geologists as having an almost perfect cone shape. Inside its crater lies magnificent, tropical rainforest of towering mahogany trees, wild bananas, air plants and trailing vines festooned with wild orchids and flowering air plants. Wood doves and sulfur-yellow butterflies flutter in the shadows, and at full moon, torch-bearing Statians hunt scuttling land crabs.

Steep limestone cliffs interspersed with a few stretches of black-sand beach dominate the island's western coast. Its eastern shores shelve into a wide strip of dark sand and pebbles. There are few roads, and donkeys are still used for exploring rocky inland trails. Offshore lie the remains of more than 200 shipwrecks.

Beautiful shallow reefs, highlighted by giant golden sea fans and lush, soft corals, skirt the ballast stones and rubble of sunken 17th-century wooden trading ships. Now dive and snorkeling sites, they are all close to shore—at most, a few minutes by boat.

A leisurely stroll through the narrow cobblestone streets of Oranjestad, Statia's capital and only village, reveals the grey-stone and yellow-ballast brick walls of historic buildings dating back to the 1600's and the now-restored Fort Oranje (pronounced "oh-rahn-ye").

The fort, perched on the cliffs overlooking Oranjestad Bay, was the scene of the first salute to the US colors back in November 1776. Nearby, the ruins of an 18-century synagogue and graveyard, and a Dutch Reformed Church nestle among the pink and yellow homes of today's Statians. This area is Upper Town, the uphill section of town.

Contributor: Mark Padover, marine biologist and former Dive Statia instructor.

From the center of the village, just past a monument erected in honor of Queen Wilhelmina's Golden Jubilee, the stone-paved Fort Road zig-zags down to Lower Town, once the Caribbean's most bustling port.

In the mid-1700's Lower Town stretched for two miles along the Bay. Warehouses, taverns, slave markets and merchants' stalls lined the double roadway. The lively traffic, both licit and illicit, made St. Eustatius the richest port in the West Indies. Today, gentle-faced donkeys browse among its ruins.

Sheep and cows graze on small farms and pastures outside Oranjestad. On the opposite side of the island, surf tumbles onto a long strand where beachcombers find a treasure of shells, glass floats and sun-bleached driftwood.

Overall, the island is perfect for vacationers seeking an unhurried, peaceful haven. There is virtually no crime on the island. Everyone is safe walking the streets at night. Doors are rarely locked and the people are extremely friendly. When an elderly resident of St. Eustatius was asked if many tourists visited the island, the old gentleman looked hurt. "My dear sir," he replied, "we don't have tourists on Statia, we have guests!"

And, Statians do have a knack for making "guests" feel welcome. Passers-by exchange greetings in the narrow streets; young boys offer to lead newcomers to hunt for the island's favorite treasure—blue "slave beads"—found nowhere else in the Caribbean.

When to Go
Visibility is best in winter, though seas occasionally get rough. Summer brings calm seas, warmer water and more fish. Water temperature varies from 76° in February to 82° in October.

History
Statia played a key role in America's war for independence. It was a major trans-shipment point for European arms and supplies intended for George Washington's troops. Muskets and gunpowder, frequently shipped in casks marked "Tea," were stored in yellow brick warehouses that stretched for a mile along the Bay. From there, blockade runners in swiftly moving brigantines would carry the supplies to the ports of Boston, New York and Charleston.

It was on November 16, 1776, that the cannons of Fort Oranje roared forth the first official salute to the American colors by a foreign power. The armed American merchant ship *Andrew Doria* sailed into the harbor and fired a 13-gun salute to the Dutch flag fluttering above Fort Oranje. Commander Johannes de Graaff, sympathetic to the cause of the American rebels, ordered the cannons of the fort to return the courtesy with an 11-gun salvo. By this act he unwittingly set in motion events that would bring to a violent end the age of prosperity on Statia.

De Graaff's salute turned out to be the world's first official recognition of the sovereignty of the rebellious colonies, though he was obviously unaware of its historic importance. Getting wind of it, however, the British were understandably infuriated.

By 1781, the situation had become desperate for the British. Not only was the war going badly for George III's troops in North America, but the stream of supplies passing through St. Eustatius was unabated, despite a British blockade. Turnabout came on February 3, 1781, when British Admiral George Brydges Rodney attacked what he called "this nest of vipers."

Storming ashore with 650 troops he demanded the surrender of the Dutch garrison and began systematically looting not only the well-stocked warehouses, but the personal possessions of the merchants as well. In all, he destroyed the harbor and ransacked the town while accumulating five million pounds' worth of booty. Rodney also kept the Dutch flag flying above the ramparts of the fort, thereby luring more than 150 ships into his trap. Less than a year later the British troops were expelled from the island by the French.

Today, the island is an autonomous part of the Netherlands and is self-governing. But, on each anniversary of De Graaff's salute, the island band strikes up *The Star Spangled Banner*, as the American flag is hoisted to the top of the flagpole in the center of the compound.

Sunken Treasure Hunting

The remains and treasures of 17th- and 18th-century sailing ships are played up in many Statia dive articles, but the island's real treasures are her lovely shallow reefs. The ship's wooden hulls rotted away centuries ago. What's left are some wonderful old anchors and piles of stone ballast where small fish play hide and peek.

A few sites have, in fact, given up treasures of jewels and exotic pottery, but any charted wrecks not yet salvaged are buried in the sand and would require extensive and expensive excavation work to uncover. Plus, if a diver happens upon an intact artifact, it must go to the St. Eustatius Historical Foundation. Treasure hunting is discouraged—metal detectors are prohibited, as is "fanning" of the bottom to find artifacts. Exceptions which divers may keep are fragments of clay pipe stems or bowls and blue beads (slave beads), Uninhabited shells and broken pieces of dead coral may also be taken.

Best Dive and Snorkeling Sites

There are approximately 20 dive/snorkel sites around Statia ranging from extreme shallows to 130 ft. Visibility often exceeds 100 ft, with water temperatures averaging 80° F. Divers must dive with a buddy, stay within the no-decompression limits, have a pressure gauge, depth gauge, flotation device and timing device. C-cards are required.

☆☆☆ **The Snorkeling Museum** is an underwater cannon display established for the St. Eustatius Historical foundation at Oranje Bay in Lower Town through the Golden Rock Dive Center (*see Dive Operators*).

☆☆☆☆ **Carolines Reef** is a spectacular site in the center of the southern reef complex. Several long ledges meet, forming a circular hub. Big barrel sponges, tube sponges, sea fans, brain coral, sea whips and volcano sponges adorn the tops of the ledges. Hoards of small critters are in residence—blennies, lightbulb tunicates, pistol shrimp in their corkscrew anemones, lavender cleaning shrimp, cleaning gobies and arrow crabs. Big angels are common, as are rock beauties, barracuda, scrawled file fish, Bermuda chub, butterfly fish, sharptail eels and groupers. Nurse sharks and turtles cruise the area.

The hub is a keyhole in the coral, about 18 inches in diameter. Used as a shortcut by fish traversing one side of the ledge to the other, it also serves as an excellent photo-subject frame. Maximum depth is 65 ft. Recommended for novice and experienced divers.

☆☆☆ **False Shoal**, outside of Kay Bay off the southwest shores, is an unusual formation of huge boulders that rise from the bottom at 25-30 ft to within a foot of the surface. Coral cover is minimal, but fish life is superb, with big congregations of tiger groupers, French and queen angels, several species of parrot fish and swarms of reef fish. Good for snorkeling and novice divers.

☆☆☆☆ **Anchor Reef** is named for an enormous anchor hooked under a ledge. The anchor is seven feet across and 14 feet long with an 18-inch ring. It is surrounded by a pretty reef with a colorful array of elephant-ear, moose antler, and green, lavender and red vase sponges. Cracks and crevices reveal feather dusters, shrimp anemones, barber shrimp and gorgonians. Bushy sea whips, sea plumes and sea fans decorate the ledges. Maximum depth is 60 ft.

☆☆☆☆ **Dropoff**, the southernmost dive on Statia and the most dramatic wall, starts at 85 ft and drops vertically to about 130 ft. The face of the wall is a collage of mountainous star coral, black wire coral, and sponges. Enormous French and queen angels, Nassau and tiger grouper, black durgons, spotted eagle rays and occasional reef sharks and hammerheads frequent the area. For experienced divers.

☆☆☆ **Barracuda Reef** is a 700-ft-long mini-wall at 45 ft that drops to a sand pit at 70 ft. A 12-ft long, five-ft-wide coral-encrusted anchor earmarks this site. As the name implies, schools of barracuda frequent the area, as do some more unusual creatures. On one occasion a friendly humpback whale cruised smack into a group of snorkelers and hung out with them for 15 minutes. Whale season on Statia is from Dec to mid-March. Healthy soft corals, a host of invertebrates, reef fish, spotted morays, stingrays and nurse sharks typify the area. Recommended for all level divers.

☆☆☆☆ **Outer Crooks Reef** is a pretty, shallow reef, five minutes by boat south of the city pier. The reef's ledges form a V shape, which might stand for variety. Every imaginable hard and soft coral thrives within its bounds. Fish life, too, is diverse, with schools of smallmouth and striped grunts, black durgons, blue head wrasse, coneys, rock hinds, banded and four-eyed butterflyfish, rock beauties, blue tang, bar jacks, damsels, fairy basslets, princess parrots, queen parrots, stoplight parrots, Spanish hogfish, sharknose gobies, spotted drums, honeycomb cowfish, burrfish, and huge porcupine fish—some over three ft long.

There are also secretary blennies. It takes a sharp eye to spot these tiny fish, but if you can, try watching them for a few minutes. You'll see them dart out for food that's drifting by, then quickly shoot tail-first back into their holes. They are unafraid of divers and make great subjects for close-up photography.

Invertebrates include flamingo-tongue snails, small crinoids, corkscrew anemones, giant anemones, pistol shrimp, pederson shrimp, thor shrimp, feather dusters, fire worms, crabs and spiny lobster. At night, divers have spotted rare copper lobsters and orange-ball anemones.

Outer Crooks is a best pick for getting reacquainted with the water and your gear after a long dry spell. Also, a great spot for night dives or snorkeling. Maximum depth, 40 ft.

☆☆ **City Wall** is 40 yds out from shore in front of Dive Statia and the hotels in Lower Town. The rock wall parallels the shore from 75 yds south of the Golden Era Hotel to the pavilion at Smoke Alley. This was the old sea wall for Lower Town back in the days of sailing ships. Storms, erosion, a freak earthquake and wave action have since repositioned the shoreline and the wall underwater. The top is at six ft, the bottom at seven to 13 ft. In many areas the wall is folded or crumpled, forming deep crevices where fish and creatures stand guard. There is not much coral cover, but reef fish are plentiful and invertebrate life is good. Watch out for sea urchins. The deepest point of the wall is 12 ft. Suggested for snorkeling and warm-up dives.

☆☆☆ **Stingray Wreck** is one half-mile offshore to Oranjebaii. Named for a great number of stingrays in residence, the site has been studied by William and Mary University and found to be the remains of a Dutch trading ship that went down in 1768.

St. Eustatius (Statia)

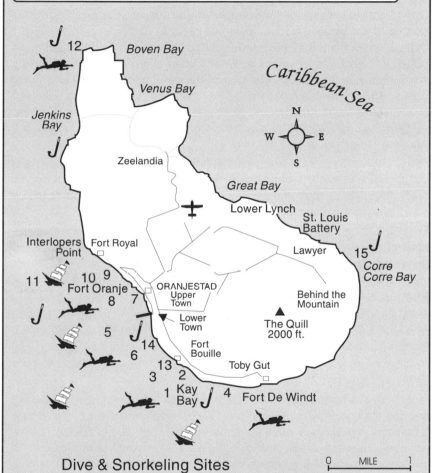

Boven Bay

Venus Bay

Caribbean Sea

Jenkins Bay

N
W — E
S

Zeelandia

Great Bay

Lower Lynch

St. Louis Battery

Interlopers Point

Fort Royal

Lawyer

15

Corre Corre Bay

11   10   9
Fort Oranje

8   7

ORANJESTAD
Upper Town

Behind the Mountain

The Quill
2000 ft.

5

Lower Town

14

Fort Bouille

6

13   2

Toby Gut

3

1   Kay Bay

4   Fort De Windt

12

Dive & Snorkeling Sites

1. Caroline's Reef
2. False Shoal
3. Anchor Reef
4. Dropoff
5. Barracuda Reef
6. Outer Crooks Reef
7. City Wall
8. Stingray Wreck
9. Double Wreck
10. Supermarket
11. Tommy's Temptation
12. North Point
13. Darlene Bay
14. Inner Crooks
15. Corre Corre Bay

0   MILE   1

The sea moss beds at the south end of the wreck attract hawksbill turtles and flying gurnards. Average depth is 50 ft.

☆☆☆ **Double Wreck** is a colorful dive, five minutes from Oranjebaii. Two wrecks, one on top of the other are overgrown with red-vase sponges and giant anemones. Bring your dive light to see the colors. Basket starfish curled into balls rest inside the sponges during the day. Patches of sea grass double as conch beds for four different species. The most common is the queen conch; the rarest, the rooster conch. At night, helmet conchs crawl out of the sand. Empty conch shells are often taken over by giant hermit crabs scavenging for food. Mantis shrimp, spotted snake eels and flying gurnards are curious residents. The northern wreck is littered with centuries-old broken bottles and pottery shards. Good for scuba, all levels.

☆☆ **Supermarket**, just outside of Double Wreck, is another dual wreck site. The remains are encrusted ballast, overgrown with branching corals, barrel and vase sponges, and plumes. A number of stems and bowls from old clay pipes—some dating back to the 1600's—have been unearthed by the shifting sands. But, remember, no fanning the bottom and anything intact goes to the museum.

Fish include cottonwicks, queen triggerfish, scorpionfish, stingrays, coneys, parrot fish, chalk bass and an occasional hawksbill turtle. Conchs reside in the sandy patches off the wreck. Depth is 70 ft.

☆☆☆☆ **Tommy's Temptation** is a photographer's delight. A 15-minute boat ride from town, this site is a lava finger that runs parallel to shore and just over a mile and a half straight out. The top is at 70 ft and the bottom at 100 ft. Soft corals and coral rubble umbrella the sides of the finger. The big attraction is the mega-sized old anchors hooked under the ledge. They average seven ft across and 14 ft in length with hawsers (the rings the ropes were tied to) about 18 inches in diameter.

Hundreds of schooling great barracuda, black margates, grouper, triggerfish and French angels sail by the ledges. This is also a good place to see turtles. If you spot one, stay still. Dive guide and contributor, Mark Padover reports frequent advances on the turtles' part when the divers are motionless. "If you charge them, they get scared and vanish at lightening speed."

Currents often rule out a dive to this area, but when sea conditions are calm and currents light, this is a super spot for intermediate to advanced divers. If the ocean isn't flat, it is a bad choice.

☆☆ **North Point** is an outstanding dive and snorkeling site at the north point of the island. The bottom slopes off steeply from shore, bottoming out in sand at 70-100 ft. The area is strewn with huge boulders, some up to 40 ft tall. The boulders are covered with corals, sea fans and gigantic barrel sponges—up to five ft across. Fish life is extraordinary. On one dive expect to see schoolmasters, black margates, hogfish, whitespotted filefish, blue tangs, rock beauties, sergeant majors and squirrel fish. Huge two-ft French and gray angels swim by. Spotted eagle rays and reef sharks cruise the area. Good for all experience levels.

☆☆ **Darlene Bay** is excellent for snorkeling when the seas are calm. The dive (or snorkel) boat anchors in a sandy area off the shallow reefs or will drift with you as you swim among lava outcrops and fingers. Maximum depth is 20 ft. The lava and corals come up to the surface at the south end of the bay. Good fish life— turtles, sea fans, sea whips and branching corals.

It is easiest to reach this site by a five-minute boat ride. It is a most difficult hike for a shore entry, with large rocks and loose gravel to negotiate, but if you are very rugged, you can reach it by heading south along the coast for half an hour after passing the ruins of Crooks Castle.

Additional good snorkeling is found at **Inner Crooks**, just north of Crooks Castle (max. depth 18 ft); **Jenkins Bay** (max. depth 25 ft) on the northwest corner of the island; and **Corre Corre Bay** (max. depth 40 ft), opposite town on the Eastern shores.

Dive Operators

Blue Nature Water Sports, Cherry Tree, offers scuba courses, rentals, scuba and snorkeling tours. ☎ (011) 599-3-82725, fax (011) 599-3-82756.

Dive Statia is a full-service PADI training facility and NAUI PRO facility offering introductory courses through instructor and guided reef and wreck trips. Their boats range from inflatables to a 31-ft cabin boat. Every dive is accompanied by a certified instructor or dive master. Rental gear and dive/accommodation packages are offered. ☎ (011) 599-3-82435, fax (011) 599-3-82539. Write PO Box 158, St. Eustatius, NA.

Golden Rock Dive Center, Oranjestad, features resort courses, dive and snorkeling trips, rentals. ☎ (800) 311-6658 or (011) 599-3-82946. Web site: www.divetrip.com/goldenrock/.

Dive Tours

Caribbean Connection Plus, PO Box 261, Trumbull, CT 06611, ☎ (800) 692-4106 (US & Canada). Custom packages. Five nights at the King's Well hotel with one two-tank dive per day, breakfast and airport transfers costs from $588 per person.

Dive Saba Travel, 1220 Brittmoore Road, Houston, TX 77043, customizes tours with any of the resorts. ☎ (800) 883-7222 or (713) 467-8835, fax (713) 461-6044.

Island Trails offers guided hiking/snorkeling tours. ☎ (800) 233-4366.

Accommodations

Statia hotels add a 5-10% service charge and 7% government room tax unless otherwise stated. Note: St. Eustatius and Saba are marketed jointly in the US and offer dual-destination packages that include dives, accommodations and more. Contact the **Statia Tourist Office**, PO Box 6322, Boca Raton, FL 33427, ☎ (800) 722-2394 or (561) 394-8580. E-mail: 10565.536@compuserve.com.

King's Well offers eight lovely rooms on Orange Bay, each with a fridge and cable TV. Great views! Rates are $60-$90 per night, breakfast included. Walk to beach and Dive Statia. ☎ (800) 692-4106, direct (011) 599-3-82538. The hotel pub, a favorite après-dive meeting place, serves steaks, jaeger and wiener schnitzels.

The Golden Era Hotel offers 20 air-conditioned rooms on Oranje Bay, with a pool and seaside restaurant. Rates start at $88 per night, per room for a double. Cable TV, phones, fridges. Dive shop next door. ☎ (800) 223-9815 or (011) 599-3-82345/82545, fax (011) 599-3-82445. Canada, ☎ (800) 344-0023. Dive packages through Caribbean Connections, ☎ (800) 692-4106. **Talk of the Town,** with eight standard and efficiency rooms and its own restaurant, is located on the edge of town. Room rates are $88 for a double, seven nights accommodations for $516. Includes buffet breakfast daily. US ☎ (800) 223-9815, direct (011) 599-3-82236, fax (011) 599-3-82640. Web site: www.antyrus.com/tot/talk.html.

Other Activities and Sightseeing

Swapping dive stories, nature hikes, historic walks, and hunting for blue slave beads highlight a visit to Statia.

Historical sites

In spite of British Admiral, Lord Rodney's savaging of the island in 1781, numerous historical buildings remain, from large monumental structures to small workers' homes. Many are currently being restored in Upper Town.

Among those are Fort Oranje and Fort de Windt, the Historical Foundation Museum, old ruins at Oranje Bay and remains of *Honen Dalim*, the second oldest synagogue in the Western Hemisphere.

Don't miss the Underwater Snorkeling Museum tours offered by the Golden Era Dive Shop.

Blue Bead Hunts

Remnants of a curious past, these five-sided blue-glass beads were used to buy and sell slaves during the 17th and 18th centuries, and to reward the slaves. Upon accumulation of enough beads, a male slave could buy freedom or a woman. The woman was priced by the number of beads that fit around her waist. Today, to some, a heavy woman is still considered more valuable than a thin one.

Beads are most often found on the beach between the end of the city pier and the ruins of Crooks Castle, headquarters of the slave trade way back when.

Hiking Trails

Be sure you are OK to fly on your dive tables before climbing The Quill. Hiking Statia is strenuous. Certain trails are often slippery and dangerous. Hikers should be properly attired and in good physical condition. Trails are marked with numbered signposts. Pick up a trail guide at the tourist office in the airport or at the Historical Museum, ☎ 2288.

The most exhilarating trails lead along the rim and down through the rainforest-covered crater of the Quill. The main trail starts at Welfare Road (south end of Oranjestad) at a telephone pole marked **"Quill Track 1,"** (nos. 1-20). This trail brings you up the mountain to the rim of the volcano. It is a strenuous hike and may be slippery in places. The climb up takes about 45 minutes; down in 30.

Dining

The Golden Era specializes in West Indian, International and Creole cuisine. Sunday night buffet. At the sea in Lower Town. ☎ 599-38-2345.

The **Chinese Restaurant** on Prinseweg 9 serves West Indian and Chinese food. **No credit cards.** ☎ 599-3-82389

Talk of the Town serves West Indian, international and local dishes, sandwiches and ice cream. All major credit cards accepted. ☎ 599-3-82236 or 599-3-82681.

The Cool Corner in the heart of Oranjestad serves a tasty cross between West Indian and Chinese cuisine. ☎ 599-38-2523.

Sunny's Place on the Oranjestraat serves sandwiches and tasty local dishes. ☎ 599-38-2609.

Super Burger, in the heart of Oranjestad on the Graaffweg, specializes in burgers, all types of sandwiches, chicken and fries. ☎ 599-3-82609.

L'Etoile is a brightly decorated café noted for the spiciness of its *pastechis* (deep-fried turnovers stuffed with meat). Local specialties. Located on Heiligerweg. ☎ 599-38-2299. No credit cards.

King's Well Restaurant features steaks, wiener schnitzel and local favorites. ☎ 599-3-82538.

Facts

Helpful Phone Numbers: Police, ☎ 599-3-82333; hospital, ☎ 599-38-2211 or 599-38-2371; airport, ☎ 599-3-82361; Tourist Board, ☎ 599-3-82433; USA Tourist Office, ☎ (800) 722-2394 or (561) 394-8580, fax (561) 488-4294. E-mail: nrhv11f prodigy.com.

Nearest Recompression Chamber: Saba, 17 miles away.

Airlines: Windward Island Airways, WINAIR, ☎ (800) 634-4907, connects daily from Princess Juliana Airport, St. Maarten. Flight time is 20 minutes. Passengers from the US and Saba are considered "in-transit" and do not need to clear immigration in St. Maarten.

Driving: On the right.

Seaport: Gallows Bay.

Documents: US and Canadian citizens need official proof of citizenship—a valid passport, birth certificate or voter registration card. Others need a passport or alien registration card. You need an onward or return ticket.

Customs: No customs.

Currency: Netherlands Antilles Guilder. American dollars are accepted everywhere on the island.

Language: Dutch is the official language; English is widely spoken.

Climate: Air temperature ranges from 78° to 82° F year-round. Winter evenings may cool to 60°. Rainfall averages 45 inches per year.

Clothing: Casual, lightweight. Light wetsuit or wetskin suggested during winter.

Electricity: 110 volts, 60 cycles (same as US).

Time: Atlantic Standard (Eastern Standard + 1 hr).

Departure Tax: US $5.

Religious Services: Limited.

Additional Information: St. Eustatius Tourist Office, PO Box 6322, Boca Raton, FL 33427. ☎ (800) 722-2394 or (561) 394-8580, fax (561) 488-4294. *In St. Eustatius:* ☎ (011) 599-3-82433, (599) 3-82213 or (599) 3-82209, fax (599) 3-82433. E-mail: 105065.536@compuserve.com. Web site: www.turq.com/statia.

St. Kitts & Nevis

Cradled between St. Maarten and Antigua in the Eastern Caribbean, the sister islands of St. Kitts and Nevis call themselves "The Secret Caribbean," but the way tourist accommodations have expanded in the last 10 years, the islands won't be "secrets" too much longer. New tourist interest, sparked by Princess Di's visit in 1993, has brought world-wide attention to the area's unique natural beauty and subsea wonders. And a change in government planning has set the islands' sights on increased tourism.

Physically beautiful, the islands are a patchwork of rolling green mountains surrounded by miles of unexplored, shallow reefs, swim-through caves and grottoes. More than 400 shipwrecks, dating back to the 1600s, lie below their clear waters. Narrow strips of black and gold sand beaches skirt much of the coast.

St. Kitts is an oval-shaped landmass that stretches out into a long, narrow peninsula extending like a guitar handle from its southeastern corner. Formed from volcanic eruption, its central area is a rugged mountain range, whose highest point is the dormant volcano, Mount Liamuiga, at 3,792 feet. Tropical forests, ridges and waterfalls at the high elevations contrast with its lowlands where spacious and fertile valleys produce an abundance of sugar cane, sea-island cotton and peanuts. Most of the beaches are black volcanic sand, though white, sandy beaches can be found along the southeast peninsula of Frigate Bay and Salt Pond. Overall, the island is 23 miles long, covering an area of 68 square miles.

On the seacoast lies Basseterre, the capital, with a population of about 15,000. Its ambience is decidedly old-world Caribbean with an informal produce market and rows of weather-beaten pastel buildings along the waterfront. Narrow streets lead from the town pier to a four-block made-for-tourists area known as the "Circus," a town square, or actually town circle, dominated by a tall, grandfather clock, where three streets converge in the center of town.

Contributors: Tim Bedford; H.V. Pat Reilly; Kenneth Samuel, Kenneth's Dive Centre; John Yearwood, Oualie Beach Hotel; Ellis Chaderton, Julian Rigby, Scuba Safaris Ltd.; Auston MacLeod, Pro Divers; Gary Pereira, Turtle Beach Club; Jennifer Woods, Caribbean Explorer.

The Circus, Basseterre, St. Kitts.

Old sugar plantations on both islands have been transformed into wonderfully stylish inns. These classic "great houses," once the homes of the plantation owners, sit high in the foothills of the volcanic mountains that dominate the skylines. Surrounding the great houses are the remains of old windmills where the sugar cane was crushed, and the boiling houses where the sweet liquid was processed. Before the "around the island" narrow-gauge railroad was completed in 1926 to transport the cane to the central sugar factory in Basseterre, each plantation was a kingdom unto itself, growing, cutting, crushing, boiling and selling sugar. The downside of that free enterprise was air pollution. During the boiling season, the tall stone smokestacks on more than 50 estates would belch smoke into the atmosphere for 18 to 20 hours a day. To eliminate the problem, the government purchased the sugar-producing land and began transporting the cane to a central boiling house in Basseterre.

The majority of plantation owners sold their great houses to entrepreneurs who refurbished them as delightful inns. Most are furnished with a potpourri of antiques or West Indian furnishings.

Separated from St. Kitts by a two-mile strait known as the "Narrows" lies Nevis, the sister island Columbus named for its mountainous resemblance to the snow-capped "Nieve" peak of Spain. Dubbed *Queen of the Caribees* by 17th- and 18th-century European visitors for its therapeutic hot springs and fertile soil, this island encompasses 36 square miles of spectacularly beautiful land. The tip of the island's dominant central peak, usually encircled by clouds, rises into an almost perfectly formed cone of 3,232 ft. The capital city and only town is Charlestown, with a population of 1,200.

The terrain of Nevis encompasses numerous fertile hillsides and narrow, golden sand beaches. Most of the inhabitants are vegetable and coconut farmers.

Low-cost passenger ferries operate daily once or twice a day except Thursdays and Sundays from Basseterre, St. Kitts, to Charleston on Nevis. Nevis Express air service shuttles between the two islands for US $20 per person. The trip takes about 45 minutes. Private air service at $100 for a four-passenger twin is also available. The ferries run twice a day and are not synchronized with airline arrivals. It is often difficult to make the connection. Be sure to call or write to the tourist board for a ferry schedule before planning a trip to Nevis. Phone numbers and addresses at end of chapter.

Diving

Diving is diverse, with ledges, mini-walls, white holes teeming with fish, caves and drift diving in some areas. Most reefs on the Atlantic side and offshore on the Caribbean side are pristine, with monster-sized sea fans and sponges growing over piles of lava rocks. Regularly visited reef and wreck sites are on the sheltered Caribbean side of the islands and in the cut (the Narrows) between Nevis and St. Kitts, but trips to the Atlantic where the mysterious white holes lie and large pelagics are encountered may be arranged when seas are calm.

St. Kitts offers the most dive sites, with alternate sheltered areas on the Caribbean side when the seas are rough on the Atlantic side or at the Narrows. Nevis dive sites are more vulnerable to swells when the winds are high, even on its Caribbean side, but currents are usually light and the sites are spectacular. Average visibility is 80 to 100 ft, with exceptional water clarity at the cut and offshore Caribbean and Atlantic reefs. Water temperature is 80-85° year-round. Depths for scuba range from 30 to 90 ft, averaging 50 ft. Certification, referrals and resort courses with PADI and NAUI instructors are offered. The average boat trip to a dive site takes 15 minutes. Following rainy periods, freshwater runoff from the mountains will lower visibility on the close-in reefs and wrecks, especially off Basseterre. Coral collecting and spear fishing are prohibited only off Turtle Beach on the southeast (guitar handle) peninsula of St. Kitts.

Be sure to let the boat captains know if you prefer to dive a sheltered area as the diver population is tiny—diving is new on these islands—and some of the captains who double as fishing guides may want to share their best spots rather than the calmest ones.

Stay shallow and keep a close eye on your bottom time. The nearest recompression chamber is on Saba, a 15-minute flight from St. Kitts airport. But getting to that airport and arranging for a flight may take the good part of a day or more. Avoid exhausting mountain hikes and climbs after a dive or you risk the shaken soda bottle effect.

When to Go

The best weather is from Dec to April, though air and water temperatures are good for diving year-round and reduced-rate dive packages are offered between May and Dec. The best months for diving the Caribbean side are

View of St. Kitts from Oalie Beach, Nevis.

April and May. June through mid-Nov brings the most rain and a chance of a hurricane. Late December brings the "Christmas wind," which churns up the seas.

History

First named *Liamuiga*—The Fertile Isle—by the Carib Indians, St. Kitts was renamed "St. Christopher" by discoverer Christopher Columbus in 1493. He apparently was so taken by its beauty that he honored it with the name of his patron saint. The name was later shortened to St. Kitts.

Latter day historians equate St. Kitts with its most notable site, Brimstone Hill, a spectacular 18th-century fort turned national park and nicknamed the "Gibraltar of the West Indies." An architectural and engineering marvel, the fortress spreads across 40 acres on a bluff 800 ft above the sea.

Settled in 1623 by Sir Thomas Warner, St. Kitts was the first island in the West Indies to be colonized by the English. The French, under D'Esnambuc, colonized another part of the island in the following year.

During the 17th century, intermittent warfare was waged between the French and British settlers. In 1713, St. Kitts was ceded to Britain by the Treaty of Utrecht. Fighting over possession of the island occurred for the last time in 1782, when the French captured the British fortress of Brimstone Hill. Later that year, the British were victorious over the French in a battle off the island of Dominica and regained possession of St. Kitts in 1783 under the terms of the Treaty of Versailles.

Nevis was colonized in 1628 by British settlers living in neighboring St. Kitts. Like its sister island, Nevis suffered stormy attacks from both the French and Spanish throughout the 17th and 18th centuries. On September 19, 1983 St. Kitts and Nevis gained independence.

Best Dive and Snorkeling Sites

Dive sites in the cut and around the southeast peninsula are shared by both islands' dive shops. Caribbean sites off Basseterre are most often dived by Kenneth's Dive Shop.

Note: The "sunken city of Jamestown" on Nevis, reputed to have been washed away by a hurricane, is listed in at least one guide as a great dive. Unfortunately it is nonexistent, more myth than fact. There is some small mention of it in historical records, but if it exists on the sea floor, no diver has discovered it. Historians feel that Jamestown simply fell into disuse as marshlands moved over it.

☆ **Turtle Bar Reef,** off the unpopulated southwestern tip of the St. Kitts, is a spur and groove reef growing over a rocky bottom. Pillar corals and sea plumes rise from a rocky bottom that slopes from 15 ft down to 65 ft. Seas are always calm. The shallows are a good dive for novices and snorkelers. Ten-minute boat ride from the Turtle Beach Watersports Center, 20 minutes from Basseterre.

☆☆☆☆ **Monkey Reef** is 2½ miles off the peninsula and Nevis, a longer boat ride than most, but worth the trip when seas are calm for the wonderful array of fish and invertebrate life, including blackbar soldierfish, coneys, sharks, barracuda, turtles and rays. The reef is a labyrinth of small caves, canyons and ledges ablaze with pink-tipped anemones, orange tube sponges, encrusting sponges, mounds of club finger corals, and seafans. Big barrel sponges. Excellent visibility. Average depths are from 45 to 60 ft. Suggested for experienced ocean divers only. Sea conditions are often choppy with four- to six-ft swells.

☆☆☆ **Coral Gardens**, a hilly reef off Oalie Beach, Nevis, has huge pillar coral formations and gigantic barrel sponges. It's a good place to spot big turtles, schools of spade fish, nurse sharks, rays, remoras, lobsters. Depths are 50-80 ft. Seas average three to four ft with little current. Excellent visibility. For experienced divers only. Ten minutes from Scuba Safaris.

☆☆☆ **Lobster Walk** is inside Coral Gardens, about 1½ miles from Oalie Beach, Nevis. The dive is similar to Coral Gardens, but inhabited by numerous lobsters. Depths start at 70 ft and drop to 110 ft. Experienced ocean divers only. Visibility and water clarity are outstanding. Expect some swells.

☆☆☆☆ **The Caves,** off the southwestern coast of Nevis, are a series of large caverns formed of ancient lava flows. The once-molten tubes are now home to schools of grunt, snapper, chubs, stingrays, nurse sharks and black tip reef sharks. Huge 200-lb turtles and rays have been spotted. Maximum depth is 40 ft. Good for all divers and snorkelers.

Scuba Safaris Dive Shop, Oalie Beach, Nevis.

☆☆☆☆ **Redonda Reef,** off the southern end of Nevis, is a wilderness area—an extensive series of caverns, and mini-walls just beginning to be explored. Depths average 60-70 ft. Sea conditions vary with the wind. Spectacular visibility and marine life. It is a 45-minute or longer boat ride. Seas must be exceptionally calm for the dive boats to visit this site.

☆☆ **Nags Head Reef** is at the southernmost tip of St. Kitts where the Caribbean and Atlantic meet. About a 55-minute boat ride from Basseterre, 10 minutes from Turtle Beach, this area is **the** place for spotting eagle rays, huge stingrays and other large pelagics. Even whales occasionally blast by. This site is weather-dependent, sometimes rough and with strong currents, suggested only for experts. But, when the sea is calm, it is good for novice divers. Depths range from 25 to 110 ft. The reef is a mix of mini-walls and canyons with superb and varied marine life.

☆ *Taleta* **Wreck** sank in 1985 off the west coast of St. Kitts and lies in 50 ft of water. A quick boat ride from Basseterre, it is one-half mile offshore, surrounded by coral rubble. Its steel hull attracts schooling fish, barracuda and lobster. The wreck is subject to murky conditions after a storm.

☆☆☆☆ **Sandy Point** is the photographers' favorite, with huge barrel sponges, lavender seafans, gorgonians and orange, elephant-ear sponges. A mini-wall and canyon, depths range from 45 to 100 ft. Unfortunately, this site is a long trip for St. Kitts dive operators and is visited only on request by groups who are then bussed to the site (15 miles north of Basseterre), where they rendezvous with the dive boats.

☆☆☆ **The White Holes**, off the Atlantic side of Nevis, are clear, sandy hollows packed with fish and surrounded by coral. Depths range from 15 to 45 ft. Fishlife and visibility are incredible, but the seas are often rough and the trip uncomfortable. On a calm day, this is an exceptional dive.

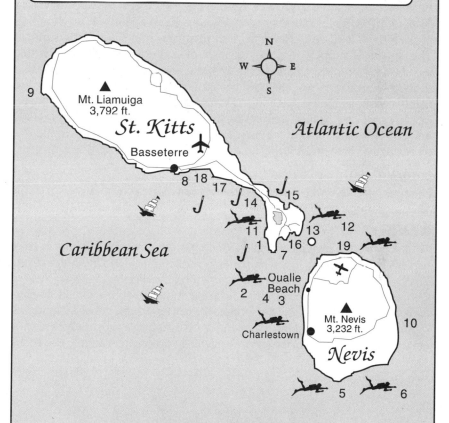

St. Kitts & Nevis
(ST. CHRISTOPHER)

Mt. Liamuiga
3,792 ft.

St. Kitts

Basseterre

Atlantic Ocean

Caribbean Sea

Oualie
Beach

Charlestown

Mt. Nevis
3,232 ft.

Nevis

Dive & Snorkeling Sites

1. Turtle Bar Reef
2. Monkey Reef
3. Coral Gardens
4. Lobster Walk
5. The Caves
6. Redonda Reef
7. Nags Head Reef
8. "Taleta" Wreck
9. Sandy Point
10. The White Holes
11. Green Point
12. GridIron
13. Turtle Beach
14. White House Bay
15. Sand Bank Bay
16. Cockleshell &
    Banana Bays
17. Timothy Beach
18. Bird Rock Beach
19. Long Hall Bay,

☆☆☆ **Green Point**, off the Caribbean side of the southeast peninsula on St. Kitts, is alive with black corals, big barrel and tube sponges and a variety of soft corals. Abundant lobster and fish. A 15-minute trip from either St. Kitts dive shop. Twenty-five minutes from Nevis. Depth is 50 ft. Sea conditions are always calm. Good for all level divers.

Another Atlantic dive is ☆☆☆ **Grid Iron**. This reef starts at New Castle Airport on Nevis and extends out past Booby Island and the North shoreline of St. Kitts. It is an undersea shelf that rises to within 15 ft of the surface. The shallows support a dense growth of well-formed elkhorn stands, fan-shaped hydroids, colonies of giant brain coral, yellow and orange tube sponges, barrel sponges, elephant ear sponges, and plate corals. There are plenty of fish, including blue tangs, French angelfish, porcupine fish, chubs, lobster, scrawled filefish, and yellowtail. Sea conditions vary. High winds and currents may rule out the area, but when conditions are favorable it is a spectacular dive and snorkeling site.

Snorkeling

Note: All St. Kitts and Nevis beaches are open to the public. Access in some cases is through hotel property.

NEVIS

☆☆ **Longhaul Bay** has good snorkeling on the inner side of the barrier reef off Nisbets Plantation. The water is shallow and visibility quite good. The beach is gorgeous. Get there by driving down to the beach at Nisbets Plantation Inn (near the airport) and walk south along the beach. Facing the sea, turn right and follow the shore to the last jetty. Experienced snorkelers should go outside the jetty, swim out to the reef and turn right to find a protected inner reef. Novice snorkelers will find many fish among the rocks

Pro Divers off Turtle Beach, St. Kitts.

*Dive boat leaves
Kenneth's Dive Center,
Basseterre, St. Kitts.*

closer to shore inside the last jetty. The current will bring you back to the Nisbet beach bar, which serves cool drinks and an excellent lunch! Always calm inside the barrier reef. A wonderful spot for swimming and picnics too.

ST. KITTS

☆☆ **Turtle Beach**. Facing the cut, walk to your left along the beach and swim out about 20 yards to the reef where you'll find the beginning of Ballast Bay Reef. Turtle Beach is a watersports facility at the end of the southeast peninsula. Signs lead the way. Snorkeling gear may be rented from Pro Divers on the beach. Turtle Beach Bar & Grill serves drinks and lunch daily from 12 pm to 5 pm.

☆ **White House Bay** is at the end of the first dirt road to your right as you reach the Great Salt Pond Area. You'll know it by the two sections of tugboat sticking out of the water. If the road is muddy, you may have to park near the main road and walk part of the way back. Choose the dirt road to the left. Lots of fish and corals inhabit the wreck, which was washed ashore by Hurricane Hugo in 1989. Depths range from shallow to 25 ft in the bay.

☆☆ **Sand Bank Bay** is the first turn-off to your left before reaching the Great Salt Pond area. The Bay is on the Atlantic side and subject to waves on windy days. Walk to your right along the cove and swim over to the rocks, where a bevy of beautiful reef fish await.

☆☆ **Cockleshell & Banana Bays** are one bay south of Turtle Beach. To reach it, drive straight to the end of the scenic drive. There is a construction sight with framework for an unfinished—with no definite plans to be finished—hotel at the end of the road. Park next to it and walk toward the old Cockleshell Hotel (devastated by Hurricane Hugo) on the bluff. Directly in front of the bluff is a pretty reef. Watch out for fire coral. Both bays are calm with good visibility. Beautiful white sand beaches skirt the area. At press time the hotel property was sold to Sandals for a future resort.

☆ **Timothy Beach Resort**, just south of Basseterre, has a small reef off the beach. Shallow depths.

☆☆ **Bird Rock Beach Hotel**, two miles south of Basseterre on the Caribbean, has a narrow strip of jet-black sand at the bottom of its property. Just off the shore are several rocks and a pretty reef which drops off enough for a shallow dive. Always calm, never a current. Decent visibility. Reach the area by boat or by climbing down the three steep flights of stairs behind the multi-terraced hotel. On the climb back up you'll find cold drinks and meals at the hotel's open-air restaurant.

Dive Operators

Prices for a two-tank boat dive range from US $70 to $80 and include all the equipment, if desired. One-tank dives are $45.

St. Kitts

St. Kitts Scuba, next to the Bird Rock Beach Resort, features new boats and equipment, and dive packages with Bird Rock. Rates for a seven-night stay with six day of diving, one night dive, transfers, taxes are from $599. ☎ (800) 621-1270, (869) 465-8914, fax (869) 699-7583. E-mail: birdrock@ caribbeans.com. Web site: www.caribbeans.com.

Kenneth's Dive Centre on Bay Road East, Basseterre, offers full PADI certification programs, rental gear and two fast dive boats. Owner, Kenneth Samuel, has been diving St. Kitts for more than 20 years and is an expert on the reefs and wrecks, tides and currents. Friendly service is provided by a professional staff. Comfortable, roomy, twin-hull, twin-engine, flat-bottom dive boats tour the Caribbean sites around Basseterre. Trips to the cut and Monkey Reef on request. ☎ (800) 359-0747 or (869) 465-2670, fax (869) 465-7723. (Note: spearfishing is allowed with this operator.)

Pro Divers is based at Turtle Beach on the Southeast Peninsula. This PADI instruction center, owned and operated by Auston MacLeod, offers dive packages and dive/accommodation packages with Ocean Terrace Inn which provides guests with daily shuttle service to the beach. All gear rentals, Nikonos camera and strobe rentals. The shop offers a full range of services, resort courses and PADI certification (open water to assistant instructor). Reef tours aboard a fast 30-ft, twin-engine dive boat. Pro Divers circles the peninsula and always visits the best sites. When the wind is too high on the Atlantic, they dive the cut. When weather rules out the cut the dive boats go around the bend to a protected Caribbean cove. Pro divers also rents gear for beach dives. No spear fishing in this protected area. ☎ (869) 465-3223, fax (869) 465-1057.

MV *Caribbean Explorer* is a live-aboard that departs from St. Maarten and tours St. Kitts and Saba.

The yacht has nine air-conditioned cabins, and is fully equipped for scuba, u/w photography and video. ☎ (800) 322-3577 or write to Sara Moody, 10 Fence Row Drive, Fairfield, CT 06430. The *Explorer* visits some of the outer Caribbean reefs that are out of range for the dive shops.

Nevis

Dive uncrowded and unhurried Nevis with **Scuba Safaris** at the Oualie Beach Hotel. Owner Ellis Chaderton is a NAUI instructor offering personalized cave, wreck, and reef dives at **The Caves, Monkey Shoals** and **Redonda Bank,** noted for hammerheads, dolphin and whale sightings. ☎ (800) 359-0747 or direct (869) 469-9518, fax (869) 469-9619. E-mail: oualie@caribsurf.com.

Snorkeling Tours

Day-sail snorkeling tours aboard a sleek 70-ft catamaran are offered by **Leeward Islands Charters,** ☎ (869) 465-7474. For customized tours, try **Tropical Tours,** ☎ (869) 465-4039, on Canyon Street, Basseterre.

Travel Tours

Money-saving air/hotel/dive packages from the US are offered by **Rothschild Travel,** ☎ (800) 359-0747, **ICS Scuba,** ☎ (800) 722-0205, **Landfall Productions,** ☎ (800) 525-3833, and **Into the Blue,** ☎ (800) 6-GETWET.

Accommodations

A list of all accommodations, including rooms in the historic inns (most are not air conditioned), apartments, and guest houses, is available from the tourist board. See details at end of chapter.

Dive packages, including room (double occupancy), airport transfers, tax, service charge and 10 dives, are offered by the resorts listed below. A 7% government hotel tax and 10-15% service charge are added to the rates shown.

ST. KITTS

Bird Rock Beach Hotel is high on a bluff overlooking Basseterre, with a panoramic view of the Caribbean. The inn has 24 deluxe rooms and two-story cottages complete with TV and telephone. Divers and snorkelers are bussed to waiting dive boats. Gear may be stowed at the dive shop. The hotel features an excellent, adjacent restaurant, pool, coffee shop, bar. Nice snorkeling off the rock beach. Winter room rates start at $140, summer rates are from $75. Dive/hotel packages with St. Kitts Scuba start at $599 per person for seven nights. ☎ (800) 621-1270, (869) 465-8914, fax (869) 699-7583. E-mail: birdrock@caribeans.com. Web site: www.caribeans.com.

Frigate Bay Resort, overlooking Frigate Bay, features spacious air-conditoned rooms and suites, restaurant and pool. The beach and golf course is a short stroll away. Winter rates start at $123 for a room to $373 for a two-bedroom suite; summer rates are from $75 to $215. Their PADI dive package with Kenneth's costs $895 (winter) for seven nights, six days diving (two-tank dives) and one night dive, transfers and breakfast daily. ☎ (800) 266-2185, (869) 465-8935, fax (869) 465-7050.

Ocean Terrace Inn (OTI), perched on a hill overlooking the capital city of Basseterre and its snug harbor, is a multi-terraced resort. Modern guest rooms are air-conditioned, have satellite TV, and tubs with showers. The inn features two bars, two pools and a jacuzzi. OTI is headquarters for Pro Divers. Room rates are from $116 for a double to $346 for a two-bedroom (4 persons) per night. Dive packages with Pro Divers or Kenneths are $870 per person for seven nights accommodations, six days of diving and airport transfers. ☎ (800) 524-0512, (800) 223-5695 or (869) 465-2754, fax (869) 465-2754. E-mail: tdcoticaribsurf.com.

Diving and snorkeling guests are shuttled by mini-van from the hill-top resort to Turtle Beach and the dive boats on the southeast peninsula—a 20-minute drive.

Sun' N Sand Beach Villas are one- and two-bedroom air-conditioned cottages with kitchenettes. Located on Atlantic Beach in the Frigate Bay area with a golf course, restaurants and casino nearby. Baby sitters (on request), pool, restaurant, mini mart, gift shop, TV. Studio apartments have one queen-size bed and kitchenette. Winter rates start at $160 for a studio, $270 for a cottage, summer $90 for a studio, $150 for cottage. Add $20 for a third person in studio or fifth person in cottage. Add $35 per day for full breakfast and dinner. Beach-side restaurant known for creative burgers and Caribbean dishes. ☎ (800) 223-6510 or (800) 621-1270, (869) 465-8037/8, fax (869) 465-6745.

NEVIS

Nisbet Plantation Beach Club is by far the most picturesque spot on Nevis. Built as a sugar plantation in 1778, the resort is situated on a mile-long, white-sand beach on the island's reef-protected north shore. Units are housed in 13 duplex cottages with spacious bedrooms, showers and enclosed screened patios. All have small fridges, hairdryers (a rarity on these islands), tea- and coffee-smaking facilities, and telephones. Cooled by ceiling fans. The club's gourmet restaurant is outstanding and worth a visit. Winter (Dec 21-Apr 14) rates for two people are $425 to $525 per day, including breakfast, afternoon tea and dinner daily. Summer packages are $935 per person for seven nights with meals, taxes, daytime flight from St. Kitts and airport transfers (no diving). Nice snorkeling inside the reef off the resort beach.

Shore scuba possible, but you need to make your own arrangements with the dive shop to get tanks. ☎ (800) 742-6008 or (869) 469-9325, fax (869) 469-9864.

Oualie Beach Hotel, headquarters for Nevis dive vacations, sits on a lovely black-sand beach on the island's leeward side. The hotel offers 22 standard and deluxe rooms and suites with ceiling fans and telephones. A few have air conditioning and cable TV.

The resort restaurant opens early for breakfast. Winter rates for a room, double occupancy,

Beach at Nisbet Plantation, Nevis.

run from $175 to $255 per day; summer, from $140. Scuba Safaris, currently the island's only dive center, is next to the hotel. Children under 12 are free with parents. Nice swimming beach. ☎ or (869) 469-9176, fax (869) 469-9176. Dive packages ☎ (800) 359-0747. E-mail: oualie@carib-surf.com.

The Mount Nevis Hotel on the slopes of Mt. Nevis offers breathtaking views of St. Kitts and the Caribbean. Air-conditioned, modern rooms have 11-channel cable TV, VCRs, phones and private balconies. Suites with kitchens are available. Restaurant, pool, shuttle to beach. Diving with Scuba Safaris at Oualie Beach. ☎ (800) 359-0747 or (869) 469-9373/4, fax (869) 469-9375. E-mail: mtnevis@aol.com. Web site: www.mountnevishotel .com.

Hurricane Cove Bungalows, perched on a hilltop above the beach, provides a private setting in one- , two- and three-bedroom bungalows complete with kitchens. Freshwater pool, snorkeling equipment. Diving with Scuba Safaris. Cottages for two people run from $235 to $335 per day. Add $45 per day, per person for breakfast and dinner. Book through your travel agent or ☎/fax (809) 465-9462.

Sightseeing and Other Activities

ST. KITTS

Among the sporting activities are golfing (18-hole international championship course at Frigate Bay and a nine-hole course at Golden Rock, St. Kitts); tennis; horseback riding along the beaches of Friar's Bay and Conaree Beach. Traveling on land is done by taxi, auto, moped or bicycle. Or one can venture through town by horse and carriage. Taxis are expensive and allowed to jack up their rates at night. Be sure to have the published rates in hand and note the hours they are in effect. Taxis with Ts on the license plates mean the driver is able to recite the local history and give sightseeing tours. Cars can be rented from $30 per day from TDC, ☎ (869) 465-2991, in St. Kitts; Nevis, ☎ (869) 469-5690. Avis and other local agents have booths at the airports.

Tours of St. Kitts start at Basseterre and "The Circus," an area patterned after London's famous Piccadilly Circus. Its centerpiece is a memorial to Thomas Berkeley. Surrounding it are a few craft boutiques, restaurants and galleries. Souvenir shops offer locally hand-screened fabrics, straw and coconut products, and jewelry fashioned from conch shells and volcanic rocks—many "Made in St. Kitts." Batik clothing and fabrics crafted on the island are found below the Ballahoo Restaurant on "The Circus" at **Island Hopper**. From town, rent a car or taxi and travel north along the west coast, island road. You'll pass several former "great houses," some newly converted into restaurants or shops. Continue to **Old Road Bay,** the island's first capital city. Near the English colony Carib drawings are sketched on the boulders. A short distance away is **Romney Manor,** the home of **Caribelle Batik,** where local artists work colorful designs into fabric with wax and dyes.

Continue to **Brimstone Hill,** a national park and fort that spreads over 40 acres above the sea and offers glorious views of St. Kitts and surrounding islands. The fort, which took 106 years of slave labor to build, is connected to a museum displaying photos and memorabilia honoring those who fought here.

Heading north from the fort brings you to **Sandy Point**, once headquarters for the Dutch tobacco industry. Continue along the island road, around the island past miles of sugar cane fields until you come to the **Black Rocks,** rugged cliffs formed of ancient lava flows from Mt Liamuiga. A left will lead you to the Frigate Bay area, the site of luxury hotels, casinos, and the yacht club. From here head up the mountain on the new scenic road out through the uninhabited **South East Peninsula** and **The Salt Ponds,** habitat to green vervet monkeys, herons, sea turtles and wild deer. The ponds are a source of salt to the islanders.

The scenic road winds, dips and soars through seven miles of the most gorgeous, lush, green mountains and breathtaking ocean views on earth. On the Atlantic side there are panoramic views of waves crashing against rocky cliffs and washing over secluded, golden beaches and snorkeling coves. Rounding the mountains brings the turquoise Caribbean and distant mountains of Nevis into view. Near the end is the Great Salt Pond. Watch for monkeys and, near the ponds, cows crossing the road.

Hikes into the rainforest, windsurfing, deep-sea fishing, horseback riding, sunset cruises, and historic tours are easily arranged through the resorts or individual operators. Rainforest tours, cave tours, volcano tours and plantation tours are offered by **Greg's Safaris**, ☎ 465-4121.

NEVIS

If you arrive on Nevis by boat, you can walk to Charlestown. You'll first encounter the **Cotton Ginnery**, still used to gin cotton, and **Market Place,** where local merchants sell fresh fruits, spices and seafood. But more interesting is the **Nevis Philatelic Bureau,** which offers beautiful color plates of marine life, historic aircraft and space subjects, and local flora—unique souvenirs, all suitable for framing. **The Nevis Museum and Hamilton House**, birthplace of statesman and first Secretary of the US Treasury, Alexander Hamilton, will also be found here.

Heading north on the coast road past Oualie Beach, you'll come to **Newcastle Pottery**, where centuries-old methods create natural red pottery—-from small ashtrays to flower pots and the coalpots used by many villagers. The best prices on the pottery are at the factory.

South of town turn left across from the Esso station to find the **Bath Hotel and Spring House,** once THE grand hotel and health spa of the Caribbean. Much of the original structure was destroyed by an earthquake in 1950, but visitors can enjoy a mineral bath or just stick a toe in and tour the hotel.

Horseback riding and rain forest walks may be arranged through the hotels.

Dining

Local seafood, lobster dishes, and West Indian cuisine highlight St.Kitts and Nevis menus. Many fine restaurants are in the "great houses." Fast food and pizza shops are found in towns. Menus list prices in EC (East Caribbean Dollars), one of which is about US $2.70. When you are quoted a price in "dollars" ask which one. Credit cards are NOT widely accepted.

ST. KITTS

Fisherman's Wharf, on the harbor in Basseterre, offers fresh seafood and local dishes. Seating is on a broad deck a few inches over the water. Much

The Baths, Nevis.

like eating on a yacht that doesn't rock. Great views of Basseterre at night. Don't miss the pumpkin fritters. Informal. Open for dinner nightly, and for lunch on weekends. Moderate. ☎ 465-2695.

The Ballahoo, center of town, Basseterre at the Circus, open Mon-Sat, serves seafood and local dishes, 8 am to 11 pm. ☎ 465-4197.

J's Place, at the foot of the Brimstone Hill Fortress, serves sandwiches and cold drinks. Open Tues-Sun from 11 am to 11 pm. ☎ 465-6264.

PJ's Pizza Bar and Restaurant features pizza, sandwiches, vegetarian and Italian dinners. Eat-in or take-out. ☎ 465-8373.

NEVIS

Oualie Beach Hotel, open daily from 7 am to 11 pm, serves lunch and dinner. Enjoy West Indian cuisine in an informal atmosphere at the water's edge. Excellent broiled lobster and pineapple mousse. Moderate prices. No credit cards. ☎ 469-5329.

Unella's Waterfront Bar & Restaurant serves refreshing tropical drinks, sandwiches, local and seafood dishes, including curried lamb, spare ribs and conch, at reasonable prices. By the ferry pier in Charlestown. ☎ 469-5574.

Nisbet Plantation offers elegant settings and taste-tempting creations such as chilled avocado and apricot soup, marinated salmon over asparagus mousse with caviar-stuffed quail eggs, amberjack with hollandaise sauce or sumptous meat dishes. Expensive. Meals average US $55 per person without drinks, plus gratuities and tax and an "optional" tip. If you are staying at Nisbet, be sure to get the money-saving meal package, which includes breakfast, afternoon tea and dinner daily. ☎ (869) 469-9325.

Facts

Helpful Phone Numbers: Police, ☎ 465-2241. Hospital, ☎ 465-2551. Airport, ☎ 465-8472. Tourist Board: *St. Kitts,* ☎ (869) 465-4040; *Nevis,* ☎ 469-5521. Doctor, ☎ 465-8252/465-4083/465-2837. Ferry, ☎ 465-2521.

Nearest Recompression Chamber: Saba, a 15-minute flight from St. Kitts. Getting from the dive boat to the airport and arranging for air transport may be dangerously time-consuming. Avoid decompression dives.

Getting There: American Airlines, ☎ (800) 433-7300, is the main carrier with direct flights from major US cities to San Juan, connecting to American Eagle, which serves Golden Rock Airport, St. Kitts. Other North American and international carriers have direct flights to San Juan, Antigua and other Caribbean islands that connect with American Eagle, BWIA, LIAT, and Windward Islands Airways to and from the island of St. Kitts. Golden Rock Airport on St. Kitts can handle wide-body jets, while Newcastle Airport on Nevis can accommodate smaller twin-engined, prop aircraft. Daily ferry service connects Basseterre to Charlestown. Several cruise lines stop at St. Kitts.

Driving: Traffic moves on the left. A local license is required and can be obtained from the Police Traffic Dept for about US $10. Rental car steering wheels are on the left also.

Language: English.

Documents: Passports are required of all visitors except US and Canadian citizens who may use a voter registration card or original birth certificate.

Airport Tax: Departure tax of US $8 (EC $20).

Currency: Eastern Caribbean dollar (EC) $2.70=US $1.

Climate: Average temperate of 79° F. Annual rainfall is 55 inches.

Clothing: Casual, lightweight clothing. Beach attire, short shorts, bikinis or bare chests are NOT ALLOWED in public places—town, restaurants or shops. Snorkelers should wear wetskins or long-sleeve shirts to protect from the sun. Wetsuits unnecessary, though a shortie or wetskin is nice for winter diving and when making several deep dives. On land, casual lightweight clothing.

Electricity: 230 volts, 60 cycles AC. Some hotels have 110 volts, AC. Transformers and adapters are generally needed.

Religious Services: Seventh Day Adventist, Anglican, Baha'i, Baptist, Catholic, Church of God, Jehovah's Witnesses, Moravian, Methodist, and Pentecostal. Contact hotel desk for details.

Additional Information: *In the US—St. Kitts & Nevis Tourist Board,* 414 East 75th St, N.Y. 10021, ☎ (800) 582-6208 or (212) 535-1234, fax (212) 879-4789; or 1464 Whippoorwill Way, Mountainside, NJ 07092, ☎ 908-232-6701, fax 908-233-0485. *In Canada*—11 Yorkville Ave, Suite 508, Toronto, M4WIL3, ☎ 416-921-7717, fax 416-921-7997. *In the UK*—10 Kensington Court, London W8 5DL, ☎ 071-376-0881. *In St. Kitts and Nevis*—Department of Tourism, Church St., PO Box 132, Basseterre, St. Kitts, WI, ☎ (869) 465-2620/4040, fax (869) 465-8794. E-mail: skbnev@ix.netcom.com. Web site: www.interknowledge.com/stkitts-nevis.

St. Lucia

Saint Lucia, (pronounced loó sha), is the second largest of the Windward Islands. An independent state, the 238-square-mile island is about 1,300 miles southeast of Florida, 24 miles north of St. Vincent and 21 miles from Martinique.

Mountainous and scenic, the island is characterized by Morne Gimie, the highest peak at 3,145 ft, and two spectacular ancient forest-covered volcanic cones—Gros Piton (2,619 ft) and Petit Piton (2,461 ft)—that rise abruptly from the sea near Soufriere, an old colonial town on the west coast. Nearby, hot sulfurous springs bubble and spout steam from muddy, black craters. Lush, jungle-like vegetation covers much of the island and seems to grow as you pass through it.

St. Lucia's coast is lined by miles of beautiful beaches interspersed with sheer volcanic cliffs that dive straight into the sea, where they are covered with a blaze of orange and yellow corals and sponges. Most diving and snorkeling is off Anse Chastanet (pronounced "ants-shas-tan-ay") and Soufriere Bay, both sheltered coves on the island's southwest corner. Within 150 ft of their shorelines lies a 30-mile-long coral reef on a shelf at 10- to 30-ft depths. Farther out are shallow caves and a sheer wall. Beyond the coves, strong currents mandate drift diving. The entire area is protected as a marine park.

St. Lucia is heavily populated. Its 150,000 people are mostly African or of mixed African and European descent. English is the official language, although there is also a local patois that owes much to early French domination of the island. One-third of the population resides in Castries, the capital and deep water port.

The economy is agricultural, with bananas as the main export crop. Cocoa beans, coconut oil, and copra (dried coconut) also are exported. Industries include rum making, fishing, and brick manufacturing. There are two airports, Hewanorra International at the southern tip of the island, and Vigie in the north. American Airlines serves both airports. In summer, bug repellent is necessary from the moment you step off the plane.

When to Go

Dive St Lucia from Jan to April, the dry season. The rainiest months are from June through Nov; Aug-Sept are the worst. Annual rainfall varies from 55 inches on the south coast to 140 inches in the interior. Air temperatures average 80° F.

History

No one is certain when St. Lucia was discovered, or by whom, though some credit Christopher Columbus in 1502. The British tried to settle the island in 1605 and 1638, but were driven off with fierce attacks by the native Carib Indians. French claims to the island were confirmed by a treaty with the Caribs in 1660. St. Lucia subsequently changed hands several times before being captured by the British in 1803 and ceded to them by the Treaty of Paris in 1814. In 1838, it became part of Britain's Windward Islands administrative group.

On Feb 22, 1979, St. Lucia attained full independence. The British monarch continues to be head of state and to be represented by a governor general, who appoints the prime minister. Parliament consists of a Senate and House of Assembly, and there is a supreme court.

Best Dive and Snorkeling Sites

☆☆☆ **The Wreck of the *Lesleen M*** is a 165-ft freighter sunk by the Department of Fisheries in 1986 to create an artificial reef. The wreck is intact, lying upright at 65 ft. Its hull, covered with soft corals, slender tube sponges and hydroids, provides shelter to many juvenile fish. Divers can explore the pilot house at 35 ft. It is possible to explore inside the hold and in the engine room. Good visibility.

☆☆☆☆ **Anse Chastanet Reef**, which lies off the Anse Chastanet Hotel, has three distinct dive areas. New divers and snorkelers enjoy a nice shallow area with a small cavern, sponges, large brain and boulder corals at depths of five to 25 ft. A resident school of squid is joined by goat fish, a frog fish, parrot fish, chromis and wrasse.

Farther out, the reef slopes off to a wall that plummets to 140 ft. Most dives are at 50-60 ft, where the coral ledges sparkle with ruby sea whips, pink anemones, lacy corals, teal vase sponges, and crimson rope sponges. Crabs, lobster, trumpet fish, peppermint-stick lobster, blackbar soldier fish, brown chromis, batfish, peacock flounders, flying gurnards, moray eels, and margates inhabit the area.

Below 100 ft are larger fish, black corals and porcelain-like plate corals.

☆☆ **Anse la Raye Reef** is a slope covered in huge boulders near the wreck of the *Lesleen M*. The shallow areas have lots of colorful fire corals, while deeper there are iridescent vase sponges, huge barrel sponges and bushy soft corals. Schools of jacks, bermuda chub and spotted drums frequent the area.

☆☆☆ **Fairyland**, outside the Anse Chastanet cove, is always done as a drift dive. Subject to occasional strong currents, this area has outstanding visibility and vibrant corals. The plateau slopes from 40 to 60 ft and is strewn with huge boulders. Finger corals, anemones and lavender tube sponges attach to the rocks with plenty of nooks and crannies for fish and invertebrates.

☆☆☆☆☆ **Pinnacles** are four spectacular seamounts that rise from the depths to within a few ft of the surface. These coral-covered subsea cliffs are a macro-photographer's dream—alive with octopi, feather dusters, arrow crabs, seahorses, squid, and shrimp. Cleansing currents nurture big barrel and vase sponges and a lattice of soft corals—sea plumes, sea whips and sea fans. Lots of fish. Black corals at depth.

☆☆☆ **Piton Wall**, at the base of Petit Piton, falls from the surface to hundreds of ft below. Sea whips, gorgonians, big feather dusters give way to a profusion of fish. Strong currents possible. Experienced divers only.

☆☆☆ **Superman's Flight** is a 15-minute boat trip across Soufriere Bay to the base of the Petit Piton Mountain. It was used as a setting for the film *Superman II*. Strong currents make this an exciting drift drive. You'll "fly" the wall underwater. Good fish life and excellent visibility.

☆☆ **Turtle Reef**, a crescent-shaped shoal north of Anse Chastanet Bay, starts at 40 ft, then drops to over 150 ft. Divers enjoy spectacular pillar coral and barrel sponges in the shallows. Lots of crustaceans, squid, parrot fish, starfish and soft corals.

When occasional calm seas occur off the southeast coast you can dive two wrecks—an airliner and a freighter. But more often than not rough seas and strong currents rule them out as safe sites.

Dive Operators

Scuba St. Lucia is a PADI five-star training facility located at Anse Chastanet. The seven-instructor shop offers introductory and advanced open-water and rescue courses plus specialty courses in marine life identification, underwater navigation, drift diving, wreck diving and UW photography. E6 processing and photo rentals are available. Five custom dive boats. Hotel-dive packages with Anse Chastanet Hotel. ☎ (800) 223-1108, (758) 459-7000 or (758) 459-7355. Write to PO Box 7000, Soufriere, St. Lucia. WI.

St. Lucia Undersea Adventures, at the Wyndham Morgan Bay Resort, has a fast 40-ft dive boat that takes divers to Anse Cochon, the Pinnacles and Anse Chastanet reefs. Packages available. ☎ (800) 327-8150 or (758)

451-7716. E-mail: nealwatson@aol.com. Web site: www.twofin.com/twofin/ stlucia.htm.

Buddies Scuba at Vigie Marina, Castries, is a full-service PADI facility. Buddies offers resort courses and reef and wreck tours. Six-dive packages are available. ☎ (758) 452-5288 or (758) 452-7044. Write to Buddies Scuba, Vigie Marina, Castries, St. Lucia, WI.

The Moorings Scuba Centre, at Club Mariner, Marigot Bay, offers reef and wreck dives, rentals, instruction and night dives. ☎ (758) 451-4357.

Accommodations

St. Lucia has a wide range of accommodations for all budgets, some as low as US $30 per night. Space dictates we list only those with or near dive facilities, but a complete list is available from the tourist board offices listed at the end of this chapter.

For apartment or private home rentals contact: **Happy Homes,** PO Box 12, Castries, St. Lucia; **Caribbean Home Rentals,** PO Box 710, Palm Beach, FL 33480; or **Tropical Villas,** PO Box 189, Castries, St. Lucia, ☎ (758) 452-8240.

Anse Chastanet Beach Hotel is the island's premier dive resort. It is named for one of the French aristocratic families who settled on the island during the 18th century. The Chastanets originated in the Bordeaux region. "Anse" is antique French for "Bay."

Anse Chastanet is a beautifully scenic resort set amidst a lush 400-acre plantation and edged by a secluded, quarter-mile-long, soft sand beach. Some of the resort's 48 rooms are scattered on a hillside, others are beachside. All rooms have fridges, electric tea/coffee makers, wall-mounted hair dryers, clay tile or tropical hardwood floors, private showers, and ceiling fans. Scuba St. Lucia is a part of the resort. Snorkeling and shore dives are possible from the resort beach. Dive-hotel package rates for a double, with meals, start at $2,798 (Dec 20 to April 15). For a single from May 16 to Oct 31, dive-hotel package rates start at $1,029 without meals. All packages include seven nights accommodations, airport transfers, six days of diving (two tanks), weights, local plantation tours and beach towels. Night dives may be substituted. Non-diver rates, without meals, start at $849 in summer. MAP supplement is mandatory during the high season. Group packages available. ☎ (758) 459-7000, fax (758) 459-7700. Telex: 0398/6370. Write to PO Box 7000, Soufriere, St. Lucia, WI.

Marigot Beach Club Bay Resort is nine miles from Vigie Airport and Castries on picturesque Marigot Bay. The resort features 47 villas set in the hillside around the bay and marina. Cottages rent from $90 per day in summer and $140 per day in winter. The Moorings dive shop on the premises offers diving for $65 per day. Bareboat or crewed charters are on Beneteau 32s or Bordeaux 104s. Package rates for a room with a day sail are $425 per person in spring and summer, $585 per person in winter. For current rates and reservations, ☎ (800) 334-2435 or 813-538-8760, fax 813-530-9747. In St. Lucia, ☎ (758) 451-4357, fax (758) 451-4353.

Wyndham Morgan Bay Resort's 250 guest rooms sprawl across 22 green acres on secluded Choc Bay, a short trip from the airport. Luxury rooms have satellite TV, large balconies, high ceilings, and tropical decor. Beach, pool, fitness center. Dive packages are with St. Lucia Undersea Adventures. Per person rates, based on double occupancy, run from $820 for five nights to $1,200 for seven nights. Oceanfront rooms range from $970 to $1,410. Non-divers pay from $700 for five nights to $1,150 for seven nights. Boat ride to dive sites averages 40 minutes. Package includes room, airport transfers, breakfast, lunch and dinner daily, unlimited wine and bar drinks (excluding champagne), three two-tank dives on a five-night package, five two-tank dives on a seven-night package. Tanks, weights and belts, full use of all facilities. ☎ (800) 327-8150. E-mail: nealwatson@aol.com. Web site: www.twofin.com/twofin/stlucia.htm.

Small Inns

St. Lucia also has a number of lovely small inns that rent rooms for an average of $85 to $125 per day in winter, with some as low as $35. For a complete listing, call the tourist board at ☎ (800) 456-3984 or fax (212) 867-2795; or call the small inn association, ☎ (758) 452-4599, fax (758) 452-5428.

Dining

Menu prices are in EC. EC $1=US $2.70. Credit cards are **not** widely accepted, but major restaurants do take credit cards. Prices following are in US $.

Fast-food lovers will find good burgers, salads and pizza at two **Peppino's Pizza** locations: in Castries on upper Bridge Street and in Gros Islet at the north end of the island. All available for takeout. No credit cards. ☎ 452-3942.

Dasheene in Soufriere is on a 1,300-ft ridge in a lush setting at LaDera Resort. Good Creole and seafood dishes. Open seven days for breakfast, lunch and dinner. ☎ 459-7850. Reservations.

For steaks, ribs and fresh seafood, try the **Charthouse**, overlooking Rodney Bay (northwest corner). Entrées start at US $15. ☎ 452-8115.

On Tuesday evenings there are beach barbecues at **Anse Chastanet**. Festivities begin at the hotel at 7:30 pm. Each Friday night in **Gros Islet,** also known as "The Village," there is an all-out street party with music, dancing, food and loads of local color. It can get rowdy.

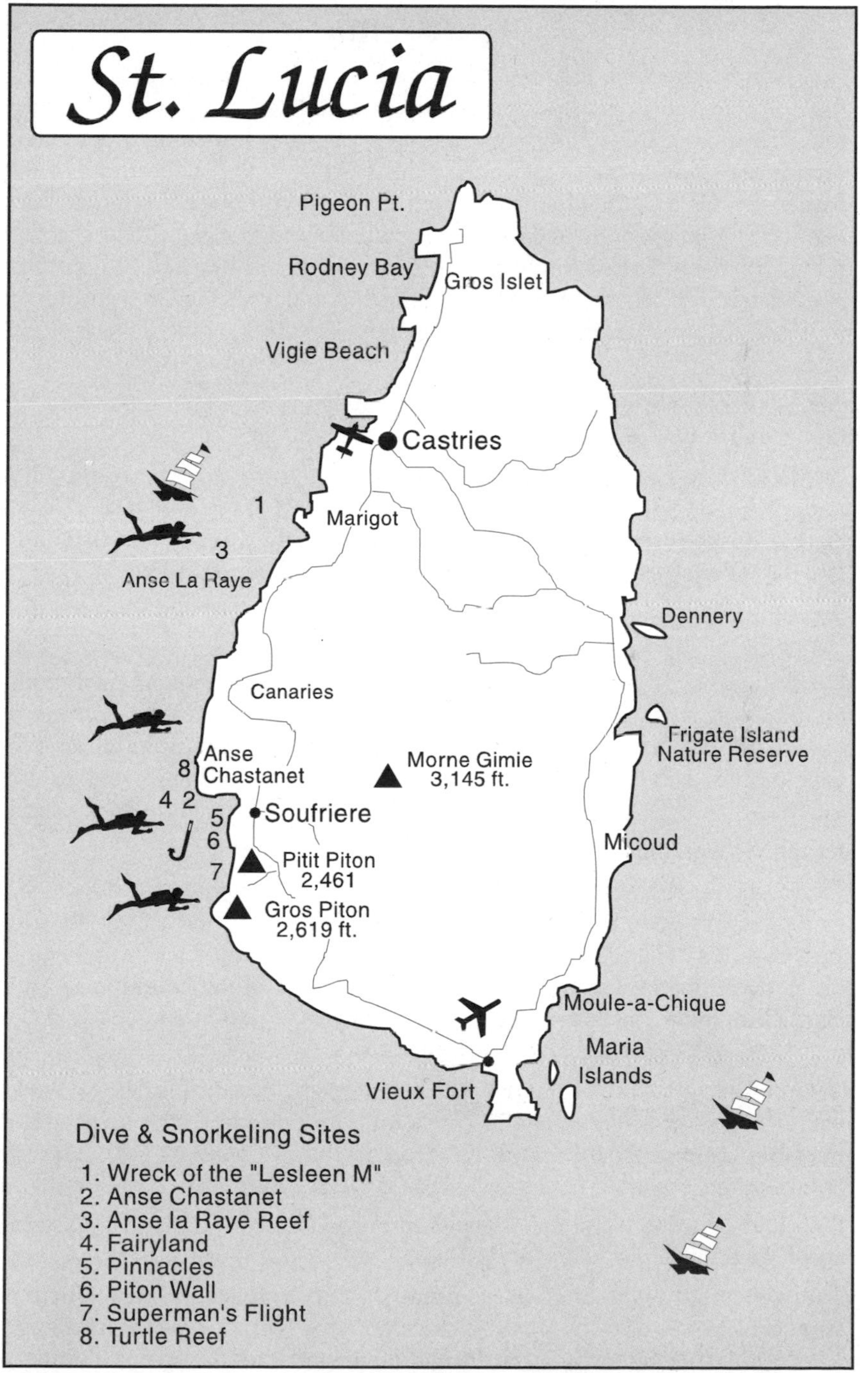

St. Lucia

Pigeon Pt.

Rodney Bay

Gros Islet

Vigie Beach

● Castries

1

Marigot

3

Anse La Raye

Dennery

Canaries

Frigate Island
Nature Reserve

8

Anse
Chastanet

▲ Morne Gimie
3,145 ft.

4 2

5

● Soufriere

6

7

▲ Pitit Piton
2,461

Micoud

▲ Gros Piton
2,619 ft.

✈

Moule-a-Chique

Maria
Islands

Vieux Fort

Dive & Snorkeling Sites

1. Wreck of the "Lesleen M"
2. Anse Chastanet
3. Anse la Raye Reef
4. Fairyland
5. Pinnacles
6. Piton Wall
7. Superman's Flight
8. Turtle Reef

Sightseeing

St. Lucia has recently improved the roads. The 30-mile trip to Soufrieres that formerly took three hours can now be negotiated in an hour. A driving tour of the west coast affords breathtaking views of the bays, mountains, rainforests, and surrounding countryside. Starting at the southern tip of St. Lucia is Moule à Chique Peninsula, marked by a lighthouse. From here you can see St. Vincent and the Grenadines. Heading north along the west coast brings you to the **Sulfur Springs**, billed as the world's only drive-in volcano. A walk-through takes you past steaming hot sulfur springs and bubbling mud craters. An ever-present smell of rotten eggs usually makes this a quick stop.

Just north of the springs is the 18th-century village of Soufriere, the island's breadbasket, where local fruits and vegetables are grown.

The **Soufriere Estate** offers tours where you can learn about the harvesting and processing of copra (dried coconut meat yielding oil) and cocoa. Adjacent to the estate are the **Diamond Falls and Mineral Baths,** where you can take a "therapeutic" hot dip and enjoy the surrounding gardens.

Take the dirt road (very slowly) south of town for spectacular views of the Pitons.

Continuing north brings you to **Anse-la-Raye**, a fishing village where dugout canoes are made. Beyond lies **Mt. Parasol** and **Mt. Gimie**. From here the road winds and dips through banana country to **Marigot**, a world-famous yacht harbor and resort community. There are two hotels and restaurants.

The road from Marigot to Castries curves and bends sharply with the rugged terrain through miles of banana plantations.

When you reach **Castries** take the John Compton Highway to the center of town where you'll find duty-free shopping. Behind the city is **Morne Fortune**, the "Hill of Good Fortune." A scenic drive up the Morne begins on Bridge Street. From the top are splendid views of the countryside and **Fort Charlotte**, an 18th-century French fort.

From Castries you can cross the island to the Atlantic coast or head north to Gros Islet, a sleepy fishing village, and **Pigeon Island National Park** with 40 acres of forts, ruins and caves that are reputed still to hold pirate treasure. Beyond Pigeon Island lies **Cap Estate**, covering 1,500 acres of fine beaches, secluded coves and a golf course.

Full- and part-day water excursions are offered down the island's western coast. Most offer snorkeling and lunch.

The windward Atlantic coast is home to the **Frigate Island Nature Reserve**. A one-mile walk encircles the park area and takes you to a lookout where you can view outlying islets. During the summer the area is a nesting site of frigate birds and timid boa constrictors. Half-day tours may be arranged by the National Trust (☎ 425-5005). Avoid swimming in the Atlantic. Strong currents and powerful waves make it dangerous. Offshore from **Vieux** on the south tip is the **Maria Islands Nature Reserve**, which houses unique grass snakes and ground lizards, plus many species of birds. Tours may be arranged when it's open.

Guided hikes in the Pitons and into the rain forest are offered by the Forest Service. ☎ 452-3231 or 452-3078.

Facts

Helpful Phone Numbers: Police, ☎ 999; St. Jude's Hospital, Vieux Fort, ☎ 454-6041; Victoria Hospital, Hospital Road, Castries, ☎ 452-2421.

Nearest Recompression Chamber: Barbados, ☎ 011-590-828888, Dr. Dramor; ☎ 011-590-829880, Dr. Serina.

Getting There: American Airlines (☎ 800-433-7300) has service from Miami, New York and other gateway cities with a stop in San Juan. BWIA (☎ 800-327-7401) flies direct from New York and Miami. Air Canada (☎ 800-422-6232) flies from Montreal and Toronto with connections through Barbados. LIAT connects with other Caribbean destinations.

Island Transportation: Car rentals—**Avis,** Vide Boutielle, ☎ (758) 45-24554/22700, fax (758) 45-31536; **National**, Gros Islet, ☎ (758) 45-28721, fax (758) 45-28577; **Dollar**, Reduit, ☎ (758) 45-20994; and **Budget,** Marisule, ☎ (758) 45-20233/28021, fax (758) 45-29362.

Cab service is readily available from Hewanorra International Airport at the south end of the island. Taxis are unmetered and unregulated. Be sure to ask the cost *before* getting in the cab and whether it is in EC $ or US $.

Driving: You must be 25 or older and hold a valid driver's license. Buy a temporary St. Lucian license for $11 at the airport or police headquarters on Bridge St in Castries. Steering wheels are on the right. Driving is on the left. Drivers should exercise extreme caution while negotiating St. Lucia's rugged mountainous roads and hairpin curves.

Documents: Citizens of the US, UK and Canada must produce proof of identity. Passports are suggested, but a birth certificate with a raised seal and some form of photo ID will suffice. Visitors must have onward tickets.

Currency: The Eastern Caribbean dollar which is exchanged at the rate of US $1=EC $2.70 ($2.60 in hotels and stores); US and Canadian dollars are also accepted. Credit cards accepted in many stores, but not all restaurants. Check when making reservations or accommodations.

Climate: In winter temperatures range between 65° and 85° F; summer, between 75° and 95°. Summers are rainy. Light wetsuits are suggested for winter diving.

Clothing: Lightweight and casual. Some of the fancier restaurants at the hotels in Castries require a jacket and tie.

Electricity: 220 volts. Adapters are required.

Time: Atlantic Standard (EST + 1 hr).

Language: English.

Tax: An 8% government tax is added for accommodations. A service charge of 10% is added for restaurants. Note: hotels often calculate the taxes and charges in the rates.

Religious Services: Most of the island is Catholic, but Anglican, Methodist, Baptist, Seventh Day Adventist, and Jehovahs Witness faiths are also represented.

For Additional Information: Contact the St. Lucia Tourist Board. *In New York:* 820 Second Ave., NY, NY, ☎ (212) 867-2950, fax (212) 370-7867. *In Canada:* 151 Bloor St. West, Suite 425, Toronto, Ontario, Canada M5S 1S4, ☎ (416) 961-4317. *In London:* 10 Kensington Court, London W8 5DL, England, ☎ (011) 44-71-937-1969, fax (011) 44-71-937-3611. *In St. Lucia:* PO Box 221, Castries, St. Lucia, ☎ (758) 45-24094/25968, fax (758) 453-1121. Web site: http://info@stlucia.com/.

St. Maarten/St. Martin

St. Maarten/St. Martin is a good spot for divers, snorkelers or non-divers to share a vacation. The island is surrounded by extremely shallow reefs, perfect for snorkeling or learning to dive. There are some areas suitable for children. For the more experienced diver, there are advanced reef, cave and wreck sites off the south coast. The island also serves as a jump-off point to three neighboring "best dive" islands — Saba, St. Eustatia, and Anguilla.

It is the largest of the Dutch Windward Islands, though still compact enough for you to stay on one end and easily explore the other. The north half (St. Martin) is French, the south half (St. Maarten) is Dutch. It is the only Caribbean island shared by two governments.

The island's dual personality, coupled with its reputation as the gourmet capital of the Caribbean, exciting nightlife, duty-free shopping, endless watersports and extraordinary scenery have contributed to its popularity as a prime vacation spot. The bustling tourist population may seem too busy for the devout naturalist, yet, given half a chance, this island's beautiful beaches and endless creature comforts can seduce, surprise and entertain just about anyone.

Residents of this small island point proudly to more than 300 years of peaceful co-existence. They are fond of describing their 37-square-mile island as "the smallest bit of real estate in the world shared by two countries" and they are quick to add, "probably the friendliest."

A single border monument bracketed by a pair of flags, stands beside the road connecting Philipsburg and Marigot, the Dutch and French "capital villages." There are no real boundaries or borders.

History

St. Maarten/St. Martin was discovered by Christopher Columbus on Nov 11, 1493. Though Spain claimed the island, it was deserted in 1648 when the Spaniards no longer needed a Caribbean base. The Dutch commander of St. Eustatius promptly sent Captain Martin Thomas to take possession. Thomas found French troops who, after a few skirmishes, signed a treaty

Contributors: Tom Burnett; Trade Winds Dive Center: Dominique & LeRoy French; Ocean Explorers.

dividing the island between France and Holland. Legend portrays a Frenchman and a Dutchman walking from opposite ends of the island to see how much territory each could claim for his side in one day.

Unfortunately, that early agreement didn't last as long as the legend, and St. Maarten changed hands 16 times before becoming permanently Dutch.

During the 17th and 18th centuries, fishing, sugar plantations, and salt harvesting became the base for the island's economy. By the middle of the 18th century, however, the tiny nearby island of St. Eustatius began to overshadow St. Maarten/St. Martin in prosperity. Farms on St. Maarten/St. Martin supplied grapes for the tables of wealthy Statian merchants.

St. Maarten/St. Martin remained little noticed by the outside world until Princess Juliana Airport opened in 1943. With the end of World War II, American and European travelers, eager for an unspoiled Caribbean getaway, began to discover the island. In 1947, St. Maarten's first hotel, the Sea View, opened.

The decades following 1960 brought an increase in tourism. Today St. Maarten/St. Martin is one of the most popular vacation spots in the Caribbean.

Diving

There are a few snorkeling sites near shore, but the best dive and snorkeling spots are about a mile offshore and must be reached by boat.

The Windward side of St. Maarten, extending from Philipsburg up the coast to Dawn Beach, is known for brilliant rock formations and a moon hole created by the impact of a meteor. The Leeward side of St. Maarten has scattered coral heads.

Off the northeast coast of St. Martin, dive sites include Ilet Pinel, a small out island good for shallow diving, Green Key, a prolific barrier reef and Flat Island (also known as Ile Tintamarre), for sheltered coves and sub-sea geological faults. To the north, Anse Marcel is a good choice.

Best Dive and Snorkeling Sites

☆☆☆ **Wreck of the _Proselyte_** sits one mile off the south coast of St. Maarten in 50 ft of water. Remains include three 14-ft anchors, cannons, ballast bars and brass barrel hoops from the powder kegs. Divers still find square nails and spikes. Schools of sergeant majors, hordes of angelfish, yellow tail snappers and grunts inhabit the wreck, with an occasional sighting of an eagle ray or grey reef shark. The ship, first named _Jason,_ began her 31 years afloat as a Dutch war frigate at Rotterdam, Holland. She was taken over by a mutinous crew in 1796 and given to the British. The ship sank in 1801 after striking a submerged reef.

Bobby's Marina (left) and Great Bay Marina, Philipsburg.

The reef surrounding the *Proselyte* is pretty, with stands of elkhorn and soft corals. Reef depths are from 15 to 45 ft. A swim behind the reef reveals two new wrecks, a 30-ft sailboat and a 100-ft steel barge, sunk in 1989.

Seas average three to four ft. No spearfishing or coral or shell collecting. Good for novice divers.

☆☆ **The Alleys** and **Cable Reef** are a two-reef complex just east of the *Proselyte* wreck. Maximum depth is 65 ft. The reefs are riddled with small caves crowded with fish and lobster. Besides the usual parade of tropicals there are a few nurse sharks, an occasional hammerhead, eagle rays and turtles. In winter, the barracuda population quadruples. Coral rubble interspersed with sea fans and gorgonians carpets the bottom. Visibility varies with sea conditions from 50 to 100 ft. This area is recommended for novice divers when the seas are calm. Expect two- to four-ft swells. No spearfishing or collecting.

☆☆ **The Maze,** a huge shallow reef off Little Bay Beach on the south tip of St. Maarten, starts at 20 ft, dropping to a sandy bottom at 50 ft. Elkhorn corals predominate. There are a number of mini-caves and swim-throughs. One section, a hangout for hundreds of barracuda, has been dubbed Barracuda Alley.

☆☆☆☆ **One Step Beyond**, a seven-mile boat ride off St. Maarten's southeast tip, features huge eagle rays, sharks, turtles, big morays, schools of grunts and spadefish, surrounding a big coral hill that branches into arches and swim-throughs.

High winds often rule this area out, but when seas are calm it is a great dive. Expect three- to four-ft seas on the calm days. Maximum depth is 90 ft.

Average visibility ranges from 80 to 100 ft. Suggested for experienced divers only.

☆☆☆ **Fish Bowl Reef** lies between One Stop Beyond and Cable Reef, off the southeastern corner of the island. Noted as one of the prettiest spots in the area, the reef attracts walls of tropicals, huge nurse sharks, stingrays and barracuda. The terrain is shot through with ledges and caves. Depths are between 40 and 60 ft. Good for novices. Visibility varies from 60 to 100 ft. No spearfishing or collecting.

Snorkeling

Sail-snorkeling tours to the best snorkeling sites off the small islands surrounding St. Martin/St. Maarten may be arranged at Bobby's Marina and Great Bay Marina in Philipsburg, Simpson Bay Lagoon and Port La Royale Marina at Marigot Bay.

Snorkelers and novice divers will find some shallow reefs and wrecks off the northern and western coasts.

Long Bay Reef is close to shore at Long Bay off the western peninsula. This is a good choice when the outer reefs are weathered out. Watch for occasional currents. **French Reef** is close to shore off Cole Bay on the south coast. With depths from 12 to 25 ft, this protected reef is a good choice for beginners. Lots of tropicals.

BEACH SNORKELING exists off **Plum Beach** and **Rouge Beach** on the western peninsula, **Mullet Bay**, the point between Lay Bay and Cole Bay, the point between Cay Bay and Little Bay. When the Atlantic is calm there is excellent snorkeling on the reef off **Dawn Beach** and **Orient Beach** on the east coast. (Orient Beach is clothing-optional. Long Bay and Plum Bay have topless bathing.)

To reach Dawn Beach from Philipsburg, take the road on the northeast side of Salt Pond for two miles, then turn right and continue down the steep hill.

Grand Case Beach on the French side has crowds of small tropical fish and corals off the north end at Creole Rock. Depths are from 10 to 25 ft (boat or beach access). Seas are always calm with no currents and visibility is usually good. To reach it follow the paved road through Grand Case; when it turns to the right, take the dirt road straight ahead.

Dive Operators

ST. MAARTEN

Ocean Explorers Dive Center is on a quiet beach on the south coast at Simpson Bay. It is owned and operated by LeRoy & Dominique French, long-time residents of St. Maarten, who personally escort tours aboard a

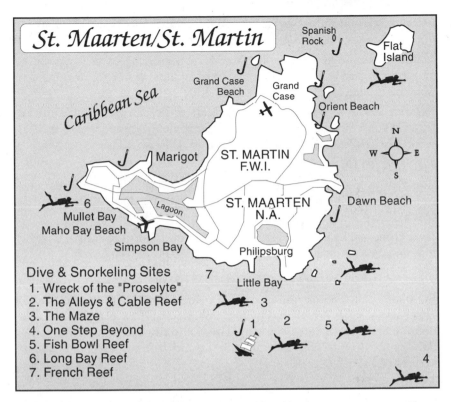

St. Maarten/St. Martin

Caribbean Sea

Spanish Rock

Flat Island

Grand Case Beach

Grand Case

Orient Beach

Marigot

ST. MARTIN F.W.I.

N
W — E
S

6
Mullet Bay
Maho Bay Beach

Lagoon

ST. MAARTEN N.A.

Dawn Beach

Simpson Bay

Philipsburg

Dive & Snorkeling Sites
7
Little Bay

1. Wreck of the "Proselyte"
2. The Alleys & Cable Reef   3
3. The Maze
4. One Step Beyond   1   2   5
5. Fish Bowl Reef
6. Long Bay Reef   4
7. French Reef

fast, 26-ft Robalo dive boat. A maximum of seven divers per trip are taken. Ocean Explorers provides stab jackets with auto inflators, 80 cubic ft tank, regulators with high pressure gauges, and wet suits. The shop has been appointed a NAUI Dream Resort. C-cards required. Resort and certification courses available. ☎ (011) 599-5-45252, fax (011) 599-5-45252. Local 45252. Yachts may contact the shop on VHF 16. Seven night dive/accommodation packages from $400.

Leeward Islands Divers at the Simpson Bay Yacht Club offers PADI, SSI, CMAS and HSAS certification, and resort courses, dive tours to reefs and wrecks, live-aboard sail charters, snorkeling trips, deep sea fishing. Dive/hotel packages are offered from $399 per person, double occupancy for five nights at the Treasure Island Hotel & Casino, five dives, transfers, breakfast daily. ☎ (011) 599-42262, fax (011) 5995-42262. Local 42262. Dive guides speak English, French, German, Dutch, Italian and Spanish.

Trade Winds Dive Center is on the dock at Great Bay Marina, Philipsburg near Chesterfield's Restaurant. The shop visits the south coast dive areas with a 25-ft Mako and a 27-ft, ridged-hull Avon inflatable powered by twin 120-hp outboards. PADI certifications available. Introductory lessons are taught in calm Mullet Bay. ☎ (011) 599-5-54387, fax (011) 599-5-23605; from the French side, 03-54387. Local 54387.

Maho Watersports is on the beach at Mullet Bay on the western peninsula. The shop offers PADI courses, resort courses, trips. ☎ (011) 599-5-54387; from the French side 03-54387. Local 54387.

Pelican Watersports at the Pelican Marina, Pelican Resort in Simpson Bay offers dive and snorkeling excursions. Equipment sales and rentals. ☎ (011) 599-5-42640/42503, ext. 1092 or 1553, fax (011) 599-5-42476.

ST. MARTIN

Lou Scuba Club at the Laguna Beach charges $45 per dive. PADI and CMAS courses. Dive packages are available. ☎ (011) 590-872258, fax (011) 590-8-72014.

Blue Ocean at Le Pirate in Marigot is a PADI and CMAS operation offering trips and courses. ☎ (011) 590-8-78973, fax (011) 590-8-72636.

Accommodations

St. Maarten/St. Martin resorts are not geared specifically toward scuba. Hotel/air packages are offered by tour operators and travel agents. Private home and villa rentals are offered by **Island Hideaways**, ☎ (800) 832-667-9652 or (202) 667-9652. Expect a 5% tax and 15% service charge added to most resort bills.

ST. MARTIN

Grand Case Beach Club, a condo resort on the beach at Grand Case offers 62 air-conditioned studios and suites with balconies or patios and kitchenettes. Oceanview rooms are $290 for two in winter; gardenview rooms are $230. Diving is nearby and can be arranged at the desk. ☎ (800) 223-1588 or (011) 590-875187. Write Box 339, Grand Case 97150, St. Martin.

Green Cay Village, on Orient Beach, offers spacious, private villas in a resort setting. Services include airport pickup, daily maid service, bookings for restaurants, tours and cruises, beach guest privileges. Winter rates start at $2,400 per week. ☎ (800) 832-667-9652 or (202) 667-9652. (Note: Orient Beach is clothing-optional.)

La Flamboyant Hotel Resort, on the lagoon at Nettle Bay, features 271 suites in a colonial setting, two pools, tennis, volleyball, water-sports center, pool bar, beachfront restaurant, meeting rooms and children's playground. Each unit has a private balcony, some with a fully-equipped kitchen. Room rates in winter for a junior suite, double occupancy are $230; one-bedroom suite $295. Summer rates are from $150. No charge for one or two children 2-12 years old sharing their parent's room. For an all-inclusive supplement, add $85 per person per day, $43 per child. ☎ (800) 221-5333 or 305-599-2124, fax 305-599-1946. Write 8390 NW 53rd St, Suite 313, Miami, FL 33166.

ST. MAARTEN

Great Bay Beach Hotel & Casino is a 225-room hotel on the beach at the edge of Philipsburg. Recently renovated rooms have marble baths, air-conditioning, phones. Resort features include casino, restaurants, disco, shopping arcade, two pools, entertainment, tennis. Tradewinds Dive Shop on premises. Winter room rates start at $190 for a mountain view, $225 for ocean view. Add 20% for room tax. ☎ (800) 223-0757, fax (212) 969-9227.

Maho Beach Hotel & Casino features 615 rooms, several restaurants, meeting rooms, freshwater pool, casino, tennis, gym, disco and dive shop. Room rates in winter range from $185 per night to $590. In summer, from $155 to $460. One-tank dives are $45, three boat dives for $120, five for $185. ☎ (800) 223-0757 or (212) 969-9220

Oyster Bay Beach Resort has a dive shop on premises offering equipment rentals, diving and snorkeling tours. The resort, located where the Caribbean meets the Atlantic, offers 40 lovely rooms with private balconies, splendid views and tropical tranquility. French-Caribbean restaurant serves breakfast, lunch and dinner. Decent snorkeling off adjacent, mile-long Dawn Beach, around the rocky point, when seas are calm. Rates during the high season are $170 to $310; low season, $120 to $200. ☎ (800) 231-8331, (011) 599-5-36040 or 36208, fax (011) 599-5-36695.

Pelican Beach Resort & Casino on Simpson Bay offers air-conditioned suites and rooms with color TV, ocean views, kitchens. Amenities include Pelican Watersports, ☎ (011) 599-5-24317, fax (011) 599-5-30080, on premises, five pools, jacuzzis, restaurant, shopping arcade, marina and health spa. Winter room rates are from $95 per night. ☎ (800) 626-9637, fax (954) 927-1007. Web site: www.mangomaxx.com.

Lovely small inns, hotels and guesthouses are widely available, with rates from $65 per night for **Joshua Rose Guest House,** ☎ (011) 599-5 24317, fax (011) 599-5-30080; $70 per night for the **Great Bay Marina Inn,** ☎ (011) 599-5-22167, fax (011) 599-5-24940; $88 for **The Beach House** on Great Bay Beach; $180 for **LaVista,** ☎ (011) 599-5-43005, fax (011) 599-5-43010; and $225 for the magnificent **Ocean Club,** ☎ (011) 599-5-54362 or (203) 227-7017, fax (203) 227-0270. There is also the **Blue Beach Hotel** at Oyster Pond, ☎ (011) 590-8-27-3344, fax (011) 590-87-4213. All may be booked through **ITR,** ☎ (800) 365-8484 or (212) 251-1703.

Secluded Cove, St. Maarten.

Dining

St. Maarten/St. Martin has more than 400 restaurants, featuring a wide variety of international cuisine. For classic French sidewalk cafés, head for Marigot. Philipsburg and Grand Case restaurants offer everything imaginable from Cuban or Mexican aperitifs, Brazilian or Indonesian entrées and Vietnamese desserts, along with Creole, Italian and Continental cuisine. There are also rib shacks or *lolos* where local cooks barbecue chicken, ribs and lobster. Following is a small sampling.

Rick's Place, on Front Street in Dutch St. Maarten, offers great American burgers, Phillie steaks, nachos, burritos and traditional food for breakfast, lunch and dinner. Reasonable prices. ☎ 43005.

Seafood Galley at Bobby's Marina specializes in seafood. ☎ 23253.

Rainbow Seaside Restaurant, 176 Boulevard de Grand Case, offers French cuisine in a beachside setting. ☎ 875580.

The Fish Pot Restaurant, 82 Boulevard de Grand Case, overlooking Grand Case Bay, features classic French cuisine. ☎ 875088.

Captain Oliver's and Marina, at the entrance of Oyster Pond, features an aquarium and mini-zoo. French cuisine. Moderate. ☎ 873000.

Stop & Shop Restaurant and Deli on the waterfront, across from Princess Juliana Airport, ☎ 52626, and at the Simpson Bay Yacht Club, ☎ 43419, offers early breakfasts, freshly made sandwiches on French bread, chili and deli specials. Open seven days for breakfast and lunch, 7:30 am to 8:30 pm.

Find fast food at **McDonalds** on Front Street and **Kentucky Fried Chicken** at Cole Bay on the Dutch side and in Marigot on the French side.

Sightseeing and Other Activities

For guided island tours try **St. Maarten Sightseeing Tours,** ☎ 22753.

You can get a good bird's-eye view of St. Maarten from **Fort Willem** in Philipsburg, but walk up to it rather than drive as the road is treacherous.

The new three-acre **Sint Maarten Zoo and Botanical Gardens** are on the Arch Road in Madame Estate on the Dutch side. The collection focuses on plants and animals of the Caribbean area, including a large reptile collection. Open Mon-Fri, 9 am- 5 pm, weekends 10 am to 6 pm. ☎ 22748.

Windsurfing, jet-skiing, water-skiing, parasailing, sailing, horse-back riding and deep-sea fishing can be arranged through hotel activity desks.

St. Maarten's duty-free shopping is among the best in the Caribbean. Philipsburg features a wide assortment of goods, including perfumes, liquors, cigarettes, crystal, linen and European designer fashions at 25-50% less than the US and Canada. Shops in Philipsburg are open 8 am to 12 pm; 2 pm to 6 pm. Mon through Sat.

Casino gambling is offered by many hotels on the Dutch side.

On the French side, a climb to the top of **Fort Louis at Marigot** affords exceptional views of the surrounding bays and lagoons. Built in 1767 under Louis XVI, it is the islands biggest historical monument. On the road to Bay-Side and Galion, look for the **Butterfly Farm** where rare species offer a visual delight. **The Pottery Workshop**, on the hilltop overlooking the eastern bay, creates original and unique souvenirs.

Facts

Helpful Phone Numbers: Police—Dutch side, ☎ 111; French side, ☎ 87 50 04. Ambulance—Dutch side, ☎ 130; French side, ☎ 87 86 25. Hospital—Dutch side, ☎ 140; French side, ☎ 87 50 07. Pharmacies—Central Drugs, Philipsburg, ☎ 522321.

Nearest Recompression Chamber: Saba (30 miles from the south coast).

Getting There: Major carrier service is available to St. Maarten. American Airlines, ☎ (800) 433-7300, has daily non-stop service from New York, Miami and San Juan. Continental, ☎ (800) 231-0856, offers daily service from Newark; USAir from Baltimore; ALM from Aruba, Curacao and Bonaire.

Driving: On the right. Major car rental offices are at the airport.

Language: English is widely spoken, though Dutch is the official language of St. Maarten and French is the official language of St. Martin.

Documents: US citizens need a passport or original birth certificate with the raised seal. Canadian and UK citizens must have a valid passport and an onward ticket.

Customs: None, but luggage is checked for illegal drugs and contraband.

Airport Tax: $12 per person over two years of age.

Currency: On the Dutch side, the Netherlands Antilles florin or guilder. FL 1.77=US $1. On the French side, the Franc (F). 5 F=US $1.

Climate: Mean temperature is 80° F year-round; 45 inches rainfall annually.

Clothing: Lightweight, casual.

Electricity: 110 volts, 60 cycles.

Religious Services: Roman Catholic, Seventh Day Adventist, Anglican, Baptist, Jehovah's Witness, Methodist.

For Additional Information:

St. Maarten: St. Maarten Tourist Office, 675 Third Ave, NY, NY 10017. ☎ (800) 786-2278 or (212) 953-2084, fax (212) 953-2145.

St. Martin: French West Indies Tourist Office, 444 Madison Avenue, NY, NY 10022. ☎ (900) 990-0040, fax (212) 838-7855. E-mail: sxmto@aol.com. There is a 95¢ charge for the 900 number.

Web site: http://www.interknowledge.com/st-maarten.

St. Vincent and the Grenadines

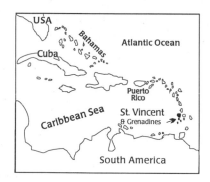

St. Vincent and the Grenadines, a multi-island nation in the eastern Caribbean, is known to just a few discriminating divers and snorkelers, but sailors have been enjoying her sheltered coves, beautiful beaches and protected harbors for centuries.

The capital and chief port is Kingstown on St. Vincent, the main island at 18 miles long and 11 miles wide. St. Vincent is also the most densely populated, with 100,000 residents. Black and white sand beaches loop most of the island's coastline. La Soufriere, an active volcano and the highest point, reaching 4,048 ft, dominates the mountainous north end. It erupted last on Good Friday, the 13th of April 1979, causing extensive damage to farmland, houses and roads.

The Grenadines comprise 32 small islands and cays strung out like emerald stepping stones between St. Vincent and Grenada. All but two, Carriacou and Petit Martinique, are a part of this nation. Many are uninhabited or the site of a single estate or resort. A favorite for many yachtsmen and divers are the tiny, uninhabited Tobago Cays, a five-island national park celebrated for its translucent waters and adjacent Horseshoe Reef—a magnificent snorkeling area.

The larger Grenadine islands include Bequia (beck-way), Carib for "Island of the Clouds," Canouan (Can-o-wan), Mayreau (My-row), Mustique, Union, and Carriacou. All are postcard-perfect, fringed in part by soft, white sand beaches and towering palm trees. Dive trips take off from St. Vincent, Bequia, and Union Island, a tiny, mile-long rock 40 miles south of St. Vincent.

Also tiny Palm Island (formerly Prune Island) and Petit St. Vincent are world class, one-resort islands offering guests luxurious jungle hideaways.

Intrepid divers, snorkelers, birdwatchers and hikers are slowly expanding the small tourist population, but the country's economy is chiefly agricultural

---

Contributors: Dennis and Karen Sabo, Landfall Productions; Bill Tewes, Dive St. Vincent.

with exports of bananas, arrowroot, coconuts, cotton, sugar, cassava and peanuts.

Two main airports, one at Arnos Vale on St. Vincent's south coast, and another on Bequia, nine miles south of St. Vincent, serve the area. The most direct air service from the US is through Barbados. Mustique Airways offers excellent inter-island service. Mustique, Canouan and Union Island have airstrips with scheduled and charter flights. Sailing and yacht charters are available at the marinas. By boat, the trip from St. Vincent to Bequia, the largest of the Grenadines, takes about an hour.

When to Go

The dry season is from Dec to April. Average rainfall on the coastal areas is 60 inches. The climate is tropical, tempered by the trade winds with a mean temperature of about 80° F.

Insects are a problem year-round, especially for hikers. Pack plenty of bug repellent.

History

The first inhabitants of St. Vincent and the Grenadines came by small craft from South America. First the Ciboney settled in, then the peaceful Arawak Indians, who later fell to the Caribs. Slaves who escaped from Barbados plantations literally "blew" in by makeshift craft with the prevailing winds, along with those who survived shipwrecks near St. Vincent and Bequia. These freed Africans, known as the Black Caribs, fought off Europeans side-by-side with the yellow Caribs. Despite a claim of "discovery" by Christopher Columbus in 1498, Europeans did not settle for 200 years. During the 17th and 18th centuries the island and surrounding rocks and islets changed hands between the British and the French. In 1763 the area was ceded to the British crown, but it wasn't until 1969 that the United Kingdom declared St. Vincent an associated state. The northern Grenadines, from Bequia to Petit St. Vincent, were administered by St. Vincent, while Carriacou and islets south of it were governed by Grenada. On Oct 27, 1979, St. Vincent and the Grenadines became an independent state.

Best Dive and Snorkeling Sites

Distinctive underwater landscapes encompass rocky canyons, caves, ledges and grottoes carved into mountain-sized boulders. Black corals exist at much shallower depths than normal.

ST. VINCENT

St. Vincent's best dive sites lie off the southwest corner of the island where calm sea conditions prevail. Strong currents, which maintain outstanding water clarity, occur in some areas. Private boaters should check local conditions before diving or snorkeling.

☆☆☆☆ **Bottle Reef**, a wall and reef dive located off a point under Fort Charlotte near Kingstown, takes its name from a huge collection of antique rum and gin bottles tossed down from the fort during the 18th century. Reef fish, including huge tarpons and morays, abound. Swim round the point of the wall to spot tuna, amber jacks, and bonito. Immense sea fans, towering gorgonians and sponges shelter hermit crabs, octopi and mini-critters. Bottle Reef is fine for all level divers and experienced snorkelers. Sea conditions range from calm to choppy, depending on the wind.

☆☆☆ **Turtle Bay Reef**, a shallow wall near Bottle Reef, brims over with giant gorgonians, sponges, club fingers, and star corals. Masses of fish swarm the area. Crabs, turtles, huge spotted eels and rare yellow frogfish are frequently spotted. The reef bottoms at 30 ft with more shallow areas for snorkeling. Good for novice divers. Visibility exceeds 80 ft. Seas are calm.

☆☆☆☆ **The Wall**, 200 yds off the western shore, starts with a shallow ledge at 18 ft, then slopes off into a stream of monster-sized boulders. Countless fish and mini-critters hide in the crevices and cracks. Big basket sponges bedeck the mammoth rocks. Large numbers of snappers, copper sweepers, squirrel fish, grunts, barracuda, and kingfish inhabit the reef. Black coral trees grow at depth. Average scuba depths are from 45 to 90 ft. Good for all level divers and experienced snorkelers.

☆☆☆☆☆ **New Guinea Reef**, just 10 minutes from Dive St. Vincent's dock, drops down a sheer cliff from a beautiful cove of orchids and lush vegetation. The reef starts at 40 ft, where an outpost of pastel gorgonians and finger sponges gives way to eight-ft-wide purple and orange sea fans. A cave at 80 ft shelters hard and soft black corals that bloom in shades of yellow, pink, green, white and red. Sea horses, large schools of reef fish, big angels and morays inhabit the ledges and overhangs. A great dive! Good, too, because of its shallow spots, for advanced snorkelers. Seas usually calm.

☆☆☆ **The Wrecks** refer to the rubble, anchors and cannons of two old wrecks in Kingston Harbor, and the nearby *Seimstrand*, an intact 120-ft freighter in 80 ft of water. All attract huge groupers, rays and eels. Better for diving than snorkeling, but the clear water gives good views to snorkelers. Sea conditions are calm.

☆☆☆☆☆ **The Gardens** is a spectacular shallow reef located 15 yds from the shoreline, just north of Kingston. Frogfish, hordes of angelfish, creole wrasse, gray snapper, kingfish, parrots and soldierfish crowd a profusion of soft, club and finger corals. Big boulders, brain corals, and colonies of iridescent yellow tube sponges cover the bottom. Perfect for shallow dives and snorkeling. Seas are calm. Boat access.

BEQUIA

Bequia's leeward side is a marine park protecting eight miles of pristine reefs. Ferry and air service is available from St. Vincent.

☆☆☆☆ **L'Anse Chemin**, a 30-minute trip from Admiralty Bay, is a drift dive. Healthy corals and a big fish population popularize this spot. Seawhips, feather corals, orange-cup coral, lettuce and brain corals, blue sponges and mauve seafans envelop the rocky bottom. As many as 20 flamingo tongues may be attached to one seafan. Fish life is superb with large parrot fish and groupers, queen trigger fish, queen and French angels, spotted and juvenile drums, gray snapper, Spanish mackerel, tuna, creole wrasse and schooling reef fish. Nurse sharks are seen beneath the ledges of the reef. Depths range from 60 to 90 ft.

☆☆☆ **Ship's Stern** is a maze of swim-through tunnels, pinnacles, caverns and grottoes, all lavish with a thick cover of lacy corals, gorgonians and sponges. Big groupers and schooling fish abound. The site is a five-minute boat ride from the dock at Admiralty Bay. Depths are between 40 and 90 ft. Seas are calm.

☆☆☆ **Northwest Point**, a five-minute boat ride from the dock, is a seascape of coral buttresses. Throngs of squirrel fish, margate, trumpetfish, parrotfish, morays, chromis, grunts and creole wrasse are in residence. Micro life is abundant with corkscrew anemones, flamingo tongues, flaming scallops, arrow crabs, neon gobies, barber shrimp and octopi. Seas generally calm. *The* spot for night dives.

☆☆ **West Cay**, off Bequia's southernmost tip, is the meeting point of the Atlantic and Caribbean. Mixing currents make this an exciting wall/drift dive and the best place to spot huge grouper, reef sharks, turtles, durgons, jack and spadefish. Photogenic with big sponges and dramatic overhangs. Depths are from 15 to 115 ft. For experienced divers.

☆☆ **Wreck of the *M.S. Lirero*.** This 110-ft freighter was scuttled in 1986 to create an artificial reef. She sits upright in 60 ft of water, covered over with red and yellow sponges and soft corals. The hull may be penetrated.

OUT ISLANDS

Dive trips to Union Island, Tobago Cayes, Petit St. Vincent, Palm and Mayreau take off from Union Island and Canuoan. World's End Reef shelters these areas from wind-driven seas and storms.

☆☆☆ **Mayreau Gardens**, a 20-minute boat ride from the dock at Union Island, is a sparkling forest of branching and plate corals. Tornados of fish, stingrays and exotic fish drift with you as the current carries you along the walls and channels of this colorful reef. Average depth is 60 ft.

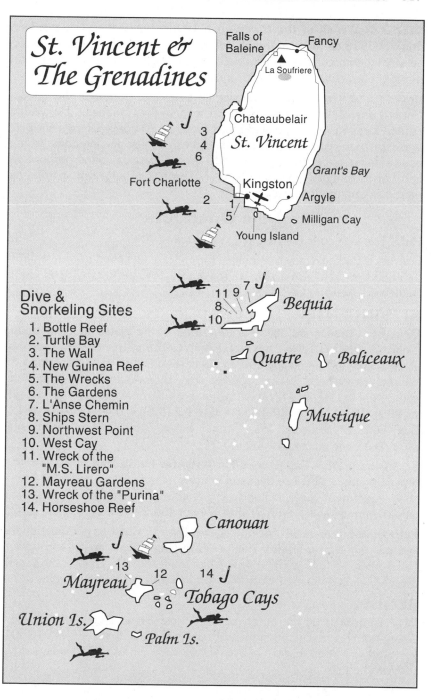

St. Vincent &
The Grenadines

Falls of Baleine

Fancy

La Soufriere

Chateaubelair

St. Vincent

Grant's Bay

Fort Charlotte

Kingston

Argyle

Milligan Cay

Young Island

Bequia

Quatre

Baliceaux

Mustique

Canouan

Mayreau

Tobago Cays

Union Is.

Palm Is.

Dive & Snorkeling Sites

1. Bottle Reef
2. Turtle Bay
3. The Wall
4. New Guinea Reef
5. The Wrecks
6. The Gardens
7. L'Anse Chemin
8. Ships Stern
9. Northwest Point
10. West Cay
11. Wreck of the "M.S. Lirero"
12. Mayreau Gardens
13. Wreck of the "Purina"
14. Horseshoe Reef

☆☆☆☆ **Wreck of the *Purina*** is a 140-ft merchant trawler that went down in 1918 off Mayreau Island. Intact, the wreck at 40 ft is the center of activity for communities of yellow tail, huge French and grey angels, spotted morays, barracuda, nurse shark, squirrel fish and sergeant majors.

☆☆☆☆☆ **Horseshoe Reef,** which skirts four islands in the Tobago Cays, is one of the top five snorkeling spots in the Caribbean. Despite the remote location, it is populated by as many as 70 boats per day. Visibility is exceptional—you can see the reef and fish by just peering down from a boat. Depths range from the surface to 80 ft. Gigantic seafans, gorgonians, and barrel sponges highlight the reef. Throngs of angelfish, grunts, big parrotfish and grouper cluster about.

Dive Operators

Note: The area code is scheduled to change to 784.

Dive/travel packages may be arranged through Landfall Productions. ☎ (800) 525-3833 or (510) 794-1599, fax (510) 794-1617. Write to 39189 Cedar Boulevard, Newark, CA 94560.

ST. VINCENT

Dive St. Vincent sits on the southern tip of the island opposite Young Island. Owner Bill Tewes, a NAUI, PADI, CMAS instructor, offers personalized scuba and snorkeling trips to the best reef and wall dives around St. Vincent. Resort and C-card courses. Bill is an outstanding underwater photographer. He and his work appear on St. Vincent postage stamps. ☎ (809) 457-4714 or (809) 457-4928, fax (809) 457-4948. Write to PO Box 864, St. Vincent, WI. E-mail: bill2s@caribsurf.com. Web site: www.divestvincent.com.

St. Vincent Dive Experience/Underwater Unlimited offers dive and snorkeling tours, NAUI certification courses, resort courses and a full line of rental equipment. Sleek, canopied boats whisk divers to the best sites, most only 10 minutes away. ☎ (809) 456-9741 or 456-2768, fax (809) 457-2768.

Petit Byahaut dives St. Vincent's leeward coast. The shop packages diving and five nights at a 50-acre nature resort with private beach and decent shore dives. $1,020. ☎ (809) 457-7008, fax (809) 457-7008. E-mail: petit byahaut/@outahere.com. Web site: www.outahere.com/petitbyahaut.

BEQUIA

Dive Bequia is on the beach at the Ginger Bread Hotel. Owner, New Jersey-born Bob Sachs, offers tours aboard a 22-ft Mako. ☎ (809) 458-3504, fax (809) 458-3886. E-mail: bobsax@caribsurf.com. Web site: www.empg.com/divebequia.

Sunsports Diving Bequia a full-service PADI facility on Admiralty Bay at the Gingerbread Complex, offers three trips daily to nearby dive sites. Boats carry a maximum of 10 people, making three trips daily to sites within a 15-minute radius. Staff sets up, rinses and stores your dive gear. ☎ (809) 458-3577, fax (809) 457-3031. Packages from the US, ☎ (800) 525-3822. E-Mail: sunsport@caribsurf.com. Web site: www.vincy.com/sunsport.htm.

UNION

Grenadines Dive at the Anchorage Yacht Club tours the Tobago Cays and other southern Grenadine dive and snorkeling spots. ☎ (809) 458-8138, fax (809) 458-8122. Yacht rendezvous. Write to Glenroy Adams, Grenadines Dive, Union Island, St. Vincent, WI.

Snorkeling excursions aboard a 60-ft catamaran are offered by **Grenadine Tours**, ☎ (809) 435-8451.

Accommodations

Rates listed are based on double occupancy and, unless othewise stated, do not include a 10% service charge and 7% government tax, which is added to the bill.

Money-saving accommodation/dive travel packages for groups, individuals and agents are offered through **Landfall Productions**. ☎ (800) 525-3833 or (510) 794-1599, fax (510) 794-1617. Write to 39189 Cedar Boulevard, Newark, CA 94560. Island area code may change to 784.

ST. VINCENT

Coconut Beach Inn, at Villa Beach in Kingston, is a tiny inn with an excellent open-air bar and restaurant. The garden patio extends to the water's edge. Black sand beach. Room rates are from $52 to $65 per day. Dive St. Vincent picks you up on the hotel beach. Major credit cards. ☎ (809) 457-4900, fax (809) 457-4900, or book through your travel agent. Write to them at Indian Bay, Box 355, St. Vincent, WI.

The Umbrella Beach, one mile from the airport, is a nine-room hotel adjacent to Dive St. Vincent. Rooms are simple with ceiling fans, private bath. Porches overlook the gardens or waterfront. Each unit has a fully-equipped kitchen. Low per-person package rates for seven nights, 10 dives run from $565. Includes transfers. Non-divers pay $245. ☎ (809) 458-4651, fax (809) 457-4930.

The Grand View Beach Hotel at Villa Point is a plush 19-room resort set in a renovated plantation house on eight tropical acres. The dining room has a great view of the neighboring islands. Tennis, pool, AC, TV, bar, fitness center. Good snorkeling off the beach. Transportation is provided to Dive St. Vincent's dock. Room rates in winter are $150 for a single, $210 for a double. Rates with diving during the high season range from $1,438 per person for seven nights and six dives. Non-divers pay from $845. Prices drop dramatically during summer. ☎ (800) 525-3833, (800) 424-5500, (800) 223-1108, (809) 458-7421 or (809) 458-4811. E-mail: granview@caribsurf.com. Web site: www.cpscaribnet.com/ads/grandview/grandview.html.

Young Island is a short 200-yd hop by boat from the southern tip of St. Vincent. This 25-acre tropical-garden island offers 29 individual cottages featuring king or twin beds, a refrigerator, ceiling fan and private patio. Life is ultra-casual. Packages offer an optional two nights aboard one of the resort's 44-ft sailing yachts, complete with captain and cook. No children under five years accepted between Jan 15 and March 15. Diving is with Dive St. Vincent's. Snorkelers walk to the reef! Breakfast, lunch and dinner are included in seven-night dive packages. Rates per person for seven nights, 10 dives are from $2,075 for superior rooms (nearest the beach) in the high season, from $1,230 in summer. Room rates with breakfast and dinner (double) are from $500 per day. Summer (April 14-Dec 19) rates are $1,600 for a dive package, $1,275 for a non-diver, $180 per person for each extra night. Deluxe and luxury accommodations at higher prices. No children under 5 between Jan 15 and March 15. For dive packages, ☎ (800) 525-3833. Hotel only, ☎ (800) 223-1108. In the UK, 0800-373742. In St. Vincent, (809) 458-4826, fax (809) 457-4567. Write to PO Box 211, St. Vincent, WI.

Beachcombers Hotel, originally a seaside family home, has 12 hilltop rooms with private bath and covered patios where your breakfast of fresh fruits, assorted homemade bread and beverages is served. The Beach House restaurant and bar offers fresh seafood and local vegetables. Weather permitting, dive boats will pick up and drop off at the hotel beach. Gear storage is provided at the Dive Center. Room rates are $60 to $80 per day. Rates for a diver are from $699 per week. Non-divers pay $390 per week. Dive/hotel packages are through Landfall, ☎ (800) 525-3833. Direct, ☎ (809) 458-4283, fax (809) 458-4385. Tailor-made vacations staying at the hotel and sailing on Beachcomber's 44-ft motor-sail yacht can be arranged.

Petit Byahaut, a secluded 50-acre valley on the leeward coast of St. Vincent, is accessible only from the sea. There are no roads, no phones and no TVs. This unique naturalist outpost provides ferry service from Kingstown by prior arrangement. Diving and snorkeling are offered in Petit Byahaut Bay and other walls and reefs along the coast. Guests stay in room-sized tents on large roofed decks on a hillside overlooking the sea and beach. Each tent features a queen-sized bed, hammock, solar powered lights and fresh water showers. Facilities include a restaurant, cocktail bar, boutique, secluded beach, dive shop, small sail and paddle boats, kayaks, water taxi service, moorings and air fills. Per person rates, which include all meals, snorkeling and use of small boats, year-round for five days, are $695; by the day, $125 to $145. Scuba packages are $325 for 10 dives, including shore, night and boat dives or unlimited self-guided shore diving for $200 per person, per week. Good snorkeling off the shore. ☎ (809) 457- 7008, VHF 68. Transfers for stays of three nights or longer. E-mail: petitbyahaut@outahere.com. Web site: www.outahere.com/petitbyahaut.

BEQUIA

From St. Vincent you can reach Bequia by Mustique Airways or ferry. The nine-mile ferry ride takes 70 to 90 minutes. Trips depart the main dock in Kingstown. Direct flights from Barbados are available.

Frangipani, on the shore of Admiralty Bay, accommodates guests in eight hillside garden cottages built of stone and hardwood. Units have two beds, modern bath, ceiling fan and sun deck over the bay. Bar and excellent restaurant on premises. Adjacent to Sunsports Dive Center. Per-person rates are from $775 for seven nights/10 dives. ☎ (800) 525-3833 or (809) 458-3255.

The Gingerbread Complex is on Admiralty Bay and adjacent to Sunsports Dive Center. The complex is three apartments, a restaurant and boutique. Good for an extended stay. Apartments have large porches, full kitchens and modern baths. Divers pay $665 for seven nights, 10 dives. Non-divers pay $305. ☎ (800) 525-3833 or (510) 794-1599. Write to 39189 Cedar Boulevard, Newark, CA 94560.

Friendship Bay Hotel sits on a hilltop overlooking distant green islands and the sea. The 60-room resort has a tennis court, dive shop and its own jetty for visitors with boats and for watersports. Decent snorkeling off the hotel beach. Swedish owners Lars and Margit pamper guests with gourmet cuisine in the lovely outdoor dining room and bar. Near Port Elisabeth, the capital of Bequia, and the Tobago Cays for diving and snorkeling. Room rates range from $90 to $200 per day. Winter package rates for a diver at $1,219, oceanfront, $1,015, oceanview, for seven nights including five days of diving (10 dives), breakfast daily, tax, service charge and airport transfers. Non-divers pay $615. Summer rates (April 21 to Nov 30) drop to $1,015 for oceanfront, $850 for oceanview, $450 and $615 for non-divers. ☎ (800) 525-3833; direct (809) 458-3222, fax (809) 458-3840.

Plantation House offers 25 pastel cottages, each with a private veranda, king or twin beds, ceiling fan and stocked mini-bar. Resort features a sunken pool lounge, open-air dining room and weekly entertainment. Divers pay $1,450 each for seven nights and 10 dives—including breakfast and dinner. Non-divers pay $1,030. Add 17% government tax/service charge. Dive Bequia is on the resort beach. ☎ (800) 525-3833, (809) 458-3425 or (212) 599-8280. Write to Box 16, Admiralty Bay, Bequia, St. Vincent, WI.

Petit St. Vincent is a private 113-acre island touted as the Caribbean's most luxurious and romantic hideaway. Accommodations are in 22 cottages, each with spectacular views. Each cottage has a living room, bedroom, bathroom and patio. Meals are served in the main pavilion, at your cottage or on the beach if you wish. Diving is provided by Grenadines Dive with pickup at the resort's dock. Week-long dive packages are offered from $2,645 per person—breakfast, lunch and dinner included and round-trip transfer from Union Island airport. Add 15% tax. ☎ (800) 525-3833, (800) 654-9326 or (809) 458-8801. No credit cards. Closed Sept and Oct.

Julie's Guest House, in the center of Bequia's main harbor town, may be the bargain spot of the Caribbean. This small hotel features 19 clean rooms, each with private bath and shower. Julie's restaurant offers good seafood and fresh fruits and vegetables from their own garden. Rates with 10 dives, breakfast and dinner daily for seven nights are $599 per diver. Non-divers pay $224. Extra night per person with meals costs $32. Dive gear stores at the Sunsports Dive center. ☎ (800) 525-3833, (809) 458-3304, fax (809) 458-3812.

Dawn's Creole Garden, at the end of Lower Bay, offers studio apartments, rec room, restaurant and bar. Good snorkeling off the beach. Sunsports Dive Center will store gear and will pick up and drop off on the beach, wave action permitting. Apartment with diving, but without meals, costs $640 per person, per week. Non-divers pay $280. ☎ (800) 525-3833 or (809) 458-3154, fax (809) 458-3154.

CANOUAN (Island of the Turtles)

Jump-off point to the Tobago Cays and the magnificent Horseshoe Reef, Canuoan sits 25 miles south of St. Vincent between Mustique and Union Island. A popular anchorage for sailors, this island has recently begun a multi-million-dollar expansion program on the airport with plans for night landings, an extended runway and new terminal building. In addition, the new 60-unit **Canouan Beach Resort,** ☎ (800) 961-5006, (809) 458-8888, fax (809) 458-8875, was under construction as we went to press. Canouan is about a one-hour flight from Barbados.

Tamarind Beach Hotel & Yacht Club offers 42 luxurious rooms on Grandbay Sandy Beach. The resort services yachts with provisions and free mooring. Two good restaurants and a beach bar serve a variety of pizzas and pastas, grilled fish and meats. Room rates per day for a double, including breakfast, lunch and dinner, are $300 in season. Guests are met at the airport. ☎ (800) 223-1108 or (809) 458-8044, fax (809) 458-8851. Kayak diving and snorkeling from the beach. Dive/hotel accommodations with meals for seven nights are from $1,385 per person. ☎ (800) 510-1599.

UNION

More developed than Mayreau or Canouan, Union is St. Vincent's customs and clearance point of entry for yachts. The island's lush appearance, splendid mountainous terrain and beautiful beaches attract more and more visitors each year. Near Tobago Cays.

Sunny Grenadines Hotel is a very simple, inexpensive place to stay (under $60 per night—room only). Guest rooms are in two-story stone cottages with twin beds and small porches. Kitchen units available. ☎ (809) 458-8327.

Anchorage Yacht offers comfortable cottages at the marina. ☎ (809) 458-8221. Expensive.

PALM ISLAND

Palm Island, a privately owned resort, lies about a mile east of Union Island. To get there, fly from Barbados to Union, where a resort launch picks you up for the 10-minute trip to Palm Island.

Palm Island Beach Resort is owned and operated by the Caldwell family. They sailed around the world to find this "remote hideaway in the tradewinds" and transformed it from the jungle-covered, swamp-ridden, mosquito-infested "Prune Island" into the intimate oasis it is today. Guests stay in beach-front cottages with king or twin beds, private bath, refrigerator, fans, coffee maker, hot water, screens, beach furniture, floats and patio. Diving and snorkeling trips take off from the resort Dive Shack, run by local dive instructor David Allen. Thirty staff members cater to 48 guests' whims. Amenities include a boutique, yacht club, game room with ping pong, TV, table games and books (no TV in the rooms), superb gourmet restaurant, beach bar that serves burgers, fast food, ice cream and beverages. Rates between Dec 2 and Jan 9 run $365 per couple, per day. A third person pays $106. From Jan 10-Jan 31, rates are $290 per couple, per day; a third person pays $95 and singles pay $245. From Feb 1 to Apr 14, it's $365 for a couple per day, $245 for single occupancy; Apr 15-Dec 20, $270 per couple per day, $174 for a single. Rates include three meals, tea, laundry, transfers, tennis and most watersports. Good snorkeling exists about 100 ft from off the beach amidst boulders that shelter throngs of fish. ☎ (800) 999-PALM, (212) 242-4700, fax (212) 242-4768, direct (809) 458-8824, fax (809) 458-8804.

Dining

ST. VINCENT

The Aquatic Club, on the waterfront, offers local and international dishes. Open from 11 am till 2 pm for lunch, from 6 pm to closing for dinner. For yachtsmen, they offer laundry, ice water, boarding and cleaning facilities. ☎ 456-1232.

Basil's in the Cobblestone Inn, a converted 1800's sugar warehouse, offers a buffet lunch, seafood pastas, lobster and excellent French wines. On Bay St in Kingstown. Buffet on Fridays. Entrées from $10 to $30. ☎ 457-2713.

Beachcombers, on the beach in an exotic garden, offers an interesting à la carte menu and Friday night barbecue. Open from 7 am till the last guest leaves. From $8 to $30. ☎ 458-4283.

The Bounty Restaurant and Art Gallery on Halifax Street in Kingstown offers inexpensive steaks, *rotis*, pizza, burgers, pastries and homemade ice cream. No credit cards. ☎ 456-1776.

French Restaurant, adjacent to the Umbrella Hotel, is one of the finest and one of the most expensive in the islands. The restaurant features its own lobster/crab pool from which guests select their entrée. Menu specialties are charcoal-grilled lamb chops, or beef tenderloin in garlic butter, crêpes, curried conch and steamed fish in a green pepper sauce. Reservations needed in season. Entrées from $23 to $44. Open daily 9 am to 9:30 pm. ☎ 458-4972.

The Lagoon and Green Flash Bar, at the Lagoon Marina & Hotel, features breakfast, lunch and dinner. Good conch fritters, smoked fish and fresh seafood. Dinner entrées are from $22 to $35. ☎ 458-4308.

Join the locals at **Lime N Pub** two doors down from the Umbrella Beach Hotel. Specials are pumpkin, lobster and callaloo soups, veal, chicken, steak, burgers and pizza. No credit cards. Moderate. ☎ 458-4227.

Young Island, directly across the channel from the French Restaurant, features a super barbecue and steel band on Saturdays (about $20 per person). Call for the Young Island water taxi from the phone at the dock adjacent to the French Restaurant. ☎ 458-4826.

BEQUIA

Credit cards are not accepted. Most restaurants close on Sundays.

Mac's Pizzeria, seen on *Lifestyles of the Rich & Famous,* serves a world class lobster pizza, tangy pita sandwiches and mouth watering brownies and lime pie. It's on the beach at Port Elizabeth. Call for reservations. ☎ 458-3474. No credit cards. Moderate.

Other diver-dinner favorites are **Old Fig Tree** overlooking the harbor, **Port Hole** in Port Elizabeth for great rotis, **Harpoon Saloon** for a cold drink and **Daphne's** for home cooking.

For a special treat try **Le Petit Jardin** in Port Elizabeth. ☎ 458-3318. No credit cards. Expensive.

Sightseeing and Other Activities

Prime topside sightseeing attractions are on St. Vincent, the most popular being the **Botanical Gardens.** Located north of Kingstown on the west coast, the 20-acre gardens are the oldest in the Western Hemisphere, established for growing herbs, spices and medicinal plants.

Garden paths wind through passion flowers, breadfruit, ironwood, and blooming jacaranda trees; sealing wax palms (a sticky gum taken from the base is used for sealing envelopes), coconut, avocado pears, huge mahogany, nutmeg, cocoa and fragrant ylang-ylang trees—oil from the ylang-ylang is used to make perfumes. The oldest tree sprouted about 1765.

Rugged hiking trails criss-cross St. Vincent's 33,000 acres of forest. The nicest are the **Vermont Nature Trails** in the upper part of the Buccament Valley, directly north of Kingstown—home to a community of 100 parrots which may be spotted early mornings or late afternoons.

Fort Charlotte, named for the wife of King George III, is only a few minutes drive from Kingstown. Situated on a 600-ft ridge, the fort is complete with a moat and drawbridge to the mainland. Visitors enjoy panoramic views of the Grenadines from the old gunner ports.

Baleine Falls is reached by boat and a short hike through a rocky stream. Wear boat shoes or aqua socks and plan on most of a day for the trip (about a one-hour boat ride, arranged through either dive shop), which includes snorkeling and diving stops. Rum punch and lunch are usually a part of the deal. The falls, which would befit a Hollywood set, are 60 ft high and drop into a deep crystalline pool. They are located on the northwest coast near the northern tip of the island.

Shop for batiks, tie-dyed sarongs, and crafts in **Kingstown**—a charming port town with cobblestone sidewalks, old stone buildings and a cluster of three churches.

Facts

Helpful Phone Numbers: Police, ☎ 457-1211; hospital, ☎ 456-1185; Department of Tourism, ☎ 456-2610; E.T. Joshua Iinternational Airport, St. Vincent, ☎ 458-4379. Pharmacies: Kingstown, Reliance, ☎ 456-1734, or Deane's, ☎ 457-1522; Bequia, ☎ 458-3296. Note: The small islands do **not** have phones.

Nearest Recompression Chamber: Barbados.

Airlines: From the US, American Eagle, ☎ (800) 433-7300, flies direct from San Juan to St. Vincent with 46-seat turboprops. Flights from the US also connect with LIAT, ☎ (809) 457-1821, and Mustique Airways, ☎ (800) 223-0599 or (800) 526-4789) in Barbados. Mustique flies from Barbados to St. Vincent, Bequia, Union, and Mustique. Other carriers with connecting flights are BWIA, British Airways, Air Canada and Air France.

Island Transportation: Taxis and buses are available at the airports.

Driving: On the left. A temporary license is required and costs about US $9. Rental cars are available on St. Vincent at the airport. Johnson's U-Drive, ☎ 458-4864.

Documents: US and Canadian citizens must have a passport and onward ticket.

Currency: The Eastern Caribbean Dollar exchange rate is approximately EC $2.70=US $1. Major credit cards are accepted at large hotels and restaurants on St. Vincent. With some exceptions, cash is necessary in the Grenadines.

Language: English is spoken everywhere.

Climate: Average air temperature is 86° F; water, 80°.

Clothing: Very casual. Pack light. Bring sneakers or light hiking shoes if you plan to hike the trails. Aqua socks are good for mucking about the shallows.

Electricity: 220 volts, 50 cycles. Bring an adaptor.

Time: Atlantic Standard (EST + 1 hr).

Departure Tax: EC $20 (US $7).

Religious Services: Catholic, Methodist.

Additional Information: *In the US*—☎ (800) 729-1726, fax (212) 949-5946; 801 2nd Ave. 21st floor, NY, NY; or (214) 239-6451, fax (214) 239-1002. *In Canada*—100 University Ave., Suite 504, Toronto, Ontario M5J 1V6. *In the UK*—☎ 071-937-6570. Web site: http://www.discover-stvincent.net/.

Tobago

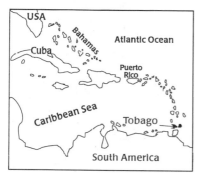

Tobago, the "Robinson Crusoe Island," is Trinidad's small sister island. Separated by 22 miles of sea, both islands lie about seven miles off Venezuela's coast. Tobago sits on the South American continental shelf at the southernmost tip of the Lesser Antilles arc. It has a land area of 116 square miles and a mountainous interior, with a central backbone known as Main Ridge that runs most of its length. Pigeon Peak, its highest point, reaches 1,700 ft. The hillsides and lowlands are dotted with thatched cottages, each with an array of prayer flags on bamboo poles. Most of the people live on lower ground and are fishermen or farmers. The northwestern Caribbean coast is ribboned with smooth beaches fringed by palms, breadfruit, mango and banana trees.

Inland jungles support exotic wildlife and luxuriant vegetation, including flowering trees such as the crimson immortelle, pink poui, with its large bunches of trumpet-shaped flowers, its cousin, the yellow poui, and the purplish queen of flowers (pride of India). There are more than 700 species of orchids. The country's national flower is the chaconia, or wild poinsettia. Among the animal species are 60 kinds of bats, rodents such as the agouti and spotted paca (lappe), the pig-like peccary, the armadillo, the caiman (related to alligators), many types of snakes (including poisonous ones), and a great variety of birds and butterflies. This is the only place outside New Guinea where birds of paradise exist in their wild state.

The main tourist areas are Scarborough, the capital, and along the Caribbean coast between Plymouth and the island's southern tip.

About half of Tobago's 40,000 people are of black African descent, including those of mixed race, 40% have South Asian ancestry (the "East Indians") and the rest are of European or Chinese descent. Many languages are spoken, but English is the official and common medium of communication.

DIVING

Diving Tobago is adventure diving at its best. It's not just a visual experience, but a delight for the entire body and spirit. There are drift dives, "flights" through churning cuts, holes swarming with huge pelagics, monster coral forms, caves, grottoes, fish and more fish. For the diver grown weary of the ordinary, it is therapeutic.

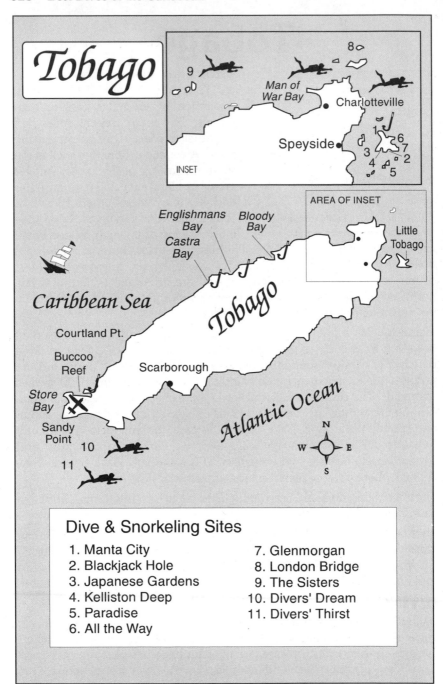

Tobago

INSET

9

8

Man of
War Bay

Charlotteville

Speyside

1
6
7
2
3
4
5

AREA OF INSET

Little
Tobago

Englishmans
Bay

Bloody
Bay

Castra
Bay

Caribbean Sea

Tobago

Courtland Pt.

Buccoo
Reef

Scarborough

Atlantic Ocean

Store
Bay

Sandy
Point

10

11

N
W   E
S

Dive & Snorkeling Sites

1. Manta City
2. Blackjack Hole
3. Japanese Gardens
4. Kelliston Deep
5. Paradise
6. All the Way

7. Glenmorgan
8. London Bridge
9. The Sisters
10. Divers' Dream
11. Divers' Thirst

Tobago's best dive areas are nurtured by fresh and saltwater currents that attract an ever-present population of manta rays, huge turtles, dolphins and sharks. Less spectacular, but calmer, shallow-reef areas exist that are good for snorkeling and novice divers. The most famous spot, but not necessarily the most interesting is Buccoo Reef off the island's northwest corner.

When to Go

January through June brings the best visibility and the fewest mosquitoes. Rainfall is heaviest from July to Dec, although it occurs in every month. Yearly precipitation varies in different parts of the islands but almost everywhere averages at least 50 inches. The islands are south of the normal hurricane belt.

The climate of the country is tropical, with little seasonal variation in temperature but with a significant contrast between day and night readings. Northeast trade winds moderate the heat.

History

Christopher Columbus discovered Trinidad in 1498, but never mentioned Tobago. The island later made up for this neglect by changing hands more frequently than perhaps any other Caribbean island. For two centuries, the Dutch, English, and French fought for control. The Treaty of Amiens gave Tobago to France, but the island was ceded to Great Britain in 1814. For a while the island was declared neutral territory. This, however, made it irresistible to pirates and Tobago turned into such a dangerous outpost of rogues that in 1762 the British invaded just to clear them out.

Subsequently, a prosperous sugar industry developed on the island and "as rich as a Tobago planter" became a familiar saying.

In 1976, Trinidad and Tobago severed its ties with the British crown and in 1980 Tobago was granted limited autonomy, exercised through its new House of Assembly.

Tourism increased greatly after World War II, becoming the country's second-largest industry as fast air service brought the islands within easy reach of North America. Tobago was discovered by tourists seeking a quiet, unspoiled tropical island.

Best Dive and Snorkeling Sites

Freshwater overflow from the Orinoco and the Amazon rivers is carried past the south and east coasts of Tobago by the Guyana Current. This mix of salt and freshwater nutrients produces massive plankton blooms that support a huge range of marine life. Many deep-sea fish are found much closer to the surface here than normal.

Manta rays, turtles and dolphin are the star attractions, with huge, silvery tarpon, spotted eagle rays, stoplight parrotfish, queen angels, electric eels, durgons, squid, jewfish, lizard fish, spadefish, triggerfish, occasional black tip sharks and hammerheads as a splendid supporting cast. Little Tobago is also a haven for every imaginable critter, including multi-colored barber shrimp, banded shrimps, arrow crabs, spider crabs, Christmas trees and feather worms, slugs, nudibranchs and urchins. One diver reports three sightings of a whale shark.

The main areas for diving are off Speyside around the out islands: Little Tobago; Goat Island; off the north coast around the islets known as The Sisters; and off the southern tip of the island.

The best snorkeling areas are along the Caribbean coast at Arnos Vale Bay, Englishman's Bay, Castra Bay, Fort James, Courtland Bay, Buccoo Bay, Store Bay and off Speyside at Tyrells Bay.

SPEYSIDE MARINE AREA DIVE SITES

All of the reefs in this area fringe the out islands. There is a prevailing northerly current and most dives are drift dives. Check with dive shops before diving or snorkeling on your own. Water temperature averages 82° F.

☆☆☆☆☆ **Manta City**, on the north side of Little Tobago, is *the* single most popular dive in Tobago. As the name implies, it is where manta rays are most commonly seen. Several of the mantas are used to interacting with divers and will approach to play. Avoid the temptation to hitch a ride as you may inadvertently harm the animal. Other residents are big French angels, urchins, crabs, blue tangs, jacks, damselfish, sharpnose puffers, and barracuda. Dive depths range from the extreme shallows near the shore to 50 ft. The bottom is a magnificent landscape of boulders and big rocks with good growth of star, brain and flower corals. Large barrel sponges and tube sponges are found at depth. The rays are usually spotted along the edge of a drop-off. Seas are generally calm with an occasional surge. The shallows are suitable for experienced snorkelers and novice divers. Unparalleled photo opportunities.

☆☆☆ **Blackjack Hole**, also off the south shore of Little Tobago, is a gentle slope allowing divers to choose their own depth preference. A beautiful dive with loads of fish, as well as loads of corals, big and small. Peak interest on the reef lies between 45 and 90 ft. The surface is calm, protected by the nearby island. Currents, if any, are gentle.

☆☆☆ **Japanese Gardens**, another manta-watch point, lies off the western tip of Goat Island. The reef's rich and varied soft corals take on a flower-garden appearance with a landscape of odd shapes, colors and patterns. The surface is usually choppy, but there is little or no current below except at the center of a reef where you will catch a good "flight" for some minutes through a narrow canal. The first part of the dive is on a slope, and the last part is in an area with big reef-boulders and reef-patches on a sandy bottom. Sunlight reflecting in the sand adds a lot of color to the dive. Angels, grunts, moray eels, and parrots are always about. Divers select depths for their skill level—between 30 and 60 ft or between 50 and 100 ft for the very experienced.

☆☆ **Kelliston Deep**, the site of the biggest recorded brain coral head in the world—16 ft wide and 12 ft high—sits off the southwest tip of Little Tobago. It starts at a shelf between 30 and 50 ft, then slopes down to a sandy bottom at 120 ft. Typical reef fish are abundant with occasional sightings of nurse sharks and manta. The outer edge starts in 50 ft. This beautiful area is destined to become a marine reserve.

☆☆ **Paradise** is an almost circular arena with a sandy bottom. The site is off an islet just south of Little Tobago. You enter at the edge of a hole, go through a narrow canal, around a corner and over an edge. Above you, heavy wave action forms clouds and clouds of white foam, and right under the white foam drift loose schools of tarpons four to eight ft long. A magnificent sight. Nearby and a part of this dive is a gently sloping reef with lots of coral and fishlife. Suggested experience level depends on sea conditions. Average depth is 60 ft.

☆☆ **All the Way** is a playground of gigantic boulders—a secretive dive where you don't know what's around the next corner. The reef slopes are a marvelous seascape rich with coral and sponge growth. Depths average 40 to 50 ft. "All the Way" is off the northeast tip of Little Tobago.

☆☆☆ **Glennmorgan** lies in a sheltered area off the eastern coast of Little Tobago. Soft corals and slender tube sponges color the canyons and walls of the reef. Average depth is 60 to 80 ft. Seldom any current. Expect to meet white-tip sharks and other pelagics. Suggested experience level depends on sea conditions. Often calm.

CARIBBEAN DIVE SITES

☆☆☆ **London Bridge**, at St. Giles Island off the northern tip of Tobago, is a rugged dive on a good day. St. Giles is a small rocky island with a hole going through both above and beneath the surface—like a bridge. As you enter the hole you experience a Venturi effect and are whirled through by a rush of water. Exhilarating! The depth in the hole is 30-40 ft, and the rest of the dive is normally at 60 ft. Maximum depth is 110 ft. Fish life is superb with 30-lb parrot fish, huge green morays, lobster, schools of tarpon and pelagics between the walls and boulders. Big sponges, sea fans and corals. Experienced ocean divers except on extremely calm days. Boat dive.

☆☆ **The Sisters** are a group of small islands off Bloody Bay on the northern coast. Reaching the site requires a 30- to 45-minute boat ride over

Manta Ray.

choppy seas, but if you crave a dramatic wall dive with huge pelagics, it's worth it. The wall is strewn with big boulders and rocks. At times you might find current and at times you might find surge. For experienced divers.

SOUTHEAST DIVE SITES

Water temperature on this Atlantic side is about 79° F. Dives on this Atlantic side are drift dives with strong currents and some surge. Currents often run in one direction on the surface and the opposite way at depth, with occasional upwellings and downwellings. Not suggested for the timid or inexperienced diver.

☆☆☆☆ **Diver's Dream**, an awesome stone formation with towering fissures, cracks, canyons and caves, packs in an incredible wealth of fish and crustaceans. Once in the "Dream," you'll encounter giant vase sponges measuring six ft across, and·finger corals that are 10 ft high. Large schooling reef fish mingle with black-tip sharks, nurse sharks, huge turtles, barracudas, and mantas. Surface conditions are calm, with gentle rollers. Always a drift dive with a one- to three-knot current. Recommended for experienced drift divers.

☆☆☆ **Diver's Thirst** is a mix of rock and reef which forms an amphitheater populated by big grouper, black-tip sharks, eagle rays and midnight parrot fish. Maximum depth is 45 ft. Always a drift dive. Surface conditions are light. Experienced drift divers.

Photo by Rick Ockelmann

Dive Operators

All Tobago dive operators require a C-card and request a logbook. Rates for a two-tank dive average $50. Prices subject to change.

Note: Tobago diving is fairly rugged, weather-dependent, with seas that often run five to six ft. Suggested for experienced ocean divers.

Aquamarine Dive Ltd., at the Blue Waters Inn, Speyside, tours Coral Gardens, Book Ends and Japanese Gardens. Fast boats and modern equipment. ☎ (809) 639-4416, fax (809) 639-4416. US, ☎ (800) 6-GET WET. E-mail: amdtobago@trinidad.net. Web site: www.trinidad.net/bwitobago.

Man Friday Diving is at Man-O-War Bay, Charlotteville, near Speyside. Danish owner and dive manager Finn Rinds tours the best sights around Little Tobago and the northeastern spots. He is personal friends with a few mantas too! The PADI/NAUI shop has storage lockers and equipment rentals. Finn whisks divers out to the reefs aboard a 28-ft custom dive boat. Dive packages can be arranged with Blue Waters Inn at Speyside or Man-O-War Bay cottages. ☎ (809) 660-4676, fax (809) 660-4676. Write to Man Friday Diving, Charlotteville, Tobago, WI.

Tobago Dive Experience is at the Rex Turtle Beach Hotel on the northern, Caribbean coast and at Manta Lodge in Speyside. Dive master, Sean Robinson, offers trips to all the Caribbean spots and around the south tip to the rugged Atlantic sites. This NAUI/PADI shop offers basic and advanced courses, dive equipment and photo rentals. Plus personalized videos. In Grafton: ☎ (809) 639-0191, fax (809) 639-0030. In Speyside: ☎ (809) 639-7034, fax (809) 639-0030. E-mail: divemanta@trinidad.net. Web site: www.trinidad.net/tobagodive.

Tobago Marine Sports Ltd is at the Crown Reef Hotel, Store Bay. Operated by Keith Darwent, this full-service PADI shop offers all courses, and tours the southeast tip of Tobago—Caribbean and Atlantic dives. Contact Keith or John Darwent at ☎ (809) 639-0291. Write to PO Box 300, Crown Reef Hotel, Store Bay, Tobago, WI.

Dive Tobago Limited at Pigeon Point is Tobago's oldest dive operation. It caters to the beginner and advanced diver. Resort courses, $60. One-tank dive with equipment, $30. ☎ (809) 639-0202, fax (809) 639-2727. E-mail: cohel@tstt.net.tt. Write to PO Box 53, Scarborough, Tobago, WI.

Accommodations

Dive-accommodation packages including seven nights accommodations, 10 dives, three meals daily, transfers and taxes, are offered by **Into the Blue Tours** starting at $875 per person for a double. ☎ (800) 6-GET-WET. E-mail: cvdt@aol.com. Web site: www.intotheblue.com. Scuba Voyages offers similar tours. ☎ (800) 544-7631. E-mail: scubavoy@ix.netcom.com.

Manta Lodge, a lovely, low-rise dive resort in Speyside, offers 22 deluxe rooms with private verandas and an ocean view. Your choice of ceiling fan or air-conditioning. Tobago Dive Experience on site. Pool, beautiful beach. Rates for five nights, including eight dives and breakfast daily, are $575 from April to Dec, $635 from Dec to April. ☎ (800) 544-7631, direct (809) 660-5268, fax 660-5030.

Grafton Beach Resort, in Black Rock, is the island's leading hotel. Situated on the Caribbean, this 100-room luxury resort is set amidst five acres of tropical splendor. Features are a swim-up bar, pool, air-conditioned squash courts, gym, restaurant, palm-lined beach, entertainment, dive shop and an 18-hole golf course nearby. Guest rooms have air-conditioning, cable TV, private bath and mini-fridge. Book through your travel agent or direct. ☎ (809) 639-0191, fax (809) 639-0030. Near Tobago Dive Experience.

Mt Irvine Bay Hotel is a 64-room, two-story complex with 42 adjacent cottages on the site of a 17th-century sugar plantation. It is located on the south end of the Caribbean coast. Beaches are across the street. Facilities include a pool, restaurant, spa, tennis and meeting room. Rates for a double are from $140 per day. ☎ (800) 544-7631, direct (809) 639-8871, fax 639-8800. Write Box 222, Tobago, WI.

Turtle Beach Hotel at Plymouth is just 15 minutes from the airport on Courland Bay. Rooms have private bath, air-conditioning, balcony or patio overlooking the beach. Beach bar, small pool, Creole Restaurant. Entertainment. ☎ (809) 639-2820, fax (809) 639-1495. Write PO Box 201, Plymouth, Tobago, WI.

Blue Waters Inn, Batteaux Bay, Speyside, is at the heart of the Speyside Marine area. Rustic and rural, it is a haven for nature lovers, far away from the tourist area in its own private bay with 46 acres of grounds. Snorkel from the beach. The inn has 28 guest rooms and four cottages. All are cooled by ceiling fans. Snorkel from the beach. Dive shop on premises. Room rates for double occupancy are from $121.20 in winter, $80 in summer. With meals, add $32 per person per day. Cottages are from $150 in winter, $105 in summer for one bedroom; $258 in winter, $150 in summer for two bedrooms, two persons; from $170 for four people. ☎ (800) 742-4276, (809) 660-4341, (809) 660-4077, fax (809) 660-5195.

Man-O-War Bay Cottages, near St. Giles and Little Tobago Islands, are for nature lovers and bird watchers. Far from the tourist area, the Caribbean-side cottages are part of Charlotteville Estate, a 1,000-acre cocoa plantation 36 miles from the airport. The cottages are plain and simple, each with one to four bedrooms, twin beds, kitchenette, shower, jalousie windows. No AC. (Air temperature averages 82° F year-round.) ☎ (809) 660-4327,

Manta City, off Little Tobago.

fax (809) 660-4328. Write to Charles and Pat Turpin, Charlotteville Estate, Charlotteville, Tobago, WI.

Dining

Curried crab and dumplings highlight Tobago's menus, along with fish and lobster dishes prepared with callaloo (like spinach), coconut and cornmeal. Peas and rice are a frequent side dish.

Manta Lodge Restaurant in Speyside features local and continental seafood favorites. ☎ 660-5268.

The Village at Kariwak Village in Crown Point offers island atmosphere and a fabulous Creole menu. Fresh seafood and fruit concoctions are special. ☎ 639-8442. Moderate.

The Corico Inn in Plymouth offers fabulous seafood dishes in simple surroundings. At North and Commissioner St. ☎ 639-2661. Moderate.

The Blue Crab in Scarborough is a tiny spot offering lunches daily and dinner on Wed and Fri. Fresh fish and local vegetables are prepared with island spices. ☎ 639-2737.

Sightseeing and Other Activities

A two-hour drive from Scarborough, the capital, at the northern tip of Tobago, will lead you through most of the sightseeing spots on this tiny, rural island.

While in **Scarborough** visit the **Botanic Gardens,** the 18th-century **Fort King George** and the **National Fine Arts Gallery and Museum.** The fort commands a magnificent view of southern Tobago and the Atlantic coast.

Pigeon Point is the island's most famous beach, with offshore **Buccoo Reef.** A stop at **King's Bay Waterfall** is a necessity for the photo buff. It's about 20 miles from Scarborough along the Windward Road to Charlotteville. Bring your bathing suit for a dip in the natural pool at the base of the falls.

Two of Tobago's loveliest spots are **Argyll Waterfall** near Roxborough on the north end of the Atlantic coast and **Courland Bay** on the leeward coast, named for early settlers from Latvia.

Diving and bird watching dominate the sports scene, but golfers will enjoy the **Mt. Irvine Golf Course** (☎ 639-8871), founded in 1892. Windsurfing is big off Speyside (☎ 660-5206) and horseback riding is offered at the **Palm Tree Village Beach Resort** (☎ 639-4347).

Facts

Helpful Phone Numbers: Police, ☎ 999 or 622-5412; medical help, ☎ 623-2551; fire or ambulance, ☎ 990; Scarborough Hospital, ☎ 639-2551.

Nearest Recompression Chamber: Trinidad, Port of Spain Hospital. A chamber was under construction in Tobago, but not completed at press time.

Getting There: American Airlines, ☎ (800) 433-7300, flies to San Juan, connecting with American Eagle, which flies direct to Tobago. BWIA, ☎ (800) 327-7300, has frequent flights to Piarco Airport, Trinidad, from New York, Miami and Toronto, with connections to Tobago via Air Caribbean.

Island Transportation: Taxis are very expensive in Tobago. If you drive, rent at Crown Point Airport (☎ 639-0644), or AR Rentals (☎ 639-5330). Some of the roads are narrow and muddy during spring and summer.

Driving: On the left. A valid license is required.

Documents: Passport valid for length of stay, return or onward ticket.

Currency: The Trinidad and Tobago dollar (TT $). currently TT $6=US $1. Credit cards are widely used in tourist areas.

Climate: Average water temperature is 78° F. Air temperature averages 85°. Humidity is high, with frequent showers, especially from June to December. Biting insects are a problem.

Clothing: Ultra-casual and lightweight. Long-sleeve shirts, long pants and closed shoes are best for hiking the rainforest trails. Light wetsuit suggested for deep dives. Snorkelers should wear protective covering from the midday sun.

Security: Avoid walking alone at night. Don't stop if flagged down while driving. Use hotel safes, lock cars and hotel rooms. Avoid wearing flashy jewelry.

Electricity: 110 and 220 volts, 60 cycles.

Time: Atlantic Standard (EST + 1 hr).

Tax: 15% government tax is added to hotel rates. A departure tax of TT $75 must be paid in local currency. A 10% service charge is added or expected at restaurants.

Religious Services: Catholic, Protestant.

For Additional Information: The Trinidad and Tobago Tourism Development Authority. *In the US*— 7000 Blvd East, Guttenberg, NJ 07093, ☎ (800) 595-1TNT or (888) 595-4TNT, (201) 662-3408, fax (201) 869-7628. *In the UK*—Morris Kevan International Limited, International House, 47 Chase Side, Enfield, Middlesex, EN2 6NB, England, ☎ 0-(800) 960-0057, (181) 367-3752, fax (181) 367-9949. *In Canada*—The RMR Gourp Inc., Taurus House, 512 Duplex Ave, Toronto, M4R 2E3, ☎ (800) 595-1TNT or (888) 595-4TNT. E-mail: tourism-info@tidco.co.tt. Web site: www.tidco.tt.

US Virgin Islands

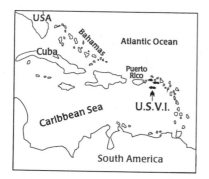

Discovered by Columbus in 1493, the US Virgin Islands (USVI) comprise three main islands: St. Croix, St. John and St. Thomas. Each has a distinct personality and flavor, and since they are close together you can choose one island as your base and still catch the fun of the other two. They offer an enormous variety of reefs, wrecks and drop-offs, all in crystal clear water protected from strong currents and heavy seas.

Before becoming an American territory, the USVI lived under six different flags and it still preserves a rich and varied culture. Wander through old Danish arcades covered with tropical flowers in the historic town of Christiansted on St. Croix; visit Bluebeard's Castle on St. Thomas; or stroll around the partially restored ruins of the Annaberg Plantation on St. John.

ST. CROIX

The largest of the USVI, St. Croix plays host to over 50,000 visiting snorkelers and divers per year, the main attraction being Buck Island National Park—the most famous snorkeling spot in the world. Scuba divers will find their share of reefs, walls and wrecks to dive.

Picturesque St. Croix, once a Danish territory, is known for its easy lifestyle and warm hospitality. The streets of Christiansted, its tiny capital, are lined with 18th-century buildings in pastel pinks, blues and yellow. Tropical flowers greet the visitor everywhere. At night, shops, restaurants and nightclubs come alive with reggae music and island hospitality.

The small town of Frederiksted is laced with wide tree-shaded streets that lead to a lovely waterfront with arcaded sidewalks. After a devastating fire in 1878, Frederiksted was rebuilt in the Victorian style. Flowering vines now cling to the balustrades of the "gingerbread" frames the Cruzans built over the Danish masonry. Much of the best diving and snorkeling around St. Croix is accessible by beach entry.

Area contributors: Luana Wheatley, Virgin Rhythms; Michelle Pugh, Dive Experience; Lucy Portlock, Pelagic Pleasures.

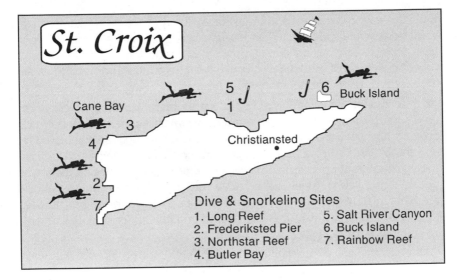

St. Croix

Cane Bay

5
1

6 Buck Island

3

4

Christiansted

2

7

Dive & Snorkeling Sites
1. Long Reef   5. Salt River Canyon
2. Frederiksted Pier 6. Buck Island
3. Northstar Reef   7. Rainbow Reef
4. Butler Bay

Best Dives of St. Croix

☆☆☆ **Long Reef**, a six-mile-wide shallow reef on the outskirts of Christiansted Harbor, offers a variety of reef dives. The bottom terraces gently from the shallows to an average depth of 50 ft, reaching 80 ft at some spots. Hundreds of small coral caves and crevices along the reef shelter French angels, parrotfish, rays, turtles, morays, octopi, lobsters and goatfish. A docile nurse shark makes frequent appearances. Huge brain and elkhorn coral formations prevail. An old barge intentionally sunk at 60 ft near the harbor channel attracts a healthy fish population. Visibility varies. Recommended for snorkelers and novice divers.

☆☆☆☆ **The Frederiksted Pier** offers the ultimate night dive at St. Croix. Underwater pilings, carpeted with red, yellow and orange sponges, provide cover for seahorses, iridescent tube sponges, octopi, baby morays, juvenile fish, brittle stars, puffers, featherdusters, parrot fish and tube anemones. Take your dive light. Beware the stinging corals and red "do not touch me" sponge. Entrance to the dive site is by climbing down a steel ladder or taking a giant stride off the end of the pier. Before entering the water, be sure to see the Harbor Master at the pier, C-card in hand. ☎ 772-0174. Diving is prohibited when a ship is in.

☆☆☆☆ **Northstar Reef**, a spectacular wall dive at the east end of Davis Bay, is recommended for intermediate or experienced divers. Beach entry is possible here but most divers opt for boat access because of the rocky terrain.

Beautiful staghorn thickets and brain corals decorate the wall. A sandy shelf at 50 ft leads to a spooky cave and a hefty green moray eel. Huge anchors from 18th-century sailing ships lie scattered about. Marine life includes a superb collection of schooling tropicals, pelagics, turtles, morays and eagle rays. Expect an occasional moderate current.

☆☆☆ **Butler Bay,** on the island's west shore, harbors four shipwrecks: the 170-ft *Rosaomaira*, which sits in 100 ft of water; the 140-ft *Suffolk Maid*, an old fishing trawler at 90 ft; the *Northwind*, a retired tugboat at about 60 ft; and the *Virgin Island*, a 300-ft barge sunk in 1991, resting at 70 ft. The wrecks are part of an artificial reef system which also includes old cars and trucks, music boxes, typewriters, and a vast array of other items. Wreck residents include goat fish, groupers, snappers, hogfish, parrotfish, turtles, rays, and angelfish. Recommended for intermediate to experienced divers.

☆☆☆ **Salt River Canyon,** a deep, submerged canyon formed by the outflow to the Salt River, features two distinct dives off its east and west walls. **Salt River East**, with interest between 40- and 100-ft depths, is famed for the massive orange elephant ear sponges and black corals that decorate its precipice. The area's usual good visibility allows a long look at resident bigeyes, grunts, barracuda, blue chromis and sting rays. Suggested for intermediate divers.

Salt River West plunges from 40 to more than 130 ft. Plate corals cascade down the reef slope and large purple tube sponges make a wonderful foreground for wide-angle photography.

When seas are calm, it is an excellent spot for novices. Visibility, normally good, may decrease during stormy weather.

☆☆☆ **Cane Bay Drop-off** is the favorite beach dive. The drop-off lies about 140 yds off the beach and is suitable for scuba and snorkeling, with depths ranging from the surface to 120 ft. Inside the reef, calm waters and a decent fish population make this spot a favorite of snorkelers. Light surf along the shore. Light current at the drop-off. Park along the road at Cane Bay Beach.

Additional shore-entry dives are best at Davis Bay and Butler Bay. Visibility close to shore is weather-dependent and decreases when a lot of rain and wind churn the bottom. Equipment may be rented at any of the dive shops.

Best Snorkeling of St. Croix

☆☆☆ **Buck Island Reef** continues to capture the hearts of Caribbean tourists despite noticeable wear from hurricanes and a daily blitz of snorkelers. Established by President John F. Kennedy as a national monument, this 850-acre sanctuary houses the world's only underwater national park.

Christiansted Harbor, St. Croix.

As in most national parks, Buck Island has its own rangers, only here they sport swim trunks and patrol in power boats. There are also the standard park guide markers, but at Buck Island they stand at a depth of 12 ft, embedded in the sands along the ocean floor. Each day, catamarans, trimarans, sloops, and yawls unload what the islanders call "the wet set." The Buck Island welcoming committee includes green parrotfish, snappy sergeant majors, grouper, rainbow-striped angel fish and the silvery Bermuda chub. Beginners and experienced snorkelers alike can experience this underwater fantasy in an unusually safe atmosphere. The reefs of Buck Island lie only 100 yds off the coast and no trail is more than 15 ft deep. As snorkelers enter the park, they are welcomed by a blue and white plaque shimmering below the surface. One marker (number 8) next to an unusual round coral full of veins inquires, "What would you name this coral?" The next marker says, "You are right. Brain Coral." Arrows and signs guide the swimmer along the underwater trail and give the precise names of coral and other growths below the surface.

More than 300 species of fish are identified. One species that audibly demands attention is the small striped grunt, a fish that can be clearly heard underwater. The National Park Service maintains a careful watch, but one familiar park rule—Don't Feed the Animals—does not apply here. Swimmers can feed the fish as often as they like. Grouper, a favorite fish to hand-feed, come readily at the slightest beckoning.

Since the reef park is strictly non-commercial, you are advised to rent gear before heading out. Whether you're coming from St. Thomas, St. Croix or St. John, you can obtain equipment readily on all three islands. And getting there is half the fun. Most hotels on St. Croix offer a shuttle service to Christiansted, where you can select almost any kind of boat imaginable. Charter boats of every description line the docks of the Christiansted harbor. Boats to Buck Island are widely available at low cost.

Make sure you stop over on Buck Island Beach, a pristine stretch of powdery, white sand created in part by parrotfish gnawing on the coral reef and excreting sand. From the beach, a wildlife trail leads 200 ft to an observation tower, which gives a grand view of the lagoon and reef. A trip to Buck will be one of the most memorable experiences of your visit to the Virgin Islands. Areas of Buck Island reef away from the snorkeling trail are suitable for scuba.

Dive Operators of St. Croix

All of the dive operators on St. Croix require a C-card.

Cane Bay Dive Shop, on the beach at Cane Bay, offers "walk in" dives to the Cane Bay Drop-off, which sits about 140 yds off the beach. Snorkeling tours. Hotel and dive packages available. ☎ (800) 338-3843 or (340) 773-9913. Write to PO Box 4510, Kings Hill, St. Croix, USVI 00851.

Dive Experience is at the Club St. Croix in Christiansted. Owner, Michelle Pugh is a diver-medic instructor as well as a PADI instructor. This PADI five-star facility offers all certifications, including a four-day certification, a resort course, rentals, photography equipment . Dive Experience offers boat dives around the island and will shoot personalized videos. Hotel and dive packages are available. ☎ (800) 235-9047, (340) 524-2049 or write Box 4254, Christiansted, St. Croix, USVI 00822.

Dive St. Croix in Christiansted offers wall and wreck diving trips, night dives, Buck Island trips, camera rentals, resort through certification courses, and accommodation package tours with several different resorts. ☎ (800) 523-3483 or (340) 773-3434, fax (340) 773-9411. Write to 59 Kings Wharf, Christiansted, St. Croix, USVI 00820.

Virgin Island Divers is located at the Pan Am Pavilion in Christiansted. All certification ratings and rentals. Beach dives, boat, night and wreck dives, custom dive boats. ☎ (340) 773-6045 or write Pan Am Pavilion, Christiansted, St. Croix, USVI 00820.

Anchor Dive Center is a PADI five-star, IDC training facility. Resort to instructor courses. Located at the Salt River Marina, they are three minutes from Salt River Canyon. ☎ (340) 778-1522 or (800) 532-3483. Write to PO Box 5588, Sunny Isle, St. Croix, USVI 00823.

Cruzan Divers, Inc. offers boat, beach and pier dives plus wall and reef dives. Resort, rescue, dive master and advanced courses. ☎ (800) 352-0107 or (340) 772-3701. Write to 12 Strand St., Frederiksted, St. Croix USVI 00840.

Sea Shadows is in Cane Bay and at Kings Wharf. Owners Libby Wessel and Steve Fordyce are beach diving specialists. The shop also operates two dive boats that tour all the sites around St. Croix.

Scuba Tech at the Salt River Marina is a full-service dive facility. Accommodation packages available. ☎ (800) 233-7944 or (340) 778-9650. Write to PO Box 5339, St. Croix, USVI 00820.

Accommodations

St. Croix offers a wide range of luxury resorts, villas, condominiums, inns and guest houses. Like the neighboring British Virgin Islands, the waters around the USVI are excellent for sailing. Many visiting divers combine a week of bare boating or live-aboard sailing with sub-sea exploring. The following are resorts that cater to divers and offer package deals. (Add 8% tax to room rates.)

The Buccaneer Hotel in Christiansted also offers packages with Caribbean Sea Adventures. The Buccaneer is a sprawling resort with three beautiful beaches, three restaurants, a spa, shopping arcade, eight tennis courts, an 18-hole golf course and all water sports. Dive and snorkeling trips leave from the resort dock for Buck Island. Rates are from $170 (summer), $210 (winter) per night for a double in a standard room. Cottages range from $225 to $1,370 per week (summer), $335 (winter) per night. For singles, deduct $20 per night. Dive packages are $190 for six dives, $295 for 10 dives. ☎ (800) 223-1108 or (340) 773-2100; write PO Box 800, Waccabuc, NY 10597.

Chenay Bay Beach Resort offers beachfront cottages with kitchens for $185 to $205 per day. ☎ (800) 548-4457, fax (340) 773-2918.

Hisbiscus Beach Hotel, a small, friendly Caribbean-style hotel, rents oceanfront rooms with patios or balconies for $130 to $140 per night. TV, phone, restaurant. White sand beach. ☎ (800) 442-0121, fax (340) 773-7668.

The Waves At Cane Bay offer spacious seaside studios with balconies, pool, beach, restaurant. Scuba and snorkeling off the beach. Rooms are from $140 to $195 per night. TV, no phones. ☎ (800) 545-0603 or (340) 773-0463, fax (340) 778-4945. PO Box 1749, Kingshill, St. Croix, USVI 00850.

Cane Bay Reef Club features six two-room suites with full kitchens, balcony overlooking the sea. Saltwater pool. Rates are from $140 to $230 per day. PO Box 1407, Kingshill, St. Croix, USVI 00851. ☎ (340) 778-2966.

Dining

The US Virgin Islands are considered the mecca of haute cuisine in the Caribbean. From the islands' rich mixture of cultures—Spanish, French, English, Danish, Maltese, Dutch and American—its pungent local spices and fresh tropical fruits, local chefs create dishes to dream about. So many fine restaurants have opened up within the last five years, we can only give a hint of the many options.

The Buccaneer Hotel's **Brass Parrot** on St. Croix promises a feast to remember. Situated just 20 minutes outside of historic Christiansted, the restaurant combines a taste of past glory with a stunning modern decor. The Haitian chef prepares fine continental cuisine with a touch of the islands. Specialties include conch with hot lime sauce; shrimp Bahia, giant shrimp sautéed in garlic butter and topped with brandy and pineapple liqueur; or a rack of lamb carved at your table. In a more informal setting, diners will enjoy the lively **Club Comanche Restaurant**, on the second floor of an old Danish townhouse in Christiansted. Favorites here are cucumber soup, prime ribs, rack of lamb, and lobster. For dessert, try key lime pie.

The Wreck Bar on Hospital Street is the place for West Indian atmosphere. Opens for dinner 4 pm, Mon through Sat. Specials are fish and chips, fried shrimp and beer batter onion rings. Entertainment includes crab races and guitar music. Cash only.

ST. JOHN

The smallest and most verdant of the USVI, St. John is truly the most "virgin." The island is an unspoiled sanctuary of natural beauty and wildlife. Two-thirds of the 28-square-mile island and most of its stunning shoreline comprise the Virgin Islands National Park, part of the US National Park system. Here nature flaunts her majestic mountains, emerald valleys and lush tropical vegetation. St. John is the best choice for beach-front camping.

Best Dives of St. John

The best dives of St. John are from the out islands, Congo Cay and Carvel Rock. Shallow dive sites are found around the south shores of Reef Bay and west shores of Cruz Bay.

☆☆ **Congo Cay** is a favorite dive site for dive boats based at St. John and St. Thomas. It is a rocky islet located between them. Visibility is usually good. As with many of the small cays, the rocky submerged areas are home to large schools of fish. The coral mounds, some of which have been beaten up by the sea, are decorated with soft corals and brightly colored sponges. Currents are occasionally strong here.

☆☆☆ **Carval Rock** is a short boat ride from the north end of St. John. Try this dive only if weather and sea conditions permit, as strong currents may exist under less than perfect circumstances. Recommended for very experienced divers only. The attraction here is the schools of very large fish and eagle rays. The submerged part of the rock is covered with sponges, gorgonians, basket stars, and false corals.

☆☆ **Fishbowl Reef**, just south of Cruz Bay, is a nice shallow dive for novices and snorkelers. Divers swim along ledges sparkling with beautiful elkhorn and staghorn coral. Soft corals undulate in the shallows. Many kinds of small reef fish are found hiding in the crevices.

Best Snorkeling Sites of St. John

Half-day and full-day snorkeling excursions by boat or exploring outer reefs or shipwrecks, are available. Lucy Portlock, **Pelagic Pleasures**, ☎ (340) 776-6567, at the Caneel Bay Resort, offers boat snorkeling excursions to all the best sites around St. John. If you're not staying at Caneel Bay, sign up at Hurricane Alley in the Mongoose Junction Mini Mall.

☆☆☆ **Trunk Bay** on the north shore of the island has a clearly marked underwater trail, with abundant soft and hard corals, yellowtail, damsel fish, and occasional turtles. The reef is shallow and is just off beautiful Trunk Bay Beach. Top-side here is great for snapshots. Average depths: 10 to 15 ft.

☆☆☆ **Salt Pond Bay,** at the southeast end, is never crowded and is blessed with ample shade trees. Coral reefs stretch from both points of the Bay, offering snorkelers a full day's worth of adventure. Many fish and marine animals make their home here.

☆☆☆ **Chocolate Hole**, located at the east side of the mouth of Chocolate Bay, is distinguised by several rocks sticking up out of the water. The reef is just to the west of these. Reef depths are from four to 15 ft. Hordes of fish, including grunts, squirrelfish, blue chromis, parrot fish, rays and turtles, wander about. Seas are usually very calm unless the wind is from the south. Good for all levels.

☆☆ **Waterlemon Cay**, a national park, offers terrific fish watching for experienced swimmers. To get there, drive to Annaberg Sugarmill ruins, park and hike down the road to the beach (half a mile). Swim along the east side of the bay to Waterlemon Cay. There are loads of big Caribbean starfish in the sand and walls of fish all around the island, including big yellowtail snapper and jawfish. This spot is usually calm in summer, but choppy in winter when the wind is out of the northeast. Tidal currents may exist.

☆☆ **Caneel Bay Snorkeling Trail** is limited to guests of the Caneel Bay Resort or boaters who enter from the sea, but Caneel Bay's main beach is open to the public and offers some nice fish watching.

☆ **Francis Bay** is easiest by boat, but you can reach it by driving to the Annaberg Sugar Mill, then left to Francis Bay. The last stretch of road is gravel and dirt. Rocks, corals and plenty of fish.

☆☆ **Cocoloba Cay,** a bare rocky site "attached" to St. John by rock, coral and sand, requires boat access. The east side has huge coral formations, some 15-ft high, which died long ago, but now have new coral growing on top. Large coral patch reefs exist along the west side. Depths range from five to 30 ft. Highlights are angel fish, schools of blue tang, spadefish, jacks, pompano and an occasional shark. This area is usually rough, good only on days with the wind from the north or northeast. Experienced ocean swimmers only. Boaters should anchor about 100 yds east of the cay.

Dive Operators

Coral Bay Watersports Center offers diving rentals, snorkeling gear, sailing, windsurfing, fishing, and parasailing. ☎ (340) 776-6857 or write 14 Emmaus, Coral Bay, St. John, USVI 00830.

St. John Watersports Inc. offers rentals and dive trips. ☎ (340) 776-6256. Or write PO Box 431, Cruz Bay, St. John, USVI 00830.

Cinnamon Bay Watersports Center, located at Caneel Bay Resort, operates a 42-ft custom dive boat complete with compressor. Dive trips are offered to the outer islands (cays) and reefs. Day trips to the *R.M.S. Rhone*, an outstanding wreck dive, located nearby in the British Virgin Islands, can be arranged for groups. Dive packages with Caneel Bay Resort are available. ☎ (340) 778-8330. Write to PO Box 720, Cruz Bay, St. John USVI 00831.

Accommodations

Caneel Bay Resort occupies a 170-acre peninsula that adjoins the Virgin Islands National Park. There are 171 guest units in low-profile buildings scattered about the grounds, three restaurants, seven white sand beaches and seven tennis courts. The resort is known for the gardens where over 500 tropical plant species grow. Divers may combine a week with Little Dix Bay resort on Virgin Gorda (transfers handled by resort) or sailing on Hinckley yachts ranging from 40 to 50 ft. Room rates are from $250 to $450 per day, high season from $350 to $850 per day. All-inclusive packages that cover room and all meals for seven nights range from $4,000 to $7,500 per week, per couple. ☎ (800) 928-8889 or see your travel agent.

Westin Regency St. John sprawls over 34 exotic acres with a gigantic freshwater pool covering a quarter-acre and offers 280 luxury guest rooms with all amenities. Under 18 stay free. Good snorkeling off the beach. Cruz Bay Watersports (☎ 693-8000), on premises, offers dive and snorkeling trips. Winter room rates for a double start at $300 to $395; summer, from $265. ☎ (800) 228-3000 or (340) 693-8000, fax (340) 779-4985.

Condos and Apartments

Cruz Bay Villas, high on the mountainside near town, rent for $160 per night. ☎ (340) 776-6416.

Gallows Point Suite Resort, on the waterfront, features suites with full kitchens, private patios and bathrooms. Pool, gourmet shop and restaurant. Good snorkeling from the beach. From $265 to $355 per day. ☎ (800) 323-7229, fax (340) 776-6520.

Moonsong & Sundance are charming two-bedroom villas. Five-minute walk to secluded beach. Jacuzzi, sunset views. $1,330 per week. ☎/fax (340) 693-8495.

For additional rentals try **Tropic Retreats**, ☎ (800) 233-7944, fax (340) 778-3557 or **Island Villas,** ☎ (800) 626-4512, fax 773-8823.

Campgrounds

Camping/snorkeling trips are popular on St. John. Bring your own gear.

Cinnamon Bay Campground, PO Box 720, Cruz Bay, St. John, USVI 00830. Costs $15 to $98 per day. Cottages, campsites and tents on Cinnamon Bay Beach in the national park. ☎ (800) 539-9998 or (340) 776-6330, fax (340) 776-6458. Dive packages available, windsurfing and sailboat rentals.

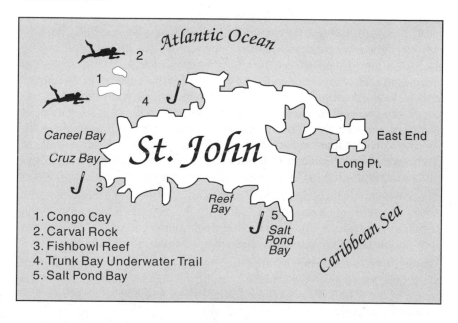

1. Congo Cay
2. Carval Rock
3. Fishbowl Reef
4. Trunk Bay Underwater Trail
5. Salt Pond Bay

Trunk Bay, St. John.

Maho Bay Camps, PO Box 310, St. John, USVI 00830. Luxury camping, white sand beach, watersports and gourmet restaurant. From $60 per day. ☎ (800) 392-9004.

ST. THOMAS

St. Thomas is the second largest of the USVI and site of the capital, Charlotte Amalie. Provincial yet cosmopolitan, modern yet rich in history, it can be seen in a day. Divers should save an afternoon for shopping. Duty-free prices and keen competition make it a bargain-hunter's dream. In the narrow cobblestone streets and arcades of Charlotte Amalie you'll find designer shops housed in 200-year-old restored warehouses that were once full of molasses and rum. For those content to idle away some topside time, St. Thomas boasts sugar-white beaches. It is in these calm sands that St. Thomas's history, rich and tumultuous, lies hidden. The sheltered coves once harbored some of the most bloodthirsty pirates in Caribbean history.

The architecture and people of St. Thomas reflect the island's many-cultured past. Dutch, French and Spanish historic sites sit side-by-side with contemporary resorts. For those mixing scuba diving and sailing, St. Thomas is the home port to a number of charter operators.

Though some beach-entry diving exists here, the prettiest reefs and clearest waters are found around the outer cays. Some dive shops offer trips to the wreck of the *R.M.S. Rhone*. Cruise ship visitors will find an abundance of snorkeling opportunities.

Best Dives of St. Thomas

☆☆☆ **French Cap Cay** is well south of St. Thomas, but worth the long boat trip for both divers and snorkelers. This reef complex displays an enormous array of corals, caves, tunnels, and a spectacular sea mount. Visibility is often unlimited. The reef is teeming with fish, rays and critters. Beautiful lavender, orange, and yellow vase and basket sponges grow on the walls, interspersed with orange and red corals and unblemished stands of elkhorn. A light current is usually encountered here.

☆☆ **Capella Island** is just east of Little Buck Island. The reef here begins at 25 ft. Divers swim down through coral-encrusted canyons to a beautiful rocky bottom where basket sponges, soft corals and pillar coral grow. The visibility, often excellent, is weather-dependent. Fish life is abundant.

☆☆ **Saba Island**, a short boat trip from the St. Thomas's harbor, is a favorite one-tank dive. Depths are 20 to 50 ft. The reef at Saba Island is very pretty; divers swim through staghorn thickets and pillar corals. Large boulders cover the bottom, which is at a depth of about 50 ft. You may encounter surge; a number of divers have been tossed into the fire coral on the reef.

Best Snorkeling Sites

Coki Beach, on the north shore of St. Thomas, is a favorite beach dive and snorkeling site. The beach is adjacent to Coral World, an underwater viewing tower. The reef here ranges in depth from 20 to 50 ft. Divers swim down a sand slope amid schools of snappers, French and queen angels, and an occasional baby shark. The reef has small coral arches and recesses, a favorite hiding place for small fish, sea turtles and stingrays. Star coral, sponges, crinoids, and rock are characteristic of the reef at Coki Beach. This is an excellent first dive also.

☆☆☆ *Cartanser Senior*, a 190-ft wreck, sits just off Little Buck Island in 35 ft of water. It is filled with schools of squirrel fish, morays, angels, butterfly fish, sergeant majors, angels and damsels, all of whom are accustomed to being hand-fed and will approach you looking for a snack. Visibility is often good here.

French Cap Cay has the best visibility for snorkeling and free diving photography (see overall description above). The reef has many shallow areas full of large sea fans, antler coral, and elkhorn.

Additional good beach snorkeling exists at **Hull Bay** on the north coast and **Bolongo Bay**, plus the resort beaches at Sugar Bay Resort, Renaissance Grand Beach, Secret Harbor Beach, Sapphire Beach, Point Pleasant Resort, Marriott's Morning Star Resort, Grand Palazzo, and Carib Beach.

St. Thomas

Big Hans Lollick

Thatch Cay

• Dorothea

4

Charlotte Amalie

Red Hook

Great St. James Island

3

5   2   1

1. Frenchcap Cay
2. Capella Island
3. Saba Island
4. Coki Beach
5. "Cartanser Senior"

St. Thomas Dive Operators

Aqua Action, at Secret Harbour Beach Hotel, features custom dives to area sites. Accommodation packages. ☎ (340) 775-6285 or write Red Hook, Box 15, St. Thomas, USVI 00802.

Chris Sawyer Diving Center has three locations, one at the Renaissance Grand Beach Resort at Coki Beach, American Yacht Harbor and the main operation at Compass Point Marina. The shops offer resort courses as well as PADI and NAUI scuba certifications. All gear, including underwater photo equipment, is available for rental. A fast 42-ft dive boat shuttles divers to all the best dives around St. Thomas and its outer islands. Escorted beach-snorkeling tours. ☎ (800) 882-2965 or (340) 775-7320. Write to 6300 Estate Frydenhoj, St. Thomas, USVI 00802. E-mail: sawyerdive@world-net.att.net. Web site: insightsintl.com/dive.

Caribbean Divers, at Red Hook, has boat dives and PADI certification classes. ☎ (340) 775-6384.

Dive In!, at the Sapphire Beach Resort, a full-service PADI facility, visits the sites around St. Thomas. Snorkelers may join the dive tours when sites are shallow. Equipment rentals and scuba courses. ☎ (800) 524-2090.

St. Thomas Diving Club, at the Bolongo Bay Beach Club, specializes in dive and snorkel excursions to local and BVI sites. ☎ (340) 776-2381.

Dive World. If you're arriving by cruise ship, Dive World will pick you up at the dock, take you diving, and drive you back to the ship. Beach diving for novices and experienced divers around St. Thomas. ☎ (340) 698-8816 or write PO Box 12140, St. Thomas, USVI 00801.

Accommodations

St. Thomas has a seemingly endless variety of accommodations. You'll find charming antique guesthouses and cozy in-town hotels, resorts on secluded beaches, romantic mountain-top villas, condos, and hotels.

Bolongo Bay Beach & Sports Club offers diving packages in cooperation with the on-premises St. Thomas Diving Club. The all-inclusive resort has 75 air-conditioned beachfront units with telephone, color TV, kitchenettes, and balconies. Nightly entertainment. Sport facilities include four tennis courts, a Sunfish sailboat fleet, resort yacht *Heavenly Days*, snorkeling, volleyball courts and board games. Informal atmosphere. Children under 15 free in room. Beach bar. Winter rates run from $325 per person, per day, including all meals, taxes, and service charge; $460 for a double. Room only, double occupancy, is from $165 to $225 per day in winter; age 17 and under, $75 per day. Good snorkeling off the beach. ☎ (800) 524-4746 or (340) 779-2844, fax (340) 775-3208 or write 50 Estate Bolongo, St. Thomas, USVI 00802.

Renaissance Grand Beach Resort is a deluxe beachfront resort located at Pineapple Beach on the east shores of St. Thomas. It has 315 rooms, all air-conditioned, two pools, three restaurants, entertainment, and TV. There are dive packages with Chris Sawyer Diving Center, on the property. Room rates in winter are from $335 for garden view to $445 for ocean view. Summer rates start at $235 per night, double occupancy. Child under 18 free in room. Guided beach snorkeling excursions with dive shop. Write PO Box 8267, St. Thomas, USVI 00801. ☎ (800) HOTELS1 or (340) 775-1510, fax (340) 775-2185.

Marriott's Frenchman's Reef Resort, a full-service 423-room luxury beachfront resort, offers diving and snorkeling tours, freshwater pool, tennis and seven restaurants. Recently renovated rooms have TV, phones and tropical decor. ☎ (800) 524-2000, fax (340) 776-3054.

Sapphire Beach Resort, on the northeast coast, offers suites with full kitchens, TV, phone, handicap access, day-long children's program. Under 12 free in room. Dive In! dive shop on premises offers PADI courses, equipment rentals, dive and snorkeling tours. Freshwater pool, tennis, three restaurants. Suite rates are from $295 per day to $440 in winter, $195 per day in summer. ☎ (800) 524-2090, fax 775-4024.

Best Western's Carib Beach Resort on south coast Lindbergh Bay, features affordable ocean-view rooms with private balconies. Two miles from town. Freshwater pool, phones, TV. Winter dive package for seven nights, eight days, including room, tax, service charge, 12 dives, one night dive, costs $869 per person, based on double occupancy; summer rates for same are $669 per person. ☎ (800) 792-2742 or (340) 774-2525, fax (340) 777-4131.

Best Western's Emerald Beach Resort, a quarter-mile from the airport, two miles to downtown, features 90 deluxe, beachfront rooms overlooking beautiful Lindberg Bay. Rooms have balconies, cable TV, direct dial phone, hair dryers, coffee makers. There is a freshwater pool. Admiralty Dive Shop on premises offers boat dives. Nice white sand beach. Winter room rates are $245; summer, $185. Dive package rates for three nights, four days, including the room, tax and service charges, eight dives, $460; summer, $395. For seven nights in winter, $1,125; summer, $965. Children under 12 stay free. ☎ (800) 233-4936, fax 776-3426.

Secret Harbor Beach Resort on Nazareth Bay, the southeast Caribbean side, offers 171 luxury rooms in a tranquil beachfront setting. Per day room rates run from $265 for one bedroom to $495 for a two-bedroom suite; in summer, from $169 for a studio, $199 for a one-bedroom suite, $299 for two bedrooms. Children under 13 stay free. Good snorkeling off the beach on a small reef with tropicals, turtles and rays. Aqua Action Dive Shop on premises offers rentals, courses, dive and snorkeling boat trips. Dive packages available. ☎ (800) 524-2250 or (340) 775-6550, fax 775-1501.

Small Hotels and Condos

Admiral's Inn offers 16 ocean-view rooms from $99 to $149 per day with cable TV, AC, phone. Sea pool with sandy beach area. Diving and snorkeling must be arranged through local dive shops. ☎ (800) 544-0493, fax (340) 774-8010.

Blazing Villas, adjacent to Renaissance Grand Beach Resort, features boat diving and shore snorkeling excursions with Chris Sawyer Diving, on property. Guests use all of Rennaissance Resort's facilities. Suites feature full kitchens or kitchenettes, phones, TV, handicap access, tennis, beach. Winter rates range from $150 per night; Christmas, from $250; summer rates, from $100 per night. Under 12 stay free with adults. Add 10% service charge. ☎ (800) 382-2002 or (340) 776-0760, fax 776-0760.

Cowpet Bay Villas, one mile from the St. John ferry, faces Great St. James Island, where good snorkeling and diving via boat is found. White sandy beach. Two- , three- and four-bedroom condos are fully equipped with daily maid service. Rates from $1,890 per week. ☎ (800) 524-2038 or (340) 775-7531, fax (340) 775-7531.

Live-Aboards

Virgin Islands Charter Yacht League will rent you a sailing yacht and teach you how to sail. On some yachts crew includes a divemaster; some also have compressors aboard. Others arrange rendezvous with dive boats. ☎ (800) 524-2061 or (340) 774-3944. Advance reservations suggested.

Regency Yacht Vacations offers dive vacations aboard fully-crewed, liveaboard yachts from 40 to 100 ft. Scuba instruction, if desired, must be arranged in advance. ☎ (800) 524-7676, (340) 776-5950. Write to 5200 Long Bay Rd, St. Thomas, USVI 00802.

Sightseeing and Other Activities

The USVI provide opportunities for a wide variety of activities. Check with your hotel or the tourist newspapers (available everywhere) for historic tours, rum factory tours, golf, tennis, deep sea fishing, bird walks, day sails, visits to the new national park on Hassel Island, parasailing, and board sailing. Check nightclub listings for broken bottle dancing, fire eating, limbo dancing, steel bands, and island entertainment acts. Be sure to see a performance of the **Mocko Jumbis** on their 17-foot stilts or the **Mungo Niles Cultural Native Dancers and Musicians**. The dancers, ranging in age from 20 to well over 70, swirl and twirl in their bright red and white floral-motif costumes to the sounds of Qelbe or "scratch" music. For schedules, call the Reichhold Center on St. Thomas at ☎ (340) 774-9200 or Island Center on St. Croix at (340) 778-5272.

Dining

The rich history of the USVI is reflected in the wonderful restaurants. You can dine on the finest continental cuisine or sample exciting local dishes. Savor a Caribbean lobster bouillabaisse in one of the restored 19th-century inns or try a delicious fish-fry on the beach while listening to strains of reggae or calypso. Check the tourist newspaper for complete restaurant listings.

Hotel 1829 was originally built by a sea captain and completed in the year of its name. This is a formal restaurant with an interior resembling an Italian villa. The chef specializes in rack of lamb and various pasta dishes. Located in the heart of the harbor. ☎ 776-1829.

The Chart House, located in Frenchtown's historic Villa Olga, serves dinner on a lovely terrace. The favorite here is the 40-dish salad bar. Entrées include ribs, chicken, lobster, fish and shrimp. ☎ 774-4262.

Additional restaurants worth a try are **La Scala** (☎ 774-2206), moderate, **Café Lulu** at Blackbeard's Castle (☎ 776-1234), low to moderate, and **The Old Stone Farmhouse** (☎ 777-6277), moderate to high.

Facts

Recompression Chamber: St. Thomas.

Getting There: There are daily direct flights from the US mainland, via American Airlines, ☎ (800) 433-7300, USAir, Delta and Prestige. Other airlines serving the newly expanded Cyril E. King Airport are American Eagle, Air Anguilla and Seaborne Seaplane. Inter-island connections can be made by ferry, seaplane shuttle or one of the island airlines. US citizens must carry a passport if also traveling to the BVI.

Island Transportation: Taxi service is readily available on all three islands. Taxi rates are determined by law and those rates are available from your driver. Bus service and tours are available on St. Thomas and St. Croix. Car rentals: ABC Auto Rentals, ABC Jeep, Avis, Budget, Hertz.

Driving: Traffic keeps to the left on all three islands. A US driver's license is required.

Customs: US residents are entitled to take home $1,200 worth of duty-free imports. A 10% tax is levied on the next $1,000.

Currency: US $, travelers checks, major credit cards. No personal checks accepted.

Climate: Year-round temperatures range from 76 to 82° F.

Clothing: Casual, lightweight, with sweaters for winter; jackets and ties needed for some resorts and eating establishments.

Electricity: 110 volts AC, 60 cycles (same as US).

Time: Atlantic Standard, which is one hour earlier than Eastern Standard.

Language: English.

Taxes: No sales tax. 8% hotel tax. Service charge may apply at some hotels and restaurants.

Religious Services: All denominations.

For Additional Information: United States Virgin Islands Division of Tourism, PO Box 6400, Charlotte Amalie, USVI 00804. *In New York:* 1270 Avenue of the Americas, NY, NY 10020. ☎ (800) 372-USVI, (212) 332-2222, fax (212) 332-2223. Web site: http://www.usvi.net.

What About Sharks?

Sharks have generated more sensational publicity as a threat to divers than any other animals, even though their bites are among the least frequent of any injuries divers sustain. Two opposing attitudes seem to predominate: either irrational fear or total fascination.

Nowhere is this fascination more apparent than at the "Jaws" exhibit at Universal Studios in Orlando, Florida, where people wait in long lines for the opportunity to be drenched, buffeted and threatened by a huge, relentless great white shark.

Paul Sieswerda, collection manager of the New York Aquarium, warns divers about taking either approach to this honored and feared species. Common sense and a realistic understanding of the animals should be used, he says, adding that "anything with teeth and the capability of biting should be treated with the same respect we give to any large animal having potential to inflict injury." The vast majority of sharks are inoffensive animals that threaten only small creatures; but some sharks will bite divers that molest them. Included are such common forms as nurse sharks and swell sharks. These animals appear docile largely because they are so sluggish, but large individuals can seriously injure a diver when provoked. Sieswerda cites an incident with a "harmless" nurse shark as the cause of 22 stitches in his hand—the result of aquarium handling.

The answer to "What about sharks?" from divemasters is usually a shrug of the shoulders. Experience tells us that most sharks are timid animals. Fewer than 100 serious assaults by sharks are reported worldwide each year with the average being closer to 50. Less than 35% of these are fatal. Statistics isolating attacks on divers alone are not available, but they would be far fewer than 50. A majority of those few fatal attacks on man are not cases of the infamous great white shark biting the diver in two; they involve four- or five-foot sharks causing a major laceration in an arm or leg. Loss of blood due to lack of immediate medical attention is usually the cause of death.

Overplaying the danger is equally unrealistic. Encounters with dangerous sharks by divers on shallow reefs or shipwrecks are rare. Divers interviewed for this book who have sighted dangerous sharks all report the same thing—getting a long look at a shark is tough. When a shark encounters man, it tends to leave the area as suddenly as it appeared.

Sharks are largely pelagic animals found out in deep open water. Dangerous sharks are seldom found in shallow areas where most novice sport diving takes place—certainly not on shallow snorkeling reefs. Most dive guides agree. They would change their line of work if they thought a huge set of jaws were awaiting them on each day's dive.

So use common sense. Avoid diving in areas known as shark breeding grounds. Avoid spearfishing and carrying the bloody catch around on the end of the pole. If you do see a shark and are uncomfortable about its presence, leave the water. Above all do not corner or provoke the shark in any manner.

One crowd of bathers in Miami, fearful after seeing a well-known shark terror movie, clubbed a baby whale to death in the surf, thinking it was a shark. Our favorite shark danger story comes from Florida divemaster, Bill Crawford. A young diver begged to see a shark in the water. Finding one presented quite a problem. The area was largely shallow reefs so shark sightings were rare indeed. Thinking hard, the divemaster remembered a big old nurse shark who could be found sleeping under a ledge on one of the outer reefs. She had been there for years totally ignoring the daily stampede of divers and snorkelers. So he took the young man to that spot and, as luck would have it, there was the shark. Upon seeing it sleeping under the ledge, the young diver became frozen with fear. In a wild panic he backed into a wall of coral, putting his hand deep into a hole where a big green moray eel lived. The nurse shark, true to its calm reputation, just kept sleeping. But the moray, incensed at the intrusion, defended its home by sinking its sharp teeth deep into the diver's hand.

Photo by Jon Huber

"Jaws" at Universal Studios, Orlando, Florida.

Nitrox

Nitrox, a mixture of nitrogen and oxygen, replaces compressed air in your scuba cylinder. We are often asked about Nitrox diving and especially about its use in the Caribbean. Should you dive Nitrox? Do you have a technical bent? Do you want to learn a new skill? You need to examine your style of diving and goals to determine if the advantages of Nitrox will prove valuable. Nitrox can extend your bottom time and reduce your nitrogen load. Some people say you will feel less tired and warmer, both during and after a dive. As can be seen below, the time or depth advantage of Nitrox is significant.

Equivalent Nitrox Depths

Air Depth (feet)	With a mix of 32% oxygen, 68% nitrogen	With a mix of 40% oxygen, 60% nitrogen
40	51	63
50	63	76
70	75	89
80	86	99 (Max)
90	109	
100	121	
110	132 (Max)	

Nitrox diving can be as simple or complex as anything you will encounter in scuba diving. Basic Nitrox dive training will have you in the water with your standard scuba gear. No need to buy new gear or learn how to use and maintain it. This is the easiest, least expensive and probably the safest way for a sport diver to reap the benefits of Nitrox.

With that said, the maximum benefits of Nitrox can only be achieved with rebreather equipment. A rebreather is a self-contained breathing device which reuses at least part of each breath. Regular scuba equipment expels the entire breath into the surrounding water when the diver exhales. Although rebreathers have some significant advantages in technical diving applications, their use and the training are outside the scope of this book.

Contact your local dive shop or certifying agency about training (listed in *Planning* chapter).